Lecture Notes in Computer Science 724
Edited by G. Goos and J. Hartmanis

Patrick Cousot Moreno Falaschi
Gilberto Filè Antoine Rauzy (Eds.)

Static Analysis

Third International Workshop, WSA '93
Padova, Italy, September 22-24, 1993
Proceedings

Springer-Verlag
Berlin Heidelberg New York
London Paris Tokyo
Hong Kong Barcelona
Budapest

Series Editors

Gerhard Goos
Universität Karlsruhe
Postfach 69 80
Vincenz-Priessnitz-Straße 1
D-76131 Karlsruhe, Germany

Juris Hartmanis
Cornell University
Department of Computer Science
4130 Upson Hall
Ithaca, NY 14853, USA

Volume Editors

Patrick Cousot
DMI, Ecole Normale Superieur
45 rue d'Ulm, F-75230 Paris Cedex 05, France

Moreno Falaschi
Dipartimento di Elettronica e Informatica, University of Padova
Via Gradenigo 6/A, I-35131 Padova, Italy

Gilberto Filè
Dipartimento di Matematica Pura e Applicata, University of Padova
Via Balzoni 7, I-35131 Padova, Italy

Antoine Rauzy
Departement Informatique, IUT "A", Université Bordeaux I
F-33405 Talence, France

CR Subject Classification (1991): D.1, D.2.8, D.3.2-3, F.3.1-2, F.4.2

ISBN 3-540-57264-3 Springer-Verlag Berlin Heidelberg New York
ISBN 0-387-57264-3Springer-Verlag New York Berlin Heidelberg

Printed in Germany

Typesetting: Camera-ready by author
Printing and binding: Druckhaus Beltz, Hemsbach/Bergstr.
45/3140-543210 - Printed on acid-free paper

Foreword

This volume contains the proceedings of the Third Workshop on Static Analysis (WSA'93), held in Padova (Italy) September 22-24, 1993. The previous workshops in this series, JTASPEFL and WSA'92, took place in Bordeaux (France). The aim of WSA'93 is to illustrate the use of static analysis in different programming paradigms. WSA'93 is a step towards improving contacts and promoting cross-fertilization among the numerous researchers in this area. The program committee has selected 20 papers out of the 68 submitted. These papers contribute to the following topics:

- generic algorithm for fixpoint computation
- program transformation
- strictness analysis
- static analysis techniques for logic, functional, concurrent and parallel languages and for term rewriting systems.

The workshop also includes system demonstrations and three invited lectures delivered by Pascal Van Hentenryk, Peter Van Roy and Paul Hudak. The abstracts or papers of these lectures are included in this volume.

We thank all members of the program committee and all the referees for their care in reviewing the submitted papers.

The organization of WSA'93 was supported by:

- Consiglio Nazionale delle Ricerche
- Department of Pure and Applied Mathematics, University of Padova
- University of Padova.

Finally, we express our gratitude to the members of the Organizing Committee for their enthusiastic contribution to the success of WSA'93.

July 1993 Patrick Cousot, Moreno Falaschi, Gilberto Filè, Antoine Rauzy
Co-chairpersons

Program Committee

Charles Consel (OGI)
Patrick Cousot (ENS; Chair)
Radhia Cousot (Polytechnique)
Olivier Danvy (CMU)
Bart Demoen (KUL)
Gilberto File (Padova; Co-chair)
Pascal Van Hentenryck (Brown)
Manuel Hermenegildo (UPM)
Neil Jones (DIKU)
Pierre Jouvelot (ENSMP)
Baudouin Le Charlier (Namur)
Giorgio Levi (Pisa)
Kim Marriott (Monash)
Alan Mycroft (Cambridge)
Antoine Rauzy (Bordeaux; Co-chair)
Helmut Simonis (Cosytec)

Organizing Committee

Annalisa Bossi (Padova), Michele Bugliesi (Padova), Moreno Falaschi (Padova; Chair), Giuseppe Nardiello (Padova), Sabina Rossi (Padova), Kaninda Musumbu (Bordeaux), Michel Billaud (Bordeaux), Pierre Casteran (Bordeaux), Marc-Michel Corsini (Bordeaux).

List of Referees

J.R. Abrial,
T. Amtoft,
P. H. Andersen,
N. Andersen,
L.O. Andersen,
R. Bagnara,
R. Barbuti,
P. Bazet,
M. Bellia,
L. Birkedal,
A. Bondorf,
A. Bossi,
D. Boulanger,
F. Bourdoncle,
S. Brookes,
M. Bruynooghe,
F. Bueno,
D. Cabeza,
M. Carro,
M. Chiara Meo,
M. Codish,
C. Codognet,
P. Codognet,
L. Colussi,
M. M. Corsini,
A. Cortesi,
R. Cridlig,
P. L. Curien,
D. De Schreye,
B. Demoen,
M. Denecker,
P. Deransart,
A. Deutsch,
A. Dovier,
J. C. Fernandez,
P. Ferragina,
G. Filé,
A. Filinski,
M. García de la Banda,
R. Giacobazzi,
R. Glück,
E. Goubault,
P. Granger,
K. Havelund,
T. Hospel,
J. Joergensen,
N. D. Jones,
P. Jouvelot,
P. López García,
K. Lackner Solberg,
G. Levi,
G. Longo,
P. Mancarella,
A. Marien,
T. Marlowe,
B. Martens,
F. Masdupuy,
B. Monsuez,
J. J. Moreno-Navarro,
A. Mulkers,
A. Mycroft,
F. Nielson,
C. Palamidessi,
J. Palsberg,
A. Pettorossi,
C. Queinnec,
B. Ryder,
B. Salvy,
D. Sands,
H. Søndergaard,
M. Welinder,
P. Zimmermann

Invited Talk

Challenges in developing useful and practical static analysis for logic programs 111
P. Van Roy (Digital Research Labs, Paris)

Transformation

Occam's razor in metacomputation: the notion of a perfect process tree .. 112
R. Glück (University of Technology, Vienna)
A. Klimov (Russian Academy of Sciences, Moscow)

Tupling functions with multiple recursion parameters 124
W-N. Chin (National University of Singapore)
S-C. Khoo (National University of Singapore)

Avoiding repeated tests in pattern matching 141
P. Thiemann (Wilhelm-Schickard-Institut, Tübingen University)

Logic Programs

Freeness, sharing, linearity and correctness — all at once 153
M. Bruynooghe (Katholieke Universiteit Leuven)
M. Codish (Katholieke Universiteit Leuven)

Synthesis of directionality information for functional logic programs 165
J. Boye (Linköping University)
J. Paakki (Linköping University)
J. Maluszyński (Linköping University)

Term Rewriting Systems

Abstract rewriting 178
D. Bert (IMAG-LGI, Grenoble Cedex)
R. Echahed (IMAG-LGI, Grenoble Cedex)
B. M. Østvold (Norwegian Institute of Technology, Trondheim)

Invited Talk

Reflections on program optimization 193
P. Hudak (Yale University)

Strictness

Finiteness conditions for strictness analysis 194
F. Nielson (Aarhus University)
H. R. Nielson (Aarhus University)

Strictness properties of lazy algebraic datatypes 206
P. N. Benton (Cambridge University)

Contents

Invited Talk

The impact of granularity in abstract interpretation of Prolog 1
P. Van Hentenryck (Brown University)
O. Degimbe (Namur University)
B. Le Charlier (Namur University)
L. Michel (Namur University)

Fixpoint Computation

Optimization techniques for general purpose fixpoint algorithms:
practical efficiency for the abstract interpretation of Prolog 15
B. Le Charlier (Namur University)
O. Degimbe (Namur University)
L. Michel (Namur University)
P. Van Hentenryck (Brown University)

Chaotic fixpoint iteration guided by dynamic dependency 27
N. Jørgensen (Roskilde University Center)

Fast abstract interpretation using sequential algorithms 45
A. Ferguson (Glasgow University)
J. Hughes (Chalmers Tekniska Högskola, Göteborg)

Concurrency

Abstract interpretation and verification of reactive systems 60
J. C. Fernandez (VERIMAG, Grenoble)

Semantics and analysis of Linda-based languages 72
R. Cridlig (Ecole Normale Supérieure, Paris)
E. Goubault (Ecole Normale Supérieure, Paris)

Parallelism

Compiling FX on the CM-2 87
J-P. Talpin (CRI, Ecole des Mines de Paris)
P. Jouvelot (CRI, Ecole des Mines de Paris)

Combining dependability with architectural adaptability by means of
the SIGNAL language 99
O. Maffeïs (GMD I5-SKS, Sankt Augustin)
P. le Guernic (IRISA/INRIA-Rennes)

Minimal thunkification 218
T. Amtoft (Aarhus University)

Reasoning About Programs

An efficient abductive reasoning system based on program analysis 230
S. Kato (Nagoya Institute of Technology)
H. Seki (Nagoya Institute of Technology)
H. Itoh (Nagoya Institute of Technology)

A congruence for Gamma programs 242
L. Errington (Imperial College, London)
C. Hankin (Imperial College, London)
T. Jensen (Imperial College, London)

Types

Usage analysis with natural reduction types 254
D. A. Wright (Tasmania University)
C. A. Baker-Finch (Canberra University)

Polymorphic types and widening operators 267
B. Monsuez (LIENS, Paris)

Poster Session

Demonstration: static analysis of AKL 282
D. Sahlin (SICS, Kista)
T. Sjöland (SICS, Kista)

The Impact of Granularity in Abstract Interpretation of Prolog

Pascal Van Hentenryck[1], Olivier Degimbe[2], Baudouin Le Charlier[2], Laurent Michel[2]

[1] Brown University, Box 1910, Providence, RI 02912 (USA)
[2] University of Namur, 21 rue Grandgagnage, B-5000 Namur (Belgium)

Abstract. Abstract interpretation of Prolog has received much attention in recent years leading to the development of many frameworks and algorithms. One reason for this proliferation comes from the fact that program analyses can be defined at various granularities, achieving a different trade-off between efficiency and precision. The purpose of this paper is to study this tradeoff experimentally. We review the most frequently proposed granularities which can be expressed as a two dimensional space parametrized by the form of the inputs and outputs. The resulting algorithms are evaluated on three abstract domains with very different functionalities, `Mode`, `Prop`, and `Pattern` to assess the impact of granularity on efficiency and accuracy. This is, to our knowledge, the first study of granularity at the algorithm level and some of the results are particularly surprising.

1 Introduction

Abstract interpretation of Prolog has attracted many researchers in recent years. This effort is motivated by the need for optimization in logic programming compilers to be competitive with procedural languages and the declarative nature of the languages which makes them more amenable to static analysis. Considerable progress has been realised in this area in terms of the frameworks (e.g. [1, 4, 2, 7, 18, 21, 22, 25, 37]), the algorithms (e.g. [2, 5, 11, 16, 17, 18, 30]), the abstract domains (e.g. [3, 14, 27]) and the implementation (e.g. [11, 13, 18, 36]). Recent results indicate that abstract interpretation can be competitive with specialized data flow algorithms and could be integrated in industrial compilers.

As can be seen from the above references, abstract interpretation of Prolog has led to the development of many frameworks and algorithms. One of the reasons for this proliferation is the fact that program analysis can be defined ar various granularities achieving specific tradeoffs between accuracy and efficiency.[3] The granularity of an algorithm is influenced by numerous parameters, including the choice of program points and the form of the results (e.g. how many output abstract substitutions are related to each program point). In fact, combinations of these two parameters cover most existing algorithms.

The first parameter, **`program point`**, concerns the number of abstract objects considered per procedure. At least, three possibilities (**`single, call, dynamic`**)

[3] Note that the tradeoff between efficiency and accuracy can be studied at the abstract domain level as well, as for instance in [10].

have been investigated and they differ in the way different call patterns for a procedure are dealt with. **single** associates a unique abstract object with each procedure as, for instance, in the algorithm of Taylor [31, 32]. As a consequence, different call patterns are merged together within this granularity. Mellish [25] also associates a unique abstract object with each procedure. Contrary to Taylor however, the abstract object is a set of abstract substitutions and not a single substitution. **call** associates an abstract object with each procedure call in the *text of the program*, as in the framework of Nilsson [28, 29].[4] Different call patterns for a procedure are not merged but rather distributed among the procedure calls. Of course, different call patterns are merged inside each program point. **Dynamic** associates an abstract object with each pair (β, p) in the program, where β is an abstract substitution and p is a predicate symbol. This granularity is adopted in many frameworks (e.g. [2, 4, 11, 13, 17, 18, 22, 23, 37, 38]) and keeps different call patterns separate. It is interesting to note that, for the first two granularities, it is possible to generate a priori a finite set of equations whose variables represent the abstract substitutions adorning the program points. This is not possible for the third granularity whose semantics defines a functional equation. However, this equation can be approximated by a dynamic set of finite equations. As a consequence, it is more difficult to produce an algorithm for **dynamic** since the static analyzer must combine the fixpoint computation with the generation of the equations.

The second parameter, **abstract result**, concerns the form of the result stored at each program point. At least two possibilities (**single, multiple**) have been proposed and differ in the way they handle the results of the clauses to produce the result of a procedure. **single** stores a single result per program by using, an upper bound operation on the clause results. This granularity is used in many frameworks and algorithms (see all the above references). **multiple** stores a set of results per program point by collecting the results of all clauses and possibly applying a filter (e.g. a subsumption test). This granularity is used in the frameworks based on **OLDT**-resolution (e.g. [5, 10, 12, 16, 33, 35]).

The two parameters, when combined, produce a two-dimensional design space depicted in Figure 1. Other granularities exist. For instance, the **single** and **call** entries can be doubled by allowing set of abstract objects for the forms of the inputs. These granularities are related to **OLDT**-based abstract interpretation but are not studied here.

The purpose of this paper is to study experimentally this two dimensional space. The experimental results are given for a variety of benchmarks and for three abstract domains: **mode**, a domain containing same-value, sharing, and mode components [26], **pattern**, a domain containing same-value, sharing, mode, and pattern components [26, 18], and **Prop**, a domain using Boolean formulas to compute groundness information [8, 20, 24].

The rest of this paper is organized in the following way. Section 2 reviews informally the various granularities considered in this paper. Section 3 presents the experimental results. Section 4 contains the conclusion of this research. Most of the

[4] In the presentation of Nilsson, program points are associated with clause entry, clause exit, and any point between the literals in the clause. As discussed later in the paper, this is equivalent to adorning each procedure call in the text of the program with an input and an output substitution.

input / output	single	call	dynamic
single	AISISO	AICISO	AIDYSO
multiple	AISIMO	AICIMO	AIDYMO

Table 1. The Design Space of Granularities

results given here are described in detail in two technical reports [34, 33].

2 The Granularities

In this section, we give an informal overview of the various granularities. We assume that the frameworks use abstract substitutions to represent sets of concrete substitutions and that *Abs* is an abstract domain of this type (e.g. a pointed cpo with an upper bound operation). We use *Pred* and *Call* to denote the set of predicate symbols and the set of procedure calls in the text of the program. Abstract substitutions are denoted by β (generally subscripted), predicates by the letter p, and procedure calls by the letter C.

2.1 Dynamic/Single

This granularity is probably the most popular in the logic programming community and corresponds to what is called a *polyvariant* analysis in the functional programming community. It is used for instance in [4, 2, 13, 17, 18, 11, 22, 23, 38, 37].

The key idea is to associate with each predicate symbol p multiple abstract tuples of the form $(\beta_{in}, p, \beta_{out})$. More precisely, the result of the analysis is a partial function of signature $Pred \rightarrow Abs \rightarrow Abs$ which, given a predicate symbol p and an input abstract substitution β_{in}, returns a result β_{out} satisfying the following informal condition:

> "the execution of $p(x_1, \ldots, x_n)\theta$, where θ is a substitution satisfying the property expressed by β_{in}, produces substitutions $\theta_1, \ldots, \theta_n$, all of which satisfy the property expressed by β_{out}."

The main features of this granularity are as follows:

- The abstract semantics at this granularity define a functional and cannot be reduced to a finite set of equations. As a consequence, the fixpoint algorithm needs to interleave the generation of the equations and their solving.
- Since the semantics preserve multiple input patterns, it can be used to implement advanced program transformations such as multiple specializations [37] which associates multiple versions to each procedure (possibly one for each input patterns).

`GAIA` [18], which is the basis of the experimental work described later on, is a top-down algorithm working at this granularity. It can be viewed as an instance of a general fixpoint algorithm [19] or, alternatively, as an implementation of Bruynooghe's framework [2]. The algorithm is query-directed, providing an algorithmic counterpart to the notion of minimal function graph [15]. It also includes many optimizations such as caching of the operations [11] and a dependency graph to avoid redundant computations. Finally, in the case of infinite domains, the algorithm uses a widening operator to ensure the finiteness of the analysis for domains satisfying the ascending chain condition. Another closely related algorithm is **PLAI** [13]. The algorithm at this granularity is referred to as **AIDYSO** in the following.

2.2 Single/Single

Single/Single is the coarsest granularity studied in this paper and corresponds to what is called a *univariant* analysis in the functional programming community. Taylor's algorithm [31, 32] is an example of analyzer working at this granularity.

The key idea here is to associate with each predicate in the program a unique pair $\langle \beta_{in}, \beta_{out} \rangle$, where β_{in} (resp. β_{out}) is an abstract substitution representing the properties of the concrete input (resp. output) substitutions of p. More precisely, the result of the analysis is a partial function of signature $Pred \rightarrow Abs \times Abs$. The result $\langle \beta_{in}, \beta_{out} \rangle$ of the analysis for a predicate symbol p can be read informally as follows:

> "p is executed in the analyzed program with input substitutions satisfying β_{in} and produces answer substitutions satisfying β_{out}".

The loss of efficiency compared to **AIDYSO** occurs because input patterns from different procedure calls may be merged together resulting in a less precise input pattern for analyzing the procedure.

The main features of this granularity are as follows:

- The granularity collapses all the input patterns into a single input substitution. As a consequence, it produces the coarsest granularity studied in this paper. We expected this granularity to give rise to the fastest algorithm.
- The granularity precludes certain types of program transformations such as multiple specializations.
- The abstract semantics defined at this granularity can be expressed as a finite set of equations and the fixpoint algorithm does not need widening operators when the abstract domain satisfies the ascending chain property.

The fixpoint algorithm **AISISO** for this granularity can be deduced from **AIDYSO** by computing before the execution of a procedure an upper bound on the memoized input abstract substitution to be refined and a new input abstract substitution under consideration. The upper bound is used both as the new memoized abstract substitution and to continue the analysis.

2.3 Call/Single

The granularity **Call/Single** was proposed by Ulf Nilsson [28, 29] and is intermediary between the previous two granularities.

Its key idea is to associate with each *procedure call* a pair of abstract substitutions $\langle \beta_{in}, \beta_{out} \rangle$. More precisely, the fixpoint algorithm computes a partial function $Call \rightarrow Abs \times Abs$ which, given a procedure call C, returns a pair $\langle \beta_{in}, \beta_{out} \rangle$ whose informal semantics is described as follows:

"during the program execution, the substitutions encountered before the execution of a procedure call C satisfy the property expressed by β_{in} while the substitutions encountered after the execution of the call satisfies the property expressed by β_{out}."

Although it seems to be fundamentally different from the previous two, this granularity can be reexpressed in the same framework by considering simply that the function computed is of signature $Pred \rightarrow Call \rightarrow Abs \times Abs$. Viewing it this way, it becomes clear that the granularity is intermediary between **Single/Single** and **Dynamic/Single**. Instead of collapsing all input patterns into a single input, **Call/Single** distributes them among a finite number of procedure calls. The gain in precision compared to **Single/Single** comes from the fact that different procedure calls do not interfere with each other. The loss of precision compared to **Dynamic/Single** comes from the merging of abstract substitutions for a given procedure call.

The key features of this granularity are as follows:

- The granularity is coarser than **Dynamic/Single** and finer than **Single/Single**. We expected the algorithm to be faster than **AIDYSO** and slower than **AISISO**.
- The granularity allows for multiple specializations although their full potential may not be realized because of the merging.
- The semantics defined at this level can be reduced to a finite set of equations.

Once again, the algorithm for this granularity **AICISO** can be obtained from **AIDYSO** by computing upper bound operations appropriately. The key insight, mentioned earlier, is to associate with each predicate symbol p as many pairs as there are program points corresponding to procedure calls to p.

It is also interesting to note that a finer granularity can be obtained from *Dynamic/Single* and *Call/Single* by associating multiple pairs $\langle\beta_{in}, \beta_{out}\rangle$ to a procedure call. This results in an analysis returning a partial function of signature $Call \rightarrow Abs \rightarrow Abs$. This granularity is not explored here for reasons that will appear clearly in the experimental results.

2.4 Dynamic/Multiple

Dynamic/Multiple is another popular granularity in the logic programming community. It was used for instance in [5, 10, 12, 16, 33, 35]. The main reason is that the algorithm for this granularity can be obtained automatically by applying **OLDT**-resolution to an abstract version of the program as shown in [6, 35]. This is due to the interesting termination properties of **OLDT**-resolution.

The key idea here is to associate with each predicate symbol p in the program multiple abstract tuples of the form $\langle\beta_{in}, S_{out}\rangle$, where S_{out} is a set of abstract substitutions (i.e. $S_{out} \in 2^{Abs}$). More precisely, the result of the analysis is a partial function of signature $Pred \rightarrow Abs \rightarrow 2^{Abs}$ which, given a predicate symbol p and an input abstract substitution β_{in}, returns a set S_{out} whose informal semantics is given by:

"the execution of $p(x_1, \ldots, x_n)\theta$, where θ is a substitution satisfying the property expressed by β_{in}, will produce substitutions $\theta_1, \ldots, \theta_n$, all of which satisfy the property expressed by some β_{out} in S_{out}"

In general, for efficiency reasons, it is important to add some more structure on 2^{Abs} to eliminate redundant elements from the output sets (i.e. the elements β' such there exists another element β satisfying $\beta' \leq \beta$). The relational powerdomain (i.e. Hoare powerdomain) can be used instead of the powerset for that purpose.

This granularity is the most precise studied in this paper. The gain in accuracy compared to `Dynamic/Single` comes from the multiple outputs which give rise to more precise input patterns, especially when the abstract domain maintains structural information.

The key features of this granularity are as follows:

- It is the finest granularity defined in this paper and is obviously appropriate for multiple specializations [37].
- The abstract semantics at this granularity define a functional transformation.

The algorithm `GAIA` can be generalized to work at this granularity but the task is non-trivial, since each procedure call gives rise to multiple clause suffix and special care should be given to avoid redundant work. In [33], we report how optimizations such as the suffix optimization, caching, and output subsumption are important to achieve a reasonable efficiency. With this optimization, the resulting algorithm `AIDYMO` spends over 90% of its time in the abstract operations.

Another point to stress is that a new widening operator is necessary to make sure that an output cannot be refined infinitely often in case of infinite abstract domains. This new widening is used when a new output, say β, is about to be inserted in an output set, say S. Instead of inserting β, the algorithm inserts $\beta \nabla S$ for a given widening operator ∇. There are a variety of possible widening operators, some of them being domain-dependent and others being domain-independent. In our experiments, we use the operators ∇_d. The operator is domain-dependent, is defined on the domain `Pattern` to be discussed later, and relates to the depth-k abstraction sometimes used in abstract interpretation. Informally speaking, ∇_d widens the new substitution by taking its lub with all the substitutions having the same outermost functors (depth-1). Since there are finitely many function symbols in a program, the output set is guaranteed to be finite.

2.5 Single/Multiple

`Single/Multiple` is an hybrid between `Single/Single` and `Dynamic/Multiple`. It is close to the early proposal of Mellish [25], the only difference being that the single input in Mellish is also a set of abstract substitution. This granularity will thus give us an idea on how appropriate this early proposal was.

The key idea is to associate with each predicate symbol p in the program a single abstract tuple $\langle \beta_{in}, S_{out} \rangle$.

The key features of this granularity are as follows:

- The abstract semantics can be reduced to a finite set of equations.
- The granularity is coarser than `Dynamic/Multiple` and finer than `Single/Single`. It is difficult to compare to the other granularities proposed earlier. The granularity is not appropriate for multiple specialization.

The algorithm `AIDYMO` can be specialized to produce an algorithm `AISIMO` for this granularity, once again by taking appropriate upper bound operations.

3 Experimental Results

We now turn to the experimental results. We start with a brief description of the abstract domains before considering the experimental results for efficiency and accuracy. The Prolog programs used in the experiments are described in previous papers (e.g. [11]) and are available by anonymous ftp from Brown University.

3.1 Abstract Domains

The Domain **Mode**: The domain **Mode** of [26] is a reformulation of the domain of [2]. The domain could be viewed as a simplification of the domain **Pattern** described below, where the pattern information has been omitted and the sharing has been simplified to an equivalence relation. Only three modes are considered: **ground**, **var** and **any**. Equality constraints can only hold between program variables (and not between subterms of the terms bound to them). The same restriction applies to sharing constraints. Moreover, algorithms for primitive operations are significantly different. They are much simpler and the loss of accuracy is significant.

The Domain **Prop**: In **Prop** [24, 8, 20], a set of concrete substitutions over $D = \{x_1, \ldots, x_n\}$ is represented by a Boolean function using variables from D, that is an element of $(D \rightarrow Bool) \rightarrow Bool$, where $Bool = \{false, true\}$. **Prop** only considers Boolean functions that can be represented by propositional formulas using variables from D, the truth values, and the logical connectives $\vee, \wedge, \Leftrightarrow$. $x_1 \wedge x_2$ and $x_1 \Leftrightarrow x_2 \wedge x_3$ are such formulas. The basic intuition behind the domain **Prop** is that a substitution θ is abstracted by a Boolean function f over D iff, for all instances θ' of θ, the truth assignment I defined by $I(x_i)$ = true iff θ' grounds x_i $(1 \leq i \leq n)$ satisfies f.

The Domain **Pattern**: The abstract domain **Pattern** contains patterns (i.e. for each subterm, the main functor and a reference to its arguments are stored), sharing, same-value, and mode components. It should be related to the *depth-k abstraction* of [16], but no bound is imposed a priori to the terms depth. Since the domain is infinite, widening operations must be used by many of the algorithms. The domain is fully described in [26, 18] and reference [26] contains also the proofs of monotonicity and safeness. This is an infinite domain and the experimental results are reported with a simple widening technique which applies an upper bound operation on each recursive call.

3.2 Efficiency

This section reports our experimental efficiency results on a variety of domains. For lack of space, we only report a summary of the results, the full tables being available in the technical reports associated with this paper.

Table 2 reports the efficiency results for the algorithms on the domain **Mode**. We give the ratios between the cpu times of the algorithms wrt **AIDYSO** and the absolute time in seconds of **AIDYSO** on a Sun Sparc 10/30. There are two important results in this table:

1. The first and more surprising result is that **AICISO** is in fact 13% slower than **AIDYSO**, indicating that a coarser granularity does not imply necessarily a better

	Ratio on AIDYSO			Time
	AISISO	AICISO	AIDYMO	AIDYSO
cs	0.89	1.03	1.01	1.44
cs1	0.85	1.01	1.03	1.18
disj	0.99	1.14	1.00	0.74
disj1	0.93	1.05	1.01	0.81
gabriel	0.71	0.89	1.03	0.35
kalah	0.74	0.83	1.02	1.21
peep	0.90	1.14	1.71	1.11
pg	0.76	0.82	1.07	0.17
plan	1.00	1.09	1.45	0.11
press1	0.63	1.14	1.07	1.53
press2	0.65	1.14	1.07	1.55
qsort	1.00	1.00	2.00	0.01
queens	1.00	1.00	1.50	0.01
read	0.71	2.51	1.31	1.40
Mean	0.84	1.13	1.15	

Table 2. Ratios on the Efficiency Results on Domain Mode

efficiency. This negative result can be attributed to the fact that some redundant computations occur because the same results are stored twice in different program points. This forces AICISO to perform many more iterations and, although most of the redundancy is removed by the caching optimization, the loss in efficiency is still important.

2. The second result is that the algorithms are really close. AISISO gains about 16% over AIDYSO on this domain, while AIDYSO is 1.15 times faster than AIDYMO.

Table 3 depicts the efficiency results for the domain Pattern. The table also contains some interesting results.

1. The most surprising result is the significant loss of efficiency incurred by AIDYMO which is more than 17 times slower than AIDYSO in the average. For some large programs (e.g. program disj1), AIDYMO is about 54 times slower than AIDYSO. The analysis time is in the worst case (i.e. program press1) about 2 minutes. The main reason for this poor result is the fact that domain Pattern is both more precise and richer than domain Mode. In particular, the pattern component forces AIDYMO to maintain outputs whose modes are similar but which have different functors as is typical in analyzing recursive programs. This can lead to additional precision as we will see but it also entails some duplicated effort as indicated by the efficiency results.
2. The second surprising result is that AISIMO is significantly slower than AIDYMO indicating once again that a coarser granularity does not necessarily mean a better efficiency.
3. The remaining results confirm some of the previous results on the domain Mode. They indicate that AISISO brings an improvement of 29% over AIDYSO in the average while AICISO is about twice as slow as AIDYSO, confirming the relatively poor results of AICISO. It is important to stress the impact of the widening

	Ratio on AIDYSO				Time
	AISISO	AICISO	AIDYMO	AISIMO	AIDYSO
cs	0.87	0.98	7.17	8.30	2.13
cs1	0.87	0.96	6.94	7.96	2.18
disj	0.88	1.68	45.21	55.05	1.19
disj1	0.89	1.62	54.64	56.56	1.22
gabriel	0.39	0.81	3.95	3.86	0.90
kalah	0.59	0.75	4.72	5.46	2.97
peep	0.66	1.02	28.98	19.38	2.36
pg	0.34	0.51	2.10	2.31	0.71
plan	0.73	1.23	2.00	2.33	0.22
press1	0.32	1.01	13.41	31.69	8.70
press2	1.08	3.45	10.38	101.81	2.60
qsort	1.00	11.00	56.00	48.00	0.01
queens	1.00	2.00	12.00	12.00	0.01
read	0.29	1.27	6.86	10.42	5.53
Mean	0.71	2.02	17.52	22.14	

Table 3. Ratios on the Efficiency Results on Domain Pattern

techniques on AIDYSO. The fact that widening is implemented through a general upper bound operation explains why AISISO and AIDYSO are rather close. The main difference between the two algorithms on recursive calls is that AIDYSO keeps distinct tuples when it takes the upper bound on two recursive calls while AISISO merges them. The need to update the various tuples should explain the small difference in efficiency and iterations between the two algorithms. On the other hand, keeping distinct versions can lead to important differences in accuracy for non-recursive calls with very different input patterns (i.e. multi-directional procedures).

Table 4 depicts the efficiency results for the domain Prop. The results indicate that AISISO brings an improvement of 5% over AIDYSO in the average while AICISO is about 1.57 as slow as AIDYSO. The gain of AISISO over AIDYSO is rather small in this case. The best improvement occurs for program Press1 (29%) but most programs show little or no improvement. AICISO is the slowest program and is about 5 times slower on Read.

3.3 Accuracy

To evaluate the accuracy of the various algorithms, we use the number of unification specializations made possible by the modes inferred by the algorithms. We consider that $x_i = x_j$ (i.e. AI_VAR) can be specialized when one of its arguments is either ground or variable and that $x_{i_1} = f(x_{i_2}, \ldots, x_{i_n})$ (i.e. AI_FUNC) can be specialized when its first argument is either ground or a variable. Once again, we report the results for all domains. In measuring unification specializations, we assume that there is only one version of each procedure (i.e. no multiple specialization), since AISISO and AICISO do not support several versions. The measure is of course unfair to AIDYSO but helps understanding the tradeoff between efficiency and accuracy.

	Ratio on AIDYSO		Time
	AISISO	AICISO	AIDYSO
cs	1.01	1.14	1.58
cs1	1.00	1.12	1.60
disj	1.01	1.10	1.27
disj1	1.08	1.15	1.21
gabriel	0.95	1.53	0.58
kalah	1.00	1.23	1.00
peep	1.08	1.66	1.43
pg	0.95	1.20	0.20
plan	0.93	1.07	0.14
press1	0.71	1.69	6.76
press2	0.75	1.74	6.69
qsort	1.00	1.00	0.01
queens	1.00	1.00	0.01
read	0.77	5.31	2.12
Mean	0.95	1.57	

Table 4. Ratios on the Efficiency Results on Domain Prop

		AIDYSO		AISISO		AICISO		AIDYMO		AISIMO	
	P	E	$\%E/P$	E	$\%E/P$	E	$\%E/P$	E	$\%E/P$	E	$\%E/P$
peep	543	527	97.05	527	97.05	527	97.05	538	99.07	526	96.87
press1	434	259	59.68	258	59.45	258	59.45	259	59.68	258	59.45
press2	435	421	96.78	259	59.54	259	59.54	421	96.78	259	58.57
read	405	299	73.83	274	67.65	274	67.65	299	73.83	274	67.65
Mean			90.18		87.07		87.07		90.96		87.07

Table 5. Accuracy Results on Domain Pattern

For the domain Mode, all specialization results are the same for all algorithms.

Table 5 depicts the specialization results for which there is a difference between the programs and the average over all programs. We report the number of possible specializations (P), the number of effective specializations deduced from the analysis (E), and the ratio (E/P) in percentage for the three program. The results for Pattern indicate that AISISO, AICISO, AISIMO lose precision on three programs compared to AIDYSO: **press1**, **press2**, and **read**. These are also the programs for which AISISO produces more significant efficiency improvements. AIDYMO produces a small improvement over AIDYSO on **peep** but this is rather marginal in the overall accuracy results. The good accuracy of AISISO on the above two domains can be explained by two important features of our algorithms and domains: operation EXTG and the same-value component of domains Mode and Pattern. Operation EXTG performs a form of narrowing [9] at the return of the procedure call. Hence much of the accuracy lost in the upper bound operation of the procedure call is recovered through operation EXTG. The same-value component contributes to the precision recovered by providing EXTG with strong relations on the variables. For instance, it is possible that a call pattern (ground,any) returns (any,any) in AISISO. However, if the result also concludes that the two arguments are equal thanks to the same-value component, operation **EXTG** will concludes that both arguments are ground achieving a form of narrowing operation.

For the domain **Prop**, no difference in accuracy is exhibited by the algorithms. This interesting result can be explained by the fact that the upper bound operation (implemented by applying the **LUB** operation of the domain) does not lose accuracy in **Prop**. It is thus equivalent to consider several input patterns or a single one which is the **LUB** of the encountered patterns. Any domain with this property is probably worth investigating and **AISISO** is clearly the most appropriate algorithm in this case. Note also that **Prop** is not particularly appropriate for specialization, since only groundness and not freeness is computed.

In summary, **AIDYSO** improves the accuracy of **AISISO** and **AICISO** on a certain number of programs for the domain **Pattern** and the domain **Mode** with reexecution. The improvement occurs for the larger programs in general and correlates well with the programs where **AIDYSO** spends more time than **AISISO**. **AIDYMO** improves slightly over **AIDYSO** on a single program.

4 Conclusion

Abstract interpretation of Prolog has received much attention in recent years leading to the development of many frameworks and algorithms. One reason for this proliferation comes from the fact that program analyses can be defined at various granularities, achieving a different trade-off between efficiency and precision. The purpose of this paper is to study this tradeoff by considering various granularities for the program points. Three algorithms have been considered and extended with reexecution. The first three algorithms have been evaluated on three abstract domains, **Mode**, **Prop**, and **Pattern** with respect to accuracy and efficiency, while the reexecution algorithms have been studied on the domain **Mode**.

The experimental results lead to several conclusions.

- **AISISO** is in general the fastest analyzer but it may lose some precision for programs using the multidirectionality of logic programming. **AISISO** seems best on domains which enjoy an exact **LUB** operation, since it seems faster and as accurate as **AIDYSO**.
- **AICISO** seems not to be very interesting in practice. It is slower than **AIDYSO** in the average although it works at a coarser granularity. The difference in efficiency is not dramatic but there is no reason to choose **AICISO** over **AIDYSO**.
- The algorithms **AIDYMO** and **AISIMO** seems to work at a too fine granularity. They incur a substantial loss without really improving the accuracy.
- The differences in accuracy between these algorithms on our benchmarks were rather small.

It is tempting for us to argue that **AIDYSO** can be considered as a "best-buy" since

1. its loss in efficiency compared to **AISISO** is rather small on our domains;
2. it is more accurate than **AISISO** on arbitrary domains and this difference would show up more clearly on benchmarks exploiting the multi-directionality of logic programs which was not really the case of our benchmark programs;

3. it can be more easily tuned to accommodate the specificities of the domains. With the standard widening scheme, **AIDYSO** is close in efficiency to **AISISO** although more precise. Other widening schemes can be used however to produce more accurate results at the cost of a more time-consuming analysis.

Acknowledgements

Pascal Van Hentenryck is partly supported by the National Science Foundation under grant number CCR-9108032 and the Office of Naval Research under grant N00014-91-J-4052 ARPA order 8225 and a National Young Investigator Award.

References

1. R. Barbuti, R. Giacobazzi, and G. Levi. A General Framework for Semantics-based Bottom-up Abstract Interpretation of Logic Programs. (To appear in *ACM Transactions on Programming Languages and Systems*).
2. M. Bruynooghe. A Practical Framework for the Abstract Interpretation of Logic Programs. *Journal of Logic Programming*, 10:91–124, 1991.
3. M Bruynooghe and G Janssens. An Instance of Abstract Interpretation: Integrating Type and Mode Inferencing. In *Proc. Fifth International Conference on Logic Programming*, pages 669–683, Seattle, WA, August 1988.
4. Bruynooghe, M. et al. Abstract Interpretation: Towards the Global Optimization of Prolog Programs. In *Proc. 1987 Symposium on Logic Programming*, pages 192–204, San Francisco, CA, August 1987.
5. C. Codognet, P. Codognet, and J.M. Corsini. Abstract Interpretation of Concurrent Logic Languages. In *Proceedings of the North American Conference on Logic Programming (NACLP-90)*, Austin, TX, October 1990.
6. P. Codognet and G. Filé. Computations, Abstractions and Constraints in Logic Programs. In *Proceedings of the Fourth International Conference on Programming Languages (ICCL'92)*, Oakland, CA, April 1992.
7. A. Corsini and G. Filé. A Complete Framework for the Abstract Interpretation of Logic Programs: Theory and Applications. Research report, University of Padova, Italy, 1989.
8. A. Cortesi, G. Filé, and W. Winsborough. Prop revisited: Propositional formulas as abstract domain for groundness analysis. In *Proc. Sixth Annual IEEE Symposium on Logic in Computer Science (LICS'91)*, pages 322–327, 1991.
9. P Cousot and R. Cousot. Abstract Interpretation: A Unified Lattice Model for Static Analysis of Programs by Construction or Approximation of Fixpoints. In *Conf. Record of Fourth ACM Symposium on Programming Languages (POPL'77)*, pages 238–252, Los Angeles, CA, 1977.
10. S. Debray. On the complexity of dataflow analysis of logic programs. In *Proc. 19th ICALP*, Vienna, Austria, July 1992.
11. V. Englebert, B. Le Charlier, D. Roland, and P. Van Hentenryck. Generic Abstract Interpretation Algorithms for Prolog: Two Optimization Techniques and Their Experimental Evaluation. *Software Practice and Experience*, 23(4), April 1993.
12. G Filé and P Sottero. Abstract Interpretation for Type Checking. In *Third International Symposium on Programming Language Implementation and Logic Programming (PLILP-91)*, Passau (Germany), August 1991.
13. M. Hermenegildo, R. Warren, and S. Debray. Global Flow Analysis as a Practical Compilation Tool. *Journal of Logic Programming*, 13(4):349–367, 1992.
14. D. Jacobs and A. Langen. Accurate and Efficient Approximation of Variable Aliasing in Logic Programs. In *Proceedings of the North-American Conference on Logic Programming (NACLP-89)*, Cleveland, Ohio, October 1989.

15. N.D. Jones and A. Mycroft. Dataflow Analysis of Applicative Programs using Minimal Function Graphs. In *Proceedings of 13th ACM symposium on Principles of Programming Languages*, pages 123–142, St. Petersburg, Florida, 1986.
16. T. Kanamori and T. Kawamura. Analysing Success Patterns of Logic Programs by Abstract Hybrid Interpretation. Technical report, ICOT, 1987.
17. B. Le Charlier, K. Musumbu, and P. Van Hentenryck. A Generic Abstract Interpretation Algorithm and Its Complexity Analysis (Extended Abstract). In *Eighth International Conference on Logic Programming (ICLP-91)*, Paris (France), June 1991.
18. B. Le Charlier and P. Van Hentenryck. Experimental Evaluation of a Generic Abstract Interpretation Algorithm for Prolog. *ACM Transactions on Programming Languages and Systems.* To appear. An extended abstract appeared in the Proceedings of Fourth IEEE International Conference on Computer Languages (ICCL'92), San Francisco, CA, April 1992.
19. B. Le Charlier and P. Van Hentenryck. A Universal Top-Down Fixpoint Algorithm. Technical Report CS-92-25, CS Department, Brown University, 1992.
20. B. Le Charlier and P. Van Hentenryck. Groundness Analysis for Prolog: Implementation and Evaluation of the Domain Prop. In *Proceedings of the ACM Symposium on Partial Evaluation and Semantics-Based Program Manipulation (PEPM93)*, Copenhagen, Denmark, June 1993.
21. K. Marriott and H. Sondergaard. Notes for a Tutorial on Abstract Interpretation of Logic Programs. North American Conference on Logic Programming, Cleveland, Ohio, 1989.
22. K. Marriott and H. Sondergaard. Semantics-based Dataflow Analysis of Logic Programs. In *Information Processing-89*, pages 601–606, San Francisco, CA, 1989.
23. K. Marriott and H. Sondergaard. Abstract Interpretation of Logic Programs: the Denotational Approach, June 1990. To appear in ACM Transaction on Programming Languages.
24. K. Marriott and H. Sondergaard. Analysis of Constraint Logic Programs. In *Proceedings of the North American Conference on Logic Programming (NACLP-90)*, Austin, TX, October 1990.
25. C. Mellish. *Abstract Interpretation of Prolog Programs*, pages 181–198. Ellis Horwood, 1987.
26. K. Musumbu. *Interpretation Abstraite de Programmes Prolog.* PhD thesis, University of Namur (Belgium), September 1990.
27. K. Muthukumar and M. Hermenegildo. Determination of Variable Dependence Information Through Abstract Interpretation. In *Proceedings of the North American Conference on Logic Programming (NACLP-89)*, Cleveland, Ohio, October 1989.
28. U. Nilsson. *A Systematic Approach to Abstract Interpretation of Logic Programs.* PhD thesis, Department of Computer and Information Science, Linkoping University, Linkoping (Sweden), December 1989.
29. U. Nilsson. Systematic Semantic Approximations of Logic Programs. In *Proceedings of PLILP 90*, pages 293–306, Linkoping, Sweeden, August 1990.
30. R.A. O'Keefe. Finite Fixed-Point Problems. In J-L. Lassez, editor, *Fourth International Conference on Logic Programming*, pages 729–743, Melbourne, Australia, 1987.
31. A. Taylor. Removal of Dereferencing and Trailing in Prolog Compilation. In *Sixth International Conference on Logic Programming*, Lisbon, Portugal, June 1989.
32. A. Taylor. LIPS on MIPS: Results From a Prolog Compiler for a RISC. In *Seventh International Conference on Logic Programming (ICLP-90)*, Jerusalem, Israel, June 1990.
33. P. Van Hentenryck, O. Degimbe, B. Le Charlier, and L. Michel. Abstract Interpretation of Prolog Based on OLDT-Resolution. Technical Report No. CS-93-05, CS Department, Brown University, 1993.
34. P. Van Hentenryck, O. Degimbe, B. Le Charlier, and L. Michel. The impact of Granularity in Abstract Interpretation of Prolog. Technical report, CS Department, Brown University, 1993. Forthcoming.

35. D.S. Warren. Memoization for Logic Programs. *Communication of the ACM*, 35(3), March 1992.
36. R. Warren, M. Hermedegildo, and S. Debray. On the Practicality of Global Flow Analysis of Logic Programs. In *Proc. Fifth International Conference on Logic Programming*, pages 684–699, Seattle, WA, August 1988.
37. W. Winsborough. Multiple Specialization using Minimal-Function Graph Semantics. *Journal of Logic Programming*, 13(4), 1992.
38. W.H. Winsborough. A Minimal Function Graph Semantics for Logic Programs. Technical Report TR-711, Computer Science Department, University of Wisconsin at Madison, August 1987.

Optimization Techniques for General Purpose Fixpoint Algorithms Practical Efficiency for the Abstract Interpretation of Prolog

Baudouin Le Charlier, Olivier Degimbe, Laurent Michel[1]
University of Namur, 21 rue Grandgagnage, B-5000 Namur (Belgium)
Email: ble@info.fundp.ac.be

Pascal Van Hentenryck
Brown University, Box 1910, Providence, RI 02912 (USA)
Email: pvh@cs.brown.edu

Abstract

Fixpoint computation is a major issue in abstract interpretation. However, little attention has been devoted to the design and implementation of efficient general purpose fixpoint algorithms. This paper provides an experimental evaluation of several general-purpose optimization techniques: stabilization detection, manipulation of the sets of call patterns, and caching of abstract operations. All techniques can be included in a general fixpoint algorithm which can then be proven correct once for all and instantiated to a large variety of abstract semantics. For the sake of the experiments, we focus on a single abstract semantics for Prolog and shows the instantiations of the general-purpose algorithms to this semantics. The experiments are done on two abstract domains and a significant set of benchmarks programs. They seem to demonstrate the practical value of the approach.

1 Introduction

Fixpoint computation is a major issue in abstract interpretation [2]. However, little attention has been devoted to the design and implementation of efficient general purpose fixpoint algorithms. More attention has been devoted to generic algorithms tailored to a particular language or paradigm (see [1, 4] for Prolog) and various optimizations have been proposed. However, the impact and the general nature of these optimizations is not properly understood and their correctness is often difficult to prove since they intermingle semantic and optimization issues.

This paper tries to improve this situation by studying the impact of several general-purpose optimization techniques: stabilization detection, manipulation of the sets of call patterns, and caching of abstract operations. All optimizations are general-purpose and are straightforwardly included in a general fixpoint algorithm such as [9], which can then be proven correct once for all and instantiated to a large variety of abstract semantics. For space reasons and for the sake of the experiments, we focus on a single abstract semantics for Prolog and shows the instantiations of the general-purpose algorithms to this semantics. The general-purpose character of the optimizations will appear clearly however (especially in the light of [9]). We also believe that the conclusions apply to many other contexts including other programming paradigms, although this needs to be supported by experimental results. In the context of logic programming, experimental results for other abstract semantics working at different granularities have already been obtained and are consistent with the results presented in this paper.

The rest of this paper is organized as follows: section 2 presents our fixpoint approach to abstract interpretation and its application to Prolog. Section 3 presents

[1] Part of this research was done when O. Degimbe and L. Michel were visiting Brown university.

three generic abstract interpretation algorithms using different stabilization detection strategies and some related optimization techniques. Finally, section 4 contains the experimental results.

2 Fixpoint Approach to Abstract Interpretation of Prolog

In this section, we review our approach to abstract interpretation. The approach we follow consists mainly of three steps: 1) the definition of a fixpoint semantics of the programming language, called the concrete semantics; 2) an abstraction of the concrete semantics to produce a particular abstract semantics; 3) the design of an algorithm to compute relevant parts of the least fixpoint of the abstract semantics.

We applied the above approach to the abstract interpretation of Prolog programs in [6, 7, 8]. The semantics and algorithms are defined on normalized logic programs. This greatly simplifies the semantics, the algorithms, and their implementation. Figure 1 presents a normalized version of the classical list concatenation program as generated by our implementation. Normalized programs are built from an ordered set of variables $\{x_1, \ldots, x_n, \ldots\}$. The variables are called *program variables.* A normalized program is a set of clauses $p(x_1, \ldots, x_n) : -l_1, \ldots, l_r$ where $p(x_1, \ldots, x_n)$ is called the head, and $l_1, \ldots, l_r$ the body. If a clause contains m variables, these variables are necessarily $x_1, \ldots, x_m$. The literals in the body of the clause are of the form: $q(x_{i_1}, \ldots, x_{i_n})$ where $x_{i_1}, \ldots, x_{i_n}$ are distinct variables or $x_{i_1} = x_{i_2}$ with $x_{i_1} \neq x_{i_2}$ or $x_{i_1} = f(x_{i_2}, \ldots, x_{i_n})$ where f is a function of arity $n-1$ and $x_{i_1}, \ldots, x_{i_n}$ are distinct variables. The second and third forms enable us to achieve unification of terms. It is not a difficult matter to translate any Prolog program into its normalized version. Additional built-in predicates can be accommodated in the framework and several of them (e.g. arithmetic predicates) were used in the experiments. They are not discussed in the paper for simplicity.

```
append(x1, x2, x3) :- x1=[], x3=x2.
append(x1, x2, x3) :- x1=[x4|x5], x3=[x4|x6], append(x5, x2, x6).
```

Fig 1. An Example of Normalized Program: List Concatenation

The abstract semantics is close to the works of Winsborough [12] and Marriott and Sondergaard [10], although it was designed independently as a mathematical tool to prove formally the correctness of the first version of Bruynooghe's framework [1]. It is defined in terms of abstract tuples of the form $(\beta_{in}, p, \beta_{out})$ where p is a predicate symbol of arity n and β_{in}, β_{out} are abstract substitutions on variables $x_1, \ldots, x_n$. Informally speaking, an abstract tuple can be read as follows: "the execution of $p(x_1, \ldots, x_n)\theta$, where θ is a substitution satisfying the property expressed by β_{int}, will produce substitutions $\theta_1, \ldots, \theta_n$, all of which satisfy the property expressed by β_{out}." To define the semantics, we denote by UD the underlying domain of the program, i.e. the set of pairs (β_{in}, p) where p is a predicate symbol of arity n and β_{in} is an abstract substitution on variables $\{x_1, \ldots, x_n\}$. The abstract substitutions on variables $D = \{x_1, \ldots, x_n\}$ are elements of a pointed cpo $(AS_D, \leq)$. Operations on abstract substitutions are defined informally here. Formal definitions are given in [6, 7, 11].

$TSAT(sat) = \{(\beta, p, \beta') : (\beta, p) \in UD \text{ and } \beta' = T_p(\beta, p, sat)\}.$

$T_p(\beta, p, sat) = \texttt{UNION}(\beta_1, \ldots, \beta_n)$
where $\beta_i = T_c(\beta, c_i, sat)$,
$c_1, \ldots, c_n$ are the clauses of p.

$T_c(\beta, c, sat) = \texttt{RESTRC}(c, \beta')$
where $\beta' = T_b(\texttt{EXTC}(c, \beta), b, sat)$,
b is the body of c.

$T_b(\beta, <>, sat) = \beta.$
$T_b(\beta, l.g, sat) = T_b(\beta_3, g, sat)$
where $\beta_3 = \texttt{EXTG}(l, \beta, \beta_2)$,
$\beta_2 = sat(\beta_1, p)$ if l is $p(\ldots)$
$\texttt{AI\_VAR}(\beta_1)$ if l is $x_i = x_j$
$\texttt{AI\_FUNC}(\beta_1, f)$ if l is $x_i = f(\ldots)$,
$\beta_1 = \texttt{RESTRG}(l, \beta)$.

Fig. 2. The Abstract Semantics

UNION($\beta_1, \ldots, \beta_n$) returns an abstract substitution representing all the substitutions satisfying at least one β_i. It is used to compute the output of a procedure.

AI_VAR(β), where β is an abstract substitution on $\{x_1, x_2\}$is used to execute literals of the form $x_i = x_j$ in normalized programs. Similarly, AI_FUNC(β, f) is used for literals $x_{i_1} = f(x_{i_2}, \ldots, x_{i_n})$.

EXTC(c, β) where β is an abstract substitution on $\{x_1, \ldots, x_n\}$ and c is a clause, returns the abstract substitution obtained by extending β to accommodate the new free variables of the clause. It is used at the entry of a clause to include the variables in the body not present in the head.

RESTRC(c, β) returns the abstract substitution obtained by projecting β on the variables in the head and is used at the exit of the clause.

RESTRG(l, β), where l is $p(x_{i_1}, \ldots, x_{i_m})$, $x_{i_1} = x_{i_2}$ or $x_{i_1} = f(x_{i_2}, \ldots, x_{i_m})$, returns the abstract substitution obtained by projecting β on $\{x_{i_1}, \ldots, x_{i_m}\}$ obtaining β' and expressing β' as an input abstract substitution for p/m by mapping x_{i_k} to x_k.

EXTG(l, β, β'), where β is an abstract substitution on $D = \{x_1, \ldots, x_n\}$, the variables of the clause where l appears, l is a literal $p(x_{i_1}, \ldots, x_{i_m})$ (or $x_{i_1} = x_{i_2}$ or $x_{i_1} = f(x_{i_2}, \ldots, x_{i_m})$) with $\{x_{i_1}, \ldots, x_{i_m}\} \subseteq D$ and β' is an abstract substitution on $\{x_1, \ldots, x_m\}$ representing the result of $p(x_1, \ldots, x_m)$ β'' where β''=RESTRG(l, β), returns the abstract substitution obtained by instantiating (abstractly) β to take into account the result β' of the literal l. It is used after the execution of a literal to propagate the results of the literal to all variables of the clause.

The abstract semantics is defined as the least fixpoint, denoted $\mu(TSAT)$, of the transformation $TSAT$, depicted in figure 2. In the construction, sat is a set of abstract tuples and is functional (i.e. there exists at most one β_{out} for each pair (β_{in}, p) such that $(\beta_{in}, p, \beta_{out}) \in sat$ and we denote that abstract substitution by $sat(\beta_{in}, p)$), total and monotonic. See [6, 7, 8, 11] for more details about the abstract semantics.

3 The Generic Abstract Interpretation Algorithms

In this section, we describe three generic abstract interpretation algorithms. They can be viewed as three different implementations of Bruynooghe's framework [1], removing the explicit (memory-consuming) handling on the AND/OR-tree. Alternatively, they can be viewed as instances of general purpose fixpoint algorithms whose applicability is not restricted to Prolog but assumes that the transformation is given by an effective procedure (see [9]).

Local Iteration Strategy The approach used in our algorithms consists in focusing on the elements of the fixpoint relevant to the computation of (β_{in}, p) and ignoring the others. Of course, in general, we do not know which elements are relevant, but the algorithms are designed to avoid, as much as possible, considering irrelevant elements. The purpose of our algorithms is thus to converge towards a partial set of abstract tuples *sat* that includes $(\beta_{in}, p, \beta_{out}) \in \mu(TSAT)$ but as few other elements as possible[2]. To achieve this goal, the algorithms compute a series of lower approximations $sat_0, \ldots, sat_n$ such that $sat_i < sat_{i+1}$ and sat_n contains $(\beta_{in}, p, \beta_{out})$. sat_0 is the empty set. The algorithm then moves from one partial set to another by selecting an element (α, q) which is not present but needs to be computed, or an element (α, q) whose value $sat_i(\alpha, q)$ can be improved upon because the values of some elements it depends upon have been updated.

Within this framework, there are still many decisions to take into account, including the detection of termination (i.e. the ***stabilization detection strategy***) and the choice of the elements to work on (i.e. the ***iteration strategy***). Each of our three algorithms uses the same iteration strategy and works as follows: given an initial pair (β_{in}, p), it executes the function T_p of the abstract semantics. At some point, the computation may need the value of (α_{in}, q) which may not be defined or is just (lower) approximated at that stage of the computation. In this situation, the algorithm starts a new subcomputation to obtain the value of (α_{in}, q) or a lower approximation of it. This computation is carried out in the same way as the primary computation except in the case where a value for (β_{in}, p) is needed. In that case, instead of starting a new computation (that may generate an infinite loop), the algorithm simply looks up the current value of (β_{in}, p). The execution of the initial pair (β_{in}, p) is only resumed once the computation of (α_{in}, q) is completed. Note that if the computation of (α_{in}, q) has required the value of (β_{in}, p) then its resulting substitution may only be (lower) approximated (wrt its fixpoint value) and hence (α_{in}, q) will have to be reconsidered if the value of (β_{in}, p) is updated. The three algorithms mainly differ by the way they try to avoid reconsidering stable values (i.e. their stabilization detection strategy).

Manipulation of the Set of Abstract Tuples Besides the ability to look up a value, the algorithms need to construct a subset of the fixpoint containing the value of the query. Hence they need two new operations: `EXTEND` and `ADJUST`. The first operation is intended to extend a set of tuples with a new element while `ADJUST` is intended to update the result of a pair (β, p). There are various ways of implementing these operations and we will consider two.

In the more elaborate implementation, the operations take into account monotonicity of the least fixpoint and exploit as much information as available in the set of abstract tuples: `EXTEND`(β, p, sat), given a set of abstract tuples *sat* which does not contain (β, p) in its domain, returns a set of abstract tuples *sat'* containing the value $sat'(\beta, p)$ defined as the least upper bound of all $sat(\beta', p)$ such that $\beta' \leq \beta$. `ADJUST`(β, p, β', sat), where β' represents a new result computed for the pair (β, p),

[2] Therefore the algorithms can be viewed as algorithmic reformulations of the *minimal function graph* semantics [5].

returns a *sat'* such that the value of $sat'(\beta'', p)$ for all $\beta'' \geq \beta$ is equal to LUB(β', $sat(\beta'', p)$) (other values are left unchanged).

In the simpler implementation, EXTEND simply inserts a new pair together with $\perp$ as its value while ADJUST replaces the previous value $sat(\beta, p)$ by LUB(β', $sat(\beta, p)$), other values being unchanged.

The elaborate versions are the defaults in the experiments of section 4. Moreover, the algorithms use a slightly more general version of ADJUST which, in addition to the new set of abstract tuples, returns the set of pairs (β, p) whose values have been updated.

Algorithm 1: Simple Termination Test The first algorithm detects local fixpoints by means of Boolean variables attached to each "suspended" input pair (β_{in}, p). Each time a new computation is started for (β_{in}, p), the local variable *same_sat_local* is set to *true*. It is subsequently set to *false* if and only if the set *sat* is updated (increased) during the computation. Obviously, a local fixpoint is reached whenever *same_sat_local* is still *true* at the end of this computation.

The algorithm is composed of three procedures and is shown in figure 3. The top-level procedure is procedure `solve` which, given an input substitution β_{in} and a predicate symbol p, returns the final set of abstract tuples *sat* containing $(\beta_{in}, p, \beta_{out}) \in \mu(TSAT)$. Given the results, it is straightforward to compute the set of pairs (α, q) used by (β, p), their values in the fixpoint, as well as the abstract substitutions in any program point, by applying a procedure similar to procedure `collect_call` of figure 4. Procedure `solve_call` receives as inputs an abstract substitution β_{in}, its associated predicate symbol, a set *suspended* of pairs (α, q), *sat*, and a Boolean variable *same_sat*. The set *suspended* contains all pairs (α, q) for which a subcomputation has been initiated and not been completed yet. The procedure considers (or reconsiders) the pair (β_{in}, p) and updates *sat* and *same_sat* accordingly. If (β_{in}, p) is suspended, no subcomputation should be initiated. Otherwise, a new computation with (β_{in}, p) is initiated. This subcomputation may extend *sat* if it is the first time (β_{in}, p) is considered. The core of the procedure is a `repeat` loop which computes the lower approximation of (β_{in}, p) given the elements of the suspended set. Local convergence is attained when *sat* has not been modified during the execution of the loop body (*same_sat_local* remains *true*). One iteration of the loop amounts to executing each of the clauses defining p and computing the union of the results. If the result produced is greater or not comparable to the current value of (β_{in}, p), then the set of abstract tuples is updated and variables *same_sat* and *same_sat_local* are set to *false*. Note that the calls to the clauses are done with an extended suspended set since a subcomputation has been started with (β_{in}, p). Procedure `solve_clause` executes a single clause for an input pair and returns an abstract substitution representing the execution of the clause on that pair. It begins by extending the substitution with the variables of the clause, then executes the body of the clause, and terminates by restricting the substitution to the variables of the head. The execution of a literal requires three steps: restriction of the current substitution β_{ext} to its variables giving β_{aux}; execution of the literal itself on β_{aux} producing β_{int}; propagation of its result β_{int} on β_{ext}. If the literal is concerned with unification, the operations AI_VAR and AI_FUNC are used. Otherwise, procedure `solve_call` is called and the result is looked up in *sat*.

Termination The algorithm, as defined so far, is correct for finite abstract domains and partially correct for infinite abstract domains. To guarantee termination in the case of an infinite abstract domain, the algorithm has been extended with a simple

```
procedure solve(in βin,p; out sat)
begin
   sat := ∅;
   same_sat := true;
   solve_call(βin,p,∅,same_sat,sat)
end

procedure solve_call(in βin,p,suspended; inout same_sat,sat)
begin
   if (βin,p) ∉ suspended then
   begin
      if (βin,p) ∉ dom(sat) then
      begin
         sat := EXTEND(βin,p,sat);
         same_sat := false
      end;
      repeat
         βout := ⊥;
         same_sat_local := true;
         for i := 1 to m with c1,...,cm clauses-of p do
         begin
            solve_clause(βin,ci,suspended ∪ {(βin,p)},βaux,same_sat_local,sat);
            βout := UNION(βout,βaux)
         end;
         (sat,modified) := ADJUST(βin,p,βout,sat);
         same_sat_local := same_sat_local ∧ (modified = ∅)
         same_sat := same_sat ∧ same_sat_local
      until same_sat_local
   end
end

procedure solve_clause(in βin,c,suspended; out βout; inout same_sat,sat)
begin
   βext := EXTC(c,βin);
   for i := 1 to m with b1,...,bm body-of c do
   begin
      βaux := RESTRG(bi,βext);
      switch (bi) of
      case xj = xk:
         βint := AI_VAR(βaux)
      case xj = f(...):
         βint := AI_FUNC(βaux,f)
      case q(...):
         solve_call(βaux,q,suspended,same_sat,sat);
         βint := sat(βaux,q)
      end;
      βext := EXTG(bi,βext,βint)
   end;
   βout := RESTRC(c,βext)
end
```

Fig. 3. The Generic Abstract Interpretation Algorithm with the Simple Termination Test

form of widening [2]. Each time a call (β_{in}, p) is encountered, it searches for the last element of the form (β'_{in}, p) inserted in the suspended set (which should be renamed suspended stack for that purpose). If such an element exists, the computation continues with $(\beta_{in} \nabla \beta'_{in}, p)$ instead of (β_{in}, p); otherwise the computation proceeds normally. The above processing takes place at the beginning of the procedure `solve_call` and guarantees that the suspended stack only contains finitely many elements with the same procedure name. If the domain contains infinite strictly increasing chains, the widening must also be used (instead of least upper bound) in operation `ADJUST`. Of course, the above handling of termination may lead to some loss of precision (we are no longer guaranteed to find the least fixpoint but a sound approximation of it). The domain `Mode` of our experiments is finite and no widening is used. The domain `Pattern` is infinite but does not contain infinite increasing chains. Hence the widening is implemented by means of the least upper bound.

Algorithm 2: Collection of Definitive Tuples Albeit equipped with a mechanism for local fixpoint detection, algorithm 1 may entail a lot of useless computations because the local fixpoint detection method consists in recomputing the output once more in order to establish that all tuples used by the computation are stable. This approach suffers from an important drawback: all used values are also computed and so on, recursively. Collecting definitive tuples as soon as possible allows to overcome the drawback by "pruning" the computation at the level of definitive tuples. Algorithm 2 uses two additional data structures to achieve this improvement. The data structure *def* contains the current set of definitive tuples. Moreover, a set *use_local* is attached to each input pair (β_{in}, p). It is used to collect all the elements of the suspended set that are used by its computation. If the set is empty or equal to $\{(\beta_{in}, p)\}$ at the end of the computation, $sat(\beta_{in}, p)$ is guaranteed to be definitive and can be collected. In the case of mutually recursive procedures, definitiveness is only detected when the top-level call is completed. Inner calls can then be additionally collected.

The resulting algorithm is depicted at figure 4. The collection of definitive tuples is achieved by procedures `collect_call` and `collect_clause`. (Parts of procedure `solve_clause` which are identical to procedure `solve_clause` of algorithm 1 have been removed, to save space. Procedure `collect_clause` is almost the same and is omitted.) Although designed independently, algorithm 2 is quite similar to the generic algorithm *PLAI* described in [4]. (The *PLAI* system works at a coarser granularity and includes additional optimizations related to non recursive procedures.)

Algorithm 3: The Dependency Graph Although much better than algorithm 1, algorithm 2 still entails useless computations in several obvious situations. Firstly, in the case of non recursive procedures, the repeat loop of procedure `solve_call` is executed two times : the first execution computes the output value but a second execution is required to detect definitiveness. The case of mutually recursive procedures is still much worse, because algorithm 2 behaves as badly as algorithm 1 for such procedures as long as definitiveness of the top-level tuple is not detected. Both drawbacks can be overcome by introducing a dependency graph. The resulting algorithm was previously described in [7, 8] and is omitted for space reasons. The basic intuition is that $dp(\beta, p)$ represents at some point the set of pairs which (β, p) depends directly upon. The transitive closure of the dependencies, $trans\_dp(\beta, p, dp)$, represents all the pairs which, if updated, would require reconsidering (β, p). The algorithm makes sure that a pair (β, p) is not reconsidered unless an element of $trans\_dp(\beta, p, dp)$ has been improved. The reader is referred to [7, 8, 9] for a detailed account of this algorithm.

Worst Case Complexity of the Algorithms The worst case complexity of the algorithms was studied in [6] (results for algorithm 3 were published in [7]). The main results are depicted in table 1. They depend on various assumptions about the shape

```
procedure solve(in β_in,p; out sat,def)
begin
   sat := ∅; use := ∅; def := ∅; same_sat := true;
   solve_call(β_in,p,∅,use,same_sat,sat,def)
end

procedure solve_call(in β_in,p,suspended; inout use,same_sat,sat,def)
begin
   if (β_in,p) ∈ suspended then use := use ∪ {(β_in,p)}
   else if (β_in,p) ∉ def then
   begin
      if (β_in,p) ∉ dom(sat) then
      begin
         sat := EXTEND(β_in,p,sat);
         same_sat := false
      end;
      repeat
         β_out := ⊥; use_local := ∅; same_sat_local := true;
         for i := 1 to m with c_1,...,c_m clauses-of p do
         begin
            solve_clause(β_in,c_i,suspended ∪ {(β_in,p)},β_aux,use_local,
                         same_sat_local,sat,def);
            β_out := UNION(β_out,β_aux)
         end;
         (sat,modified) := ADJUST(β_in,p,β_out,sat);
         same_sat_local := same_sat_local ∧ (modified = ∅);
         same_sat := same_sat ∧ same_sat_local
      until same_sat_local;
      use_local := use_local \ {(β_in,p)}; use := use ∪ use_local;
      if use_local = ∅ then collect_call(β_in,p,sat,def)
   end
end

procedure solve_clause(in β_in,c,suspended; out β_out;
                          inout use,same_sat,sat,def)
begin
      ...
      case q(...):
         solve_call(β_aux,q,suspended,use,same_sat,sat,def);
            ...
end

procedure collect_call(in β_in,p,sat; inout def)
begin
   if (β_in,p) ∉ def then
   begin
      def := def ∪ {(β_in,p)};
      for i := 1 to m with c_1,...,c_m clauses-of p do
         collect_clause(β_in,c_i,sat,def);
   end
end
```

Fig. 4. The Generic Abstract Interpretation Algorithm which Collects Definitive Tuples

and behaviour of the programs. The domain is assumed to be finite (no widening), h and s are respectively the heigth and size of the domain. n is the size of the *static call tree* of the program. *SP* and *SI* are behavioural assumptions asserting respectively that input abstract substitutions behave as invariants and that recursive calls are executed with weaker (larger) abstract substitutions. *Locally recursive* procedures are procedures containing several recursive calls in some clause. *MRC-0* and *MRC-1* are two particular classes of mutually recursive procedures. Observe that the algorithms have the same worst case complexity for arbitrary programs. Nevertheless, they significantly differ for other interesting classes. These theoretical results will be used in section 4 to enlight the results of our practical experiments. See [6, 7] for more details and precise definitions.

Program Class	Ass.	Alg. 1	Alg. 2	Alg. 3
Hierarchical	–	$n(n+3)/2$	$2n$	n
Tail Recursive	SP	$O(n^2h)$	$n(h+1)$	nh
Tail Recursive	SI	$O(n^2hs)$	$O(nhs)$	$O(nhs)$
Tail Recursive	–	$O(n^2hs^2)$	$O(nhs^2)$	$O(nhs^2)$
Locally Recursive	SP	$O(n^2hs)$	$O(nh)$	$O(nh)$
Locally Recursive	–	$O(n^2hs^2)$	$O(nhs^2)$	$O(nhs^2)$
MRC-0	SP	$O(n^2h)$	$O(n^2h)$	$n(h+1)$
MRC-1	SP	$O(n^2h)$	$O(n^2h)$	$O(nh)$
Arbitrary	–	$O(n^2hs^2)$	$O(n^2hs^2)$	$O(n^2hs^2)$

Table 1. Complexity Results

	KA	QU	P.1	P.2	PE	CS	DS	PG	RE	BR	PL
Number of Procedures	44	5	52	52	19	32	28	10	42	20	13
Number of Literals	475	38	742	744	808	336	296	93	820	207	94
Static Tree Size	73	5	75	75	80	46	47	11	144	21	25
Tail recursive	12	4	12	12	6	9	14	6	6	11	4
Locally recursive	0	0	5	5	0	1	0	0	0	1	0
Mutually recursive	7	0	8	8	4	2	0	0	16	0	0
Non-recursive	25	1	27	27	9	20	14	4	20	8	9

Table 2. Sizes of the Programs

Caching Caching (see [3]) is an important optimization technique in the context of abstract interpretation because it allows to lower radically the time spent in redundant computations. It is particularly useful when the abstract semantics uses few but complex and time consuming abstract operations (which is the case of our semantics). Its only drawback (as far as time is concern) is the overhead due to caching itself (hashing and searching). We study at section 4 the interaction between caching and the three stabilization detection strategies.

4 Experimental Evaluation

The experimental results were obtained on the benchmark programs described in [8]. We also use two abstract domains: `Pattern` and `Mode` which are described in [8, 11].

Time Efficiency and Experimental Complexity Table 3 presents the execution times of the three algorithms working on the benchmark programs and the two domains, without caching but with the elaborate version of `EXTEND` and `ADJUST`. Column L gives the number of literals, which is used to measure the size of the programs (S=L/1000). Column M_i (resp. P_i) provides the execution time of algorithm i on the domain `Mode` (resp. `Pattern`). The experimental results are consistent with the theoretical complexity results. (We may focus on the program size and ignore the domain parameters which are experimentally bounded by a small constant [8].)

Prog	L	M1	M2	M3	M1/S	M2/S	M3/S	P1	P2	P3
append	5	0.02	0.02	0.02	4.0	4.0	4.0	0.02	0.02	0.02
qsort	22	3.58	0.47	0.27	162.7	21.4	12.3	1.11	0.41	0.28
queens	38	0.45	0.28	0.15	11.8	7.4	3.9	0.61	0.4	0.24
pg	93	3	0.88	0.44	32.3	9.5	4.7	8	2.46	1.14
plan	94	2.66	0.61	0.29	28.3	6.5	3.1	8.25	1.58	0.77
gabriel	207	6.32	1.9	1	30.5	9.2	4.8	15.4	5.72	2.11
disj	296	9.18	4.62	2.75	31.0	15.6	9.3	22.2	10.3	3.25
cs	336	42.4	8.97	4	126.2	26.7	11.9	75	23	6.13
kalah	475	57.2	4.57	2	120.4	9.6	4.2	380	17	6.73
press1	742	134	9.34	4.89	180.6	12.6	6.6	7613	78.2	39.8
press2	744	140	9.46	4.95	188.2	12.7	6.7	193	24.3	12
peep	808	130	7.34	3.44	160.9	9.1	4.3	570	18	7.63
read	820	324	177	4.86	395.1	215.9	5.9	19213	129	20.3
average	360	65.6	17.3	2.24	113	27.7	6.28	2161	23.9	7.72

Table 3. Time Efficiency

The experimental results suggest that, in practice, algorithm 3 is linear in the size of the program whereas algorithm 1 is quadratic. Algorithm 2 is also close to linearity for most programs but with a less good proportionality factor than algorithm 3. However the behaviour of algorithm 2 is less uniform and less satisfactory for programs containing locally recursive and mutually recursive procedures. The worst case is `read` on which algorithm 2 is 36 times slower than algorithm 3. Note that `read` contains a large number of mutually recursive procedures.

PROG	P	M1	M2	M3	M1/P	M2/P	M3/P	P1	P2	P3
append	1	6	5	4	6	5	4	3	3	3
qsort	4	332	31	26	83	7.75	6.5	50	15	13
queens	5	77	31	23	15.4	6.2	4.6	34	18	15
pg	10	238	44	34	23.8	4.4	3.4	264	51	38
plan	13	740	71	46	56.9	5.46	3.54	637	54	36
peep	19	8224	177	75	433	9.32	3.95	13818	157	94
gabriel	20	595	105	80	29.75	5.25	4	623	109	81
disj	28	324	84	62	11.6	3	2.21	338	88	68
cs	32	744	123	81	23.3	3.84	2.53	621	116	85
read	42	20543	2150	119	489	51.2	2.83	91883	729	209
kalah	44	2719	144	91	61.8	3.27	2.07	5926	169	117
press1	52	5302	326	238	102	6.27	4.58	58044	794	552
press2	52	5452	326	238	105	6.27	4.58	3340	306	210
average	24.8	3484	278.2	85.9	111	9.02	3.75	13506	201	117

Table 4. Number of Iterations

Table 4 depicts the numbers of iterations performed by the algorithms. The number P of procedures in a program is used to measure its size. The number of iterations is the number of executions of the body of the `repeat` loop in procedure `solve_call`. The results are consistent with the time measures: they suggest linearity of algorithm 3, non linearity of algoritm 1 and linearity of algorithm 2 for programs with few mutually recursive procedures. It is interesting to observe that the number of iterations of algorithm 2 is almost always greater than the number of iterations of algorithm 3 plus the number of procedures in the program ($M2 \geq M3+P$). Once more, this is very consistent with the complexity results of table 1.

Impact of Caching Measures about caching are given in table 5. Timings CM_i and CP_i are execution times with caching. Ratios RM_i and RP_i are equal to $CM_i/M3$

and $CP_i/P3$. The measures suggest that caching applied to algorithm 2 allows to get performances quite close to algorithm 3 except in two cases `read` on `Mode` and `peep` on `Pattern`. Note also that caching is not powerful enough to produce satisfactory timings for algorithm 1. This means that caching techniques are not a panacea: in the case of too naive fixpoint algorithms, most of the computation time can be spent in the overhead due to caching.

PROG	CM1	CM2	CM3	M3	RM1	RM2	CP1	CP2	CP3	P3	RP1	RP2
append	0.02	0.02	0.02	0.02	1	1	0.02	0.02	0.02	0.02	1	1
qsort	0.92	0.26	0.23	0.27	3.41	0.96	0.25	0.18	0.18	0.28	0.89	0.64
queens	0.23	0.13	0.13	0.15	1.53	0.87	0.18	0.19	0.17	0.24	0.75	0.79
pg	0.91	0.49	0.4	0.44	2.07	1.11	1.21	0.94	0.83	1.14	1.06	0.83
plan	0.98	0.35	0.3	0.29	3.38	1.21	1.11	0.7	0.62	0.77	1.44	0.91
gabriel	1.98	1	0.92	1	1.98	1	2.99	2.29	2.14	2.11	1.42	1.09
disj	2.81	2.10	1.92	2.75	1.02	0.76	3.73	3.53	3.39	3.25	1.15	1.09
cs	8.33	3.95	3.69	4	2.08	0.99	7.2	6.3	6.15	6.13	1.18	1.03
kalah	10.5	2.1	1.83	2	5.23	1.05	17.5	5.74	5.76	6.73	2.6	0.85
press1	30.2	4.96	4.18	4.89	6.18	1.01	304	27.4	25.9	39.8	7.66	0.69
press2	29.5	4.94	4.24	4.95	5.95	1	18.8	9.1	8.26	11.9	1.57	0.76
peep	30.3	3.51	2.94	3.44	8.81	1.02	43.2	14.3	6.57	7.63	5.66	1.87
read	63.5	24	3.8	4.86	13.1	4.94	1808	19.2	15.4	20.3	89.2	0.95
average	13.9	3.68	1.89	2.24	4.28	1.3	170	6.91	5.8	7.72	8.89	0.96

Table 5. Impact of Caching

Impact of `EXTEND` *and* `ADJUST` In table 6, we compare the standard (elaborate) implementation of `EXTEND` and `ADJUST` with the simpler one (see section 3) in order to evaluate the practical value of this optimization. It must be noticed that the simpler operations also allow a simpler management of the *sat* data structure. The experiments use algorithm 3 with caching on `Mode`. MT and MI are the timings and the numbers of iterations for the modified (simpler) implementation. ST and SI are the measures for the standard implentation. Moreover, RT=MT/ST, RI=MI/SI, DT=MT−ST, DI=MI−SI. The results show that the optimized operations bring an improvement on all the benchmark programs, albeit not extremely significant. Finally, it is interesting to note that the best improvement is obtained on `qsort` which is a locally recursive program. This was theoretically predicted in [6] where the optimized version of `EXTEND` and `ADJUST` were shown to lower the worst case complexity of locally recursive procedures.

PR	L	MT	MI	ST	SI	RT	RI	DT	DI
append	5	0.02	4	0.02	4	1	1	0	0
qsort	22	0.29	30	0.21	26	1.38	1.15	0.08	4
queens	38	0.15	24	0.13	23	1.15	1.04	0.02	1
pg	93	0.5	36	0.41	34	1.22	1.06	0.09	2
plan	94	0.33	50	0.3	48	1.1	1.04	0.03	2
gabriel	207	1.16	85	0.88	81	1.32	1.05	0.28	4
disj	296	2.64	63	1.99	62	1.33	1.02	0.65	1
cs	336	4.95	91	3.96	85	1.25	1.07	0.99	6
kalah	475	3.88	142	3.08	140	1.26	1.01	0.8	2
press1	742	5.06	251	4.01	239	1.26	1.05	1.05	12
press2	744	5.14	251	3.99	239	1.29	1.05	1.15	12
peep	808	3.78	78	2.94	75	1.29	1.04	0.84	3
read	820	4.52	123	3.92	118	1.15	1.04	0.6	5
average	400	2.89	109.1	2.30	104.3	1.24	1.05	0.59	4.82

Table 6. Impact of `EXTEND` and `ADJUST`

Conclusion Many abstract interpretation algorithms have been proposed in the logic programming community. These algorithms generally contain multiple optimizations which seem natural but have not been carefully evaluated theoretically and experimentally. The goal of this paper was to remedy this situation and to try to find out what is really important in abstract interpretation algorithms.

We studied various optimizations including the stabilization detection strategy, the manipulation of the set of abstract tuples and the caching of abstract operations. As far as the stabilization detection strategy was concerned, we propose three algorithms containing more and more sophisticated techniques. The three algorithms were studied theoretically and experimentally. As far as the manipulation of abstract tuples is concerned, we contrasted an approach exploiting monotonicity and a simple approach. Finally, the combination of caching, another orthogonal implementation technique, with all algorithms was considered.

The experimental results are consistent with the (previously unpublished) complexity study of [6]. As far as the stabilization detection is concerned, they indicate that the *dependency graph* (see [7, 9]) is an important and general purpose optimization technique for fixpoint algorithms using a local iteration strategy. Most of redundant computations are removed resulting in an algorithm which is 17 and 279 times faster on the average, than a naive one, on `Mode` and `Pattern`, respectively. *Collection of definitive tuples* ([4, 6]) is another general optimization wich is essentially twice times slower for most programs although it is significantly slower on programs containing mutually recursive procedures. The experimental results also indicate that *caching* ([3]) almost bridges the gap between the *collection of definitive tuples* and the *dependency graph* since the collection of definitive tuples has to redo many computations exactly two times. Finally, we have also evaluated usefulness of exploiting monotonicity to optimize operations which update the current set of abstract tuples. Although effective these optimizations are not very significant on our domains and benchmarks.

References

1. M. Bruynooghe. A practical framework for the abstract interpretation of logic programs. *Journal of Logic Programming*, 10(2):91–124, February 1991.
2. P. Cousot and R. Cousot. Abstract interpretation: A unified lattice model for static analysis of programs by construction or approximation of fixpoints. In *Proc.POPL'77*, January 1977.
3. V. Englebert, B. Le Charlier, D. Roland, and P. Van Hentenryck. Generic abstract interpretation algorithms for Prolog: Two optimization techniques and their experimental evaluation. December 1991. To appear in Software Practice and Experience.
4. M. Hermenegildo, R. Warren, and S. Debray. Global Flow Analysis as a Practical Compilation Tool. *Journal of Logic Programming*, 13(4):349–367, 1992.
5. N.D. Jones and A. Mycroft. Dataflow analysis of applicative programs using minimal function graphs. In *Proc. POPL'86*, 1986.
6. B. Le Charlier, K. Musumbu, and P. Van Hentenryck. Efficient and accurate algorithms for the abstract interpretation of Prolog programs. Technical Report 37/90, Namur, Belgium, 1990.
7. B. Le Charlier, K. Musumbu, and P. Van Hentenryck. A generic abstract interpretation algorithm and its complexity analysis. In *Proc. ICLP'91*, Paris, France, June 1991. MIT Press.
8. B. Le Charlier and P. Van Hentenryck. Experimental Evaluation of a Generic Abstract Interpretation Algorithm for Prolog. To appear in TOPLAS.
9. B. Le Charlier and P. Van Hentenryck. A universal top-down fixpoint algorithm. Technical Report 92-22, Institute of Computer Science, University of Namur, Belgium, April 1992.
10. K. Marriott and H. Søndergaard. Semantics-based dataflow analysis of logic programs. In G. Ritter, editor, *Information Processing'89*, pages 601–606, San Fransisco, California, 1989.
11. K. Musumbu. *Interprétation Abstraite de Programmes Prolog*. PhD thesis, Institute of Computer Science, University of Namur, Belgium, September 1990. In French.
12. W. Winsborough. Multiple specialisation using minimal-function graph semantics. *Journal of Logic Programming*, 13(4), February 1992.

Chaotic fixpoint iteration guided by dynamic dependency

Niels Jørgensen
nielsj@ruc.dat.dk

Roskilde University Center
DK-4000 Roskilde, Denmark

Abstract. An algorithm for abstract interpretation of logic programs is defined and analyzed. The algorithm is proved to be correct with respect to an abstract semantics for (a variant of) Prolog. This abstract semantics associates a given program with a function that maps each call pattern for a predicate to a distinct success pattern. The proposed algorithm employs a variant of chaotic iteration, and is based on what may be termed a dynamic dependency relation. A low worst-case complexity is achieved: the number of passes of dataflow analysis over each program clause is proved to be independent of the size of the rest of the program.

1 Introduction

Compilers for Prolog may produce more efficient low-level code if they employ static analysis to obtain information about a program's runtime behavior. An early proposal for this was made by Mellish [21]. More recent research has looked into the technique's relevance for the compilation of constraint logic programming (CLP) languages, including the case of CLP($\mathcal{R}$) as studied by Jaffar *et al.* [11] and Jørgensen *et al.* [13]. Although some optimizing program transformations may benefit from information about how predicates will succeed, as demonstrated by Marriott and Søndergaard [19], most optimizations rely on information about how predicates will be called during runtime.

Abstract interpretation as originally proposed by Cousot and Cousot [6] provides a mathematical framework for proving an analysis correct with respect to a programming language's operational semantics. Also, a formal framework may serve as a basis for describing and understanding various fixpoint computing strategies, for instance the chaotic iteration strategies discussed in [8]. An abstract interpretation-based approach for the analysis of constraint logic programs is presented by Marriott and Søndergaard [18]. This work suggests that the analysis of Prolog can be given a very simple formulation within a general CLP framework, an approach followed in the present paper.

An algorithm for an analysis problem in the context of imperative languages was proposed by Kildall [17]. This algorithm employs a *static dependency relation* to guide the fixpoint iteration. A similar idea is employed in O'Keefe's algorithm [15], which was shown to apply to the Prolog analysis problem considered by

Mellish, and in Debray's algorithm for a more refined variant of mode analysis for Prolog [9].

The top-down analysis considered in the present paper maintains a distinction between different ways in which a predicate is called. The basic analysis problem is similar to the one solved by the algorithm given by Le Charlier *et al.* [4]. The top-down algorithm we propose employs a variant of the idea proposed in [4] of guiding the fixpoint iteration by a *dynamic dependency relation*. That is, the choice of what to compute (which clause and call pattern to evaluate) in an iteration is controlled by a data structure which is modified dynamically during the fixpoint iteration.

The algorithm of [4] has been shown to be optimal for certain classes of programs, as well as to perform very well in practice [5]. The algorithm's absolute worst-case complexity has been analyzed in terms of the total number of times that a clause in the given program is entered for dataflow analysis with respect to a call pattern. This number is shown in [4] to be of the order of $DomSize^2 * DomHeight * Tree^2$, where *DomSize* is the maximum size of the domain of patterns for a predicate, *DomHeight* is the height of that domain, and *Tree* is the size of the so-called static call tree for the given program (that size in turn being of the order of the number *Atoms* of atoms in the program). The corresponding complexity measure for the top-down algorithm presented in the present paper is of the order $DomSize * DomHeight * Atoms$. Thus, the worst-case bound of [4] is improved by two orders of magnitude. Our complexity result also implies that the number of times that each clause is subjected to a pass of dataflow analysis is independent of the size of the rest of the program.

Related work includes the frontiers algorithm [22], originally developed for the analysis of functional languages. The algorithm was designed for the computation of a function with a binary codomain (say, $\{\bot, \top\}$). In a logic programming context we would like to operate with a multitude of success patterns, and indeed subsequent research [20] has extended the basic idea in the frontiers algorithm so that an arbitrary finite codomain is allowed.

In a comparative study of a number of techniques for the evaluation of queries to deductive databases, Bancilhon and Ramakrishnan [2] give particular credit to the method of semi-naive or differential evaluation, a generalized variant of which is analyzed in [1]. If used in combination with a program transformation based on magic sets [3], the method may produce information about how predicates are called in a logic program.

The main parts of the paper are sections 4 and 5. Section 4 introduces the notion of a static dependency relation, and defines an algorithm which uses such a relation in the computation of an abstract bottom-up semantics. Section 5 defines a dynamic dependency relation, and employs it in an algorithm for the computation of an abstract top-down semantics. The abstract top-down semantics of a program may express more information about the program than the bottom-up semantics; the relevant fixpoint is more difficult to compute, and emphasis in the presentation is on explaining why and how dynamic dependency is useful for solving the more complex fixpoint problem.

2 Lattices and fixpoints

This section recapitulates some definitions and results from lattice theory.

A complete lattice is a set D equipped with a partial ordering relation $\sqsubseteq$ with the property that for any subset $S \subseteq D$ the least upper bound $\sqcup S$ and the greatest lower bound $\sqcap S$ exist. We write $\bot$ for $\sqcap D$ when D is given from the context. If D is such that $\sqcap D$ does not exist we sometimes add $\bot$ to D as an "artificial" bottom element. Dually for $\sqcup D$ and $\top$. The size of D is the number of elements in D. A subset $S \subseteq D$ is a chain if $d \sqsubseteq d'$ or $d' \sqsubseteq d$ holds for all $d, d' \in S$. The height of D is the maximum size of any chain in D.

Suppose D and E are complete lattices. The Cartesian product $D \times E$, the set D^* of finite sequences of elements of D, and the function space $D \rightarrow E$ (of monotonic and nonmonotonic functions) are all assumed to be ordered pointwise. Under these ordering relations the composite lattices are complete.

The power set of D is written $\mathcal{P}\ D$.

All sets of syntactic objects (programs, clauses, etc.) are assumed to be flat domains, that is, ordered by the identity relation. If D is a flat domain and E is a complete lattice, then the function space $D \rightarrow E$ (ordered pointwise) is a complete lattice; and any function $F : D \rightarrow E$ is monotonic, i.e., $d \sqsubseteq d' \Rightarrow (F\ d) \sqsubseteq (F\ d')$ holds for all $d, d' \in D$.

A fixpoint of a function $F : D \rightarrow D$ is an element $x \in D$ which satisfies $F\ x = x$. Let $S \subseteq D$ be the set of fixpoints of F. If $\sqcap S$ exists and is itself a fixpoint of F, then it is called the least fixpoint and denoted *lfp* F.

The following theorem gives sufficient criteria for the existence of the least fixpoint of a function. It follows from Tarski's theorem [23]:

Theorem 2.1 *Let D be a complete lattice, and let $F : D \rightarrow D$ be monotonic. Then lfp F exists.*

The first of the following two propositions gives sufficient criteria for the existence of an algorithm to compute the least fixpoint of a function. The proposition is expressed using the following notation: Let a function $F : D \rightarrow D$, where D is a complete lattice, be given. Then $F \uparrow n$ denotes the element of D defined inductively by:

$$F \uparrow 0 = \bot$$
$$F \uparrow n = F\ (F \uparrow (n-1)) \text{ for } n \in \{1, 2, \ldots\}$$

Proposition 2.2 *Let D be a complete lattice having finite height, and let $F : D \rightarrow D$ be monotonic. Then there exists $n \in \mathcal{N}$ such that lfp $F = F \uparrow n$, and n is at most the height of D.*

The sequence $F \uparrow 0, \ldots, F \uparrow n, \ldots$ is called the ascending Kleene sequence for F.

The second proposition is used in proving the fixpoint algorithms correct. Both parts of the proposition are easily verified.

Proposition 2.3 *Let D be a complete lattice, and let $F : D \to D$ be monotonic. (i) Suppose the sequence $x^0, \ldots, x^n, \ldots$ of elements of D is given by:*

$$x^0 = \bot$$
$$x^n = x^{n-1} \sqcup (F_n\ x^{n-1})$$

where $F_n : D \to D$ and $F_n \preceq F$ holds for all n. Then $x^n \sqsubseteq lfp\ F$ holds for all n. (ii) Suppose that $x \in D$ is such that $F\ x \sqsubseteq x$. Then $lfp\ F \sqsubseteq x$.

3 An example: groundness analysis of Prolog programs

The example language considered in the paper is a variant of Prolog. The language is defined as a simple constraint logic language, to simplify the formulation of abstract semantics for the language, and to indicate that semantics and algorithms may be generalized so as to apply to a broad class of CLP-languages [10].

Pred is a collection of predicate symbols $p, q, \ldots$ of arity ≥ 0. *Atom* contains atoms of the form $p(T_1 \ldots T_n)$, where $p \in Pred$ and $T_i \in Term$ is a term built in the usual way from function symbols $f, g, \ldots$ of arity ≥ 0, constants $a, b, \ldots,$ and variables $X, Y, \ldots \in Var$. The function $vars : Term \to \mathcal{P}\ Var$ returns the set of variables occuring in a term. *Con* contains all equations of the form $A = A'$, where $A, A' \in Atom$, and the trivial constraint *true*. *Con* is closed under conjunction.

A constraint $\pi \in Con$ is satisfiable if it has a solution. A solution θ to π is a ground substitution (see [16]) such that the constraint $\theta\pi$ obtained from applying θ to π is true. Constraint $\theta(A = A')$ is true if θA and $\theta A'$ are identical. Constraint $\theta(\pi \wedge \pi')$ is true if $\theta\pi$ and $\theta\pi'$ are both true.

A program $P \in Progr$ is a collection of clauses. A clause $C \in Clause$ has the form $H :- \pi, B$, where $H \in Atom$, $\pi \in Con$, and $B \in Atom^*$. (The demand that constraints precede atoms in a clause body is made merely to simplify the presentation).

In the sequel we will refer to the standard top-down and bottom-up semantics of a program. We indicate how these notions can be defined:

The *standard top-down semantics* can be defined in terms of query rewriting. Query $\langle A :: G, \pi \rangle$ is rewritten, using renamed clause $H :- \pi', B$, into query $\langle B :: G, (\pi \wedge (A = H) \wedge \pi') \rangle$, if constraint $\pi \wedge (A = H) \wedge \pi'$ is satisfiable. The standard top-down semantics maps the initial query $\langle A, \pi \rangle$ to the set of all pairs $\langle A, \pi_{ans} \rangle$ such that query $\langle nil, \pi_{ans} \rangle$ can be obtained by query rewriting from the initial query.

The *standard bottom-up semantics* of a program is the set of all pairs $\langle A, \pi_{ans} \rangle$ associated by the standard top-down semantics to some initial query. The set will be referred to as the *success set* associated with the program.

Note that the notions of top-down and bottom-up semantics are unrelated to the "direction" of the fixpoint computation, which is bottom-up in all algorithms discussed in the paper.

The algorithms and abstract semantics defined in subsequent sections are generic in the sense that they accept a collection of externally given abstract domains and operators. As an example type of analysis we define a simple ***groundness analysis***. A term T is said to be ground if $(vars\ T) = \emptyset$. Constraint π grounds term T if for all solutions θ to π we have that the term $\theta\pi$ is ground. For instance, constraint $p(X, Y) = p(a, Z)$ grounds X but neither Y nor Z. The groundness analysis is defined in terms of two abstract domains (both complete lattices) and four abstract operators (all monotonic).

The first abstract domain is *Pat* which consists of a number of so-called patterns for each predicate $p \in Pred$. Each argument to a predicate is described by one of the modes G (for ground) and A (for any).

Definition 3.1 For a given predicate $p \in Pred$ with arity k, the set Pat_p is given by

$$Pat_p = \{p(m_1 \ldots m_k) \mid m_i \in \{\mathsf{G}, \mathsf{A}\}\}$$

The set *Pat* of all patterns is given by $Pat = (\bigcup_{p \in Pred} Pat_p) \cup \{\bot, \top\}$.
The ordering relation $\sqsubseteq$ on *Pat* is defined by

$$p(m_1 \ldots m_k) \sqsubseteq p'(m'_1 \ldots m'_k) \;\Leftrightarrow\; (p = p' \text{ and } (\forall i : m_i = \mathsf{G} \text{ or } m'_i = \mathsf{A}))$$

□

The second abstract domain is *Acon*. An abstract constraint $\Pi \in Acon$ is a finite set of variables.

Definition 3.2 The set *Acon* of abstract constraint is given by $Acon = \{\Pi \in \mathcal{P}\ Var \mid \Pi \text{ is finite}\} \cup \{\bot\}$ and is ordered by the superset relation. □

Note that *Acon* has top element $\emptyset$.

The four abstract operators are defined as follows.

Definition 3.3 The four abstract operators have functionalities

$$\begin{array}{ll} add & : Con \rightarrow Acon \rightarrow Acon \\ meet & : Acon \rightarrow Acon \rightarrow Acon \\ project & : Atom \rightarrow Acon \rightarrow Pat \\ generate & : Atom \rightarrow Pat \rightarrow Acon \end{array}$$

and are defined by the equations:

$$\begin{array}{ll} add\ \pi\ W & = W \cup \{V \mid \pi \text{ grounds } V\} \\ meet\ W\ W' & = W \cup W' \\ project\ p(T_1 \ldots T_k)\ W & = p(m_1 \ldots m_k) \\ \quad \text{where } m_i = \begin{cases} \mathsf{G} \text{ if } (vars\ T_i) \subseteq W \\ \mathsf{A} \text{ otherwise} \end{cases} & \\ generate\ p(T_1 \ldots T_k)\ p(m_1 \ldots m_k) & = W_1 \cup \ldots \cup W_k \\ \quad \text{where } W_i = \begin{cases} vars\ T_i \text{ if } m_i = \mathsf{G} \\ \emptyset \quad\quad \text{otherwise} \end{cases} & \end{array}$$

with $meet \perp W = meet\ W \perp = add\ \pi \perp = generate\ p(T_1 \ldots T_n) \perp = \perp$ and $project\ p(T_1 \ldots T_n) \perp = \perp$ □

Example 4.2 below indicates how the operators can be combined in the analysis of a clause. A constant $\tau \in Acon$ is used to describe the constraint *true*. τ is given by $\tau = generate\ q\ q = \emptyset$, with q being any zero-ary predicate.

A function *pred* return predicate symbols of atoms, patterns, and clauses:

$$\begin{array}{ll} (pred\ A) = p \text{ if } A = p(T_1 \ldots T_k) & (A \in Atoms) \\ (pred\ \Delta) = p \text{ if } \Delta = p(m_1 \ldots m_k) & (\Delta \in Pat) \\ (pred\ C) = p \text{ if } C = (\, p(T_1 \ldots T_k) :- \pi, B\,) & (C \in Clause) \end{array}$$

In the complexity analysis the following notation is used:
$Atoms_C$: the number of atoms in clause C, couting the head as well as the body atoms.
$DomSize_C$: the size of Pat_p where $p = (pred\ C)$ is the predicate defined by clause C.
$DomHeight_C$: the height of the largest set $Pat_p \cup \{\bot\}$ for any predicate p called in the body of C.

any predicate p defined in P. since there are four elements in any of the sets

4 Static dependency and bottom-up analysis

The bottom-up algorithm defined and analyzed in this section computes the abstract bottom-up semantics $\mathbf{P}_{\mathrm{bu}}\,[\![P]\!]$ of a given program P. The semantics $\mathbf{P}_{\mathrm{bu}}$ is defined formally, and the algorithm is proved correct with respect to the semantics. The simple nature of the bottom-up semantics allows for a chaotic iteration strategy based on a static dependency relation.

The abstract bottom-up semantics associates a single pattern with each predicate.

Definition 4.1 The semantic domain Sem_{bu} is defined by $Sem_{bu} = Pred \rightarrow Pat$. □

The intuitive idea is that the pattern associated with a predicate p is a *success* pattern. That is, the purpose of the abstract bottom-up semantics is to provide an approximation of the standard bottom-up semantics in the following sense: Let $S \in Sem_{bu}$ be the abstract bottom-up semantics of a given program, and suppose that $S\ p = p(m_1 \ldots m_k)$ for some predicate p. Then for any pair $\langle p(T_1 \ldots T_k), \pi)\rangle$ belonging to the success set of the program it must hold that constraint π grounds the i'th argument T_i whenever $m_i = \mathsf{G}$. A formal definition and proof of this property of $\mathbf{P}_{\mathrm{bu}}$ is outside the scope of the paper.

Definition 4.2 The abstract bottom-up semantics $\mathbf{P}_{\mathrm{bu}}$ is defined as follows: The semantic functions have functionalities:

$$\begin{array}{l} \mathbf{P}_{\mathrm{bu}} : Progr \rightarrow Sem_{bu} \\ \mathbf{C}_{\mathrm{bu}} : Clause \rightarrow Sem_{bu} \rightarrow Sem_{bu} \\ \mathbf{B}_{\mathrm{bu}} : Atom^* \rightarrow Sem_{bu} \rightarrow Acon \rightarrow Acon \\ \mathbf{A}_{\mathrm{bu}} : Atom \rightarrow Sem_{bu} \rightarrow Acon \rightarrow Acon \end{array}$$

and are defined by:

$$
\begin{array}{ll}
\mathbf{P}_{\mathsf{bu}}\,[\![P]\!] & = \mathit{lfp}\,(\bigsqcup_{C\in P}(\mathbf{C}_{\mathsf{bu}}\,[\![C]\!])) \\
\mathbf{C}_{\mathsf{bu}}\,[\![H:-\pi,B]\!]\,S\,p & = \text{if}\,(\mathit{pred}\;H)\neq p\;\text{then}\;\bot\;\text{else} \\
 & \quad\;\text{let}\;\Pi=\mathbf{B}_{\mathsf{bu}}\,[\![B]\!]\,S\,(\mathit{add}\;\pi\;\tau)\;\text{in}\;\mathit{project}\;H\;\Pi \\
\mathbf{B}_{\mathsf{bu}}\,[\![\mathit{nil}]\!]\,S\,\Pi & = \Pi \\
\mathbf{B}_{\mathsf{bu}}\,[\![A::B]\!]\,S\,\Pi & = \text{let}\;\Pi'=\mathbf{A}_{\mathsf{bu}}\,[\![A]\!]\,S\,\Pi\;\;\text{in}\;\mathbf{B}_{\mathsf{bu}}\,[\![B]\!]\,S\,\Pi' \\
\mathbf{A}_{\mathsf{bu}}\,[\![A]\!]\,S\,\Pi & = \text{let}\;\Pi'=\mathit{generate}\;A\,(S\,(\mathit{pred}\;A))\;\text{in}\;\mathit{meet}\;\Pi\;\Pi'
\end{array}
$$

□

$\mathbf{P}_{\mathsf{bu}}$ is well-defined, due to completeness of Sem_{bu} and monotonicity of $\bigsqcup_{C\in P}(\mathbf{C}_{\mathsf{bu}}\,[\![C]\!])$

Example 4.1 Consider the following simple Prolog program which will be referred to as P_{ex}.

(C_1) `p(a,Y):- true.`
(C_2) `p(X,Y):- true, p(Y,X).`

The abstract bottom-up semantics of the program is given by

$$
\begin{array}{l}
\mathbf{P}_{\mathsf{bu}}\,[\![P_{ex}]\!]\,p = p(\mathsf{A},\mathsf{A}) \\
\mathbf{P}_{\mathsf{bu}}\,[\![P_{ex}]\!]\,q = \quad\bot \qquad \text{if}\;q\neq p
\end{array}
$$

□

Stated in terms of the standard bottom-up semantics, the abstract semantics of program P_{ex} expresses that only queries to predicate p may possibly succeed, and that none of the arguments to p has been established to be always ground.

Example 4.2 Consider the evaluation of the expression $\mathbf{C}_{\mathsf{bu}}\,[\![C_2]\!]\,S\,p$, where S satisfies $S\;p = p(\mathsf{G},\mathsf{A})$. From the definition of clause C_2 (in example 4.1) it is intuitively clear that with the given S, the clause grounds the second argument to p. That is, one would expect the value of the expression to be $p(\mathsf{A},\mathsf{G})$. To evaluate the expression we note that

$$
\begin{array}{rl}
\mathit{add}\;\mathit{true}\;\tau = \emptyset & \text{(i)} \\
\mathit{generate}\;p(Y,X)\;p(\mathsf{G},\mathsf{A}) = \{Y\} & \text{(ii)} \\
\mathit{meet}\;\emptyset\;\{Y\} = \{Y\} & \text{(iii)} \\
\mathit{project}\;p(X,Y)\;\{Y\} = p(\mathsf{A},\mathsf{G}) & \text{(iv)}
\end{array}
$$

and obtain:

$$
\begin{array}{ll}
\mathbf{C}_{\mathsf{bu}}\,[\![p(X,Y):-\mathit{true},p(Y,X)]\!]\,S\,p & \\
\quad = \text{let}\;\Pi=\mathbf{B}_{\mathsf{bu}}\,[\![p(Y,X)]\!]\,S\,(\mathit{add}\;\mathit{true}\;\tau)\;\text{in} & \text{(by def of } \mathbf{C}_{\mathsf{bu}}) \\
\qquad\quad \mathit{project}\;\Pi\;p(X,Y) & \\
\quad = \text{let}\;\Pi=\mathbf{A}_{\mathsf{bu}}\,[\![p(Y,X)]\!]\,S\,\emptyset\;\text{in} & \text{(by (i) and def of } \mathbf{B}_{\mathsf{bu}}) \\
\qquad\quad \mathit{project}\;p(X,Y)\;\Pi & \\
\quad = \text{let}\;\Pi'=\mathit{generate}\;p(Y,X)\;p(\mathsf{G},\mathsf{A})\;\text{in} & \text{(by def of } \mathbf{A}_{\mathsf{bu}}) \\
\qquad\quad \text{let}\;\Pi=\mathit{meet}\;\emptyset\;\Pi'\;\text{in}\;\mathit{project}\;p(X,Y)\;\Pi & \\
\quad = \text{let}\;\Pi=\mathit{meet}\;\emptyset\;\{Y\}\;\text{in}\;\mathit{project}\;p(X,Y)\;\Pi & \text{(by (ii))} \\
\quad = \mathit{project}\;p(X,Y)\;\{Y\} & \text{(by (iii))} \\
\quad = p(\mathsf{A},\mathsf{G}) & \text{(by (iv))}
\end{array}
$$

□

Now we turn to the computation of $\mathbf{P}_{\mathrm{bu}}[\![P]\!]$ for a given input program P. A brute-force approach is suggested by proposition 2.2. One may simply compute the ascending Kleene sequence for $\bigsqcup_{C \in P} (\mathbf{C}_{\mathrm{bu}}[\![C]\!])$ given by

$$S^0 = \lambda p.\bot$$
$$S^n = \bigsqcup_{C \in P} (\mathbf{C}_{\mathrm{bu}}[\![C]\!])\, S^{n-1}$$

where $S^n \in \mathit{Sem}_{bu}$. At the point where $S^{n+1} = S^n$ we have $S^n = \mathit{lfp}\,(\bigsqcup_{C \in P} (\mathbf{C}_{\mathrm{bu}}[\![C]\!]))$.

The notion of chaotic iteration was introduced by Cousot and Cousot [7] [8]. Chaotic iteration may be applied in the present context to yield the following improvement over the brute-force method: Immediately upon evaluation of $\mathbf{C}_{\mathrm{bu}}[\![C]\!]\, S\, p$, the result is "added" to the iterand S. By contrast, in the brute-force method, all clauses in the program are scanned once using a fixed iterand before the iterand is modified. Chaotic iteration yields a sequence

$$S^0 = \lambda p.\bot$$
$$S^n = S^{n-1} \sqcup (\mathbf{C}_{\mathrm{bu}}[\![C_n]\!]\, S^{n-1})$$

for some sequence of clauses $C_1, \ldots, C_n, \ldots$. Several methods exist to secure that a chaotic iteration sequence eventually stabilizes at $\bigsqcup_{C \in P} (\mathbf{C}_{\mathrm{bu}}[\![C]\!])$. Perhaps the most simple is to select clauses according to their order in the program, and stop when all clauses in P has been tried and seen not to change the iterand.

The bottom-up algorithm can be seen as choosing a chaotic iteration strategy based on a static dependency relation. The strategy prescribes that if the n'th iteration leads to an ***update*** of the pattern for predicate p, i.e., if $(S^{n-1}\ p) \sqsubset (S^n\ p)$, then the clauses that ***depend*** on p should be selected for evaluation. Clause C depends on predicate p if for some atom B_i in the body of C we have $(\mathit{pred}\ B_i) = p$.

The observation underlying this approach is that if clause C does not depend on the updated predicate p, then there is no point in (re)evaluating C. This is expressed in the following proposition, which is easily proved by induction over the number of atoms in the body of a given clause.

Proposition 4.1 *Let C be the clause $(H :- \pi, B_1 \ldots B_m)$, with $(\mathit{pred}\ B_i) = p_i$. Let $S, S' \in \mathit{Sem}_{bu}$ satisfy $S' = \mathbf{C}_{\mathrm{bu}}[\![C']\!]\, S$ for some clause C'. Then $(\forall i \in [1,m] : S'\ p_i = S\ p_i) \Rightarrow \mathbf{C}_{\mathrm{bu}}[\![C]\!]\, S' = \mathbf{C}_{\mathrm{bu}}[\![C]\!]\, S$.*

The relation between predicates and the clauses they depend on is static in the sense that the relation can be computed once and for all prior to the fixpoint iteration. The dependency information can be obtained on a syntactic basis in the sense that only the predicate symbols occuring in a clause body need be examined, while it is unnecessary to consider for instance the definition of the abstract operators.

The bottom-up algorithm is defined as follows in pseudo-code.

Input: Program P.
Output: The value of S upon termination of the algorithm is $\mathbf{P}_{bu}$ $[\![P]\!]$.

```
%% initialization
workset := all clauses in P
for all predicates p defined in program P do
  S(p) := ⊥
  depend(p) = {C ∈ P | p is called in body of C} od
%% iteration
while workset ≠ ∅ do
  select and delete clause C from workset
  let (H :- π, B) = C  and  p = (pred H)
  Δ := Cbu [[C]] S p
  if Δ ⋢ S(p) then
     S(p) := S(p) ⊔ Δ
     workset := workset ∪ depend(p) fi
od
```

The definition is in terms of the following variables ranging over composite domains:

The variable $S \in Sem_{bu}$ represents the iterands. Initially, S has the bottom value $\lambda p.\bot$. Upon termination, S holds the algorithm output $\mathbf{P}_{bu}$ $[\![P]\!]$.

The variable *workset* $\in (\mathcal{P}\ Clause)$ holds the set of clauses that must be scanned in the following iterations. Initially, *workset* contains all clauses in the given program. The algorithm terminates when *workset* is empty.

The variable *depend* $\in (Pred \rightarrow \mathcal{P}\ Clause)$ represents the dependency information. For a given predicate q defined in P, clauses C belongs to $depend(q)$ if the clause contains a call to q in the body.

The variables ranging over simple domains are $P \in Progr$, $C \in Clause$, $p \in Pred$, and $\Delta \in Pat$.

The questions of what data structures should be used to represent the variables, and how the various operations on them should be implemented, are not considered. Of course, the values of $S\ q$ and $depend(q)$ are irrelevant if q is not defined by a clause in the input program.

In the following analysis of the algorithm, an iteration refers to an execution of the while-loop. S^n and $workset^n$ denote the values of S and *workset* upon the n'th iteration (say, at the point of the test $workset \neq \emptyset$). Note that $S^{n-1} \sqsubseteq S^n$ always holds, since S is only updated "upwards". We refer to the evaluation of an expression $\mathbf{C}_{td}$ $[\![C]\!]\ S\ p$ (for given C, S, and $p = (pred\ C)$) as a *clause scan*.

Example 4.3 Consider program P_{ex} from example 4.1 as input to the bottom-up algorithm. It is assumed that clauses are added to the *workset* according to their order in the program, and deleted from the *workset* on a first-in first-out basis.

At initialization, the variable *depend* is assigned the function

$$\begin{aligned} depend(p) &= \{C_2\} \\ depend(q) &= \emptyset \quad \text{if } q \neq p \end{aligned}$$

while S and *workset* are initialized as shown in the top row of the table. The bottom-up algorithm performs three iterations:

n	Clause scan	S^n	*workset*^{n}
0		$p \to \bot$	$\{C_1, C_2\}$
1	$\mathbf{C}_{\mathsf{bu}}$ $[\![C_1]\!]$ S^0 $p = p(\mathsf{G}, \mathsf{A})$	$p \to p(\mathsf{G}, \mathsf{A})$	$\{C_2\}$
2	$\mathbf{C}_{\mathsf{bu}}$ $[\![C_2]\!]$ S^1 $p = p(\mathsf{A}, \mathsf{G})$	$p \to p(\mathsf{A}, \mathsf{A})$	$\vdots$
3	$\mathbf{C}_{\mathsf{bu}}$ $[\![C_2]\!]$ S^2 $p = p(\mathsf{A}, \mathsf{A})$	$\vdots$	$\emptyset$

A field with ($\vdots$) has the same value as the field above it. The value $p \to p(\mathsf{G}, \mathsf{A})$ of the field for S^1 stands for the function that maps p to $p(\mathsf{G}, \mathsf{A})$ and other predicates to $\bot$.

In the first iteration, clause C_1 is selected. Evaluation of $\mathbf{C}$ $[\![C_1]\!]$ S^0 p leads to an update of p, and so $\{C_2\}$ is added to *workset*, which however already contains the clause. The second iteration leads to another update of p; this iteration corresponds to the computation detailed in example 4.2. The success pattern $p(\mathsf{A}, \mathsf{A}) = (S^2\ p)$ is obtained as the least upper bound of the set $\{p(\mathsf{G}, \mathsf{A}), p(\mathsf{A}, \mathsf{G})\}$; the analysis misses out the information that either the first or the second argument is ground, because each predicate is described by only a single success pattern. The third iteration is the last one since it leaves *workset* empty. □

Correctness of the bottom-up algorithm is defined with respect to the abstract bottom-up semantics: For an arbitrary program P, the output of the algorithm as executed with input P must be equal to $\mathbf{P}_{\mathsf{bu}}$ $[\![P]\!]$.

Proposition 4.2 *The bottom-up algorithm is correct.*

The complexity of the bottom-up algorithm is expressed in terms of the number of scans of each clause in a given program, i.e., the number of passes of dataflow over each clause.

Proposition 4.3 *The bottom-up algorithm performs at most $Atoms_C$ * $DomHeight_C$ scans of any clause C in any program on which the algorithm is run.*

The bottom-up algorithm's iteration strategy, being based on a static dependency relation, is similar to the strategies underlying the algorithms proposed by for instance Kildall [17], O'Keefe [15], and Debray [9]. Significantly, by the above complexity result, the number of passes of dataflow analysis over each clause in a program is independent of the remainder of the program, i.e., of any measure on the size of the rest of the program. This is the property that we would like to carry over to the more difficult problem which arises when a distinction is made between different calls to the same predicate.

5 Dynamic dependency and top-down analysis

The top-down algorithm defined and analyzed in this section computes the abstract top-down semantics $\mathbf{P}_{\mathrm{td}}[\![P]\!]$ of a given program P. The abstract top-down semantics of a program may express more information about the program than the abstract bottom-up semantics. On the other hand, it is more difficult to compute. The top-down algorithm copes with the more difficult problem by employing a chaotic iteration strategy which can be said to be based on a dynamic dependency relation.

Definition 5.1 The semantic domain Sem_{td} is defined by $Sem_{td} = Pat \rightarrow Pat$.
□

The abstract top-down semantics is intended to approximate the standard top-down semantics in the following sense: Let $F \in Sem_{td}$ be the abstract top-down semantics of a program, let $p(m_1 \ldots m_k)$ be an arbitrary pattern, and let $\langle p(T_1 \ldots T_k), \pi\rangle$ be an arbitrary initial query to the program. Suppose that constraint π grounds T_i whenever $m_i = \mathsf{G}$. Then for all pairs $\langle p(T_1' \ldots T_k'), \pi_{ans}\rangle$ associated by the standard top-down semantics to the initial query it must hold that π_{ans} grounds T_i' whenever $m_i' = \mathsf{G}$, with $p(m_1' \ldots m_k') = F\ p(m_1 \ldots m_k)$.

Definition 5.2 The top-down semantics $\mathbf{P}_{\mathrm{td}}$ is defined as follows:
The semantic functions have functionalities:

$$\begin{array}{l}\mathbf{P}_{\mathrm{td}} : Progr \rightarrow Sem_{td}\\ \mathbf{C}_{\mathrm{td}} : Clause \rightarrow Sem_{td} \rightarrow Sem_{td}\\ \mathbf{B}_{\mathrm{td}} : Atom^* \rightarrow Sem_{td} \rightarrow Acon \rightarrow Acon\\ \mathbf{A}_{\mathrm{td}} : Atom \rightarrow Sem_{td} \rightarrow Acon \rightarrow Acon\end{array}$$

and are defined by:

$$\begin{array}{ll}\mathbf{P}_{\mathrm{td}}\,[\![P]\!] & = \mathit{lfp}\,(\bigsqcup_{C\in P}(\mathbf{C}_{\mathrm{td}}[\![C]\!]))\\ \mathbf{C}_{\mathrm{td}}\,[\![H :- \pi, B]\!]\ F\ \Delta & = \text{let } \Pi = \mathit{generate}\ H\ \Delta \text{ in}\\ & \quad \text{let } \Pi' = \mathit{add}\ \pi\ \Pi \text{ in}\\ & \quad\ \text{let } \Pi'' = \mathbf{B}_{\mathrm{td}}\,[\![B]\!]\ F\ \Pi' \text{ in } \ \mathit{project}\ H\ \Pi''\\ \mathbf{B}_{\mathrm{td}}\,[\![nil]\!]\ F\ \Pi & = \Pi\\ \mathbf{B}_{\mathrm{td}}\,[\![A :: B]\!]\ F\ \Pi & = \mathbf{B}_{\mathrm{td}}\,[\![B]\!]\ F\ (\mathbf{A}_{\mathrm{td}}\,[\![A]\!]\ F\ \Pi)\\ \mathbf{A}_{\mathrm{td}}\,[\![A]\!]\ F\ \Pi & = \text{let } \Delta = \mathit{project}\ A\ \Pi \text{ in}\\ & \quad \text{let } \Pi' = \mathit{generate}\ A\ (F\ \Delta) \text{ in } \ \mathit{meet}\ \Pi\ \Pi'\end{array}$$

□

$\mathbf{P}_{\mathrm{td}}$ is well-defined, due to completeness of Sem_{td} and monotonicity of $\bigsqcup_{C\in P}(\mathbf{C}_{\mathrm{td}}\,[\![C]\!])$ (cf. theorem 2.1).

Example 5.1 The abstract top-down semantics of program P_{ex} (see example 4.1) is given by

$$\begin{array}{ll}\mathbf{P}_{\mathrm{td}}\,[\![P_{ex}]\!]\ p(\mathsf{G},\mathsf{G}) & = p(\mathsf{G},\mathsf{G})\\ \mathbf{P}_{\mathrm{td}}\,[\![P_{ex}]\!]\ p(\mathsf{G},\mathsf{A}) & = p(\mathsf{G},\mathsf{A})\\ \mathbf{P}_{\mathrm{td}}\,[\![P_{ex}]\!]\ p(\mathsf{A},\mathsf{G}) & = p(\mathsf{A},\mathsf{G})\\ \mathbf{P}_{\mathrm{td}}\,[\![P_{ex}]\!]\ p(\mathsf{A},\mathsf{A}) & = p(\mathsf{A},\mathsf{A})\\ \mathbf{P}_{\mathrm{td}}\,[\![P_{ex}]\!]\ q(m_1 \ldots m_k) = & \quad \bot \qquad \text{if } q \neq p\end{array}$$

□

The difference between the abstract top-down and bottom-up semantics is that the former takes call patterns into account: First, when a clause is entered, an abstract constraint is "generated" which may possibly ground certain variables occuring in the clause head, due to the calling pattern for the clause. Second, during scanning of a clause, when a body atom is to be evaluated, a call pattern for the atom is computed by "projecting" the information contained in the abstract constraint onto the atom. The two semantics are otherwise closely related. In fact, if the top-down version had operated on a domain which allowed only for a single call pattern per predicate, the two semantics would have been equivalent.

To compute $\mathbf{P}_{\mathrm{td}}\,[\![P]\!]$ for a given program P, one may proceed in a brute-force manner, constructing the ascending Kleene sequence for the function $\bigsqcup_{C \in P} (\mathbf{C}_{\mathrm{td}}[\![C]\!])$.

To improve efficiency, one may use some form of chaotic iteration. We first define the content of an iteration, and then consider the over-all iteration strategy.

An iteration computes iterand $F^n \in \mathit{Sem}_{td}$ from the previous one in three steps:

Step one: A clause scan. That is, the evaluation of the expression $\mathbf{C}_{\mathrm{td}}\,[\![C_n]\!]\, F^{n-1}\, \Delta_n$, with $\langle C_n, \Delta_n \rangle$ being the pair chosen for the n'th iteration.
Step two: The result of the clause scan is added to the iterand: $F = F^{n-1} \sqcup \mathbf{S}(C_n, F^{n-1}, \Delta_n)$ with

$\mathbf{S}(C, F, \Delta) = \lambda\Delta'.(\text{if } \Delta' \neq \Delta \text{ then } \bot \text{ else } \mathbf{C}_{\mathrm{td}}\,[\![C]\!]\, F\, \Delta)$

Step three: Monotonicity of the iterand is preserved. By steps one and two, at most a single pattern Δ_{upd} will have been updated, i.e., $(F^{n-1}\Delta_{upd}) \sqsubset (F\,\Delta_{upd})$; and there may exist patterns Δ where $\Delta_{upd} \sqsubset \Delta$ and $(F\Delta_{upd}) \not\sqsubseteq (F\Delta)$. Working with monotonic iterands is intended to speed up convergence by assigning $(F\,\Delta)$ the larger value $(F\,\Delta) \sqcup (F\,\Delta_{upd})$. Step three may be expressed in terms of the function $\mathbf{M}$ defined by $\mathbf{M}(F) = \lambda\Delta.(\sqcup \{F\,\Delta' \mid \Delta' \sqsubseteq \Delta\})$.

Chaotic iteration based on steps one through three yields a sequence

$$
\begin{aligned}
F^0 &= \lambda\Delta.\bot \\
F^n &= \mathbf{M}(F^{n-1} \sqcup \mathbf{S}(C_n, F^{n-1}, \Delta_n))
\end{aligned}
$$

for a sequence of pairs $\langle C_n, \Delta_n \rangle$. The problem then is to find a good strategy for selecting the sequence of pairs. That is, a strategy which ensures quick convergence to the least fixpoint, and in which the determination of the sequence of pairs is itself not too expensive. Of course, we should only select pairs $\langle C, \Delta \rangle$ where $(\mathit{pred}\, C) = (\mathit{pred}\, \Delta)$, since otherwise we trivially have that $\mathbf{C}_{\mathrm{td}}[\![C]\!]F\Delta = \bot$ (for all F).

A straightforward generalization of the method underlying the bottom-up algorithm of section 4 is to define a dependency relation as follows:

The pair $\langle C, \Delta \rangle$ depends on Δ_{upd} if there is an atom B_i in the body of C such that $(pred\ B_i) = (pred\ \Delta_{upd})$, with Δ being any pattern satisfying $(pred\ \Delta) = (pred\ C)$. As an example, consider clause C_2 in program P_{ex} from example 4.1:

```
(C2)  p(X,Y):- true, p(Y,X).
```

This dependency relation would lead to the following: If any pattern for predicate p is updated, then all four tuples $\langle C_2, p(\mathsf{G},\mathsf{G})\rangle$, $\langle C_2, p(\mathsf{G},\mathsf{A})\rangle$, $\langle C_2, p(\mathsf{A},\mathsf{G})\rangle$, and $\langle C_2, p(\mathsf{A},\mathsf{A})\rangle$ should be reprocessed.

However, this approach seems to be too coarse. It appears to be possible to achieve a more efficient analysis of program P_{ex} by relying on a more fine-grained dependency relation where

$\langle C_2, p(\mathsf{G},\mathsf{A})\rangle$ depends on $\langle p(\mathsf{A},\mathsf{G})\rangle$
$\langle C_2, p(\mathsf{A},\mathsf{G})\rangle$ depends on $\langle p(\mathsf{G},\mathsf{A})\rangle$
etc.

Defining a more fine-grained dependency relation leads to the consideration of a dynamic relation, that is, one which is modified during the fixpoint iteration. As an example, consider the following program:

```
(C1)  p(a,Y):- true.
(C2)  p(X,Y):- true, p(Y,X), q(Y,X).
(C3)  q(X,Y):-    ...
```

Suppose an iterand F^n in a chaotic sequence for the program satisfies $F^n\, p(\mathsf{A},\mathsf{A}) = p(\mathsf{G},\mathsf{A})$. If we in the $n+1$'st iteration evaluate $\mathbf{C}_{\mathrm{td}}\, [\![C_2]\!]\, F^n\, p(\mathsf{A},\mathsf{A})$, the call pattern $q(\mathsf{G},\mathsf{A})$ will be computed for $q(Y,X)$. Thus, we are led to consider $\langle C_2, p(\mathsf{A},\mathsf{A})\rangle$ as depending on $q(\mathsf{G},\mathsf{A})$. Now, suppose a subsequent iterand F^{n+d} satisfies $F^{n+d}\, p(\mathsf{A},\mathsf{A}) = p(\mathsf{A},\mathsf{A})$. That would lead us to consider $\langle C_2, p(\mathsf{A},\mathsf{A})\rangle$ as depending on $q(\mathsf{A},\mathsf{A})$. Thus given the above program we obtain:

$\langle C_2, p(\mathsf{A},\mathsf{A})\rangle$ depends on $\langle p(\mathsf{A},\mathsf{A})\rangle$ and $\langle q(\mathsf{G},\mathsf{A})\rangle$ upon iteration $(n+1)$
$\langle C_2, p(\mathsf{A},\mathsf{A})\rangle$ depends on $\langle p(\mathsf{A},\mathsf{A})\rangle$ and $\langle q(\mathsf{A},\mathsf{A})\rangle$ upon iteration $(n+d+1)$
etc.

These considerations motivate the definition of a dynamic dependency relation, where $\langle C, \Delta\rangle$ depends on Δ' if Δ' has been computed as a call pattern for an atom in the body of C, during the most recent evaluation of Δ against C.

The usefulness of a dynamic dependency relation can be traced to the definition of the semantic function $\mathbf{A}_{\mathrm{td}}$ (in definition 5.2 of the abstract top-down semantics). To evaluate $\mathbf{A}_{\mathrm{td}}\ [\![A]\!]\ F\ \Pi$, the function F must be applied to $\Delta = (project\ A\ \Pi)$, where the abstract constraint Π is the result of processing the part of the clause to the left of atom A, implying that Π depends on F. Thus, the value of $\Delta = (project\ A\ \Pi)$ cannot (at a reasonably low cost) be predicted prior to the fixpoint iteration. By contrast, definition 4.2 of the bottom-up semantics prescribes that the evaluation of $\mathbf{A}_{\mathrm{bu}}\ [\![A]\!]\ S\ \Pi$ requires the application of S to the syntactically given entity $(pred\ A)$.

The top-down algorithm is specified in figure 1 in pseudo-code. The main program is divided into an initialization and an iteration part. In the latter, procedures ***update*** and ***scan*** are called. Procedure ***scan*** implements step one. It is a function which returns the value of an expression $\mathbf{C}_{\mathrm{td}}\,[\![C]\!]\,F\,\Delta$ and as a side-effect modifies the dynamic dependency information. Procedure ***update*** implements steps two and three. Monotonicity of the iterand is preserved by recursively working upwards in the lattice of patterns for the predicate in question. The procedure also takes care of adding pairs to ***workset***.

The variables ranging over composite domains are:

The variable $F \in \mathit{Sem}_{td}$ represents the iterand. Initially, F is assigned the bottom value $\lambda\Delta.\bot$. Upon termination F is the least fixpoint of $\bigsqcup_{C\in P}(\mathbf{C}_{\mathrm{td}}\,[\![C]\!])$.

The variable *workset* $\in \mathcal{P}\,(\mathit{Clause} \times \mathit{Pat})$ holds the pairs $\langle C, \Delta\rangle$ that are waiting to be processed.

The variable *depend* $\in (\mathit{Pat} \rightarrow \mathcal{P}\,(\mathit{Clause} \times \mathit{Pat} \times \mathcal{N}))$ maps each pattern Δ to the set of tuples $\langle C, \Delta', i\rangle$ that are currently depending on Δ. The index i refers to an atom in the body of C, namely the atom for which call pattern Δ was computed during a previous scan of C with input pattern Δ'.

The variable *last_call* $\in (\mathit{Clause} \times \mathit{Pat} \times \mathcal{N}) \rightarrow \mathit{Pat}$ is continuously modified so that the value of *last_call*(C, Δ, i) is always the call pattern which has been computed for the i'th body atom of C, during the most recent evaluation of Δ against C. Initially, *last_call* maps all triples to $\bot$. Upon each iteration, *last_call* is the inverse function of ***depend*** (see the invariant (1) below). The variable serves as a means of deciding in which points the dependency relation should be modified during a clause scan.

The variable *fathers* $\in (\mathit{Pat} \rightarrow \mathcal{P}\,\mathit{Pat})$ is assigned a function which maps any pattern Δ to the set of patterns placed immediately above Δ, with respect to the ordering relation on *Pat*. This function is used by procedure *update* in the preservation of monotonicity of the iterand.

In the analysis of the algorithm, an iteration refers to an execution of the while-loop controlled by the test ***workset*** $\neq \emptyset$. F^n, *depend*$^n(C, \Delta, i)$, etc., denote the values of the variables upon the n'th iteration.

It can be shown that for all input programs P the following properties hold invariantly for all n:

$$\langle C, \Delta_{dep}, i\rangle \in \mathit{depend}^n(\Delta) \Leftrightarrow \Delta = \mathit{last\_call}^n(C, \Delta_{dep}, i) \qquad (1)$$

$$\mathit{last\_call}^{n-1}(C, \Delta, i) \sqsubseteq \mathit{last\_call}^n(C, \Delta, i) \qquad (2)$$

$$F^{n-1}(\mathit{last\_call}^{n-1}(C, \Delta, i)) \sqsubseteq F^n(\mathit{last\_call}^n(C, \Delta, i)) \qquad (3)$$

Furthermore, we have that for $n \geq 1$

$$\begin{aligned} &\langle C, \Delta\rangle \text{ is added to } \mathit{workset}^n \\ \Leftrightarrow\ &\exists i, \Delta_{upd} : (F^{n-1}\,\Delta_{upd}) \sqsubset (F^n\,\Delta_{upd}) \text{ and } \langle C, \Delta, i\rangle \in \mathit{depends}^n(\Delta_{upd}) \\ \Leftrightarrow\ &\exists i : F^{n-1}(\mathit{last\_call}^n(C, \Delta, i)) \sqsubset F^n(\mathit{last\_call}^n(C, \Delta, i)) \text{ (by inv 1)} \qquad (4) \end{aligned}$$

Input: Program P.
Output: The value of F upon termination of the algorithm is $\mathbf{P}_{td}\,[\![P]\!]$.

%% initialization
workset $:= \{\langle C, \Delta\rangle \mid C \in P$ and $(pred\ C) = (pred\ \Delta)\}$
for all relevant Δ **do** $F := \bot$ — % Δ is relevant if $(pred\ \Delta)$
for all relevant Δ **do** $depend(\Delta) = \emptyset$ **od** — % is defined in P.
for all relevant $\langle C, \Delta, i\rangle$ **do** $last\_call(C, \Delta, i) = \bot$ **od**
% i is relevant if $1 \le i < Atoms_C$.
  for all relevant Δ **do** $fathers(\Delta) = \{\Delta' \in Pat_{(pred\ \Delta)} \mid \Delta \sqsubset \Delta'$ **od**
%% iteration
while *workset* $\neq \emptyset$ **do**
  select and delete $\langle C, \Delta_{call}\rangle$ from *workset*
  $\Delta_{succ} := scan(C, F, \Delta_{call})$
  if $\Delta_{succ} \not\sqsubseteq F(\Delta_{call})$ **then** $update(\Delta_{call}, \Delta_{succ})$ **fi**
od

procedure $update(\Delta_{call}, \Delta_{succ})$
begin
  $F(\Delta_{call}) := F(\Delta_{call}) \sqcup \Delta_{succ}$
  for all $\langle C, \Delta, i\rangle \in depend(\Delta_{call})$ **do** *workset* $:=$ *workset* $\cup \{\langle C, \Delta\rangle\}$ **od**
  for all $\Delta \in fathers(\Delta_{call})$ **do** **if** $\Delta_{succ} \not\sqsubseteq F(\Delta)$ **then** $update(\Delta, \Delta_{succ})$ **fi od**
end

function $scan(C, F, \Delta_{call})$
begin
  let $(H :- \pi, B_1 \ldots B_m) = C$
  $\Pi := generate(H, \Delta_{call})$
  $\Pi := add(\pi, \Pi)$
  for $i := 1 \ldots m$ **do**
    $\Delta_{new} := project(B_i, \Pi)$
    $\Pi' := generate(B_i, F(\Delta_{new}))$
    $\Pi := meet(\Pi, \Pi')$
    $\Delta_{old} := last\_call(C, \Delta_{call}, i)$
    $last\_call(C, \Delta_{call}, i) := \Delta_{new}$
    $depend(\Delta_{old}) := depend(\Delta_{old}) \setminus \{\langle C, \Delta_{call}, i\rangle\}$ — % modifying the dynamic
    $depend(\Delta_{new}) := depend(\Delta_{new}) \cup \{\langle C, \Delta_{call}, i\rangle\}$ — % dependency relation
  od
  $\Delta_{succ} := project(H, \Pi)$
  return Δ_{succ}
end

Fig. 1. The top-down algorithm based on dynamic dependency information. The variables ranging over simple domains are $P \in Progr$, $C \in Clause$, $H, B_i \in Atom$, $\pi \in Con$, $\Pi \in Acon$, $\Delta, \Delta_{call}, \ldots \in Pat$, and $i \in \mathcal{N}$.

Since $F^{n-1} \preceq F^n$ we have that if $\langle C, \Delta\rangle \notin \textit{worklist}^n$ then the equation $F^{n-1}(\textit{last\_call}^n(C, \Delta, i)) = F^n(\textit{last\_call}^n(C, \Delta, i))$ holds for all $i < \textit{Atoms}_C$. It follows that

$$\langle C, \Delta\rangle \notin \textit{workset}^n \Rightarrow \mathbf{C}_{\mathrm{td}} [\![C]\!] F^n \Delta = \mathbf{C}_{\mathrm{td}} [\![C]\!] F^{n-1} \Delta \qquad (5)$$

Correctness of the top-down algorithm is defined with respect to the abstract top-down semantics: For an arbitrary program P, the output of the algorithm as executed with input P must be equal to $\mathbf{P}_{\mathrm{td}} [\![P]\!]$. We assume that the algorithm implements iteration steps one through three as defined above.

Proposition 5.1 *The top-down algorithm is correct.*

The complexity of the top-down algorithm is expressed in terms of the number of clause scans, i.e., evaluations of $\mathbf{C}_{\mathrm{td}} [\![C]\!] F \Delta$.

Proposition 5.2 *The top-down algorithm performs at most $\textit{Atoms}_C * \textit{DomHeight}_C * \textit{DomSize}_C$ scans of any clause C in any program on which the algorithm is run.*

Recall the definition of $\textit{Atoms}_C$ etc. from the end of section 4. Letting

$$\begin{aligned} \textit{DomSize}_P &= \textit{max}_{C \in P}\ \textit{DomSize}_C \\ \textit{DomHeight}_P &= \textit{max}_{C \in P}\ \textit{DomHeight}_C \\ \textit{Atoms}_P &= \Sigma_{C \in P}\ \textit{Atoms}_C \end{aligned}$$

we obtain from the above proposition that the total number of clause scans during anaysis of an arbitrary program P is bound by $\textit{DomSize}_P * \textit{DomHeight}_P * \textit{Atoms}_P$.

6 Discussion

An efficent algorithm for top-down or query directed analysis of logic programs has been defined in which the fixpoint iteration is controlled using a dynamic dependency relation.

The complexity result for the top-down algorithm is promising because the number of passes of dataflow analysis over each clause is independent of the size of the rest of the program. Considering all clauses in a given program, the total number of clause scans was shown to be bound by the following product: The maximum size of the domain of patterns for a predicate, times the height of that domain, times the number of atoms in the given program. Thus, the worst-case bound of [4] is improved by two orders of magnitude.

In the groundness analysis that has served as an example analysis, the number of patterns for a predicate is exponential in the arity of the predicate; and indeed, most practically useful analyses will make use of domains than even are larger than those considered here. To deal with this kind of combinatorial explosion, it may be useful to combine the application of a dynamic dependency relation with the use of widening and narrowing operators [8].

Another useful modification of the top-down algorithm is to incorporate a minimal function graph approach [14], as discussed in [12]. Execution of a minimal function graph (*mfg*) version of the algorithm begins with a set of patterns provided by the programmer, implying a constraint on how the program may be queried. Clauses are then only scanned for the externally given patterns plus those whose evaluation is required for the evaluation of the externally given ones. This approach may reduce the average cost of the algorithm. In addition, information may be provided about how predicates will be called during runtime, rather then merely about a programs input-output behavior as in the (non-*mfg*) abstract top-down semantics.

References

1. I. Balbin and K. Ramamohanarao. A generalization of the differential approach to recursive query evaluation. *J. Logic Programming* 1987, **4**, pp. 259–262.
2. F. Bancilhon and R. Ramakrishnan. *An Amateur's Intorduction to Recursive Query Processing Strategies.* MCC Technical Report No. DB-091-86, March 1986.
3. C. Beeri and R. Ramakrishnan. On the power of magic. *J. Logic Programming* 1991, **10**, pp. 225–299.
4. B. Le Charlier, K. Musumbu, P. Van Hentenryck. A generic abstract interpretation algorithm and its complexity analysis. *Proc. 8th International Conference on Logic Programming,* 1991, Paris, pp. 64–78.
5. B. Le Charlier and P. Van Hentenryck. *Experimental evaluation of a generic abstract interpretation algorithm for Prolog.* Technical Report CS-91-55, August 1991, Brown University.
6. P. Cousot and R. Cousot. Abstract Interpretation: a unified lattice model for static analysis of programs by construction or approximation of fixpoints. *Proc. 4th ACM Symposium on Principles of Programming Languages*, 1977, pp. 238–252, .
7. P. Cousot and R. Cousot. Automatic synthesis of optimal invariant assertions: Mathematical foundations. *Proc. ACM Symposium on Artificial Intelligence and programming languages,* SIGPLAN Notices, **12** (8),1977, pp. 1–12.
8. P. Cousot and R. Cousot. Abstract interpretation and application to logic programs. *J. Logic Programming* 1992 **13**, pp. 103–179.
9. S. K. Debray. Static inference of modes and data dependencies in logic programs. *ACM Transactions on Programming Languages and Systems*, **11** (3), 1989, pp. 418–450.
10. J. Jaffar and J.-L. Lassez. *Constraint logic programming.* Technical Report, Monash University, June 1986.
11. J. Jaffar, S. Michaylov, P. Stuckey and R. Yap. An abstract machine for CLP($\mathcal{R}$). *SIGPLAN PLDI,* San Francisco, June 1992.
12. N. Jørgensen. *Abstract interpretation of constraint logic programs.* Ph.D. thesis. To appear in *Datalogiske skrifter,* 1993, Computer Science Dept., Roskilde University Center.
13. N. Jørgensen, K. Marriott, and S. Michaylov. Some global compile-time optimizations of CLP($\mathcal{R}$). *Proc. International Logic Programming Symposium,* San Diego, 1991, pp. 420–434.

14. N. D. Jones and A. Mycroft. Data flow analysis of applicative programs using minimal function graphs. *Proc. 13th ACM Symposium on Principles of Programming Languages*, Florida, 1986, pp. 296–306.
15. R.A. O'Keefe. Finite fixed-point problems. *Proc. 4th International Conference on Logic Programming*, 1987, Melbourne, 729–743.
16. J.W. Lloyd. *Foundations of logic programming.* Springer-Verlag, 1984.
17. G.A. Kildall. A unified approach to global program optimization. *Proc. POPL 1973*, Boston, 194–206.
18. K. Marriott and H. Søndergaard. Analysis of constraint logic programs. *Proc. North American Conference on Logic Programming*, Austin, 1998, pp. 521–540.
19. K. Marriott and H. Søndergaard. Bottom-up dataflow analysis of normal logic programs. *J. Logic Programming* 1992, **13**, pp. 181–204.
20. C. Martin and C. Hanking. Finding fixed points in finite lattices. *FPLCA 1987* Portland, Ohio.
21. C. S. Mellish. *The automatic generation of mode declarations for Prolog programs.* DAI Research Paper 163, University of Edinburgh, 1981.
22. S. Peyton-Jones and C. Clack. Finding fixpoints in abstract interpretation, in: S. Abramski and C. Hankin (eds): *Abstract interpretation of declarative languages.* Ellis Horwood, 1987, pp. 246–265.
23. A. Tarski. A lattice-theoretical fixpoint theorem and its application. *Pacific Journal of Mathematics*, 1955, 5, pp. 285–309.

Fast Abstract Interpretation Using Sequential Algorithms

Alex Ferguson[1] and John Hughes[2]

[1] Dept of Computing Science, University of Glasgow, Glasgow G12 8QQ, SCOTLAND.
[2] Informationsbehandling, Chalmers Tekniska Högskola, Göteborg, SWEDEN.

1 Introduction

Abstract interpretation in the framework introduced by Cousot and Cousot requires finding fixpoints of continuous functions between abstract lattices [CC77]. Very often these abstract functions are expressed as typed λ-expressions, even when the language being analysed isn't functional—for example an abstract interpretation derived from a denotational semantics in the style of Nielson [Nie82] will naturally be in this form. So implementing an abstract interpreter often requires an evaluator for λ-expressions over lattices. Of course, evaluation must always terminate—even when the result is the bottom element of the lattice concerned.

In practice this evaluation is intractable. The problem is caused by function types: lattices of functions grow more than exponentially in the size of their type. λ-expressions of quite simple types therefore denote functions that are too enormous to manipulate efficiently. Attempts to find clever representations of functions (as *frontiers*) have really failed to solve the problem [HH92], and in practice the intractability is avoided by avoiding functions—function types may be abstracted as the one point type, discarding all information about function values, or analyses may be constructed from a more intensional semantics in which 'function' values are *closures* (code–environment pairs), so that true functions do not appear. Such approaches are forced to make more or less ad hoc approximations, at a cost in accuracy, and moreover cannot yield faithful implementations of the many analyses in the literature in which functions *are* abstracted as functions. In this paper we describe an approach which we hope will make evaluation of λ-expressions over finite lattices tractable in practice.

Our basic idea is to save time by computing only *part* of the value of each λ-expression. For example, to compute the value of the application $e_1\ e_2$ it's not necessary to compute the value of e_1 precisely. We only need to know what value e_1 returns when applied to e_2 —one point in the graph of the function, rather than the whole graph. Moreover, if e_1 is a constant function, we may not need to compute the value of e_2 at all. Or if e_2 is itself a function, e_1 may only apply it to a couple of different arguments, and so we may only need to know its value at a few points rather than its entire graph. Our intention is to lazily compute only as much as is needed of each expression, in the hope that in normal cases this will be only a tiny proportion of the whole. This idea is also at the heart of Young's *pending analysis* [YH86] and Launchbury's use of *minimal function graphs* [Lau91] to represent just the part of the graph that is needed, but these approaches are really confined to first-order functions. Our contribution is to extend the same idea smoothly to the higher-order case.

This idea of 'lazy abstract interpretation' can work only if we can compute a small part of the result of an expression from small parts of the values of its sub-expressions. But fixpoints cause a problem. Consider the function $f = \lambda(x, y, z).(1, x, z)$. The approximations to its fixpoint are

$$\begin{aligned} f^0(\bot,\bot,\bot) &= (\bot,\bot,\bot) \\ f^1(\bot,\bot,\bot) &= (1,\bot,\bot) \\ f^2(\bot,\bot,\bot) &= (1,1,\bot) \\ f^3(\bot,\bot,\bot) &= (1,1,\bot) \\ &\vdots \end{aligned}$$

Now suppose we want to compute the third component of fix f, and consider at what stage we know that it is definitely $\bot$. We can't know this after computing $f^1\ \bot$ since nothing so far distinguishes the second and third components, and yet the second component is defined in the fixpoint. We can't know it after computing $f^2\ \bot$ since it might be that the third component depends on the second, which is now defined. (The function $g = \lambda(x, y, z).(1, x, y)$ yields the same first three approximations, yet the third component of fix g is defined.) We can know that the third component is $\bot$ in the fixpoint only after seeing two *identical* approximations. Verifying that two approximations are identical requires evaluating them exactly, and so lazy computation of fixed points is impossible. (Note that the problem only arises because we insist that evaluation terminates in every case. There would be no need to compare approximations if we permitted the evaluator to loop when the result is $\bot$).

The difficulty in the example above is that we cannot know which other parts of the fixpoint the third component depends on. If we knew it depended only on itself, we could at once conclude that its value in the fixpoint was $\bot$. But continuous functions give us no information about dependencies between inputs and outputs. Our solution is to adopt a different notion of 'function': Berry and Curien's *sequential algorithms* [BC82]. Sequential algorithms tell us precisely which inputs each output depends on, and so enable us to define an efficient lazy fixpointing algorithm. We believe that continuous functions are 'too extensional' to admit efficient abstract interpretation, while sequential algorithms are just intensional enough.

The rest of the paper is structured as follows. Section 2 contains preliminaries. We informally introduce Berry and Curien's theory in section 3. In the next section we explain how sequential algorithms can be used to represent continuous functions and describe our lazy fixpointing algorithm. In section 5 we encounter a difficulty in using sequential algorithms for abstract interpretation. As the name suggests, sequential algorithms can represent only 'sequential' functions—excluding functions such as parallel or. But abstract interpretation requires a very important non-sequential operation: least upper bound. We describe a way of encoding abstract functions as sequential algorithms so that this difficulty is avoided. Because of this encoding, it transpires that the fixpoint of an abstract function is not encoded as the *least* fixpoint of the corresponding sequential algorithm. In section 6 we discuss the representation of encoded abstract functions as sequential algorithms—the main topic is a variant of the lazy fixpointing algorithm. The final three sections present some practical results, discuss related work, and conclude.

2 Preliminaries

For definiteness, we shall consider the class of finite domains

$$D ::= \mathbb{1} | D_\perp | D + D | D \times D | D \to D$$

where + denotes separated sum. Our abstract lattices will be any domains in this class formed without using +. This class is sufficient for a wide range of abstract interpretations, in particular Burn, Hankin and Abramsky's strictness analysis [BHA85]. In order to avoid complications caused by free variables and environments, we will consider the problem of evaluating *categorical combinator* expressions [Cur86] rather than λ-expressions. Thus the terms we consider all denote functions, and are of the form

$e ::= e \circ e$	composition
$\mid \langle e, e \rangle$	pairing ($\langle f, g \rangle\, x = (f\ x, g\ x)$)
$\mid \Lambda(e)$	currying ($\Lambda(f)\ x\ y = f(x, y)$)
$\mid \mathrm{fix}\ e$	fixed point
$\mid$ *primitive*	

where the primitives include at least

$id : \alpha \to \alpha$	identity function
$ap : (\alpha \to \beta) \times \alpha \to \beta$	function application
$\pi_i : \alpha_1 \times \alpha_2 \to \alpha_i$	projections

In general other primitives will also be necessary to define a particular abstract interpretation: in particular almost every abstract interpretation will require

$$\sqcup : \alpha \times \alpha \to \alpha \text{ least upper bound}$$

The translation from λ-expressions into categorical combinators is standard [Cur86].

3 Sequential Algorithms

In this section we give a rather simplified and informal presentation of Berry and Curien's theory. The theory is really an alternative to Scott's domain theory, in which *concrete data structures* play the role of domains and *sequential algorithms* play the role of functions. Berry and Curien's motivation was to find semantic spaces for denotational semantics which did not include inherently parallel functions like 'parallel or'. Such spaces should be better suited for giving a semantics to sequential programming languages.

A *concrete data structure* (hereafter CDS) is just a special kind of Scott domain whose elements (or 'states') can be thought of as trees with labelled edges and optionally labelled nodes. For example, one of the elements of the CDS of lists of integers is

```
      cons
  hd/     \tl
  1        cons
       hd/     \tl
       2        nil
```

The node labels (here *cons*, *nil*, 1 and 2) are called *values* and correspond to constructors in an ordinary functional language. The edge labels (here *hd* and *tl*) are called *selectors* and correspond to field names. We write such trees in the form $value\{\ldots selector : subtree \ldots\}$, omitting the braces if there are no sub-trees. For example, we write the tree above as $cons\{hd : 1, tl : cons\{hd : 2, tl : nil\}\}$.

Pair nodes are unlabelled, just as in a functional language implementation, since a value of pair type can only be of one form. For example,

```
      *
  fst/ \snd
   1    2
```

We write such trees as $\langle subtree, subtree\rangle$; the subtrees are always labelled *fst* and *snd*.

Any subtree may be undefined, which we write as $\perp$. Elements of a CDS form a Scott domain under the usual ordering on trees. In Table 1 we define several standard CDS constructions.

CDS	Elements	
$\mathbb{1}$	$\perp$	
$\sigma \times \tau$	$\langle s, t\rangle$	where $s \in \sigma, t \in \tau$
$\sigma + \tau$	$\perp$, 0 {left : s}, 1 {right : t}	where $s \in \sigma, t \in \tau$
$\sigma_\perp$	$\perp$, *lift*{lifted : s}	where $s \in \sigma$

Table 1. Standard CDS constructions

Any node in a tree can be identified by the sequence of selectors along the path to it from the root. Such a sequence of selectors is called a *cell*. The cells in the list example above are ϵ (the root), *hd*, *tl*, *tl.hd*, and *tl.tl*. An unlabelled node is not considered to be a cell: the cells in the second example are therefore just *fst* and *snd*. A cell is *filled* if the corresponding subtree is defined, and *unfilled* if it is $\perp$. We write $t[c]$ for the value labelling cell c of tree t. If the cell is unfilled, $t[c] = \perp$.

Sequential algorithms are just decision trees, in which each node may inspect a cell of the input or create a node of the output. Sequential algorithms may contain three kinds of nodes:

– **input nodes**

```
     valof c
  v1/  ...  \vn
```

which inspects cell c of the input and continues by following the branch labelled with the value found there.

- **output nodes**

```
      output v
  s1/  ...    \sn
```

which creates a node of the output labelled v with subtrees labelled $s_1 \ldots s_n$ created by the corresponding algorithms.

- **unlabelled nodes**

```
       *
  fst/ \snd
```

which creates an unlabelled node of the output with components created by the corresponding algorithms.

Note that sequential algorithms are themselves elements of a CDS! In particular, higher-order algorithms are quite possible. We write the CDS of algorithms from σ to τ as $\sigma \to \tau$.

We can define application of a sequential algorithm to an argument as follows:

$$\begin{aligned} apply\ \perp\ x &= \perp \\ apply\ (\text{output}\ v\,\{\ldots s_i : a_i \ldots\})\ x &= v\,\{\ldots s_i : apply\ a_i\ x \ldots\} \\ apply\ \langle a_1, a_2\rangle\ x &= \langle apply\ a_1\ x, apply\ a_2\ x\rangle \\ apply\ (\text{valof}\ c\,\{\ldots v_i : a_i \ldots\})\ x &= \begin{cases} \perp & \text{if } x[c] = \perp \\ apply\ a_i\ x & \text{if } x[c] = v_i \end{cases} \end{aligned}$$

Thus every sequential algorithm defines a continuous function between CDSs. The fixed point of a sequential algorithm is just the fixed point of this function.

Sequential algorithms must satisfy several 'well-formedness' constraints:

- No cell may be read twice along any path through the algorithm.
- No cell may be read until its parent has been read.
- The types of the input and output trees must be respected.

Formalising these constraints is surprisingly difficult, and is largely responsible for the apparent complication of Berry and Curien's definitions. One pleasant consequence: there are only finitely many sequential algorithms between finite CDSs. This is important for guaranteeing termination of fixed point computations using CDSs.

Sequential algorithms for id, π_i, ap and so on exist, and the operations $\langle f, g\rangle$, $\Lambda(f)$ and $f \circ g$ can be defined so that CDSs form a cartesian closed category. We don't have space to describe these operations here: the reader can find their definitions in [BC82], and a description of their implementations in [Cur86, HF92, FH92]. Suffice it to say that if we assign a sequential algorithm to every primitive of our abstract interpretation language, then every term built from those primitives denotes a sequential algorithm.

4 Representing Functions as Sequential Algorithms

We can now interpret types as either domains or CDSs, and interpret terms as either continuous functions or sequential algorithms. Our intention is of course to *represent* domain elements by CDS elements in our abstract interpreter. It turns out that we cannot define a function from a CDS element to the domain element it represents, or vice versa. To relate the interpretations we need the generality of a 'logical relation'.

For every type σ, we define a relation R_σ between the domain interpretation of σ and the CDS interpretation. Intuitively $x\, R_\sigma\, y$ holds if the domain element x can be represented by the CDS element y. R is defined by induction over the type structure in table 2.

$$
\begin{gathered}
\bot \; R_{\mathbb{1}} \; \bot \\
(x, y)\, R_{\sigma\times\tau} \left\langle x^\dagger, y^\dagger \right\rangle \triangleq x\, R_\sigma\, x^\dagger \wedge y\, R_\tau\, y^\dagger \\
\bot \; R_{\sigma+\tau} \; \bot \\
\text{inl } x\, R_{\sigma+\tau}\, 0 \left\{ \text{left} : x^\dagger \right\} \triangleq x\, R_\sigma\, x^\dagger \\
\text{inr } y\, R_{\sigma+\tau}\, 1 \left\{ \text{right} : y^\dagger \right\} \triangleq y\, R_\tau\, y^\dagger \\
\bot \; R_{\sigma_\bot} \; \bot \\
\text{lift } x\, R_{\sigma_\bot}\, \mathit{lift} \left\{ \text{lifted} : x^\dagger \right\} \triangleq x\, R_\sigma\, x^\dagger \\
f\, R_{\sigma\to\tau}\, f^\dagger \triangleq \forall x, x^\dagger . x\, R_\sigma\, x^\dagger \Rightarrow f\ x\, R_\tau\ \mathit{apply}\ f^\dagger\ x^\dagger
\end{gathered}
$$

Table 2. The Representation Relation

Note that some continuous functions have *no* representation as a sequential algorithm—for example, 'parallel or'. Some continuous functions have *several* representations, differing in the evaluation order of the parameters—for example, the greatest lower bound function $\sqcap : \mathbb{1}_\bot \times \mathbb{1}_\bot \to \mathbb{1}_\bot$ is represented by either of the algorithms below:

```
  valof fst                valof snd
     |lift                     |lift
  valof snd                valof fst
     |lift                     |lift
 output lift              output lift
     |lifted                   |lifted
    _|_                       _|_
```

Some sequential algorithms represent *no* continuous function, since it's possible to 'read the code' of a function argument and to return different results given, for example, the two representations of $\sqcap$ above—something no continuous function can do. Thus R_σ does not contain a function in either direction; the generality of a relation is really required.

Nevertheless it can be shown that if $f\, R\, f^\dagger$ and $g\, R\, g^\dagger$, then

- $f \circ g \, R \, f^\dagger \circ g^\dagger$
- $\Lambda(f) \, R \, \Lambda(f^\dagger)$
- $\langle f, g \rangle \, R \left\langle f^\dagger, g^\dagger \right\rangle$
- $\mathrm{fix}\, f \, R \, \mathrm{fix}\, f^\dagger$
- $id \, R \, id$
- $ap \, R \, ap$
- $\pi_i \, R \, \pi_i$

It follows that if we can find suitable representations of the primitives, then the CDS interpretation of any term of our abstract interpretation language will represent the domain interpretation.

This result is of no use unless we can compute the CDS interpretation of terms lazily—that is, compute a small part of the interpretation of a compound term from small parts of its subterms. There's no problem with composition, currying and tupling, but as we saw in the introduction finding fixpoints by computing the limit of a Kleene chain is not lazy. We must therefore find an alternative way to compute the fixpoint of a sequential algorithm. The problem was that testing for $\perp$ components of a fixpoint required a 'global' comparison of every part of the fixpoint. Our aim is to develop a 'local' test for $\perp$ instead, so that we can establish that a particular cell is unfilled in the fixpoint just by inspecting a few other cells.

Observe that as we apply a sequential algorithm, we can identify exactly the cells of the input that each cell of the output depends on—they are just those which are read before the output cell is written. Let us define a variant of *apply* which labels each cell of the output with the set of input cells it depends on. We shall assume that the input is also so labelled, and that an output that depends on a particular cell of the input also thereby depends transitively on all the cells that the input cell depends on. It is convenient to introduce a notional cell which is always unfilled—we write this cell as $\perp$ too. By convention, we take cells 'written' by an undefined part of a sequential algorithm to depend on this special cell. We write a tree depending on S as t^S, and define *apply* with an additional parameter, the cells already read, which we also write as a superscript.

$$apply^S \ \perp \ x = \perp^{S \cup \{\perp\}}$$

$$apply^S \ (\text{output } v \, \{\ldots s_i : a_i \ldots\}) \ x = v \left\{\ldots s_i : apply^S \ a_i \ x \ldots\right\}^S$$

$$apply^S \ \langle a_1, a_2 \rangle \ x = \left\langle apply^S \ a_1 \ x, apply^S \ a_2 \ x \right\rangle$$

$$apply^S \ (\text{valof } c \, \{\ldots v_i : a_i \ldots\}) \ x = \begin{cases} \perp^{S \cup \{c\} \cup S'} & \text{if } x[c] = \perp^{S'} \\ apply^{S \cup \{c\} \cup S'} \ a_i \ x & \text{if } x[c] = v_i^{S'} \end{cases}$$

where $x[c] = v^S$ if cell c is filled with value v and labelled with set S in tree x, and by convention $x[\perp] = \perp^{\{\perp\}}$.

Now consider the chain of approximations $x_i = (apply^{\{\}} \ f)^i \ \perp^{\{\}}$. It is clear that erasing labels gives the sequence of approximations to fix f, and so we can establish that a cell is unfilled in fix f by showing that it is unfilled in every x_i.

We make the following observations, which can be proved by induction on i:

(1) $x_i[c] = v^S \wedge v \neq \perp \Rightarrow x_{i+1}[c] = v^S$ (once we have finished computing $x[c]$, we know all of the cells it depends on).

(2) $x_i[c] = v_i^{S_i} \wedge x_{i+1}[c] = v_{i+1}^{S_{i+1}} \Rightarrow S_i \subseteq S_{i+1}$ (if we compute $x_i[c]$ a bit further, we may discover new dependencies but we cannot lose old ones).
(3) Let $x_{i+1}[c] = v^S$. Then $v = \perp \Leftrightarrow \exists c' \in S.c'$ is unfilled in x_i (unfilled output cells depend on unfilled input cells—note that unfilled cells created by undefined algorithms 'depend on' the always unfilled cell).

Inspired by this last condition, we define our local test for $\perp$.

Definition 1. Cell c is *detectably* $\perp$ in x_i, where $x_i[c] = v^S$, if

- $c \in S$, or
- $i > 0 \wedge \exists c' \in S.c'$ is detectably $\perp$ in x_{i-1}.

Note that we can determine whether a cell is detectably $\perp$ by examining only the cells it depends on. Note also that cell $\perp$ is detectably $\perp$ in every x_i, since $x[\perp] = \perp^{\{\perp\}}$. We now sketch a proof that this local test is correct.

Lemma 2. If c is detectably $\perp$ in x_i, then c is detectably $\perp$ in x_{i+1}.

Proof. By induction on i, using observations (1) and (2).

Lemma 3. If c is detectably $\perp$ in x_i, then c is unfilled in x_i.

Proof. By induction on i. The base case is trivial. For the induction case, let $x_{i+1}[c] = v^S$. Since c is detectably $\perp$, either $c \in S$ or $\exists c' \in S.c'$ is detectably $\perp$ in x_i.

In the former case, let $x_i[c] = u^T$. If $u \neq \perp$, then $S = T$ (observation (1)), so $c \in T$, so c is detectably $\perp$ in x_i, so c is unfilled in x_i (induction hypothesis). This contradicts $u \neq \perp$, and so c must be unfilled in x_i, and since $c \in S$, c must also be unfilled in x_{i+1} (observation (3)).

In the latter case, c' is unfilled in x_i (induction hypothesis), and so c is unfilled in x_{i+1} (observation (3)).

Corollary 4. If c is detectably $\perp$ in x_i, then c is unfilled in fix f.

In a finite CDS, we can also show the following.

Theorem 5. If c is unfilled in fix f, then c is detectably $\perp$ in some x_i.

Proof. Suppose $c_n = c$ is unfilled in x_n, but is not detectably $\perp$. Let $x_n[c_n] = v^S$. If $n > 0$ then by observation (3), $\exists c_{n-1} \in S.c_{n-1}$ is unfilled in x_{n-1}. But since c_n is not detectably $\perp$ in x_n, c_{n-1} cannot be detectably $\perp$ in x_{n-1}, and moreover $c_{n-1} \neq c_n$. Continuing in this fashion we can construct n *distinct* cells $c_0 \ldots c_n$ such that c_i is unfilled in x_i, but not detectably $\perp$.

Now, in a finite CDS there is a bound on the number of distinct cells—say N. So no cell can be both unfilled and not detectably $\perp$ in x_{N+1}. It follows that any cell which is unfilled in fix f must be detectably $\perp$ in x_{N+1}.

Using these results, our lazy fixpoint algorithm computes the value in a cell by computing it in successive approximations until it is either filled or detectably $\perp$.

Curien gives another operational interpretation to fix on sequential algorithms in the third chapter of his book [Cur86]. But his interpretation loops when attempting to compute the contents of an unfilled cell, as of course one would expect of an implementation of a programming language. What is new about our fixpoint algorithm is not that it works on sequential algorithms, but that (for finite CDSs) it is guaranteed to terminate, and it uses the structure of sequential algorithms to give that guarantee efficiently.

5 Encoding Abstract Functions Sequentially

We can now lazily compute any term of our abstract interpretation language as a CDS element, provided the primitives can be represented as sequential algorithms. Unfortunately our work is not done: the least upper bound operation $\sqcup_\sigma : \sigma \times \sigma \rightarrow \sigma$ cannot be represented as a sequential algorithm. The reason is that any sequential algorithm lub_σ must inspect one of its arguments first. Then if this argument is $\perp$, the result of lub_σ must be $\perp$—but this is not a correct implementation of $\sqcup_\sigma$ if the other argument is defined. Least upper bound is a function like parallel or, with no sequential implementation. So we have chosen a representation of abstract functions which cannot represent one of the most important.

However, most abstract interpreters are implemented in sequential programming languages, yet can compute least upper bounds with no difficulty. How is this possible? The trick is to represent the $\perp$ element of the abstract lattices by a special defined value, rather than by entering an infinite loop. This idea is so obvious that it is not usually considered worth mentioning: it is simply an implementation matter which need not be discussed. But by applying it at the semantic level, we will be able to encode abstract functions as *sequential* functions (still in the world of domains), which we can then represent as CDS elements. This encoding is actually not at all trivial: indeed, an unforeseen difficulty arises. We therefore describe it in detail.

We shall encode elements of the abstract lattice σ as elements of the domain $\hat{\sigma}$, and define a logical relation $E_\sigma : \sigma \leftrightarrow \hat{\sigma}$ such that $x\, E_\sigma\, \hat{x}$ is true when $\hat{x}$ is an encoding of x. $\hat{\sigma}$ and E_σ are defined in Table 3, by recursion over the type structure. The only interesting case is $\sigma_\perp$, which is encoded as $\mathbb{1} + \hat{\sigma}$, thus representing $\perp$ by a proper value.

σ	$\hat{\sigma}$	$E_\sigma : \sigma \leftrightarrow \hat{\sigma}$
$\mathbb{1}$	$\mathbb{1}$	$\perp\ E_{\mathbb{1}}\ \perp$
$\sigma_\perp$	$\mathbb{1} + \hat{\sigma}$	$\perp\ E_{\sigma_\perp}\ \text{inl}\ \perp$ $\text{lift}\ x\ E_{\sigma_\perp}\ \text{inr}\ \hat{x} \stackrel{\Delta}{=} x\ E_\sigma\ \hat{x}$
$\sigma \times \tau$	$\hat{\sigma} \times \hat{\tau}$	$(x, y)\ E_{\sigma \times \tau}\ (\hat{x}, \hat{y}) \stackrel{\Delta}{=} x\ E_\sigma\ \hat{x} \wedge y\ E_\tau\ \hat{y}$
$\sigma \rightarrow \tau$	$\hat{\sigma} \rightarrow \hat{\tau}$	$f\ E_{\sigma \rightarrow \tau}\ \hat{f} \stackrel{\Delta}{=} \forall x, \hat{x}. x\ E_\sigma\ \hat{x} \Rightarrow f x\ E_\tau\ \hat{f} \hat{x}$

Table 3. The Sequential Encoding of Lattice Elements

It is easy to show the following facts, by induction over the type structure:

- If $x\, E_\sigma\, \hat{x}$ and $\hat{x} \sqsubseteq \hat{x}'$ then $x\, E_\sigma\, \hat{x}'$.
- If $x\, E_\sigma\, \hat{x}$ and $x'\, E_\sigma\, \hat{x}$ then $x = x'$.
- $\forall x \in \sigma. \exists \hat{x} \in \hat{\sigma}. x\, E_\sigma\, \hat{x}$.

So every lattice element has an encoding—including the troublesome $\sqcup_\sigma$.

As in the previous section, it is easy to show that if $f\, E\, \hat{f}$ and $g\, E\, \hat{g}$ then

- $f \circ g\, E\, \hat{f} \circ \hat{g}$
- $\Lambda(f)\, E\, \Lambda(\hat{f})$
- $\langle f, g \rangle\, E\, \left\langle \hat{f}, \hat{g} \right\rangle$
- $id\, E\, id$
- $ap\, E\, ap$
- $\pi_i\, E\, \pi_i$

and moreover $\sqcup_\sigma$ is encoded by lub_σ, defined in Table 4, where again the only interesting case is $\sigma_\perp$. Note that this is a 'left-to-right' lub—$\sqcup_\sigma$ could equally well be encoded by a right-to-left lub, which shows that encodings are not unique. Encodings of other primitives are easily found.

$\mathrm{lub}_{\mathbf{1}}\ (\perp, \perp) \triangleq \perp$
$\mathrm{lub}_{\sigma_\perp}\ (\perp, y) \triangleq \perp$ $\mathrm{lub}_{\sigma_\perp}\ (\mathrm{inl}\ \perp, y) \triangleq y$ $\mathrm{lub}_{\sigma_\perp}\ (\mathrm{inr}\ x', y) \triangleq \mathrm{inr} \begin{cases} \perp & \text{if } y = \perp \\ x' & \text{if } y = \mathrm{inl}\ \perp \\ \mathrm{lub}_\sigma\ (x', y') & \text{if } y = \mathrm{inr}\ y' \end{cases}$
$\mathrm{lub}_{\sigma \times \tau}\ ((x, y), (x', y')) \triangleq (\mathrm{lub}_\sigma\ (x, x'), \mathrm{lub}_\tau\ (y, y'))$
$\mathrm{lub}_{\sigma \to \tau}\ (f, f') \triangleq \lambda x. \mathrm{lub}_\tau\ (f\ x, f'\ x)$

Table 4. The Encoding of Least Upper Bound

It remains to show how encodings of fixpoints can be calculated. First note that if $e\, E_\sigma\, \hat{e}$, it *does not* follow that $\mathrm{fix}\ e\, E_\sigma\, \mathrm{fix}\ \hat{e}$. The difficulty is that $\perp$ is not encoded as $\perp$—it is encoded as a total element of course. Let $\hat{\perp}_\sigma$ be the encoding of $\perp_\sigma$. Then the approximations $e^i\ \perp_\sigma$ to $\mathrm{fix}\ e$ can be encoded as $\hat{e}^i\, \hat{\perp}_\sigma$. Since every one of these approximations is a total element, they do not in general form a chain, and so we must be careful when we talk about their 'limit'.

We do know that since all our lattices are finite, the sequence $e^i\ \perp_\sigma$ eventually stabilises, and we may expect the $\hat{e}^i\, \hat{\perp}_\sigma$ to do the same. We write the limit of an eventually stable sequence as $\lim \hat{e}^i\, \hat{\perp}_\sigma$. Certainly the $\hat{e}^i\, \hat{\perp}_\sigma$ eventually encode $\mathrm{fix}\ e$, but this does not imply that the sequence stabilises! Since encodings are not unique, it is possible that the $\hat{e}^i\, \hat{\perp}_\sigma$ oscillate between different encodings of the fixpoint.

We address this by defining another partial order on the domain of encodings: intuitively $\hat{x} \lessdot_\sigma \hat{y}$ if $\hat{y}$ encodes a more defined value than $\hat{x}$, and they are encoded 'in the same way'—the arbitrary choices between for example left-to-right and right-to-left parameter evaluation are made consistently. Formally we define

$$x \lessdot_\sigma y \triangleq \mathrm{lub}_\sigma\ (x, y) = y$$

It is easy to show by induction over σ that

- $\text{lub}_\sigma\ (x, x) = x$
- $\text{lub}_\sigma\ (x, \text{lub}_\sigma\ (y, z)) = \text{lub}_\sigma\ (\text{lub}_\sigma\ (x, y), z)$
- $\text{lub}_\sigma\ (x, y) = y \wedge \text{lub}_\sigma\ (y, x) = x \Rightarrow x = y$

from which it follows that $<_\sigma$ is a partial order, and moreover $x <_\sigma \text{lub}_\sigma\ (x, y)$.

We cannot conclude from this that the sequence $\hat{e}^i \hat{\bot}_\sigma$ stabilises. But we *can* define another sequence

$$z_0 = \hat{\bot}_\sigma$$
$$z_{i+1} = \text{lub}_\sigma\ (z_i, \hat{e}^i\ z_i)$$

which encodes the same chain $e^i\ \bot$, but is a $<_\sigma$-chain. Now it follows that the z_i stabilise, and that fix $e\, E_\sigma \lim z_i$. Note the analogy between lub and Cousot and Cousot's *widening operators*.

To summarise: we have shown how to encode abstract values as elements of larger domains, and how to compute the encoded values of the terms of our abstract interpretation language.

6 Abstract Interpretation Using Sequential Algorithms

Our abstract interpreter is implemented by representing the *encodings* of the previous section as sequential algorithms. Thus the relation between the original lattice elements and the CDS elements we actually compute is the composition of E and R. We avoid the problem of representing $\sqcup_\sigma$: instead we must find a sequential algorithm for lub_σ. This is straightforward from the definition in Table 4. In fact we suspect that *every* lattice element has an encoding that can be represented as a sequential algorithm.

The only problem is the computation of fixpoints. Firstly, since each encoding may in general be represented (via R) by several sequential algorithms, we again face the problem of sequences which oscillate between different representations of the same encoding. The solution is the same as in the last section: we define a relation on sequential algorithms by

$$f < g \triangleq \text{lub} \circ \langle f, g \rangle = g$$

we show that it is a partial order, and conclude that if $e\, E\, \hat{e}$, $\hat{e}\, R\, \hat{e}^\dagger$, and $\hat{\bot}\, R\, \hat{\bot}^\dagger$ then the sequence of algorithms

$$z_0 = \hat{\bot}^\dagger$$
$$z_{i+1} = \text{lub} \circ \left\langle z_i, \mathit{apply}\ \hat{e}^\dagger\ z_i \right\rangle$$

stabilises at a representation of fix e.

The second difficulty is that the lazy fixpointing algorithm of section 4 is not applicable, since we are not computing least fixed points. Instead we need a lazy limit finding algorithm. We can define one as follows.

First note that the sequences whose limits we need to find consist entirely of *total elements*—that is, all cells are filled. Let the elements of the sequence be z_i: we say that a set of cells S are *fixed* in z_{i+1} if each cell in S has the same value in z_i and z_{i+1}, and if each cell in S depends only on other cells in S. It is clear that fixed cells in z_i contain the same values in all subsequent approximations, and moreover every cell becomes fixed eventually—at least when the limit is reached, if not before. Our lazy limit finding algorithm computes the contents of a cell in the limit by computing it in the first approximation in which it is fixed.

7 Practical Results

We have implemented an abstract interpreter based on sequential algorithms in Lazy ML. At first we represented CDS elements by Lazy ML trees: LML's lazy evaluation then ensures that only those parts of the trees which are actually needed are computed. In an effort to reduce storage requirements we later changed to a representation in which the branches of each node are represented as a function from selector names to subtrees, which saves space at the cost of recomputing trees each time they are traversed. We are experimenting with a mixture of representations, storing the results of fixpoint computations but recomputing other trees.

We implemented a version of Burn, Hankin and Abramsky's strictness analysis [BHA85] using Wadler's abstract domain for lists [Wad87]. Some care is necessary in choosing the sequential algorithms for Wadler's list primitives: a good choice of argument evaluation order can mean that in some cases, some arguments need not be evaluated at all, with a significant saving in analysis time.

Since Meyer has shown that first-order strictness analysis is complete in deterministic exponential time, we cannot hope for good worst-case performance[3]. Instead we hope to show that performance is good in practice. We take as our example the program *foldr* (++) [] which concatenates a list of lists. (Here ++ is the list concatenation operator, and *foldr* is the higher-order function that combines the elements of a list using a binary operator). Of course this is a very small example, but we choose it because since Hunt and Hankin first used it, it has been discussed in several papers and is something of a benchmark. It requires an abstract value for *foldr* to be calculated in the lattice

$$(4 \to 4 \to 4) \to 4 \to 6 \to 4$$

where 4 and 6 are chain lattices of the respective heights. This lattice has over 500,000 elements.

We compare the performance of our analyser with that of Hunt's implementation, which represents functions by the 'frontiers' where the function value changes, rather as a surface is represented by contour lines. Hunt and Hankin report that finding the frontier of *foldr* in this example takes around 15 minutes. Our analyser requires around 5 seconds on a Sun 4/75. If the same program is transformed to continuation passing style, then *foldr* must be analysed in the lattice

$$(4 \to 4 \to (4 \to 2) \to 2) \to 4 \to 6 \to (4 \to 2) \to 2$$

[3] Meyer's result is unpublished: an independent proof appears in [HY86].

Hunt's analyser cannot complete this analysis, even given 15 hours. Ours requires around 10 seconds. This illustrates the fact that at higher types the cost of computing frontiers blows up, while the cost of computing sequential algorithms does not appear to.

Our analysis is fast because we compute only a small part of the representation of *foldr*. The complete representation consists of many thousands of nodes, and requires (at least) several hours to compute—we have been unable to do so. Thus it is not practical to analyse *foldr* once and save the result in a file for re-use: we achieve good performance only by re-analysing *foldr* at each use. This has implications for separate compilation. Frontiers have an advantage here, since once it is computed the frontier for *foldr* is quite compact—around 50 elements.

A more serious problem is the space required by our analyser: the *foldr* example requires 0.5MB, and the entire representation of *foldr* cannot be computed even given 120MB! The sequential algorithms we compute are not so large: the problem is that the LML garbage collector is unable to free intermediate results during analysis. Our analyser suffers from a very serious 'space leak'. We are currently investigating this problem.

8 Related Work

The most developed way of evaluating abstract λ-expressions uses the frontiers which we have already referred to. First introduced by Clack and Peyton-Jones [CJ85] as a representation of first-order functions, they have been gradually generalised to wider classes of functions [MH87, Hun89, HH91]. The most elegant and general presentation is in Hunt's thesis [Hun91]. Hunt and Seward have independently implemented frontier-based strictness analysers for realistic programming languages. Most recently Hankin and Hunt have speeded up fixpoint computation by finding a sequence of approximate fixpoints in smaller lattices, and using each one to help find the next [HH92]. It is an implementation of this technique which we used for the comparison above—without it, the time for analysing the *foldr* example is much greater. An alternative to frontiers has been proposed by Chuang and Goldberg [CG92]: they represent functions by λ-expressions in a certain canonical form. We understand that they need around 8 minutes to analyse the *foldr* example.

The unacceptable costs of fixpoint finding have led several researchers to study *approximate* evaluation. Hankin and Hunt show how to find approximate frontiers in [HH92], and using this technique can analyse the *foldr* example in a few seconds. Baraki has shown in principle how approximate abstract values of polymorphic functions at complex instances can be obtained from the simplest instance [Bar91], and Seward has used this technique to calculate a (better) approximation in the *foldr* example in a few seconds [Sew93]. Young's pending analyser has been used extensively to evaluate higher-order abstract functions: it simply interprets the abstract functions and detects infinite recursions by comparing the parameters of recursive function calls with those of enclosing calls [YH86]. Since equality of functions is very expensive to test for, Young's analyser does not detect all infinite recursions and instead resorts to occasional 'depth bounding'—*i.e.* approximation. Finally, approximate values of abstract λ-expressions can be obtained by first performing a *closure analysis* [Ses91] to discover what function might be called where, and then approximating every call of an unknown function as a call of any function that might appear there.

The disadvantage of all approximate methods is that the quality of the results is quite sensitive to small changes in the program: for example, applying the identity function to each function valued variable could in some cases worsen the results dramatically.

9 Conclusions

We have proposed Berry and Curien's *sequential algorithms* as a representation of function values in abstract interpretation—perhaps the first 'practical' application of this theory. We have implemented an evaluator for abstract λ-expressions, and a prototype strictness analyser based on this technology. We have tested our implementation on two well-known hard cases.

Unlike the various approximate evaluation methods, our implementation delivers predictable results that accord with the theory of abstract interpretation. Moreover, it does so orders of magnitude faster than previous exact methods. We believe that, if its excessive space use can be cured, our approach will make higher-order abstract interpretations useable in practice.

Acknowledgements

We would particularly like to thank Sebastian Hunt, for both his help in making comparisons with frontiers, and his observations about earlier presentations of this work; and Phil Wadler, for his many helpful comments and suggestions. Matthias Felleison, Jean-Jaques Levy, and Pierre-Louis Curien also gave us very useful criticisms, as did the anonymous referees.

References

[Bar91] G. Baraki. A Note on Abstract Interpretation of Polymorphic Functions. In *ACM Functional Programming and Computer Architecture*, Boston, 1991.

[BC82] G. Berry and P.-L. Curien. Sequential Algorithms on Concrete Data Structures. *Theoretical Computer Science*, 20:265–321, 1982.

[BHA85] G. Burn, C. Hankin, and S. Abramsky. The Theory of Strictness Analysis of Higher Order Functions. In H. Ganzinger and N. D. Jones, editors, *Proceedings of the Workshop on Programs as Data Objects, Lecture Notes in Computer Science*, volume 217, pages 42–62. Springer-Verlag, October 1985.

[CC77] P. Cousot and R. Cousot. Abstract Interpretation: a Unified Lattice Model for Static Analysis of Programs by Construction or Approximation of Fixpoints. In *Proc. 4th ACM Symp. on Principles of Programming Languages*, Los Angeles, 1977.

[CG92] T.-R. Chuang and B. Goldberg. A Syntactic Approach to Fixed Point Computation on Finite Domains. In *Lisp and Functional Programming.* ACM, 1992.

[CJ85] C. Clack and S. L. Peyton Jones. Strictness Analysis—a Practical Approach. In *Proceedings 1985 Conference on Functional Programming Languages and Computer Architecture*, pages 35–49, Nancy, France, 1985.

[Cur86] P.-L. Curien. *Categorical Combinators, Sequential Algorithms and Functional Programming.* Research Notes in Theoretical Computer Science. Pitman, 1986.

[FH92] A. Ferguson and J. Hughes. Abstract Interpretation of Higher-Order Functions using Concrete Data Structures. In *Functional Programming*, Workshops in Computing, Glasgow, 1992. Springer-Verlag.

[HF92] J. Hughes and A. Ferguson. A Loop-detecting Interpreter for Lazy, Higher-order Programs. In *Functional Programming*, Workshops in Computing, Glasgow, 1992. Springer-Verlag.

[HH91] S. Hunt and C. Hankin. Fixed points and frontiers: a new perspective. *Journal of Functional Programming*, 1(1), January 1991.

[HH92] C. Hankin and S. Hunt. Approximate Fixed Points in Abstract Interpretation. In *European Symposium on Programming*, volume 582 of *LNCS*, Rennes, 1992. Springer-Verlag.

[Hun89] S. Hunt. Frontiers and open sets in abstract interpretation. In D. MacQueen, editor, *Functional Programming Languages and Computer Architecture.* ACM Publications, 1989.

[Hun91] S. Hunt. *Abstract Interpretation of Functional Languages: From Theory to Practice.* PhD thesis, Imperial College, London, October 1991.

[HY86] P. Hudak and J. Young. Higher-order Strictness Analysis in Untyped Lambda-calculus. In *ACM Principles of Programming Languages*, pages 97–109, St. Petersburg, Florida, January 1986.

[Lau91] J. Launchbury. *Projection Factorisations in Partial Evaluation (PhD thesis)*, volume 1 of *Distinguished Dissertations in Computer Science.* Cambridge University Press, 1991.

[MH87] C. Martin and C. Hankin. Finding Fixed Points in Finite Lattices. In G. Kahn, editor, *ACM Conf. on Functional Programming and Computer Architecture*, LNCS, Portland, Oregon, 1987. Springer-Verlag.

[Nie82] F. Nielson. A Denotational Framework for Data Flow Analysis. *Acta Informatica*, 18:265–287, 1982.

[Ses91] P. Sestoft. *Analysis and Efficient Implementation of Functional Programs.* PhD thesis, DIKU, University of Copenhagen, Denmark, October 1991.

[Sew93] J. Seward. Polymorphic Strictness Analysis using Frontiers. In *ACM Symp. on Partial Evaluation and Semantics-Based Program Manipulation*, pages 186–193, Copenhagen, June 1993.

[Wad87] Phil Wadler. Strictness Analysis on Non-Flat Domains (by Abstract Interpretation over Finite Domains. In S. Abramsky and Chris Hankin, editors, *Abstract Interpretation of Declarative Languages*, pages 266–275. Ellis Horwood, 1987.

[YH86] J. Young and P. Hudak. Finding Fixpoints on Function Spaces. Research Report YALEU/DCS/RR-505, Dept. of Computer Science, Yale University, December 1986.

Abstract Interpretation and Verification of Reactive Systems *

J.C. Fernandez

VERIMAG, B.P. 53 X, 38041 - Grenoble Cedex, France

Abstract. This paper presents a variant of a refined partition algorithm, which exploits the irrelevance of unreachable states. When the state space is infinite, the number of accessible classes may be finite and the number of inaccessible classes infinite. The underlying idea is to incorporate a reachability analysis based on the concept of abstract interpretation. The new algorithm may terminate in cases where the original algorithm diverges.

1 Introduction

Verification of reactive systems. Program verification is a part of system design whose purpose is to "prove program correctness". By *verification*, we mean the comparison of two formal specifications: those of the program, noted $\mathcal{D}$, and those of the properties, noted $\mathcal{S}$, that the program is supposed to satisfy. The specifications of the program is translated into an intermediate form, such as Labeled Transition Systems (LTS for short), event structures, Petri nets, etc ... In this paper, we are concerned by LTS and equivalence or preorder relations between LTS. According to the specification formalisms for the specifications of the properties, two main verification approaches for concurrent programs can be distinguished:

Model checking: the specifications of the properties are formulas of a temporal logic. A formula of $\mathcal{S}$ is interpreted as a set of *computations* on $\mathcal{D}$. For example, in linear time semantics a computation is a maximal sequence, whereas in branching time semantics a computation is a tree. Then, the verification consists in checking that all the computations of $\mathcal{D}$ belong to $\mathcal{S}$.

Equivalence checking The specifications of the properties is a LTS. The verification consists in comparing the two LTS $\mathcal{D}$ and $\mathcal{S}$ with respect to a given equivalence or preorder relation.

These approaches are complementary: it turns out in practice that some of the expected properties of a distributed system are easier to express using a logical formalism, and the others by giving an abstraction of the expected behavior. Moreover, a logic can *characterize* a behavioral relation: two systems are related if and only if they satisfy the same set of logical formulas.

The limit of this approach. Some difficulties arise when data structures are associated with states. An idea that has been emerging is to represent set of states symbolically [BCM*90, Bry86, CBM89]. In this case, we one must be able to compute the

* This work was partially supported by ESPRIT Basic Research Action "SPEC"

function *pre*, *post*, and intersection of classes and to decide the inclusion of classes. Such symbolic computation is possible in the boolean case, by means of Binary Decision Diagrams [Bry86, CBM89, HRR91]. Other authors [EFT91, BdS92, FKM93] investigate the application of BDDs in the case of symbolic equivalence checking. In this paper, we concentrate on an algorithm performing minimization, according to a bisimulation equivalence, the Minimal Model Generation algorithm, or MMG for short. It combines the construction of the states graph from a program, a formula or any comprehensive expression of (labeled or unlabeled) transition systems, and its reduction by a bisimulation. It computes the coarsest partition compatible with the transition relation, refinement of an initial partition. This coarsest partition is the greatest fixpoint of a split function, *split*(see below). This algorithm has been implemented in a *Lustre* compiler [HRR91] and in *Aldébaran* [FKM93], for *strong bisimulation* [Mil80, Par81], *branching bisimulation* [GW89] and a kind of *weak bisimulation* [FM91]. However, the use of BDDs is possible for source programs containing only variables ranging over a finite domain. We investigate currently other decidable theories, such as the lattice of intervals or the lattice of polyhedra [CC76, CC77, Hal79, CH77].

Motivations In the finite case, i.e. the number of classes (accessible and inaccessible classes) of the resulting partition is finite, the algorithm terminates. We wish to apply the algorithm to general systems without restrictness on the finiteness of the state space. However, this algorithm may fail, even if the model is finite: consider the case we have a finite number of accessible and stable classes, and an infinite number of inaccessible classes.
To explain the problem, let us give a very simple example: Assume we want to build,

```
x := 0 ;
do
    x= 0  ⟶ x:= x-1 ||
    x := x+1
od
```

Fig. 1. A simple program

for the program figure 1 the minimal model according to the greatest bisimulation, with respect to the initial partition $\{x \mid x \in \mathbb{Z} \wedge x = 0\}$ and $\{x \mid x \in \mathbb{Z} \wedge x \neq 0\}$, shortly noted respectively $(x = 0)$ and $(x \neq 0)$.
At the first step, we obtain three classes:

$$C_0 = (x = 0) \quad C_3 = (x = -1) \quad C_4 = (x \neq 0) \wedge (x \neq -1)$$

At the second step we obtain four classes:

$$C_0 = (x = 0) \quad C_3 = (x = -1) \quad C_5 = (x = -2)$$

$$C_6 = (x \neq 0) \wedge (x \neq -1) \wedge (x \neq -2)$$

And so on: at the step n, we obtain $n-1$ inaccessible classes ($x = -j$), for $j = 2, n$. In order to tackle the problem of dealing with infinite state space, we use the concept of *Abstract Interpretation* [CC77]. The problem of preservation of properties, expressed by logic formulas, was studied [Sif82, Sif83, BBLS92]. We choose an abstract domain on which an upper approximation of the least fixpoint of the accessibility function *Acc*, and a lower approximation of the greatest fixpoint of the split function *split* are computed. Consider the simple program. An abstract interpretation of *Acc*, figure 2, is defined on the abstract domain of intervals. So, at each step

$$Acc = \lambda X.\{0\} \cup \{x+1 \mid x \in X\} \cup \{x-1 \mid x \in X \ \wedge \ (x = 0)\}.$$

Fig. 2. The accessibility function for the simple program

of MMG, we split each class of the current partition in two subclasses: one containing states proved inaccessible, by the upper approximation of accessible states, the other being its complement. The lower approximation of the MMG fixpoint is $(x < -1), (x = 0), (x > 0)$. Note that in this case, it coincides with the greatest fixpoint.

Organization. The paper is organized as follows. Section 2, 3 and 4 recall the theoretical framework of the problem: in section 2 definitions and notations, in Section 3 the Minimal Model Generation algorithm [BFH90] and in Section 4 the notion of abstraction [CC90]. In section 5, we investigate a method to obtain a lower approximation of the greatest bisimulation. The application area of these techniques is the following: we consider a class of programs where a set of states is characterized by a propositional formula. The atomic formulas are built from numerical variables, constants and relational symbols. We compute a least solution of a system of equations, obtained by projection of the abstract space on a *basis* instead of computing a least fixpoint of an approximate function of the accessibility function. We deduce a lower approximation of the greatest bisimulation of the abstract model. This method is illustrated by a very simple example.

2 Labeled Transition Systems and Bisimulations

We recall here the main definitions related to Labeled Transition Systems (LTS, for short) and bisimulation relations, together with the associated notations.
Throughout the paper, we consider a LTS $S = (Q, A_\tau, \{\xrightarrow{a}\}_{a \in A_\tau}, q_{init})$ where: Q is a set of program *states*, $A_\tau = A \cup \{\tau\}$ is a set of *action names*, where τ is a distinguished name representing an *internal* action, $\rightarrow \subseteq Q \times A_\tau \times Q$ is the *transition relation* of the program, and q_{init} is the *initial state* of the program, i.e., a distinguished element of Q.
Associated with the LTS S, we introduce the following notations:
$\mathcal{P}$ represents the complete lattice of partitions of Q:

- it is ordered by the refinement relation $\sqsubseteq$: $\rho \sqsubseteq \rho'$ iff $\forall X \in \rho, \exists X' \in \rho'. X \subseteq X'$
- its greatest lower bound operator is $\sqcap$: $\bigsqcap_i \rho_i = \{T \neq \emptyset \mid T = \bigcap_i X_i \text{ and } X_i \in \rho_i\}$

The pre- and post-condition functions from 2^Q to 2^Q, for a given $a \in A_\tau$, are defined as usual:

$$pre^a(X) = \{q \in Q \mid \exists q' \in X \text{ such that } q \xrightarrow{a} q'\}$$
$$post^a(X) = \{q \in Q \mid \exists q' \in X \text{ such that } q' \xrightarrow{a} q\}$$

For each of these functions, say F_a, we note $F(X) = \bigcup_{a \in A_\tau} F^a(X)$ and by $[q]_\rho$ the class of the partition ρ containing the state q. Let $post^a_\rho$ the post-condition functions corresponding to a partition ρ. These functions are overloaded as follows:

from 2^Q to $\mathcal{P}$: $post^a_\rho(X) = \{[q]_\rho \mid q \in post^a(X)\}$
from $\mathcal{P}$ to $\mathcal{P}$: $post^a_\rho(\rho') = \bigcup\{post^a_\rho(X) \mid X \in \rho'\}$

Equivalence relations for distributed systems can be defined in several ways, according to their semantics and the description formalism upon which they are based. We will focus on bisimulation or simulation based equivalences defined on LTS which, when ordered by the relation "finer than", are positioned between *bisimulation equivalence* and *trace equivalence*.
Intuitively, the simulation and bisimulation relations are intended to compare LTS from a behavioral point of view: The simulation (resp. bisimulation) relation is a preorder (resp. an equivalence) relation on the LTS behavior, observed from a given abstract level. A relation $R \subseteq Q \times Q$ is a *simulation* iff it satisfies the following property:

$$(p_1, p_2) \in R \wedge p_1 \xrightarrow{a} q_1 \Rightarrow \exists q_2 \,.\, (p_2 \xrightarrow{a} q_2 \wedge (q_1, q_2) \in R)$$

The simulation equivalence is defined by $R \cap R^{-1}$ and a *bisimulation* is a simulation verifying $R = R^{-1}$. From this general definition, one can obtain several equivalence or preorder relations [FM91].
Let ρ be the partition associated to a bisimulation relation. The quotient of the LTS S by ρ is the LTS which the set of states is the set of equivalence classes and there is a transition from B_1 to B_2 labeled by a if and only if each state p of B_1 lead to a state of B_2 by a transition labeled by a (we use the notation $p \xrightarrow{a} B_2$).

Proposition 2.1 *[KS90, Fer90] The following statements are equivalent:*

- *ρ is a bisimulation,*
- $\forall B_1, B_2 \in \rho \forall a \in A_\tau \,.\, B_1 \subseteq pre^a(B_2) \vee B_1 \cap pre^a(B_2) = \emptyset$
- $\forall B_1, B_2 \in \rho \forall a \in A_\tau \forall p, q \in B_1 \,.\, p \xrightarrow{a} B_2 \Leftrightarrow q \xrightarrow{a} B_2$

Thus, if ρ is a partition, then for each $B \in \rho, pre^a(B)$ is an union of classes of ρ.

3 Minimal Model Generation

In this section we recall the algorithm proposed in [BFH90, BFH*92], which allows to compute the quotient of a LTS S with respect to strong bisimulation. First, we give its principle, introducing the main notations.

3.1 The principle of the algorithm

Given a LTS S, the principle of the MMG algorithm is to refine an initial partition ρ_{init} of the state space of S until a *reachable* and *stable* partition is obtained. More precisely, it can be defined as the computation of the greatest fixpoint of a *split function* on the partition ρ_{init}, distinguishing two subsets of classes at each step of this computation :

- The set π of *reachable classes*, i.e., the classes containing at least one element which has been found reachable so far from q_{init}.
- The set σ of *stable classes*, i.e., the reachable classes which have been found stable with respect to the current partition (assuming a class X is stable with respect to a partition ρ if and only if $\{X\} = split(X, \rho)$).

A step of the algorithm consists in scanning each reachable class of the current partition, checking whether this class is stable or not with respect to this partition. Whenever a reachable class is found unstable, it is split into stable subclasses, and its predecessors are removed from σ, since their stability is questioned (see below the definition of the *split* function). Only subclasses which are obviously reachable are put in π: those which either contain q_{init}, or are directly reachable from a reachable stable class.
It can be shown that, for a suitable *split* function, the resulting partition exactly coincides with the set of equivalence classes of the coarsest (strong) bisimulation on S containing ρ_{init} ([BFH90]). Thus, when choosing for ρ_{init} the universal partition, this algorithm computes the states of the quotient of S with respect to the strong bisimulation relation $\sim$.
In the rest of the section, we give a more formal description of this algorithm. First, we precise the definitions of the *split* function and of the stability and reachability properties [FM91]:
Let ρ be a partition of the states of S and $X, Y \in \rho$.

split function : $split(X,\rho) = \bigsqcap_{Y \in \rho} \bigsqcap_{a \in A_\tau} \{X \cap pre^a(Y), X \setminus pre^a(Y)\}$
Stability : $Stable(\rho) = \{X \in \rho \mid split(X,\rho) = \{X\}\}$
Stable(ρ) denotes the set of the stable classes of partition ρ.
Reachability : $Acc_\rho(X) = [q_{init}]_\rho \cup \bigcup_{a \in A_\tau} post^a_\rho(X)$.
Given a partition ρ, the set of reachable classes is the least fixed-point of Acc_ρ in the complete lattice 2^{2^Q}. However, note that a class belonging to this set can contain unreachable states.

The MMG algorithm computes the greatest fixpoint

$$\nu\rho.\rho_{init} \sqcap split(\mu\pi.Acc_\rho(\pi \cap Stable(\rho)), \rho).$$

which can be written in a more algorithmic fashion :

```
begin
    ρ = ρ_init; π = {[init]_ρ}; σ = ∅ ;
    while π ≠ σ do
        choose  X in  π \ σ ;
        let  π' = split(X, ρ);
        if  π' = {X} then
            σ := σ ∪ {X}
            π := π ∪ post_ρ(X) ;
        else  π := π \ {X} ;
            if  ∃Y ∈ π' such that init ∈ Y then
                π := π ∪ {Y} ;
            fi
            σ := σ \ pre_ρ(X);
            ρ := (ρ \ {X}) ∪ π';
        fi
    od
end
```

Note that the statement $\sigma := \sigma \setminus pre_\rho(X)$ can be performed by scanning the stable classes and checking if all the transitions from X to a stable class are stable.
This algorithm can be extended respectively to weak bisimulation and branching bisimulation by redefining the *split* function [FM91].

4 Abstraction of Transition Systems

Many program analysis techniques (type checking, constant propagation, data-flow and control-flow analysis, ...) use the notion of abstraction. They have been unified under the concept of *abstract interpretation* [CC77].
There are many ways to abstract a transition system.

4.1 Abstract Interpretation

Given two complete lattices $L_1(\sqsubseteq_1, \bot_1, T_1, \sqcup_1, \sqcap_1)$ and $L_2(\sqsubseteq_2, \bot_2, T_2, \sqcup_2, \sqcap_2)$, a *Galois connection* from L_1 to L_2 is a pair of monotonic functions $\alpha : L_1 \longrightarrow L_2$ and $\gamma : L_2 \longrightarrow L_1$ such that:

$$\forall x \in L_1 \,.\, \forall y \in L_2 \,.\, \alpha(x) \sqsubseteq_2 y \Longleftrightarrow x \sqsubseteq_1 \gamma(y)$$

Proposition 4.1 *[San77] The following statements are equivalent:*

- *(α, γ) is a Galois connection from L_1 to L_2,*
- *α is $\sqcup_1$-distributive and $\gamma = \lambda Y. \sqcup_1 \{X \mid \alpha(X) \sqsubseteq_2 Y\}$.*
- *γ is $\sqcap_2$-distributive and $\alpha = \lambda X. \sqcap_2 \{Y \mid X \sqsubseteq_1 \gamma(Y)\}$.*

The idea is to approximate the least fixpoint $\mu X.F(X)$ of a monotonic function $F : L_1 \longrightarrow L_1$, by the least fixpoint $\mu X.\widehat{F}(X)$ of a monotonic function $\widehat{F} : L_2 \longrightarrow L_2$ such that $\alpha \circ F \circ \gamma \sqsubseteq_2 \widehat{F}$, approximation in the sense that $\mu X.F(X) \sqsubseteq_1 \gamma(\mu X.\widehat{F}(X))$.

4.2 Widening and Narrowing operators

This approach has been discovered and developed in [CC76, CC77] and it is used to enforce the convergence of the iterations for fixpoint computations. It consists in using a *widening operator* on the abstract domain L: $\nabla : L \times L \longrightarrow L$ such that:

$$\forall x, y \in L \,.\, x \sqsubseteq_L x \nabla y$$
$$\forall x, y \in L \,.\, y \sqsubseteq_L x \nabla y$$

and for each increasing chain $x_0 \sqsubseteq_L x_1 \sqsubseteq_L \cdots$ the chain $y_0 = x_0, y_{i+1} = y_i \nabla x_{i+1}$ is not strictly increasing, i. e. the limit of the sequence can be computed in a finite number of steps. Thus, if F_L is monotonic on L, the limit $\underline{F_L}$ of the sequence

$$\begin{aligned} X_0 &= \bot \\ X_{i+1} &= X_i \quad \text{if } F_L(X_i) \sqsubseteq_L X_i \\ &= X_i \nabla F_L(X_i) \quad \text{otherwise} \end{aligned}$$

is an upper approximation of $\mu X \,.\, F_L(X)$. This approximation can be improved using a *narrowing operator* $\Delta : L \times L \longrightarrow L$ such that:

$$\forall x, y, z \,.\, ((z \sqsubseteq_L x) \wedge (z \sqsubseteq_L y) \Rightarrow (z \sqsubseteq_L (x \Delta y) \sqsubseteq_L x)$$

and for all decreasing chains $x_o \sqsupseteq_L x_1 \sqsupseteq_L \cdots$, the chain $y_0 = \underline{F_L}, y_{i+1} = y_i \Delta x_{i+1}$ is not strictly decreasing, i.e. the limit of the sequence can be computed in a finite number of steps. It follows that the limit $\overline{F_L}$ of the sequence

$$\begin{aligned} X_0 &= \underline{F_L} \\ X_{i+1} &= X_i \quad \text{if } F_L(X_i) = X_i \\ &= X_i \Delta F_L(X_i) \quad \text{otherwise} \end{aligned}$$

remains an upper approximation of $\mu X \,.\, F_L(X)$.

5 Applications

In this section, we investigate upper approximation of the accessibility function in order to avoid splitting a class, in the MMG, according to inaccessible states. We propose a lower approximation of the greatest fixpoint:
$\nu\rho.\rho_{init} \sqcap split(\mu\pi.Acc_\rho(\pi \cap Stable(\rho)), \rho)$.

5.1 Abstract Interpretation and Equivalence Checking

Let $S_i = (Q_i, A_\tau, \{\xrightarrow{a}_i\}_{a \in A_\tau}, q_{0_i})$ for i =1,2, be two LTSs where S_2 is an abstraction of S_1 (there is a monotonic function $\alpha : 2^{Q_1} \longrightarrow 2^{Q_2}$ or a relation $R_\alpha \subseteq Q_1 \times Q_2$). By using the definitions of simulation and bisimulation, and the properties of the composition of two relations, we have:

Proposition 5.1

- *R_α is a simulation if and only if* $(\xrightarrow{a}_1)^{-1} \circ R_\alpha \subseteq R_\alpha \circ (\xrightarrow{a}_2)^{-1}$
- *R_α is a bisimulation if and only if* $(\xrightarrow{a}_1)^{-1} \circ R_\alpha \subseteq R_\alpha \circ (\xrightarrow{a}_2)^{-1}$ *and* $(\xrightarrow{a}_2)^{-1} \circ R_\alpha^{-1} \subseteq R_\alpha^{-1} \circ (\xrightarrow{a}_1)^{-1}$

Let $\widehat{pre}$ an abstract interpretation of *pre*, i.e. $\alpha \circ pre \circ \gamma \subseteq \widehat{pre}$. We want to give an upper approximation of the accessible states, with respect to a partition, and then a lower approximation of the greatest bisimulation: for a class, we give a superset of accessible states within the class.

Proposition 5.2 *Let $\gamma(Y) = \cup\{X \mid \alpha(X) \subseteq Y\}$. Then, (α, γ) is a Galois connection and $R_\alpha \subseteq Q_1 \times Q_2$, the relation induced by α, is a simulation between S_1 and S_2.*

Proof. From $\alpha \circ pre \circ \gamma \subseteq \widehat{pre}$, we deduce $\alpha \circ pre \subseteq \widehat{pre} \circ \alpha$, that is the definition of simulation. ∎

Definition 5.1 *Let β be a partition of Q_2 and L be a set of subsets of Q_1. We say that β is a* basis *of L with respect to (α, γ) if and only if :*

$$\forall X \in L \,.\, \exists \beta_1 \subseteq \beta \,.\, X = \bigcup_{B \in \beta_1} \gamma(B).$$

We note by $\mathcal{B}$ the function associating with each set of states its basis:

$$\mathcal{B}(X) = \beta_1 \text{ where } X = \bigcup_{B \in \beta_1} \gamma(B).$$

This condition may be immediately applied to the class of programs where each set of states may be characterized by a propositional formula built on numerical variables, constants and relational symbols. A formula is a disjunction of conjunctions of atomic formulas. An atomic formula is a linear equation or inequation. An element of the basis represents a finite conjunction of atomic formulas.
Coming back to our example program, we want to approximate each class of the current partition, which is a finite conjunction of atomic formulas, by an union of intervals instead of the interval containing the class.
In the following, we consider a Galois connection (α, γ) such that γ is *strict*, i.e. $\gamma(\emptyset) = \emptyset$. We consider a variant of the proposition 5.1.

Proposition 5.3 *Let β be a partition of Q_2 and ρ be a partition of Q_1 such that β is a* basis *of ρ with respect to (α, γ). Suppose that, for all $a \in A_\tau$,*

1. *β is stable with respect to $\widehat{pre}^a$*
2. *$\forall B \in \beta \,.\, \gamma(\widehat{pre}^a(B)) \subseteq pre^a(\gamma(B))$*

Then there is a partition ρ_β of 2^{Q_1} such that

1. *ρ_β is stable with respect to pre^a, (ρ_β is a bisimulation),*
2. *S_1/ρ_β and S_2/β are bisimilar.*

Proof. If β is stable with respect to $\widehat{pre}^a$, then for all $Y \in \beta$, there is $\beta_1 \subseteq \beta$ such that $\widehat{pre}^a(Y) = \bigcup_{Y \in \beta_1} Y$. Thus, we choose $\rho_\beta = \{\gamma(Y_i) \mid Y_i \in \beta\}$ In order to prove ρ_β stable, we prove that

$$\forall X, X' \in \rho_\beta \,.\, X \cap pre^a(X') \neq \emptyset \Rightarrow X \subseteq pre^a(X')$$

Let X, X' be elements of ρ_β, i.e. there is Y, Y' such that $X = \gamma(Y)$ and $X' = \gamma(Y')$. If $X \cap pre^a(X') \neq \emptyset$, then $\gamma(Y) \cap pre^a(\gamma(Y')) \neq \emptyset$. By property $\alpha \circ pre^a \circ \gamma \subseteq \widehat{pre}^a$, $\gamma(Y) \cap \gamma(\widehat{pre}^a(Y')) \neq \emptyset$. By $\cap$-distributivity of γ, $\gamma(Y \cap \widehat{pre}^a(Y')) \neq \emptyset$. By strictness of γ, $Y \cap \widehat{pre}^a(Y') \neq \emptyset$. By stability of β, $Y \subseteq \widehat{pre}^a(Y')$. By monotonicity, $\gamma(Y) \subseteq \gamma(\widehat{pre}^a(Y'))$; By property (2), $\gamma(Y) \subseteq pre^a(\gamma(Y'))$. Thus ρ_β is stable. ∎

Lemma 5.1 *[Cou81] Let*

- *$L(\sqsubseteq, \perp, T, \sqcup, \sqcap)$ be a complete distributive lattice,*
- *F be a monotonic function on L,*
- *β be a partition of L,*
- *F_i be the functions : $L \longrightarrow L$ defined by $F_i(X) = F(X) \sqcap B_i$.*

Then $(P_1, \cdots, P_n)$ is the least solution of the system of equations $X_i = F_i(\bigsqcup_{j=1}^{n} X_j)$ if and only if $\bigsqcup_{i=1}^{n} P_i$ is the least fixpoint of F.

Proposition 5.4 *Assume the hypotheses of lemma 5.1 and let ∇ be a widening operator defined on L. Then the least solution of the following system of equations*

$$X_i^0 = \perp$$

$$X_i^{k+1} = X_i^k \quad \text{if } F_i(\bigsqcup_{j=1}^{n} X_j^k) \sqsubseteq X_i^k$$

$$= (X_i^k \nabla F_i(\bigsqcup_{j=1}^{n} X_j^k)) \sqcap B_i \quad \text{otherwise}$$

can be computed in a finite number of steps and is an upper approximation of $\mu X.F(X)$.

We give the main result of the paper which holds with other bisimulations, defined as in section 2. The intuitive idea is the following: we define a $\widehat{split}$ function in the following manner: take a class of S_2, split the image of this class by γ in S_1, determine a new basis of ρ_β, say β_2, then compute an upper approximation of the accessible states with respect to this basis, and split each class of β_2 under this approximation.

Proposition 5.5 *Let $\widehat{Acc}(X) = \{q_{init}\} \cup post_2(X)$, assume the hypotheses of proposition 5.4 and suppose that β_{init} is a basis of ρ_{init} with respect to (α, γ). We define $\widehat{\text{split}}(B, \beta) = \beta'$ in the following manner. Let*

- *$\beta_2 = B(\text{split}(\gamma(B), \gamma(\beta)))$, where $\gamma(\beta)$ is the image set of β wrt γ,*
- *$(a_1, \cdots, a_n)$ be the least solution of the system of equations 5.4 with respect to β_2 and $\widehat{Acc}$,*
- *$\widehat{A} = \bigcup_{i \in [1,n]} a_i$,*
- *$\beta' = \beta_2 \sqcap \{\widehat{A}, \overline{\widehat{A}}\}$. Then*

$$\nu\beta.\beta_{init} \sqcap \widehat{\text{split}}(\mu\pi.Acc_\beta(\pi \sqcap \text{Stable}(\beta)), \beta).$$

is a lower approximation of the greatest fixpoint computed by the MMG *algorithm:*

$$\nu\beta.\beta_{init} \sqcap \text{split}(\mu\pi.Acc_\beta(\pi \sqcap \text{Stable}(\beta)), \beta).$$

Moreover, If $\gamma(pre_2^a(B) \subseteq pre_1^a(\gamma(B))$, then we obtain an lower approximation of

$$\nu\rho.\rho_{init} \sqcap \text{split}(\mu\pi.Acc_\rho(\pi \sqcap \text{Stable}(\rho)), \rho).$$

Remark We still approximate the previous approximation of the greatest fixpoint computed by the MMG algorithm by taking for a class a single element of the basis, i.e. a conjunction of atomic formulas instead of a disjunction of conjunctions of atomic formulas. We obtain a reduced model containing eventually more classes than the previous one.

6 Example

Let us come back to our example program figure 1 Consider the initial partition $\rho_{init} = \{(x = 0), (x \neq 0)\}$, let L_I be the abstract lattice of intervals, and (α, γ) the Galois connection defined as usual from the set on integers to the lattice of intervals. The upper approximation of *Acc*, figure 2 is given by:

$$Acc_{L_I} = \lambda X.[0,0] \sqcup_{L_I} X \oplus [1,1] \sqcup_{L_I} ((X \sqcap_{L_I} [0,0]) \oplus [-1,-1]).$$

where $[a,b] \oplus [a',b'] = [a+a', b+b'], \bot \oplus [a,b] = [a,b] \oplus \bot = \bot$.
The widening operator [CC76] for the lattice of intervals is defined by :
$\bot \nabla X \quad = X \bot \nabla = X$
$[l_0, u_0] \nabla [l_1, u_1] = [\text{if } l_1 < l_0 \text{ then } -\infty \text{ else } l_0, \text{if } u_1 > u_0 \text{ then } +\infty \text{ else } u_0]$.

Step 1 of the MMG algorithm After the first step of the MMG algorithm, the class $(x = 0)$ is found stable. Thus $\rho_1 = \rho_{init}, \sigma_1 = \{(x = 0)\}, \pi_1 = \rho_1$.

Step 2 of the MMG algorithm After the second step of the MMG, the class $(x \neq 0)$ is split in two subclasses, $(x = -1)$ and $(x \neq -1) \wedge (x \neq 0)$. Thus, the basis is: $\beta_2 = \{[0,0], [-\infty, -2], [-1,-1], [1, +\infty]\}$. Let $Acc_{L_I}^0, Acc_{L_I}^1$, $Acc_{L_I}2$ and $Acc_{L_I}3$ be the functions defined by:

$$Acc_{L_I}^0(X) = Acc_{L_I}(X) \sqcap_{L_I} [0,0]$$
$$Acc_{L_I}^1(X) = Acc_{L_I}(X) \sqcap_{L_I} [1,+\infty]$$
$$Acc_{L_I}^2(X) = Acc_{L_I}(X) \sqcap_{L_I} [-\infty,-2]$$
$$Acc_{L_I}^3(X) = Acc_{L_I}(X) \sqcap_{L_I} [-1,-1]$$

We compute the least solution of the system of equations: $X_i = X_i \nabla Acc_{L_I}^i(\bigsqcup_{L_I}{}_{j=1}^{n} X_j)$

Initially,$X_0^0 = X_1^0 = X_2^0 = X_3^0 = \bot_{L_I}$. After three steps, we obtain the limit: $X_0^2 = [0,0], X_1^2 = [1,\infty], X_2^2 = \bot_{L_I}, X_3^2 = [-1,-1]$.
So, we obtain an upper approximation of the accessible states:$(x \geq -1)$ and a lower approximation of the greatest bisimulation:.

$$\rho_1 = (x = 0) \quad (x = -1) \quad (x \geq 1) \quad (x < -1)$$

Step 3,4,5 of the MMG algorithm The algorithm runs in a finite number of steps, each accessible class is found stable. The final result is

$$\rho_1 = (x = 0) \quad (x = -1) \quad (x \geq 1) \quad (x < -1)$$

and only the class $(x < -1)$ is inaccessible.

7 Conclusion

The practical limitation of automatic verification of concurrent programs is the generation of a state graph on which properties are checked, *equivalence checking* and *model checking*. Two approaches may be studied in order to tackle this problem: either the property is checked "on the fly" or a state graph, minimal according to some equivalence relation on the state space, is generated.
In both cases, one must be able to take into account data type structures. In the boolean case symbolic computation is achievable, by means of Binary Decision Graph. Other variables, ranging over finite domain may be coded using BDDs. This paper is a contribution to deal with state space potentially infinite. More precisely, we are interested by state space having abstract interpretation in the lattice of intervals or the lattice of polyhedra, in which symbolic computation may be possible. We combine the Minimal Model Generation algorithm and abstract interpretation, obtaining an upper approximation of the accessible function in order to avoid splitting accessible classes by inaccessible classes. However, we have not solved the termination problem, even if the reduced model is finite.
From a practical point of view we have implemented in *Aldébaran* the Minimal Model Generation algorithm be means of BDDs for various equivalences with interesting results. We study currently another kind of model where a state is a couple (*control state, memory state).* We consider memory state with numerical variables. We approximate a set of states with numerical variables by a polyhedron. All operations needed for the MMG algorithm are defined on polyhedra and computation of an approximation of the reachable states space is possible.

References

[BBLS92] A. Bouajjani, S. Bensalem, C. Loiseaux, and J. Sifakis. Property preserving simulations. In *Workshop on Computer-Aided Verification (CAV), Montréal*, page , To appear LNCS, June 1992.

[BCM*90] J.R. Burch, E.M. Clarke, K.L McMillan, D.L. Dill, and J. Hwang. Symbolic model checking: 10^{20} states and beyond. In *Proc. 5th IEEE,LICS*, 1990.

[BdS92] A. Bouali and R. de Simone. Symbolic bisimulation minimisation. In *Fourth Workshop on Computer-Aided Verification,Montreal*, june 1992.

[BFH90] A. Bouajjani, J.C. Fernandez, and N. Halbwachs. Minimal model generation. In *Workshop on Computer-aided Verification, Rutgers*, American Mathematical Society, Association for Computing Machinery, June 1990.

[BFH*92] A. Bouajjani, J.C. Fernandez, N. Halbwachs, C. Ratel, and P. Raymond. Minimal state graph generation. *Science of Computer Programming*, 18(3), June 1992.

[Bry86] R. E. Bryant. Graph-based algorithms for boolean function manipulation. *IEEE Transactions on Computers*, C-35(8), 1986.

[CBM89] O. Coudert, C. Berthet, and J. C. Madre. Verification of synchronous sequential machines based on symbolic execution. In *International Workshop on Automatic Verification Methods for Finite State Systems, LNCS 407*, Springer Verlag, 1989.

[CC76] P. Cousot and R. Cousot. Static determination of dynamic properties of programs. In *2th Int. Symp. on Programming*, pages 106,130, Dunod, 1976.

[CC77] P. Cousot and R. Cousot. Abstract interpretation: a unified lattice model for static analysis of programs by construction or approximation of fixpoints. In *4th POPL*, January 1977.

[CC90] P. Cousot and R. Cousot. *Comparing the Galois Connectionn and Widening/Narrowing Approaches to Abstract Interpretation.* Technical Report, LIX, Ecole Polytechnique, May 1990.

[CH77] P. Cousot and N. Halbwachs. Automatic discovery of linear restraints among variables of a program. In *5th. Annual Symp. on Principles of Programming Languages*, pages 84–87, 1977.

[Cou81] P. Cousot. *Semantic Foundations of Program Analysis*, chapter 10. Prentice Hall, Inc., Englewood Cliffs, 1981.

[EFT91] R. Enders, T. Filkorn, and D. Taubner. Generating bdds for symbolic model checking in ccs. In K. G. Larsen, editor, *Proceedings of the 3rd Workshop on Computer -Aided Verification (Aalborg, Denmark)*, july 1–4 1991.

[Fer90] J. C. Fernandez. An implementation of an efficient algorithm for bisimulation equivalence. *Science of Computer Programming*, 13(2-3), May 1990.

[FKM93] J. Cl. Fernandez, A. Kerbrat, and L. Mounier. Symbolic equivalence checking. In *Workshop on Computer-aided Verification, University of Crete*, to appear, July 1993.

[FM91] J.Cl. Fernandez and L. Mounier. A tool set for deciding behavioural equivalences. In J.F. Groote J.C.M. Baeten, editor, *CONCUR'91, Concurrency theory*, LNCS 527, Springer Verlag, August 26-29 1991.

[GW89] R.J. Van Glabbeek and W.P. Weijland. *Branching time and abstraction in bisimulation semantics (extended abstract).* CS-R 8911, Centrum voor Wiskunde en Informatica, Amsterdam, 1989.

[Hal79] N. Halbwachs. *Détermination Automatique de Relations Linéaires Vérifiées par les Variables d'un Programme.* PhD thesis, Université de Grenoble, 1979.

[HRR91] N. Halbwachs, P. Raymond, and C. Ratel. Generating efficient code from dataflow programs. In *Third International Symposium on Programming Language Implementation and Logic Programming*, Passau, August 1991.

[KS90] P. Kanellakis and S. Smolka. Ccs expressions, finite state processes and three problems of equivalence. *Information and Computation*, 86(1), May 1990.

[Mil80] R. Milner. A calculus of communication systems. In *LNCS 92*, Springer Verlag, 1980.

[Par81] D. Park. Concurrency and automata on infinite sequences. In *5th GI-Conference on Theorical Computer Science*, Springer Verlag, 1981. LNCS 104.

[San77] Luis E. Sanchis. Data types as lattices: retractions, projection and projection. In *RAIRO Theorical computer science, vol 11, nr 4*, pages 339–344, 1977.

[Sif82] J. Sifakis. A unified approach for studying the properties of transition systems. *TCS*, 18, 1982.

[Sif83] J. Sifakis. Property preserving homomorphisms of transition systems. In *4th Workshop on Logics of Programs, Pittsburgh*, LNCS 164, Springer Verlag, June 1983.

Semantics and Analysis of Linda-based languages

Régis Cridlig & Eric Goubault
Laboratoire d'Informatique de l'Ecole Normale Supérieure

Address: Ecole Normale Supérieure - 45 rue d'Ulm, 75230 Paris Cedex 05, France.
Electronic mail: {cridlig,goubault}@dmi.ens.fr

Abstract. In this paper we define a process algebra abstracting relevant features of the Linda paradigm to parallel computation and show how to give it a semantics based on higher-dimensional automata which is more expressive than interleaving transition systems. In particular, it is a truly concurrent operational semantics, compositional in nature.
Furthermore this semantics leads us to new kinds of abstract interpretations useful for the static analysis of concurrency. One of these addresses the correctness of implementations of Linda programs on real computers (which have a finite number of processors).

1 Introduction

Parallel languages are difficult to design and implement. On the one hand, the task of actually using at the same time several processors should be taken care of in a transparent manner for the user. On the other hand, the multiplicity of architectures and paradigms for parallel machines and languages makes it difficult to find a unified way of speaking about semantics and about efficiency of implementations. In this article, we choose a paradigm for concurrency, exemplified by the Linda based languages, which does not make any assumption on the architecture of the machine it will be implemented on. It does not assume a shared memory nor a channel based mechanism for implementing inter-process communication.

As a first step towards the analysis of such languages, we introduce a process algebra that models their basic features, abstracting the constructs dealing with concurrency and communication. We then use a classical interleaving operational semantics to define the process algebra. Unfortunately, interleaving causes a dramatic combinatorial increase in complexity and the possible schedulings of actions on a given number of processors are out of reach. Therefore, we introduce a generalised operational semantics, based on higher-dimensional automata (see [GJ92]) which expresses the truly concurrent execution of actions, thus enabling us to speak of n actions scheduled on m processors (the "mapping problem"). It has also nice properties borrowed from the denotational world, that is being compositional.

Then we develop two kinds of abstract interpretations (see [CC92]) which link the semantics to non-standard ones of interest. The first one aims at speaking about the mapping problem, whereas the second one is more classical, and can be used for instance for abstracting the actual values of tuples to types. It may also be used to shrink the domain of the semantics to a finite state one. The article ends by putting these abstract interpretations to work with two examples, for determining the possible communications and the "best" schedulings given a few constraints.

2 Overview of Linda

2.1 The Linda paradigm

How to write parallel programs? This is the subject of N. Carriero and D. Gelernter's book [CG90] that presents and uses Linda, a language they developed as a way to coordinate multiple parallel processes to achieve a given common task.

There are three different basic models for coordination:

1. The first one is still in use in most parallel extensions of imperative languages and is based upon shared memory and variables. To avoid conflicts and race conditions between processes, it usually comprises some basic forms of synchronisation like Djikstra's semaphores. It is considered as a difficult model to program in and debug, and is restricted to shared-memory architectures.
2. The best known one today is message-passing and has been widespread by the influence of Hoare's CSP [Hoa78] that inspired the Occam language [May83]. Communication is modelled by synchronous operations in the process of sending and receiving messages. Remote Procedure Calls and buffered streams are other instances of this paradigm that is quite simple and powerful, allowing distributed computing. But it can lead to cumbersome programs when message passing does not fit well with the concurrent algorithm to implement.
3. Distributed data structures are less frequently encountered, but in some ways generalise both preceding models. Linda offers the programmer a "tuple space" model, which is orthogonal to sequential processes: the data were created by a Linda *eval* operation and are merely "active" tuples that deposit their results as "passive" ones when they exit. Another way to create one (passive) tuple is via the *put* operation. Processes can only access passive tuples, reading them with *read* and also removing them with *get*. These two atomic operations specify a pattern that can only match certain kinds of tuples, thus creating potential non-determinism and possibly blocking until some well-matching object is found.

2.2 C-Linda

In Carriero and Gelernter's C-Linda realisation, there is one global tuple space. Pattern matching is usually done by giving some key that denotes a particular distributed data structure. For instance, pattern $("A", i, j, ?val)$ is used to return element $A(i, j)$ of a distributed matrix A into variable val. This language, while being well-suited for many kinds of parallel algorithms, does not support processes (or functions) as values and lacks object hiding.

2.3 Example

Here we give a merge-sort routine written in ML-Linda, our own combination of the Linda model and the ML functional language. In ML-Linda, multiple tuple spaces called "bags" can be created and each bag only contains objects of a particular type and is only accessible through its dynamic scope:

```
let rec merge_sort lf rg A =
  if lf < rg then
    let wait = new_bag()
    and middle = (lf+rg)/2
    in eval wait (merge_sort lf middle A);
       eval wait (merge_sort middle rg A);
       get wait () in get wait ()
       in << merge classical algorithm >>;
  ();;
```

Notice that:

- the third parameter `A` is a bag containing the array to be sorted; its elements are of type int $\times\ \alpha$.
- `wait` is a bag local to each invocation of `merge_sort`; its only purpose is synchronisation and it can hold nothing but objects of type unit.

3 A Linda-calculus

In this paper we are solely interested in modelling and analysing coordination through the tuple space; we shall thus ignore the details of the computation inside of sequential processes. Similarly, we do not want to take into account the values themselves carried by a given tuple.

Consequently, we shall use a kind of Linda-calculus, only describing relevant features of coordination between processes. In that way, we follow [CJY92] but define and use an even simpler form of calculus.

3.1 Syntax

Let X denote a variable for defining recursion (we shall use upper-case characters for them) and t a passive tuple or tuple pattern. Then we define a process as follows:

$$P ::= t \mid \text{out}(P).P' \mid \text{read}(t).P \mid \text{get}(t).P \mid P \| P' \mid X \mid \text{rec } X.P$$

'out' subsumes both Linda's eval and put operations, this last one being obtained by the construct out$(t).P$. We write $\mathcal{L}$ for the set of terms defined by this grammar.

3.2 Semantics by interleaving and multisets

An operational semantics for the Linda-calculus will be given by an Interleaving Transition System. It will be based on a pattern-matching relation between tuples: let us say for instance that tuples a,b,c,... are values (ground objects) while tuples x,y,z,... are formal variables. Then t matches t' iff $t = t'$ or $t' \in \{x, y, z, \ldots\}$.

For each matching pair t, t' a substitution σ upon tuples must be chosen that satisfies the property $t = \sigma t'$. We shall note the matching relation together with its associated substitution by: t σ-matches t'. Substitutions lift to terms of $\mathcal{L}$ in a straightforward manner.

3.3 SOS rules

We choose to model the tuple space by a global multiset M. We shall write $\oplus$ for both multiset construction and union.

$$
\begin{array}{cl}
\text{(out)} & M \oplus \mathrm{out}(P).P' \rightarrow M \oplus P \oplus P' \\
\text{(read)} & M \oplus \mathrm{read}(p).P \oplus t \rightarrow M \oplus \sigma(P) \oplus t \text{ if } t \ \sigma\text{-matches } p \\
\text{(get)} & M \oplus \mathrm{get}(p).P \oplus t \rightarrow M \oplus \sigma(P) \quad \text{ if } t \ \sigma\text{-matches } p \\
\text{(left choice)} & M \oplus P \| P' \rightarrow M \oplus P \\
\text{(right choice)} & M \oplus P \| P' \rightarrow M \oplus P' \\
\text{(rec)} & M \oplus \mathrm{rec}\ X.P \rightarrow M \oplus P' \quad \text{if } M \oplus P[\mathrm{rec}\ X.P/X] \rightarrow M \oplus P'
\end{array}
$$

By this semantics, all actions are synchronous even if we can add a rule mimicking true parallelism[1]:

$$\frac{M_1 \rightarrow M_1' \quad M_2 \rightarrow M_2'}{M_1 \oplus M_2 \rightarrow M_1' \oplus M_2'}$$

This is clearly unrealistic for distributed implementations of the Linda concept. Furthermore, this interleaving semantics creates a lot of undue non-determinism that can only complicate the analysis of Linda programs.

3.4 Example

Let us try to "abstract" our merge-sort program to a Linda-calculus term. The function `merge_sort` becomes a process variable S that is bound by the rec construct to a term describing the internal behaviour of the process. We shall call v the tuple corresponding to ML's () value:

$$\mathrm{rec}\ S.(v \| \mathrm{out}(S).out(S).\mathrm{get}(v).\mathrm{get}(v).v)$$

But this term is not really faithful to the original algorithm, because it can lead for example to the following execution, where instances of process S cannot distinguish between the return tuples of their own children and other ones:

$$
\begin{aligned}
S &\xrightarrow{*} S \oplus S \oplus \mathrm{get}(v).\mathrm{get}(v).v \\
&\xrightarrow{*} \mathrm{out}(S).out(S).\mathrm{get}(v).\mathrm{get}(v).v \oplus v \oplus \mathrm{get}(v).\mathrm{get}(v).v \\
&\xrightarrow{*} S \oplus S \oplus \mathrm{get}(v).\mathrm{get}(v).v \oplus \mathrm{get}(v).v \\
&\xrightarrow{*} v \oplus v \oplus \mathrm{get}(v).\mathrm{get}(v).v \oplus \mathrm{get}(v).v \\
&\xrightarrow{*} \mathrm{get}(v).v \oplus v \\
&\rightarrow v
\end{aligned}
$$

As exemplified, our calculus can only give an approximate view of Linda-based programs. It can be enriched with a more precise treatment of variables, tuples and substitution, thus leading to a calculus we call λ-linda.

[1] In the light of next section's formalism we can see this rule as allowing cartesian product of transitions $M_1 \rightarrow M_1'$ and $M_2 \rightarrow M_2'$, which represents their synchronised execution.

4 Higher Dimensional Automata

In [Pra91] and [Gla91] Pratt and Glabbeek advocate a model of concurrency based on geometry and in particular on the notion of a higher dimensional automaton. HDA are a generalisation of the usual non-deterministic finite automata as described in *e.g.* [HU79]. The basic idea is to use the higher dimensions to represent the concurrent execution of processes. Thus for two processes, a and b, we model the mutually exclusive execution of a and b by the automaton (1):

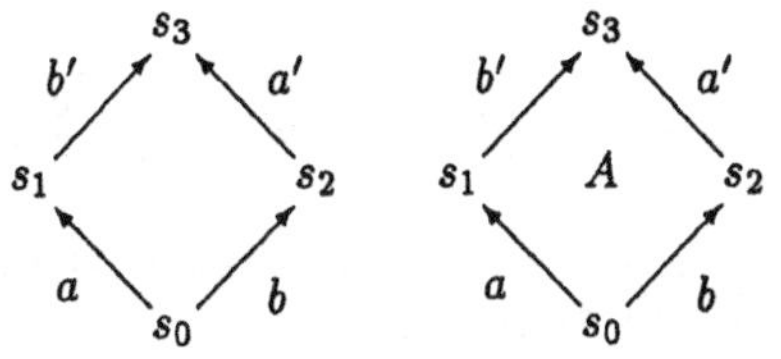

(1) (2)

whereas their concurrent execution is modeled by including the two-dimensional surface delineated by the (one-dimensional) a- and b-transitions as a transition in the automaton. This is pictured as (2).

HDA are built as sets of states and transitions between states, but also as sets of 2-transitions between transitions, and more generally n-transitions between $(n-1)$-transitions. Transitions (or 1-transitions) are usually depicted as segments, that is one-dimensional objects, whereas states are just points, i.e. 0-dimensional objects. It is therefore natural to represent n-transitions as n-dimensional objects, whose boundaries are the $(n-1)$-transitions from which they can be fired, and to which they end up. n-transitions represent the concurrent execution of n sequential processes. For instance, in automaton (2), the 2-dimensional transition A represents the concurrent execution of a and b. This 2-transition can be fired from a or from b at any time, thus the beginning of A is in some way a and b. Similarly, the end of A is a' and b'. One may want also to add coefficients (like integers) to transitions to keep track of the number of times we go through them. This motivates the introduction of vector spaces[2] generated by states and transitions and source and target boundary operators acting on them.

Definition 1. A (unlabelled) *higher dimensional automaton* (HDA) is a vector space M with two boundary operators ∂_0 and ∂_1, such that:

- there is a decomposition: $M = \sum_{p,q \in \mathbb{Z}} M_{p,q}$, verifying: $\forall p, q,\ M_{p,q} \cap (\sum_{r+s \neq p+q} M_{r,s}) = 0$.
- the two boundary operators are compatible with the decomposition and give M a structure of bicomplex:

$$\partial_0 : M_{p,q} \longrightarrow M_{p-1,q}$$

$$\partial_1 : M_{p,q} \longrightarrow M_{p,q-1}$$

$$\partial_0 \circ \partial_0 = 0, \quad \partial_1 \circ \partial_1 = 0, \quad \partial_0 \circ \partial_1 + \partial_1 \circ \partial_0 = 0$$

[2] or, more generally, free modules.

The dimension of an element of $M_{p,q}$ is $p+q$. Such an element is called a $(p+q)$-transition and we will sometimes write M_{p+q} for the sub-vector space of M generated by the $p+q$ transitions. For instance, automaton (2) is defined as,

$$\begin{array}{ccccc}
M_{1,1}=(A) & \xrightarrow{\partial_0} & M_{0,1}=(a)\oplus(b) & \xrightarrow{\partial_0} & M_{-1,1}=(s_0) \\
\partial_1\downarrow & & \partial_1\downarrow & & \partial_1\downarrow \\
M_{1,0}=(a')\oplus(b') & \xrightarrow{\partial_0} & M_{0,0}=(s_1)\oplus(s_2) & \xrightarrow{\partial_0} & M_{-1,0}=0 \\
\partial_1\downarrow & & \partial_1\downarrow & & \partial_1\downarrow \\
M_{1,-1}=(s_3) & \xrightarrow{\partial_0} & M_{0,-1}=0 & \xrightarrow{\partial_0} & M_{-1,-1}=0
\end{array}$$

with $\partial_0(A)=a-b$, $\partial_1(A)=a'-b'$, $\partial_0(a)=\partial_0(b)=s_0$, $\partial_1(a)=\partial_0(b')=s_1$, $\partial_1(b)=\partial_0(a')=s_2$ and $\partial_1(a')=\partial_1(b')=s_3$.

Let Υ be the category of HDA, whose objects are HDA and whose morphisms are linear functions $f: P \to Q$ such that for all $i,j,k, f(P_{i,j}) \subseteq Q_{i,j}$ and $f \circ \partial_k = \partial_k \circ f$. Υ is (small-) complete and co-complete, has a tensor product $\otimes$ and a Hom object such that $\mathrm{Hom}(P\otimes Q,R) \equiv \mathrm{Hom}(P,\mathrm{Hom}(Q,R))$ (see [Gou93]). Moreover, a few properties of the shape of the transition system (branchings, mergings) can be computed algebraically, and inductively for most of the constructs defined on HDA. This is done via the application of suitable n-dimensional homology functors $H_n(.,\partial_k)$ defined on objects X as being the quotient of the kernel, in X_n, of ∂_k by $\partial_k(X_{n+1})$.

Now, we have to define what we mean by a HDA semantics. In ordinary denotational semantics, we just consider the relation between input states and output states of a given program. Therefore semantic domains are made of sets of states, suitably ordered. Now, if we want to be able to observe the whole dynamics of a program, we also need all transitions between these states, and even all higher-dimensional transitions between these transitions. Then a HDA-domain (or in short, a domain) is a huge HDA which contains all possible traces and branchings. Elements of such a domain are just its sub-HDA.

A 1-transition between two states x and y is constructed as an *homotopy* between x and y. This can be coded by means of two special 1-transitions t and v defined by $\partial_0(t)=1$, $\partial_1(t)=0$, $\partial_0(v)=0$, $\partial_1(v)=1$, where 1 is a 0-dimensional element, neutral for the tensor product.

Then a 1-transition[3] going from x to y is $x \rightsquigarrow y = t\otimes x + v\otimes y$. The same formula generalises to higher dimensions, and for instance, $(x\rightsquigarrow y)\rightsquigarrow(z\rightsquigarrow t)$ is a filled-in square whose vertices are x, y, z and t.

5 A truly concurrent semantics of the Linda-calculus

Consider a denumerable family of copies of t and v, denoted by (t_i) and (v_i). Let W be the HDA defined by $W_0=(term)$ for $term$ varying in $\mathcal{L}$, $W_1=(t_i)\oplus(v_i)$. We

[3] Labelling can also be defined (as an element of a slice category Υ/L, see [Gou93]) and can be useful when performing program analysis.

construct a semantic domain D of HDA by the amalgamated sum (noted $+$)

$$D = \sum_{n \in \mathbb{N}} W^{\otimes^n}$$

This domain is easily seen to contain as sub-HDA all sub-HDA of W, and to be stable under the tensor product [4].

The semantic function $[\![.]\!] \in Hom(D, D)$ takes a term x of the Linda-calculus together with a context, the HDA describing the evaluation of the other members of Linda's tuple space, and constructs the HDA representing the possible transitions of x. The semantics of the Linda-calculus is now given by:

$$\begin{aligned}
[\![t]\!]\rho &= t \otimes \rho \\
[\![X]\!]\rho &= X \otimes \rho \\
[\![\mathrm{read}(t).P]\!]\rho &= (\mathrm{read}(t).P) \otimes \rho \rightsquigarrow r^t_P(\rho) + R^t_P(\rho) \\
[\![\mathrm{get}(t).P]\!]\rho &= (\mathrm{get}(t).P) \otimes \rho \rightsquigarrow g^t_P(\rho) + G^t_P(\rho) \\
[\![\mathrm{out}(e_1); e_2]\!]\rho &= (\mathrm{out}(e_1); e_2) \otimes \rho \rightsquigarrow e_1 \otimes e_2 \otimes \rho + [\![e_1]\!]([\![e_2]\!]\rho) + [\![e_2]\!]([\![e_1]\!]\rho) \\
[\![e_1 [\!] e_2]\!]\rho &= (e_1 [\!] e_2) \otimes \rho \rightsquigarrow e_1 \otimes \rho + [\![e_1]\!]\rho + (e_1 [\!] e_2) \otimes \rho \rightsquigarrow e_2 \otimes \rho + [\![e_2]\!]\rho \\
[\![\mathrm{rec}\ X.P]\!]\rho &= \underrightarrow{\lim} [\![P^n(X)]\!]\rho
\end{aligned}$$

where ($s_1 \hat{s_k} s_n$ meaning the product of all s_j except s_k),

$$\begin{aligned}
r^t_P(P_1 \otimes \ldots \otimes P_m) &= \sum_{P_i\ \sigma\text{-matching}\ t} \sigma(P) \otimes P_1 \otimes \ldots \otimes P_m \\
R^t_P(P_1 \otimes \ldots \otimes P_m) &= \sum_{P_i\ \sigma\text{-matching}\ t} [\![\sigma(P)]\!](P_1 \otimes \ldots \otimes P_m) \\
g^t_P(P_1 \otimes \ldots \otimes P_m) &= \sum_{P_i\ \sigma\text{-matching}\ t} \sigma(P) \otimes P_1 \otimes \ldots \otimes \hat{P_i} \otimes \ldots \otimes P_m \\
G^t_P(P_1 \otimes \ldots \otimes P_m) &= \sum_{P_i\ \sigma\text{-matching}\ t} [\![\sigma(P)]\!](P_1 \otimes \ldots \otimes \hat{P_i} \otimes \ldots \otimes P_m)
\end{aligned}$$

First equation states that the action t is to push the value t in the tuple space. Second one is trivially the same. Then the third and fourth ones mean that a read action (resp. get) is a sum of potential 1-transitions from read(t).P (resp. get(t).P) to the substitutions of P induced by the matchings of pattern t with elements of context ρ, and then carries on by the evaluation of these substitutions in the appropriate context. out first executes a 1-transition to represent the spawning and then concurrently evaluates its first argument in the context of the execution of the second one, and vice-versa. The choice operator $[\!]$ is just the union operator, that is the amalgamated sum $+$, between 1-transitions to the beginnings of the execution of its two arguments. Finally recursion is obtained by a direct limit of HDA: the

[4] From now on, we assume that, by a classical argument, we have abelianised — not taking the signs into account — the tensor product by quotienting D by $\{a \otimes b = (-1)^{(\dim a)(\dim b)} b \otimes a\}$.

colimit is taken on the diagram whose objects are the different steps of unfolding $[P^n(X)] \overset{Id}{\hookrightarrow} D$ and whose arrows are the inclusion morphisms between them.

Let us now list a few properties of interest, that one can read from this denotational semantics. These are called *geometric* since they are related to the shape of the transition system. They are extracted by using functors built from the homology functors (as defined in [Gou93]).

Deadlocks A 1-transition a leads to a deadlock, or simply is a 1-deadlock, if and only if one cannot fire any other transition b in the sequential composition *à la* CSP a;b. This leads to define it in an abstract manner, as a 1-transition a such that $\partial_1(a) = 0$, i.e. a transition of which no information whatsoever can be retrieved as soon as it has been fired. This is typically the case for the t_i's. Therefore, an elementary 1-transition which is also a generator of Ker∂_1 defines a 1-deadlock. In fact, we just need its representant modulo ∂_1 of 2-transitions. Then finding the 1-deadlocks amounts to computing the generators of $H_1(D, \partial_1)$ that are elementary 1-transitions. This generalises to what we call n-deadlocks, which are n-transitions generators of $H_n(D, \partial_1)$. These may be seen as those n-transitions that deadlock n processors simultaneously.

Serialisation A concurrent program is serialisable if it "gives the same result" as a sequential execution of it. This is a highly geometric property for HDA: this means that all paths can be deformed continuously into another. For instance, branchings of dimension one, given by the computation of the homology group of dimension one for ∂_0, are obstructions to such deformations.

Example 1. In this example, we assume that x is a variable and matches any possible value, while a and b are constant tuples that can only match themselves. Then, denoting get$(x).a$ by p and get$(a).E$ by q:

$$
\begin{aligned}
&[\![\text{out}(\text{get}(x).a);\text{get}(a).E]\!]b &&= (\text{out}(p);q)\otimes b \rightsquigarrow p\otimes q\otimes b + [\![p]\!]([\![q]\!]b) + [\![q]\!]([\![p]\!]b)\\
&[\![p]\!]b = p\otimes b \rightsquigarrow g^x_a(b) + G^x_a(b) &&= p\otimes b \rightsquigarrow a\\
&[\![q]\!]b = q\otimes b \rightsquigarrow g^a_E(b) + G^a_E(b) &&= q\otimes b \rightsquigarrow 0\\
&[\![p]\!]([\![q]\!]b) &&= (p\otimes q\otimes b \rightsquigarrow 0) \rightsquigarrow (q\otimes a \rightsquigarrow 0)\\
&[\![q]\!]([\![p]\!]b) &&= (p\otimes q\otimes b \rightsquigarrow q\otimes a) \rightsquigarrow (0 \rightsquigarrow E)
\end{aligned}
$$

Therefore, in D we have the following HDA for the program considered (where the symbol $\circ$ marks 2-transitions) :

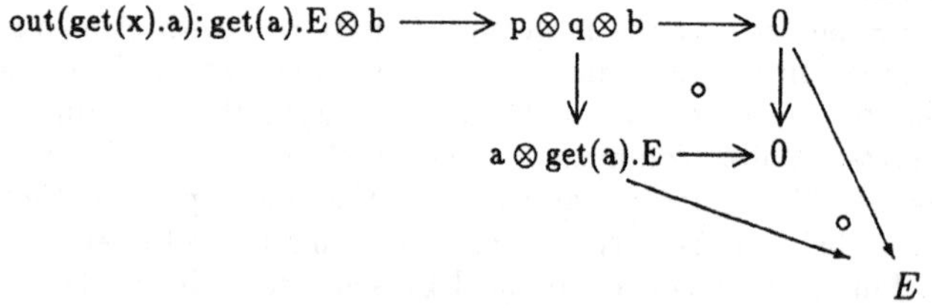

In the front square, we have two deadlocks. The only way not to deadlock the system is to schedule the execution of p with higher priority than the evaluation of q, thus creating the value a that enables the matching in q.

6 Static Analyses

6.1 Motivation

The main motivation for static analysis of Linda-based programs is to provide sufficient information for enabling efficient support of fine-grained parallelism on stock hardware. There are two sides to this goal:

1. Constructing efficient implementations of shared data structures. One could infer patterns of usage and sharing for concurrent data structures, as is proposed in [Jag91]. In some cases one can even optimise away Linda tuples (when they only carry synchronisation information for instance).
2. Managing process threads through process allocation and task scheduling. This can be done at runtime, with help from static analysis information about process causality, priority and inter-process communication.

Software validation constitutes another challenge for concurrent programming where static analysis tools can surely help. We will give a method to calculate the homology groups of HDA in a subsequent paper, thus computing relevant branching and merging properties of the associated Linda-calculus term possible executions. These properties can be directly used to show that a program is not bisimulation-equivalent (see [Gou93]) to its specification, for instance.

6.2 Abstract Interpretation

Having given a denotational semantics on a specified domain of transitions, one can interpret the semantic rules in a non-standard domain, related to the full one by a pair of adjoint functors. Let us make this a bit more precise. Let D_c be the domain on which we have given our semantics. Let D_a be another domain. We will say that D_a is an abstraction of D_c if and only if there exists a pair of adjoints functors (α,γ), α being left adjoint to γ, with $\alpha : \Upsilon/D_c \longrightarrow \Upsilon/D_a$ and $\gamma : \Upsilon/D_a \longrightarrow \Upsilon/D_c$. The slice categories Υ/D_c and Υ/D_a (see [FS90]) have as objects "generalized elements", that is, morphisms with value in D_c (resp. D_a). In particular, monomorphisms are just inclusions (in the geometric sense) of HDA in D_c (resp. D_a), that is, correspond to sub-HDA. Notice that these adjoint pairs do not always induce a Galois connection between the lattices of sub-objects (seen as sub-categories of the corresponding slice categories), for instance the relation with ordinary denotational semantics needs more morphisms than just the inclusion morphisms defining the ordering on sub-objects.

In the following, we build several such abstract interpretations.

The truncation functors The truly concurrent semantics we have given for the Linda-calculus assumes an infinite number of processors. The mapping problem is concerned with the possible implementations of such a semantics on a real machine with only n processors. We introduce first an abstract interpretation whose abstraction maps a program onto n processors. Any scheduler can then be proven correct with respect to this abstract interpretation. Questions of efficiency of the scheduling may then be asked. Notice that as a particular case, we obtain the correctness of the interleaving operational semantics (given in section 3.2) with respect to the truly concurrent one by setting $n = 1$.

Let $D_{a,n} = \sum_{0 \leq k \leq n} W'^{\otimes^k}$ where $W' = (t_i)+(v_i)+\sum_{k \in \mathbb{N}}(term^{\otimes^k})$. It is the domain of processes of dimension at most n. Let now $x : X \rightarrow D_c$ be an element of Υ/D_c. Let X' be the sub-HDA of X consisting of transitions up to dimension n ("truncation" of X of order n). We define $T_n(x)$ to be the induced morphism from X' to D_a. For f a morphism between $x : X \rightarrow D_c$ and $y : Y \rightarrow D_c$, we define $T_n(f)$ to be the induced morphism between the truncations of X and Y of order n. This defines the abstraction functor.

Take A in $\Upsilon/D_{a,n}$. Let $Y(A)$ be the diagram in Υ/D_c, whose objects are all elements x of Υ/D_c such that $T_n(x)$ is isomorphic to A, and whose arrows are all possible morphisms in Υ/D_c between these objects. We define a functor $G_n : \Upsilon/D_{a,n} \longrightarrow \Upsilon/D_c$ to be $G_n = \varinjlim Y(.)$. Then,

Lemma 2. *(T_n, G_n) is a pair of adjoint functors.*

This pair of adjoint functors induces a Galois connection between the lattices of sub-HDA of D_c and $D_{a,n}$ (viewed as a sub-category of Υ/D_c and $\Upsilon/D_{a,n}$ respectively). We apply this result for $n = 1$ to prove:

Proposition 3. *The interleaving operational semantics is correct with respect to the HDA semantics.*

As a matter of fact, T_1 maps any sub-HDA of D to the interleaved 1-transitions on its boundary. For instance automaton (2) of section 4 is mapped onto automaton (1). To prove the correctness, we just have to forget all explicitly coded deadlocks in the HDA semantics. This is also part of an adjunction we will not describe now.

The folding functors Let $\equiv$ be a given equivalence on terms, and let $p : \mathcal{L} \rightarrow \mathcal{L}/\equiv$ be the associated canonical projection. We define an abstract domain by $D_a = \sum_{n \in \mathbb{N}} W''^{\otimes^n}$ where $W'' = (t_i) + (v_i) + (term_{\equiv})$. Now, p extends to a multiplicative morphism[5] from D_c to D_a, by, $p(x \otimes y) = p(x) \otimes p(y)$ and $p(t_i) = t_i$, $p(v_i) = v_i$. More generally, we can assume that we are given an epimorphism p from D_c to a domain D_a. Then the abstraction functor is:

$$M_p(x : X \rightarrow D_c) = p \circ x : X \rightarrow D_a$$

$$M_p(f : (x : X \rightarrow D_c) \rightarrow (y : Y \rightarrow D_c)) = f : (M_p(x) : X \rightarrow D_a) \rightarrow (M_p(y) : Y \rightarrow D_a)$$

Let now N_p be the functor from Υ/D_a to Υ/D_c defined by:

- for $x' : X' \rightarrow D_a$, $N_p(x')$ is the pullback of x' along p, i.e. is the "greatest" morphism $N_p(x') : X' \times_{D_a} D_c \rightarrow D_c$ such that $p \circ N(x') = x' \circ p_1$ where $p_1 : X' \times_{D_a} D_c \rightarrow X'$ is given by the pullback diagram (see [Mac71]).

[5] i.e. a morphism which commutes with the tensor product.

- and for $f' : (x' : X' \to D_a) \longrightarrow (y' : Y' \to D_a)$, $N_p(f') : X' \times_{D_a} D_c \to Y' \times_{D_a} D_c$ is the unique morphism h in the following pullback diagram:

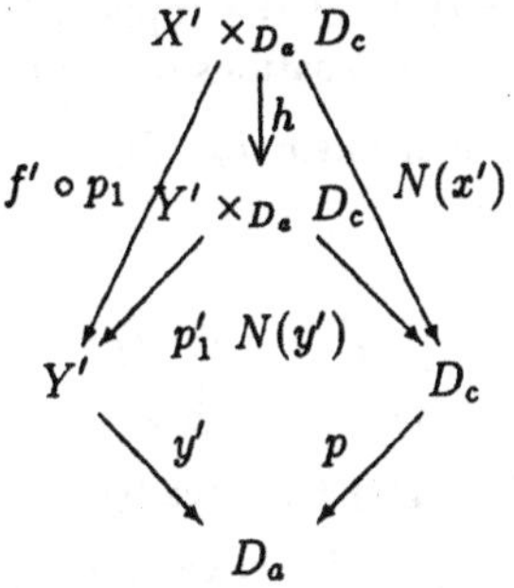

Then,

Lemma 4. *(M_p, N_p) is a pair of adjoint functors.*

We need in the following to compute the abstract operators, i.e. the abstract counterparts of $+$, $\otimes$ and $\underrightarrow{\lim}$. This will not be possible in general, and we may have to use safe approximations of them. For H any endofunctor on Υ/D_c, we say that G, endofunctor on Υ/D_a, is a safe approximation of H if and only if there exists a natural transformation from $\alpha H \gamma$ to G. Notice that it reduces to the usual definition when (α, γ) is a Galois connection. The fact that (α, γ) is a pair of adjoint functors implies that colimits in Υ/D_a are safe approximations of colimits in Υ/D_c. For instance, we can take as abstraction of $+$ and $\underrightarrow{\lim}$, $+$ and $\underrightarrow{\lim}$ respectively. This does not hold for $\otimes$ and its abstract version $\otimes_a$. But we can prove the following:

- For the adjunction (T_n, G_n), there is an "expansion law", $x \otimes_a y = x \otimes T_0(y) + T_0(x) \otimes y + \Sigma_{0<k<n} T_k(x) \otimes T_{n-k}(y)$.
- For the adjunction (M_p, N_p), if p is a multiplicative morphism then $x \otimes_a y = x \otimes y$.

6.3 Example: communication analysis

We would like to trace the communications occurring during the execution of Linda programs by collecting input operations (read and get) and tuples at each point of execution.

Annotated syntax In order to distinguish operations up to their syntactic context, we must add "control points" to Linda programs. A control point is essentially a token annotating each syntactical construct, for instance integers which are given in the textual order. As an example, out(a); read$(x).E$ becomes out$_1(a_2)$; read$_3(x_4).E_5$. We will not define this operation formally, but assume from now on that the concrete domain is changed into $D_c = \sum_k W^{\otimes^k}$ with $W = (t_i) + (v_i) + (\textit{annotated-term})$.

Adjunction For our abstract domain D_m, we take the domain of HDA generated by all terms $\mathrm{read}_k(t)$, $\mathrm{get}_k(t)$ and all tuples s_k *with the restriction that there will be at most $m > 0$ copies of the same annotated tuple s_k in each state.* Each 0-transition of these HDA describes the state of the tuple space during the evaluation of the program and the possible synchronisations occurring after it.

Let us define an abstraction morphism $u_m : D_{a,0} \rightarrow D_m$ by induction on the following equations:

$$\begin{array}{lll} u_m(\otimes^{m+k} s_j) & = \otimes^m s_j & \\ u_m(\otimes^n s_j) & = \otimes^n s_j & \text{if } n < m \\ u_m(\mathrm{read}_k(t).P) & = \mathrm{read}_k(t) & \\ u_m(\mathrm{get}_k(t).P) & = \mathrm{get}_k(t) & \\ u_m(term) & = 1 & \text{otherwise} \end{array}$$

It is clear that u_m is the canonical projection of an equivalence relation on annotated terms. So, by the result of the last section, u_m defines a pair of adjoint functors (M_{u_m}, N_{u_m}).

Abstract semantics The non-standard semantic equations are thence given by the same equations as in the truncation domain $D_{a,0}$. These equations can be further simplified when one remembers that the tensor product works in the abstract domain here, thus calculating in the equivalence classes:

$$\begin{aligned} [\![t]\!]\rho &= t \otimes \rho \\ [\![X]\!]\rho &= \rho \\ [\![\mathrm{read}(t).P]\!]\rho &= \mathrm{read}(t) \otimes \rho + R^t_P(\rho) \\ [\![\mathrm{get}(t).P]\!]\rho &= \mathrm{get}(t) \otimes \rho + G^t_P(\rho) \\ [\![\mathrm{out}(e_1); e_2]\!]\rho &= \rho + [\![e_1]\!]([\![e_2]\!]\rho) + [\![e_2]\!]([\![e_1]\!]\rho) \\ [\![e_1 \| e_2]\!]\rho &= \rho + [\![e_1]\!]\rho + [\![e_2]\!]\rho \\ [\![\mathrm{rec}\ X.P]\!]\rho &= \lim_{\rightarrow} [\![P^n(X)]\!]\rho \end{aligned}$$

The law for R^t_P remains the same, while the one for G^t_P becomes:

$$G^t_P(P_1^{\otimes^{k_1}} \otimes \ldots \otimes (P_l^{\otimes^{k_l}} = \sum_{P_i\ \sigma\text{-matching}\ t} [\![\sigma(P)]\!](P_1 \otimes \ldots \otimes P_i^{\hat{\otimes}^{k_i}} \otimes \ldots \otimes P_l)$$

$$\text{where} \quad P_i^{\hat{\otimes}^m} = P_i^{\otimes^m} + P_i^{\otimes^{m-1}}$$

$$\text{and} \quad P_i^{\otimes^{\hat{n}<m}} = P_i^{\otimes^{n-1}}$$

Example Let $m = 1$: an abstract tuple represents any number of concrete ones. We can calculate the abstract semantics of the program of the first example:

$$\begin{aligned}
&[\![\mathrm{out}(\mathrm{get}(x).a); \mathrm{get}(a).E]\!]b = b + [\![p]\!]([\![q]\!]b) + [\![q]\!]([\![p]\!]b) \\
&[\![p]\!]b = u(p) \otimes b + G^x_a(b) \quad = u(p) \otimes b + a \otimes b + a \\
&[\![q]\!]b = u(q) \otimes b + G^a_1(b) \quad = u(q) \otimes b \\
&[\![p]\!]([\![q]\!]b) \qquad = u(p) \otimes u(q) \otimes b + u(q) \otimes a + u(q) \otimes a \otimes b \\
&[\![q]\!]([\![p]\!]b) \qquad = u(q) \otimes (u(p) \otimes b + a \otimes b + a) + a \otimes b + b + a \\
&\quad \text{So, } [\![\mathrm{out}(p); q]\!]b = a + b + a \otimes b + u(q) \otimes u(p) \otimes b + u(q) \otimes a \otimes b + u(q) \otimes a
\end{aligned}$$

The result shows an upper approximation of the potential matchings between the tuples a and b and the two syntactic get operations; with $m = 2$, we would have obtained an exact result.

6.4 Example: the scheduling of constrained Linda programs

When we want to compile Linda programs, we have to keep in mind that there exists a number of different constraints due to the target machine. In this article, we will focus on two such constraints. The first one is that the machine has only n processors. The second one is that the machine has a limited amount of memory. We wish to give the compiler static information about which scheduling of the different actions is the "best" given these constraints. In the limited model we consider, "best" means that we do not want to create too many resources of some type A_i (as it may overflow the capacity of some distributed memory) but sufficiently many ones of type A_j (since they are output data we do not want to wait for). It means also that we want sufficiently many resources of type A_k for not blocking read and get operations, and not making the program deadlock, since we have only a limited number of processors that could all be waiting for a resource.

Now, we show how to abstract the semantics to have just the authorised transitions, given that we are constrained to n processors and that we do not want to have more than β_i and less than α_i tuples A_i. Let us define a morphism p from D_c to D_c by:

$$\begin{aligned}
p(A_i^{\otimes^j}) &= A_i^{\otimes^j} && \text{if } \alpha_i \leq j \leq \beta_i \\
p(A_i^{\otimes^j}) &= 0 && \text{if } j < \alpha_i \text{ or } \beta_i < j \\
p(t_i) &= t_i \\
p(v_i) &= v_i \\
p(term) &= term
\end{aligned}$$

Let then $D'_a = p(D_{a,n})$. It is the domain of traces of execution on an n-processor machine, deadlocking (thus measuring in a very definite way the ineffectiveness of the implementation) if it uses more or less resources than specified. Then we know that $(M_p \circ T_n, N_p \circ G_n)$ is a pair of adjoint functors between Υ/D_c and Υ/D'_a.

Finally, we want to collect the set of states which lead to deadlocks, as well as the deadlocking transitions. This is the information we need to tell the scheduler, "when you are in such and such states, try to delay such and such transitions".

Let $D_a = D'_a/(v_i)_i$. It is an abstract domain where transitions are deadlocks. The abstraction functor is essentially the homology functor for ∂_1 which computes deadlocks. But we do not want in the first place to bother with equivalence classes. Therefore, we set for any HDA M, $F(M) = \oplus_{i\geq 1}(\mathrm{Ker}_{|M_i}\partial_1)$ (the HDA in D_a generated by the kernel of ∂_1 on objects of dimension greater or equal than one). If $f : M \rightarrow N$ is a morphism in Υ, then f induces a morphism $f^* : F(M) \rightarrow F(N)$, since f commutes with ∂_1 (and ∂_0). It therefore defines a functor from Υ/D'_a to Υ/D_a by:

$$F(X \xrightarrow{x} D'_a) = F(X) \xrightarrow{x^*} D_a$$
$$F(f : (X \xrightarrow{x} D'_a) \longrightarrow (Y \xrightarrow{y} D'_a)) = f^* : F(x) \rightarrow F(y)$$

Let G be the functor $G(x) = \varinjlim Z(x)$, where $Z(x)$ is, for $x \in \Upsilon/D_a$, the diagram in Υ/D'_a, whose objects are the y such that $F(y) = x$ and whose morphisms are all possible morphisms between them. It is easy to see that (F, G) is a pair of adjoint functors.

Therefore, $(F \circ M_p \circ T_n, G \circ N_p \circ G_n)$ is a pair of adjoint functors. Representing objects $x^* : F(X) \rightarrow D_a$ by $x^*(F(X))$, we get the abstract semantic equations for $n = 1$, $\alpha_i = 0$ and $\beta_i = \infty$:

$$
\begin{aligned}
[\![t]\!]\rho &= t \otimes \rho \\
[\![X]\!]\rho &= X \otimes \rho \\
[\![\mathrm{read}(t).P]\!]\rho &= (\mathrm{read}(t).P) \otimes T_0(\rho) \rightsquigarrow 0 + \mathrm{read}(t).P \otimes \rho && \text{if } r^t_P(T_0(\rho)) = 0 \\
[\![\mathrm{read}(t).P]\!]\rho &= \mathrm{read}(t).P \otimes \rho + R^t_P(\rho) && \text{otherwise} \\
[\![\mathrm{get}(t).P]\!]\rho &= (\mathrm{get}(t).P) \otimes T_0(\rho) \rightsquigarrow 0 + \mathrm{get}(t).P \otimes \rho && \text{if } g^t_P(T_0(\rho)) = 0 \\
[\![\mathrm{get}(t).P]\!]\rho &= \mathrm{get}(t).P \otimes \rho + G^t_P(\rho) && \text{otherwise} \\
[\![\mathrm{out}(e_1); e_2]\!]\rho &= (\mathrm{out}(e_1); e_2) \otimes \rho + [\![e_1]\!]([\![e_2]\!]\rho) + [\![e_2]\!]([\![e_1]\!]\rho) \\
[\![e_1 \| e_2]\!]\rho &= (e_1 \| e_2) \otimes \rho + [\![e_1]\!]\rho + [\![e_2]\!]\rho \\
[\![\mathrm{rec}\ X.P]\!]\rho &= \varinjlim [\![P^n(X)]\!]\rho
\end{aligned}
$$

Example 2. We get back again to our first example.

$$
\begin{aligned}
[\![q]\!]b &= q \otimes b \rightsquigarrow 0 \\
[\![p]\!]b &= p \otimes b + a \\
[\![p]\!]([\![q]\!]b) &= p \otimes q \otimes b \rightsquigarrow 0 + a \otimes q \rightsquigarrow 0 \\
[\![q]\!]([\![p]\!]b) &= E + p \otimes q \otimes b + a \otimes q \\
[\![\mathrm{out}(p); q]\!]b &= \mathrm{out}(p); q \otimes b + [\![p]\!]([\![q]\!]b) + [\![q]\!]([\![p]\!]b) \\
&= \mathrm{out}(p); q \otimes b + p \otimes q \otimes b \rightsquigarrow 0 + a \otimes q \rightsquigarrow 0 + E
\end{aligned}
$$

Using the labelling, the result is to be interpreted as follows: the scheduler must try to delay the execution of q in favor of p.

7 Conclusion

In this article, we have presented a process algebra which is the core of the Linda based languages. Using higher dimensional automata for giving its semantics, we have been able to introduce new kinds of abstract interpretations. In particular, we have been able to formalise the link between the idealistic truly concurrent semantics, assuming an infinite number of processors, and more realistic ones, constrained to use a finite number of processors only. It is noteworthy that the approach promoted here is not restricted to Linda-based languages. Future work will have to combine our abstractions with more classical analyses like numerical ones (see [Mas92]). They could in particular be used for abstracting states or relations between states in our semantic domains.

Acknowledgements We wish to thank Chris Hankin and Lindsay Errington for the many discussions we had about the static analysis of Linda- and Gamma- like languages. We would like to thank Klaus Havelund for many valuable discussions as well, about concurrency in general and the Linda model in particular.

References

[CC92] P. Cousot and R. Cousot. Abstract interpretation frameworks. *Journal of Logic and Computation*, 2(4), 1992.

[CG90] N. Carriero and D. Gelernter. *How to write parallel programs A first course.* MIT Press, Cambridge, Mass., 1990.

[CJY92] P. Ciancarini, K. K. Jensen, and D. Yankelevitch. The semantics of a parallel language based on a shared data space. Technical Report 26, DIUP, 1992.

[FS90] P. J. Freyd and A. Scedrov. Categories, allegories. In *North-Holland Mathematical Library*, volume 39. North-Holland, 1990.

[GJ92] E. Goubault and T.P. Jensen. Homology of higher-dimensional automata. In *Proc. of CONCUR'92*, Stonybrook, New York, August 1992. Springer-Verlag.

[Gla91] R. van Glabbeek. Bisimulation semantics for higher dimensional automata. Technical report, Stanford University, 1991.

[Gou93] E. Goubault. Towards a theory of higher-dimensional automata. Technical report, Ecole Normale Supérieure, to appear 1993.

[Hoa78] C. A. R. Hoare. Communicating sequential processes. *Communications of the ACM*, 21(8):667–677, August 1978.

[HU79] J.E. Hopcroft and J.D. Ullman. *Introduction to Automata Theory, Languages and Computation.* Addison–Wesley, 1979.

[Jag91] S. Jagannathan. Expressing fine-grained parallelism using concurrent data structures. In J. B. Banâtre and D. Le Métayer, editors, *Research Directions in High-Level Parallel Programming Languages*, volume 574 of *Lecture Notes in Computer Science*, pages 77–92, June 1991.

[Mac71] S. Mac Lane. *Categories for the working mathematician.* Springer-Verlag, 1971.

[Mas92] F. Masdupuy. Array operations abstraction using semantic analysis of trapezoid congruences. In *International Conference on Supercomputing*, July 1992.

[May83] D. May. OCCAM. *ACM SIGPLAN Notices*, 18(4):69–79, April 1983.

[Pra91] V. Pratt. Modeling concurrency with geometry. In *Proc. 18th ACM Symposium on Principles of Programming Languages.* ACM Press, 1991.

Compiling FX on the CM-2*

Jean-Pierre Talpin† Pierre Jouvelot

CRI, Ecole des Mines de Paris, France

Abstract

Type and effect systems provide a safe and effective means of programming high-performance parallel computers with a high-level language that integrates both functional and imperative paradigms. Just as types describe what expressions compute, effects describe how expressions compute. Types and effects are associated with regions that describe where dynamically-allocated data structures reside in memory. We show how types, regions and effects can be used to discover when global operations on vectors are amenable to data parallelism in the presence of both side effects and higher-order functions.

To substantiate our claims that effects are an effective medium for addressing the issues of code generation for full-fledged languages on massively parallel computers, we describe the design and implementation of a CM-2 compiler prototype for the polymorphically typed FX language.

1 Introduction

The functional and imperative programming paradigms are often integrated together within sequential languages such as Common Lisp[11], Scheme[10] or Standard ML[7]. In such languages, implementors must exert care when designing code optimizers since side effects inhibit most of the nice properties of pure functional languages which are put at work in code transformations.

Going from sequentiality to parallelism, issues get significantly more complicated, both at the programmer and implementor levels. Concomitant use of side effects and parallelism leads to nondeterminism, which makes program understanding and debugging difficult because of the non-reproductibility of results. Restricting parallel programs to be deterministic, as advocated in[11], is a way of making parallel program design in higher-order imperative languages a more manageable task. Based on the concept of an effect system[5], we present here a compile-time technique that enforces such deterministic constraints and prove its effectiveness by describing a prototype compiler that targets the FX programming language[3] to the Connection Machine[1] (CM-2).

The purpose of the FX/CM compiler is to demonstrate the effectiveness of program analysis and code transformations based on type and effect information for high-level higher-order imperative languages. Our compiler uses the type and effect system presented in [13] to determine when operations on vectors are amenable to data parallelism in the presence of both side effects and higher-order functions. The absence of side-effects, for an operation mapped on every element of a vector, guarantees that its execution in parallel will not cause interferences. Such operations are run in parallel while others are conservatorily limited to sequential execution on the CM-2 front end. Our compiler uses regions to discover when the lifetime of locally allocated data structures is compatible with the memory model of the CM-2, which encourages the allocation of parallel vectors in the stack.

*This work was partially supported by MIT contract GC-R-117153.

†Current address: ECRC GmbH, Arabella Strasse 17, D-8000 Munchen 81.

[1] Connection Machine and *Lisp are trademarks of Thinking Machines Corporation.

An implementation of these compile-time techniques has been integrated to the FX system, providing a CM-2 compiler that generates *Lisp code. Test programs have been run on both a *Lisp simulator[12] and a CM-2 to evaluate the practicality and the performance of our approach.

Plan After presenting the FX language (section 2), we give (section 3) a brief overview of the Connection Machine architecture and its object language *Lisp, survey (section 4) the related work, present (beginning in section 5) the essential design ideas of our analysis and code generation techniques, discuss (section 12) the interesting implementation issues before concluding (section 13).

2 The FX Language

In order to simplify the presentation, this section introduces a core language that integrates, like FX or Standard ML, the principal features of functional and imperative programming.

2.1 Syntax

The expressions `e` of the language are the elements of the term algebra generated by the grammar described below. It uses enclosing parentheses in the reminiscence of Scheme[10].

`e ::=  x | (e e') | (op e) | (lambda (x) e) | (let (x e) e')`

`x` is a value identifier. The constructs `(e e')` and `(op e)` stand for the application of a function `e` or an operator `op` to an argument. The expression `(lambda (x) e)` defines the function whose parameter is `x` and whose result is the value of `e`. The construct `(let (x e) e')` lexically binds `x` to the value of `e` in `e'`.

2.2 Static Domains

In this section, we present the domains used in the static semantics of our language. We are first going to equip the language with a type system. The following term algebra defines the three basic kinds of the static semantics: regions, effects and types.

$$\begin{array}{lll} \rho & ::= r \mid \varrho & \text{regions} \\ \sigma & ::= \emptyset \mid \varsigma \mid \sigma \cup \sigma \mid init(\rho) \mid read(\rho) \mid write(\rho) & \text{effects} \\ \tau & ::= int \mid \alpha \mid vector_\rho(\tau) \mid \tau \xrightarrow{\sigma} \tau & \text{types} \end{array}$$

Regions ρ are either constants r or variables ϱ. Every data structure corresponds to a region which abstracts the memory locations in which it is allocated at run time. Two values are in the same region if they may share some memory locations.

Effects σ can either be the empty effect $\emptyset$, an effect variable ς, or a store effect $init(\rho)$, denoting the initialization of a mutable value in the region ρ, $read(\rho)$, which describes the access of a data in the region ρ, or $write(\rho)$, which denotes the assignment of a value to a mutable data. Effects are gathered with the infix set-union operator $\cup$ and can be compared using the set-inclusive relation $\supseteq$. Effects are introduced by operations that perform side-effects on mutable data structures such as vectors (see section 2.5).

Types τ are basic data types, such as int, type variables α, mutable vectors $vector_\rho(\tau)$ of type τ in the region ρ and function types $\tau \xrightarrow{\sigma} \tau'$ from τ to τ' with a *latent effect* σ. The latent effect of a function is the effect incurred when the function is applied.

2.3 Expansiveness

The notion of type polymorphism is the most distinguished feature of Milner's polymorphic typing discpline[6]. It reflects the property that an expression can have several different types that can be generically represented by a type scheme. Among various typing discipline, we decide here to choose the simplest one, based on the notion of *expansiveness* of expressions. An expression `e` is expansive if $exp[\![e]\!]$ holds:

$$\begin{aligned} exp[\![\mathtt{e}]\!] = \text{case } \mathtt{e} \text{ of } & \mathtt{x} \mid \mathtt{(lambda\ (x)\ e)} \Rightarrow \text{false} \\ & \mathtt{(e\ e')} \mid \mathtt{(op\ e)} \Rightarrow \text{true} \\ & \mathtt{(let\ (x\ e)\ e')} \Rightarrow exp[\![\mathtt{e}]\!] \vee exp[\![\mathtt{e'}]\!] \end{aligned}$$

In expressions such as `(let (x e) e')`, non-expansive expressions `e` can be handled by the textual substitution `e'[e/x]` of `e` for `x` in `e'`, avoiding capture of bound variables. This simple technique provides an equivalent way of expressing the property that non-expansive expressions may admit multiple types without adding the complication of introducing type schemes in the static semantics.

2.4 Static Semantics

We formulate type and effect inference by a deductive proof system that assigns a type and an effect to every expression of the language. The context in which an expressions is associated to a type and an effect is represented by a type environment $\mathcal{E}$ which maps value identifiers to types. Deductions produce typing judgments $\mathcal{E} \vdash \mathtt{e} : \tau, \sigma$ which read: "In the type environment $\mathcal{E}$ the expression `e` has type τ and effect σ".

$$\frac{\mathtt{x} \in Dom(\mathcal{E})}{\mathcal{E} \vdash \mathtt{x} : \mathcal{E}(\mathtt{x}), \emptyset} \text{ (var)} \qquad \frac{\mathcal{E}_{\mathtt{x}} + \{\mathtt{x} \mapsto \tau\} \vdash \mathtt{e} : \tau', \sigma}{\mathcal{E} \vdash \mathtt{(lambda\ (x)\ e)} : \tau \xrightarrow{\sigma} \tau', \emptyset} \text{ (abs)}$$

$$\frac{\mathcal{E} \vdash \mathtt{e} : \tau, \sigma \qquad \sigma' \supseteq \sigma}{\mathcal{E} \vdash \mathtt{e} : \tau, \sigma'} \text{ (does)} \qquad \frac{\mathcal{E} \vdash \mathtt{e} : \tau \xrightarrow{\sigma''} \tau', \sigma \qquad \mathcal{E} \vdash \mathtt{e'} : \tau, \sigma'}{\mathcal{E} \vdash \mathtt{(e\ e')} : \tau', \sigma \cup \sigma' \cup \sigma''} \text{ (app)}$$

$$\frac{\neg exp[\![\mathtt{e}]\!] \quad \mathcal{E} \vdash \mathtt{e} : \tau, \emptyset \quad \mathcal{E} \vdash \mathtt{e'[e/x]} : \tau', \sigma'}{\mathcal{E} \vdash \mathtt{(let\ (x\ e)\ e')} : \tau', \sigma'} \text{ (let)} \qquad \frac{exp[\![\mathtt{e}]\!] \quad \mathcal{E} \vdash \mathtt{e} : \tau, \sigma \quad \mathcal{E}_{\mathtt{x}} + \{\mathtt{x} \mapsto \tau\} \vdash \mathtt{e'} : \tau', \sigma'}{\mathcal{E} \vdash \mathtt{(let\ (x\ e)\ e')} : \tau', \sigma \cup \sigma'} \text{ (ilet)}$$

The rules for abstraction (abs) and application (app) show the interesting interplay between types and effects: effects flow from where functions are defined to where they are used.

2.5 Operations on Vectors

Since we are interested in studying the practical applications of effect systems to implement data parallelism, we focus on the FX module describing operations on vectors. This module integrates the facilities provided by both Scheme, Fortran90 and the scan model[1]. Vectors are represented by the abstract data type $vector_\rho(\tau)$ which denotes mutable arrays allocated in the region ρ whose elements are of type τ.

`make-vector`	initialization	$\tau \times int \xrightarrow{init(\rho)} vector_\rho(\tau)$
`vector-ref`	dereference	$vector_\rho(\tau) \times int \xrightarrow{read(\rho)} \tau$
`vector-set!`	assignment	$vector_\rho(\tau) \times int \times \tau \xrightarrow{write(\rho)} unit$
`vector-length`	length	$vector_\rho(\tau) \xrightarrow{read(\rho)} int$

The initialization performed by `(make-vector v n)` allocates a vector of length `n` initialized to the value `v`. The operation `(vector-ref v n)` dereferences the `n`th element of the vector `v`. The assignment of the `n`th element of the vector `v` to the value `e` is performed by the operation `(vector-set! v n e)`. The operation `(vector-length v)` returns the length of a vector `v`.

`identity`	identity perm.	$int \overset{init(\rho)}{\longrightarrow} vector_\rho(int)$
`permute`	regular perm.	$vector_\rho(int) \times vector_{\rho'}(\tau) \overset{read(\rho) \cup read(\rho') \cup init(\rho'')}{\longrightarrow} vector_{\rho''}(\tau)$
`cshift`	circular shift	$int \times vector_\rho(\tau) \overset{read(\rho) \cup init(\rho')}{\longrightarrow} vector_{\rho'}(\tau)$
`compress`	compression	$vector_\rho(bool) \times vector_{\rho'}(\tau) \overset{read(\rho) \cup read(\rho') \cup init(\rho'')}{\longrightarrow} vector_{\rho''}(\tau)$

Permutations implement rearrangements of vectors. When vectors are implemented by distributed data structures, as on the CM-2 (see below), permutations implement inter-process communications. Here, **(identity n)** returns the identity permutation from **1** to **n**; **(permute p v)** performs the rearrangement of **v** according to the permutation **p**; **(cshift n v)** and **(eoshift n v v′)** are the usual circular and end-off shift permutations. The expressions **(compress s v)** and **(expand s v v′)** are less usual:

```
fx> (compress #(true false true) #(1 2 3))
= #(1 3)
fx> (expand #(true false true false true) #(1 2 3) #(0 0 0 0 0))
= #(1 0 2 0 3)
```

In **compress**, the vectors **s** and **v** should be of the same size. This operation selects and concatenates the elements of $\mathbf{v}_i$ such that the $\mathbf{s}_i$ are true. In the operation **(expand s v v′)**, **s** is of the same length that v′ and bigger than **v**. When $\mathbf{s}_j$ is true for the ith time, $\mathbf{v}_i$ is selected, $\mathbf{v}'_j$ otherwise.

`vector-map`	mapping	$(\tau \overset{\sigma}{\rightarrow} \tau') \times vector_\rho(\tau) \overset{\sigma \cup read(\rho) \cup init(\rho')}{\longrightarrow} vector_{\rho'}(\tau')$
`vector-scan`	scanning	$(\tau \times \tau \overset{\sigma}{\rightarrow} \tau) \times vector_\rho(\tau) \overset{\sigma \cup read(\rho) \cup init(\rho')}{\longrightarrow} vector_{\rho'}(\tau)$
`vector-reduce`	reduction	$(\tau \times \tau \overset{\sigma}{\rightarrow} \tau) \times vector_\rho(\tau) \overset{\sigma \cup read(\rho)}{\longrightarrow} \tau$

In addition to the standard Scheme-like basic vector operations, the current vector module supports the mapping and reduction of first-class functions in the way of[1] and Fortran90 array extensions[2].

```
fx> (vector-scan and #(true false true false true))
= #(true false false false false)
fx> (vector-reduce and #(true false true false true))
= false
```

Here, **(vector-map f v)** applies the unary higher-order function **f** on every element of the vector **v** and returns the vector of the successive applications of **f**; **(vector-scan f v)** and **(segmented-scan f s v)** sum up the binary higher-order function **f** over every element of the vector **v** and returns the vector of the successive applications of **f**. In **segmented-scan**, summation is reset at $\mathbf{v}_i$ if $\mathbf{s}_i$ is false. In **vector-reduce**, the sum is returned.

3 *Lisp and the CM-2

The CM-2 is based on the SIMD model (Single Instruction Multiple Data). It is composed of up to 64k processing elements (PE), wrapped by groups of 32 processors and local memory units, connected into a global hypercube communication network. A front-end workstation issues instructions and transfers data in a time-step fashion to the CM-2.

*Lisp[12] is an extension of Common Lisp[11] that implements the PArallel Instruction Set (PARIS) and supports specific data structures: parallel variables or *pvars*. A pvar is a vector whose elements are allocated in the memory of every processing unit of the CM-2. In contrast to the usual implementation of vectors in Common Lisp systems, pvar components are unboxed values of fixed size such as booleans, fixnums or floats. The type of every pvar manipulated in *Lisp programs must be declared by the programmer.

On the CM-2, the local memory of each processing element is divided into a heap area and a stack area. By default, a *Lisp pvar expression is allocated in the current call stack frame. There are several ways of creating pvars. The most common way is to use implicit temporary allocation with the distribution operation `!!` or `coerce!!`. Pvars can also be explicitly stack allocated by using the `*let` construct:

```
*lisp> (*let ((x (coerce!! (+ 2 2) '(pvar fixnum))))
         (declare (type (pvar fixnum) x))
         (*deallocate (allocate!! x)))
```

In this example, enough space for a `fixnum` on the stack of each PE is allocated and then the value 4 is moved to this address on every PE, using the operation `coerce!!`. Note that declaring the type of `x` is required for the expression to be correctly compiled. Storage management of pvar expressions in the heap can also be explicit. The operations that perform heap allocation and reclamation respectively are `allocate!!` and `*deallocate`.

For arithmetic computations, the *Lisp system extends Common Lisp's generic operations on numbers. They are implemented by the so-called *bang-bang* functions. For example, the operation `+!!` is the equivalent of `+`. `!!` functions operate in parallel on every component of their two pvar arguments and return a pvar, such as in the following example:

```
*lisp> (+!! (!! 1) (!! 1))
= #<pvar x :general *default-vp-set* (1024)>
```

4 Related Work

In order to go beyond the crude *Lisp system[12], several other programming paradigms have been suggested. The major proposals are the APL-inspired alpha and beta global operations on xectors in CM-Lisp [4], the paralation abstract data type and its element-wise operations in Paralation-Lisp[9] or the scan operations over segmented vectors in SV-Lisp[1].

In the *Lisp language, the low-level programming features that are introduced in order to efficiently use the CM are all easy to compile. Not so for these other languages. However, their reference manuals [4, 9, 1] are quite elusive on the issue of which compile-time analysis would be necessary for programs to be effectively compiled.

Nonetheless, the data-parallel constructs designed in the SV-Lisp language[1] provide a programming model that made its way into the design of the vector module for the FX language. It proved here to be effectively compilable using our type and effect system. Our approach is thus not to introduce a new data model, but to describe how a sophisticated static system can be used to safely implement data parallel constructs on a massively parallel machine in the presence of side effects.

5 Overview of the Compiler

We introduce a series of new compile time techniques based on our type and effect inference system to detect when the use of operations on vectors is actually amenable to data-parallel execution (no inhibiting side-effects) on the CM-2 (no unimplementable parallel operations).

In FX, programs are implicitly typed, may have side-effects and may use first-class functions. Our compiler generates *Lisp programs that use pvars with explicit typing, explicit parallelism, explicit management of stack and heap storage and explicit name space assignment. (*Lisp uses multiple name spaces for function and value identifiers.) In the static semantics of FX, every expression is associated with its type and effect. The criterion of parallelizability of expressions is based on type and effect. Parallelizable expressions must manipulate scalar data structures and have no side-effects.

Parallelizable FX functions are translated into specific data structures, noted *f*-structure, built with the operator `make-f-struct`, which is a tagged pair of functions: the sequential version, the `f-seq` component, and the parallel one, the `f-par` component, operating upon pvars.

The compiler translates FX vector operations to the invocations of appropriate macros of the runtime library that implement the operations on unboxed pvars for the corresponding type of vectors operated upon.

Even though FX is a strongly typed language, the addition of `let`-bound identifiers introduces generic polymorphism. The presence of type and effect variables requires the use of run-time type dispatch for vector operations.

6 Vector Allocation

Vectors are represented by pvars. Vectors with scalar components, such as boolean or integer, are implemented by unboxed pvars. Vectors with non-scalar components, such as lists or other vectors, are represented by boxed pvars, called *front-end* pvars, which are pvars of addresses to objects that reside on the front-end i.e. front-end objects. Since *Lisp is dynamically typed, every pvar is associated on the front-end with a description header giving its actual address on every processing element and the size and type of its components.

Temporary allocation of pvars is preferred wherever possible in the generated *Lisp code in order to avoid the overhead of superfluous heap allocation. The FX compiler uses types and effects to decide when a returned value must be explicitly moved to the heap.

Definition 1 (Heap Allocation Criterion) *A vector operation (op e_1 ... e_n) that performs the allocation of a vector, of type $vector_\rho(\tau)$, must allocate its value in the heap in one of the following circumstances:*

- *The vector operation is the argument of an application expression (e $\square$) whose type is $ref_{\rho'}(\tau')$, $vector_{\rho'}(\tau')$, $list(\tau')$, or $\tau'' \xrightarrow{\sigma} \tau'$. The region ρ of the vector argument occurs free in τ' or σ.*

- *The vector operation occurs in the body of a lambda expression of the form (lambda (x) C$\square$) whose type is $\tau'' \xrightarrow{\sigma} \tau'$. The region ρ of the vector operation occurs free in τ' or in a subterm τ''' of τ'', be it a data structure $ref_{\rho'}(\tau''')$, $vector_{\rho'}(\tau''')$ or $list(\tau''')$.*

If the pvar outlives the stack frame it is allocated into, i.e. if it can be referenced in its lexical environment, it must be moved in the heap with an explicit call to `allocate!!`. The criterion presented above syntactically controls the cases in which this situations may happen and that can actually be checked by using the effect system.

7 Runtime Library

The runtime library provides *Lisp functions and macros to implement the FX vector module. For each vector operation in FX (such as `vector-ref`), specialized *Lisp macros and a generic function are defined in the runtime as follows:

- The *Lisp macros implement the data-parallel polymorphic FX operation for every type of unboxed pvars: booleans, characters, integers, reals and complex. Such an operation is also defined on front-end pvars (the macro `front-end-vector-ref` in the present example).

- The generic function (in the example, `vector-ref`) implements the operation for every type of pvars. It uses a dispatch construct depending on pvar headers to check the actual type of pvar arguments at run time and call the appropriate specialized macro.

By default, all global vector operations are performed in parallel. The FX operations that accept higher order functions, such as **vector-map**, obey a different rule which is that the front-end version, **front-end-vector-map**, implements the sequential version on generic pvar arguments.

Finally, note that *Lisp operations on pvar are restricted to the set of active PEs, or *VP set*. Similarly, parallel vector operations are in FX limited to their actual size. In the runtime library, this is implemented by the macro **(with-context-of e e')** that disables, during the execution of **e'**, the processing elements on which the pvar expression **e** is not defined.

8 Sequential Code Generation

Having briefly presented *Lisp, our FX vector module and its corresponding *Lisp runtime library, we can now describe the *Lisp code generation scheme for sequential expressions. The input of the compiler is an expression **te** decorated with its principal type τ and its minimal effect σ.

The sequential code generation scheme [14] is specified by an algorithm $SC[\![\mathtt{te}]\!]\vec{\tau}\vec{\mathtt{x}}$, which relates a typed FX expression **te** that was successfully typed checked by the algorithm of [13] with its corresponding *Lisp code, in a given compilation context $\vec{\tau}$. The context $\vec{\tau}$ is a sequence of types that are used decide when vector allocations must be performed in heap (according to Definition 1). $\vec{\mathtt{x}}$ is the sequence of parallelizable predefined functions, such as +, -, etc.

Identifiers

The compiler translates a lambda-bound identifier **x** to **x**. Identifiers **x** that appear in $\vec{\mathtt{x}}$ are predefined parallellizable functions. They are thus compiled by an *f*-structure **(make-f-struct x x!!)**.

Abstraction

To translate an abstraction **(lambda (x:**τ**) te)**:τ', the compiler compiles the body **te** of the source FX abstraction into target code *c*. If the type τ' agrees with the predicate *PF*, defined below, the lambda-abstraction is parallelizable. An *f*-structure initialization is generated, which pairs up the sequential code of the function, generated by *SC*, with its parallel version, returned by parallel code generator *PC*, presented in the next section.

If the function is not parallelizable then the compiler only returns the sequential code of the lambda abstraction. The compiler uses the following static criterion, *PF*, based on function types, to determine if a lambda of type τ' is parallelizable.

Definition 2 (Parallelizability Criterion) *A lambda-expression of type* $\tau \xrightarrow{\sigma} \tau'$ *is parallelizable (satisfies the criterion PF) if and only if its latent effect* σ *is* $\emptyset$ *or a union of effect variables, and if the types* τ *and* τ' *are scalar data types, type variables or function types that satisfy the criteria* $PF(\tau \xrightarrow{\sigma} \tau') = PA(\tau) \wedge PA(\tau') \wedge PE(\sigma)$, *where*

$$
\begin{array}{llll}
PA(\tau) = \mathit{case}\ \tau\ \mathit{of} & & PE(\sigma) = \mathit{case}\ \sigma\ \mathit{of} & \\
\mathit{bool} \mid \mathit{int} \mid \mathit{real} \mid \alpha & \Rightarrow \mathit{true} & \emptyset \mid \varsigma & \Rightarrow \mathit{true} \\
\tau' \xrightarrow{\sigma} \tau'' & \Rightarrow PF(\tau) & \sigma \cup \sigma' & \Rightarrow PE(\sigma) \wedge PE(\sigma') \\
\mathit{otherwise} & \Rightarrow \mathit{false} & \mathit{otherwise} & \Rightarrow \mathit{false}
\end{array}
$$

This criterion has both compile-time and runtime aspects. Its compile-time aspect can be informally justified in the following way. First, the lambda expression must have no side effects: no write effects *write*(ρ) must occur in σ, since they could generate non-determinism at run time. Also, no initialization *init*(ρ) or read effects *read*(ρ) may appear, as they would indicate that the function allocates or manipulates non-scalar values which are unimplementable on the Connection Machine. Second, the types τ and τ' must be scalar variables or function types.

Runtime checks are only required in the presence of effect variables in σ, to distinguish whether these effect variables actually are $\emptyset$ or not in each given instance. These effect variables are introduced by the latent effects of higher-order functions, other lambda-bound function identifiers. However, we known that every pure first-order function is compiled as an f-structure. Thus, we use the predicate `f-struct-p` to decide at runtime whether the free function identifiers of a lambda-abstraction actually correspond to other f-structures. When this condition is met, an f-structure is returned.

For instance, the code generated for `(lambda (g) (lambda (x) (g x)))` is as below. (The identifier `id` is fresh and thet *Lisp function `*funcall` applies a function value operating on pvars to its arguments.)

```
(lambda (g)
  (let ((id #'(lambda (x)
                (funcall (if (f-struct-p g) (f-seq g) g) x))))
    (if (f-struct-p g)
        (make-f-struct id #'(lambda (x!!) (*funcall (f-par g) x!!)))
        id)))
```

Application

As shown in the previous example, the compiler translate application expressions (`te te'`)$:\tau!\sigma$ by translating the subexpressions `te` and `te'` into *Lisp code c and c' and by generating the code that checks whether c is an f-structure or not.

Simplifications

More efficient compilation mechanisms for vector operations are given in the subsection 10. However, simple syntactic rewriting rules can already be used to improve the code generated by the previous technique. They are the following:

`(f-seq (make-f-struct` c c'`))`	$\Rightarrow$ `c`	`(funcall #'`c c'`)`	$\Rightarrow$ `(`c c'`)`
`(f-par (make-f-struct` c c'`))`	$\Rightarrow$ c'	`(*funcall #'`c c'`)`	$\Rightarrow$ `(`c c'`)`
`(f-struct-p (make-f-struct` c c'`))`	$\Rightarrow$ `t`	`(if t` c c'`)`	$\Rightarrow$ `c`
`(f-struct-p #'(lambda (x)` c`))`	$\Rightarrow$ `nil`	`(if nil` c c'`)`	$\Rightarrow$ c'

9 Parallel Code Generation

We describe the *Lisp parallel code generation scheme implemented by the algorithm $PC[\![\texttt{te}]\!]\vec{x} = c$ which, given a typed FX expression `te` and a sequence of parallel value identifiers $\vec{x}$, generates the parallel *Lisp code for it, for execution on the CM-2 processors. Parallel value identifiers in $\vec{x}$ are either predefined arithmetic operations, such as + or −, which are implemented on the CM-2, or user value identifiers bound by lambda abstractions.

Identifier

The compiler translates a lambda-bound identifier `x`, appearing in the sequence $\vec{x}$, by `x!!`. Free identifiers correspond to values that are imported in the parallel code. Scalar identifiers `x` (as well as constants `1,.. n`) are distributed and coerced to a pvar of the corresponding type. Functions identifiers `f` are translated to `(f-par f)`.

Identifiers of variable type use the type dispatching expression `(distribute x)` of the FX runtime library to precisely distinguish at run time between the previous cases. Other (mutable) data structure identifiers are guaranteed by the static semantics to never be used in parallel code.

Abstraction

In the compilation of lambda-abstractions, since *Lisp doesn't create real closures, the free pvar identifiers of the compiled lambda expression must be heap allocated, because the lambda abstraction may escape from the stack frame at which those pvar identifiers are allocated.

It is the case in the following example, which also shows that our compilation technique support the presence of higher order functions. The function `(lambda (f x) (lambda (y) (f x y)))` partially applies `f` to `x` and is translated it by the following parallel code:

```
#'(lambda (f!! x!!)
    (declare (type pvar x!!)
             (type (function (pvar) pvar) f!!))
    (let ((x1!! (heap-allocate x!!)))
      (declare (type pvar x1!!))
      #'(lambda (y!!)
          (declare (return-pvar-p t)
                   (type pvar y!!))
          (*funcall f!! x1!! y!!))))
```

where `x1!!` is fresh and `heap-allocate` is the generic runtime type-dispatching function for `allocate!!` on pvars. The declaration `return-pvar-p` is used to explicitly tell the *Lisp compiler that an expression returns a pvar.

Application

The parallel code generated for an application is decomposed into the code generation for its subexpressions and the invocation of the parallel function via the *Lisp construct `*funcall`.

Parallel `if` expressions are translated into *Lisp `if!!` expressions. The compilation of `if` differs from standard applications for two reasons. First, the semantics of the *Lisp expression (`if!! e e' e''`) is to execute both `e'` and `e''` and return the value of `e'` where `e` is true and `e''` otherwise. To ensure termination, we add code to check that at least one processor is active before executing the `if!!` form itself. Second, `if!!` expressions can only return pvars even though FX `if` expressions may return functions. Thus, calls to these functions must be interned within the branches of the `if` construct.

Before being compiled, the expression `((if b 1+ 1-) x)` is first transformed into the following,

```
((lambda (y) (if b (1+ y) (1- y))) x)
```

where the function expression `(if b 1+ 1-)` is abstracted over a fresh `y`. This expression gets compiled into the following *Lisp code, where `*or` performs a machine-wide reduction. If no processors are active, `nil` is returned by `*or`.

```
((lambda (y!!) (if (*or t!!)
                   (if!! b!! (1+!! y!!) (1-!! y!!))
                   (!! 0)))
               x!!)
```

10 Optimization of Vector Operations

The code generated by the scheme described above can be dramatically improved in a variety of ways by using simple type and effect based optimizations, especially on vector operations. A vector operation `(op e)` is a particular case of application statement. The default mechanism for optimizing such an operation is to look at the type of the vector $vector_\rho(\tau)$ operated upon in the expression.

When τ is a scalar data type, such as *real*, the vector is implemented by an unboxed pvar of scalar components. In this case, op is translated by a call to the appropriate *Lisp macro. When τ is a non-scalar datatype, such as a *vector*, the vector is implemented as a boxed front-end pvar, and the operation op by the macro `front-end-op` of the runtime library. Otherwise, τ is a type variable and the compiler translates the operation into a call to the generic function of the runtime library implementing the operation, named op. In a way similar to types, effects can be used to specialize some higher-order vector operations which require runtime tests. (See [14] for more details on these various optimizations.)

11 Compilation of let

Managing the `let` construct within the simplified compilation scheme shown above is easy. Value definitions such as `(let ((x e)) e')` are handled according to our basic compilation scheme by translating them into `((lambda (x) e') e)`.

An identifier `f` is defined as a function when it is bound in a `let` expression to an explicit lambda expression. Function definitions are translated by using the Common-Lisp `labels` construct. When `(lambda (x) e)`, bound to `f` in a `let` construct, is a function that can be parallelized, its parallel implementation is associated to `f!!`. The sequence of parallelized functions $\vec{x}$ is updated to associate the identifiers `f` of parallelizable functions with the lambda-bound function identifiers $\vec{f}$ on which the parallelizability of `f` actually depends at run time.

An occurrence of a function identifier `f` in function position `(f e)` is left as such during sequential code compilation. An occurrence in value position, such as in `(lambda (x) f)` or `(e f)` is translated, as previously, by the allocation of an *f*-structure if `f` was added to $\vec{x}$. If `f` is parallelizable (modulo the possible run-time check on its free function identifiers) the *f*-structure `(make-f-struct #'f #'f!!)` is returned. Otherwise, `#'f` is generated.

Example For instance, the following definition:

```
(lambda (g)
    (let ((f (lambda (x) (g x))))
        f))
```

is compiled as:

```
(lambda (g)
   (labels (((f x) (funcall (if (f-struct-p g) (f-seq g) g) x))
            ((f!! x!!) (*funcall (f-par g) x!!)))
     (if (f-struct-p g) (make-f-struct #'f #'f!!) #'f)))
```

During parallel code generation, an occurrence of a parallelizable function identifier `f` in function position is translated to `f!!`. The static semantics guarantees that non-parallelizable functions occurring in parallelizable FX expressions are never used. The occurrence of `f` in a value position, such as in `(lambda (x) f)` or `(e f)`, is translated into `#'f!!`.

12 Implementation

The FX compiler for the CM-2 was implemented by using the initial implementation of the FX-91 interpreter, consisting of a parser, a kind and type checker and a simple interpreter. The FX-91 interpreter is written in Scheme and runs under T[8] and has been adapted to *Lisp. The techniques described in this paper have all been implemented.

The FX/CM Compiler has first been tested on the *Lisp simulator[12]. We have then used the CM-2 installed at ETCA (Arcueil, France) and run more interesting data-parallel algorithms, such as a `life` program, a `quicksort` algorithm using segmented scanning and a matrix transposition algorithm.

Example We illustrate the speed-up obtained by our compiler the segmented matrix transposition algorithm **segment-transpose**, described below, which uses higher-order functions and segmented vectors as 2D matrices.

```
(define (segment-transpose m segment)
  (let ((id (segment-identity segment))
        (offset (1+ (vector-reduce max id))))
   (permute m
    (vector-map2 + (segment-index segment)
                   (vector-map (lambda (i) (* offset i))
                               id)))))
```

It was executed on 8×8 to 128×128 integer matrices on a 8K processor CM-200a. Busy times are almost independent of the problem size, except for the last case. For a 128×128 matrix, the VP set exceeds the actual machine size and thus multiple operations are performed on each processor, slowing down the overall execution.

Matrix size	8×8	16×16	32×32	64×64	128×128
Elapsed Time (s)	1.48×10^{-2}	1.51×10^{-2}	1.83×10^{-2}	1.52×10^{-2}	1.74×10^{-2}
Busy Time (s)	6.47×10^{-3}	6.48×10^{-3}	6.43×10^{-3}	6.43×10^{-3}	1.04×10^{-2}

13 Conclusion

The FX/CM compiler prototype supports the claim that effect systems can be used to integrate, for the first time, functional and imperative programming on massively parallel architectures. Effects are used to decide whether potentially parallel constructs can actually be implemented as such without leading to non-determinism or do not use local data structures that inhibit their efficient implementation on existing parallel hardware. Regions are used to optimize space allocation strategies and limit the garbage collection overhead.

Acknowledgements

We thank J. P. Massar (Thinking Machines Corporation) for discussions on the issue of implementing a pvar garbage-collector in *Lisp, C. Millour (Consultant at ETCA) for his experience in the use of *Lisp, P. Clermont and S. Petiton (ETCA) for allowing us to access the CM-2 at SEH.

References

[1] Blelloch, G. E. Vector model for data-parallel computing. The MIT Press, 1990.

[2] ANSI, *Standard for the Information Systems Programming Language Fortran: S8(X3.9-198x)*, 1989.

[3] Gifford, D. K., Jouvelot, P., Lucassen, J. M., and Sheldon, M. A. FX-87 Reference Manual. *MIT/LCS/TR-407*, MIT Laboratory for Computer Science, September 1987.

[4] Hillis, W. D. The Connection Machine. The MIT Press,1985.

[5] Lucassen, J. M., and Gifford, D. K. Polymorphic Effect Systems. In *Proceedings of the 1988 ACM Conference on Principles of Programming Languages.* ACM, New-York, 1988.

[6] Milner, R. A Theory for type polymorphism in programming. In *Journal of Computer and Systems Sciences*, Vol. 17, pages 348-375. 1978.

[7] MILNER, R., TOFTE, M., HARPER, R. The definition of Standard ML. *The MIT Press*, 1990.

[8] REES, J. A., ADAMS, N. I., AND MEEHAN, J. R. *The T Manual, fourth edition*. Yale University 1984.

[9] SABOT, G. W. *The Paralation Model*. MIT Press 1990.

[10] REES, J., AND CLINGER W., EDITORS. Fourth Report on the Algorithmic Language Scheme, 1988.

[11] STEELE, G. L. *Common Lisp, the language*. Digital Press 1990.

[12] *Lisp Reference Manual, version 4.0. Thinking Machines Corporation, Cambridge, 1987.

[13] TALPIN, J. P., AND JOUVELOT, P. Polymorphic Type, Region and Effect Inference. In the *Journal of Functional Programming*, volume 2, number 3. Cambridge University Press, 1992.

[14] TALPIN, J. P. *Aspects Théoriques et Pratiques de l'Inférence de Type et d'Effet*. Doctoral dissertation. University Paris VI, May 12th, 1993.

Combining Dependability with Architectural Adaptability by means of the SIGNAL Language

Olivier MAFFEÏS[1] Paul LE GUERNIC[2]

[1] GMD I5 - SKS, Postfach 1316, D - 5205 Sankt Augustin, Germany
[2] IRISA/INRIA-Rennes, Campus de Beaulieu, 35042 Rennes Cedex, France

Abstract. This paper introduces a new abstract program representation, namely Synchronous Flows Dependence graph, which has been induced from SIGNAL, a synchronous dataflow language based on axiomatic flow transformation operators. We have provided this graph representation with (1) architecture-independent validation tools which encompass control-consistency verification and deadlock detection and, (2) the notion of abstraction which enables some tuning of the grain of the SFD graphs according to the target architecture.

1 Introduction

In response to the spectacular technological advances in high performance computing, the programming languages community re-focused its attention on the design of intermediate program representations to get a better architectural adaptability of the software. This response has been materialized into two complementary directions:

1. upstream, *program normalization to bring portability*;
   The normalization direction tries to make explicit every program feature (e.g side-effects) which depends on a particular target architecture (e.g VON-NEUMANN architecture). Since the normalization direction goes towards the intrinsic application properties, it brings portability. For instance, this approach led to an efficient algorithm [5] which infers a *Static Single Assignment* form of sequential programs. The normalization step is often used as a front-end to abstract representation.
2. downstream, *abstract representation design to gain in efficiency.*
   This second direction intends to define finer abstract representations on which high-level optimizations may be applied to infer efficient implementations. This second approach yielded the definition of new representations like *Program Dependence Graphs* [6] and *Dependence Flow Graphs* [12].

The contribution of this paper is intended in these two directions. On the one hand, this paper presents the SIGNAL language which defines an axiomatization of flow transformations. One the other hand, it defines the concept of *Synchronous*

Flows Dependence Graph (SFD graph) and endows it with modularity through the notion of ***abstraction***.

In section 2, we present the SIGNAL language, a dataflow oriented language outcoming from the ***principles of synchrony*** [2]. We illustrate the specification capability of this language by programming a basic resource for numerous languages: a memory cell which implements a variable. In section 3, we define the algebraic model in which the control part of SIGNAL programs is encoded and synthesized. Section 4 defines the SFD graph abstract representation. This graph representation statically describes the dynamic evolution of the data flows according to the control states; it is a generalization of the Directed Acyclic Graphs (DAGs). The inference of distributed implementations from SFD graphs, a fine-grain abstract representation, onto various architectures requires a tool which enables grain-size variations. This tools is based on the notion of abstraction of SFD graphs which is presented in section 5.

2 The SIGNAL Language

As SIGNAL is a data-flow oriented language, it describes processes which communicate through sequences of (typed) values with an implicit timing: the ***signals***. For instance, a signal X denotes the sequence $(\mathbf{x}_t)_{t \in \mathbb{N}/\{0\}}$ of data indexed by time.

2.1 The kernel of the language

Two classes of operators constitute the kernel of the SIGNAL language: the operators on signals and the process operators. Four kinds of operators are acting on signals:

- *instantaneous functions* which are the extension of the usual functions on values to signals (sequences of values). Let f a symbol which denotes an n-ary function and $[\![f]\!]$ the corresponding function acting on values; the SIGNAL expression:

  $$\mathtt{Y} := f(\mathtt{X1}, \ldots, \mathtt{Xn})$$

  defines a basic process such that $\forall t \geq 1 \quad \mathbf{y}_t = [\![f]\!](\mathbf{x1}_t, \ldots, \mathbf{xn}_t)$

  For instance, the boolean and arithmetic operators belong to the set of the instantaneous functions. ***The principles of synchrony allows us to focus on the* logical relations *specified among signals occurrences.*** Hence, from the synchronous point of view, a basic process like `Y:= - X` induces the relation $\mathbf{x}_t \longrightarrow \mathbf{y}_t$ on a logical time instead of the relation $\mathbf{x}_t \longrightarrow \mathbf{y}_{t+\Delta t}$ on a physical time: the ***principles of synchrony in specification stand for assuming an ideal machine where the execution time of the operators is zero duration.***

  Basic processes built on instantaneous functions[3] require all the signals involved to simultaneously carry a value: these signals are bound to the same logical time index, the same *clock*; signals bounded to the same clock are declared ***synchronous***.

[3] Note that, due to recursive definitions like $\mathtt{X} := f(\mathtt{X}, \mathtt{Y})$, the above expression may express relations (and not only functions).

- *shift register* is the basic memory operator, it recalls the previous value carried by a signal. For instance, the process

$$\texttt{Y} := \texttt{X}\ \$1$$

defines a basic process such that $\mathtt{y}_1 = v0, \quad \forall t > 1 \quad \mathtt{y}_t = \mathtt{x}_{t-1}$ where $v0$ denotes an initial and constant value associated with the declaration of Y.

Instantaneous functions and the shift register operator deal with a single clock: they are *monochronous operators.* In addition to the first two monochronous operators, the kernel of SIGNAL includes two complementary *polychronous operators*:

- the *selection* operator allows us to draw some data of a signal through some boolean condition. In the SIGNAL process

  Y := X **when** B

  (where B must be a boolean signal), Y carries the same value than X each time X carries a data and B carries the value *true*. Otherwise, Y is absent, i.e. the value of Y is not defined.
- the *merge* operator combines flows of data. The SIGNAL process

  Y := X1 **default** X2

  defines Y by merging the values carried by X1 and X2 and giving priority to X1's data when both signals are simultaneously present.

The four operators on signals define basic processes. The specification of complex processes is achieved with the parallel composition operator. Let P1, P2 denote two processes, the composition of P1 and P2 is denoted

P1 | P2

In the composed process, the common names between P1 and P2 refer to common signals; they stand for the communication links. This parallel composition is an associative and commutative operator. In addition, the process algebra of SIGNAL includes a restriction operator which assigns a local scope to signals.

Owing to the equation-oriented style of the SIGNAL programming, specifications may be achieved using a block-diagram editor which provides the programmer with a convenient programming environment. In the next subsection, this block-diagram editor is used to specify a memory cell.

2.2 Specification of a memory cell

Externally, a variable is a device which memorizes the last written value (signal IN) and delivers it (signal OUT) when requested. The SIGNAL process VAR which specifies such a device is presented in Fig. 1.

The top box specifies the functional part of the memory: the content of the memory carried by the signal MEM is defined by IN when it occurs; otherwise, it keeps its previous value memorized by ZMEM. Implicitly, this specification induces that a memory device is more often active than the occurrences of IN.

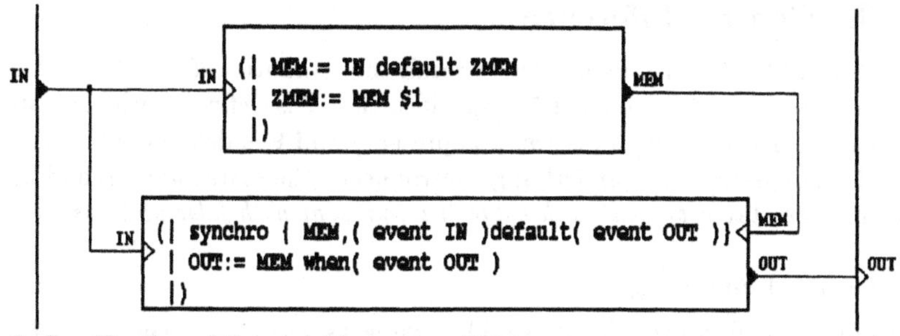

Fig. 1. Specification of the variable process **VAR**

The two basic processes included in the bottom box respectively specify:

1. *the control of the memory device.*
   The **event** operator makes explicit the transition from signals to *signal-clocks* which are signals occurring only with the value *true*. For instance, if `C` is defined by `C:= event X` , it takes the value *true* when `X` carries a value; this process is rewritten in the kernel of SIGNAL by `C:= (X=X)` (the equal operator belongs to the instantaneous functions set). The **synchro** operator is a relational instantaneous operator. It specifies the synchrony of SIGNAL expressions (this operator is rewritten in equality between signal-clocks). Hence, the upper basic process of the bottom box sets that **MEM** is defined when a write operation occurs (**event IN**) or (**default**) when an output is requested (**event OUT**).
2. *the definition of the output.* The memorized value carried by **MEM** is delivered in a demand-driven manner, when **OUT** is requested: **when(event OUT)**.

2.3 Design Methodology

The specification of this memory cell emphasizes the independence of SIGNAL programming from target architectures. This independence is achieved through the principles of synchrony and the declarative style of the SIGNAL language. By means of this independence, we consider a three steps design methodology:

1. *Specification of applications in* SIGNAL.
   Going deeper into that direction is out of the scope of this paper; the reader interested in the SIGNAL methodology of specification is referred to [11].
2. *Validation of the specification independently of target architectures.*
   The next two sections define an architecture-independent abstract representation, SFD graphs, and they present validation techniques respectively related to the control (representation, synthesis and consistency verification) and the data relations (representation and deadlock detection).
3. *Inference of efficient and semantics-preserving implementations.*
   Fine-grain parallel implementations are specified through a SFD graph transformation; this is roughly presented in subsection 4.2. Distributed implementations for large-grain architectures are envisaged by means of the notion of abstraction which is presented in section 5. This notion enables some tuning of the abstract representation grain according to the target architecture.

3 The Control Inference

To apprehend the control model, let us recall the semantics of the selection operator. The process `Y := X when B` specifies that **Y** is defined with the value of **X** if **X** carries a value (i.e., **X** occurs, **X** is present) and **B** is defined with the value *true*. Thus, expressing the underlying control needs the states *present* and *absent* for **X** and, the states *present with value true*, *present with false* and *absent* for **B**.

3.1 Control encoding

The boolean algebra over the set $\{0, 1\}$ of integers modulo 2, denoted by $\mathcal{B} =< C, \vee, \wedge, \widehat{0}, \widehat{1} >$, is taken to encode the states of signals as follows:

$$absent\ :\ 0 \qquad\qquad present\ :\ 1$$

Let us denote	C	a set of characteristic functions which denote the occurrences of the signals,
	$\widehat{x}$	a characteristic function which encodes the states of **X**; $\widehat{x}$ is said to be the *clock* of **X**; $\mathcal{B}$ is called the *clock algebra*
	$[b], [\neg b]$	the characteristic functions which respectively encode the states *present with value true* and *present with value false* of the boolean signal **B**
	$\widehat{0}$	the lowest element of $\mathcal{B}$ which stands for the never present clock; it is used to denote something that never happens
	$\widehat{1}$	the highest element of $\mathcal{B}$, the always present clock.

Among these characteristic functions, the following equivalences hold:

$$[b] \vee [\neg b] \equiv \widehat{b} \qquad\qquad [b] \wedge [\neg b] \equiv \widehat{0}$$

Hence, the implicit control relations of SIGNAL processes are encoded in equations over $\mathcal{B}$. For instance, the process `Y:= X when B` is encoded by:

$$\widehat{y} \equiv \widehat{x} \wedge [b]$$

Let us examine the control encoding of the process **UNFOLD** specified in Fig. 2. This process converts a vector **VECT**, a spatial representation of data, into a sequence of **SCALAR**, a temporal representation. Such a process may enable pipelined computations over **VECT**; it also specifies a PIO/SIO interface.

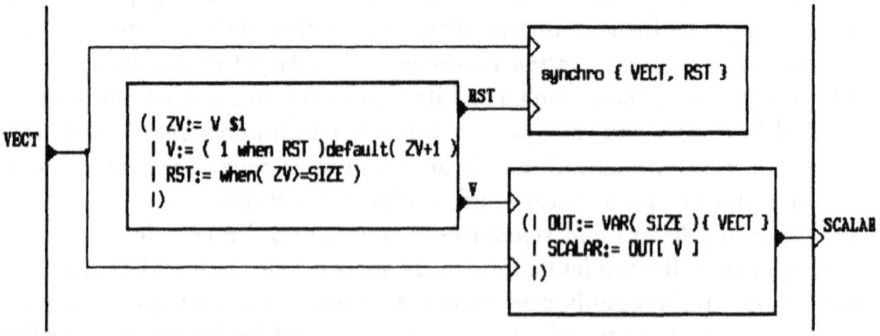

Fig. 2. Specification of **UNFOLD**

This process is made up with three components:

- left box: a *modulo counter*. The current value of this counter is held by `V`; this counter is reset to 1 when `RST` occurs; `RST` occurs when the counter reaches the limit defined by the parameter `SIZE` (a constant value);
- lower right box: an *enumeration process*. It enumerates the `SIZE` elements of a vector signal `OUT` according to the occurrences of `V`. `OUT` memorizes the last occurrence of `VECT` by means of the process `VAR` specified in Fig. 1.
- upper right box: a *control constraint*. The basic process `synchro { VECT, RST }` sets that the enumeration must be completed before accepting another input.

The `UNFOLD` process is encoded as follows, where the `VAR` instance is substituted with its definition; we have introduced a boolean signal Ψ to make clear the boolean condition defining `RST`.

`ZV := V $1`	$\widehat{zv} \equiv \widehat{v}$	(1)
`V := ( 1 when RST )default( ZV + 1 )`	$\widehat{v} \equiv \widehat{rst} \vee \widehat{zv}$	(2)
`RST := when` Ψ	$\widehat{rst} \equiv [\psi]$	(3)
Ψ `:= ( ZV >= SIZE )`	$\widehat{\psi} \equiv \widehat{zv}$	(4)
`synchro { MEM, (event VECT)default(event OUT)}`	$\widehat{mem} \equiv \widehat{vect} \vee \widehat{out}$	(5)
`MEM := VECT default ZMEM`	$\widehat{mem} \equiv \widehat{vect} \vee \widehat{zmem}$	(6)
`ZMEM := MEM $1`	$\widehat{zmem} \equiv \widehat{mem}$	(7)
`OUT := MEM when (event OUT)`	$\widehat{out} \equiv \widehat{mem} \wedge \widehat{out}$	(8)
`SCALAR := OUT[ V ]`	$\widehat{scalar} \equiv \widehat{out} \equiv \widehat{v}$	(9)
`synchro { VECT, RST }`	$\widehat{vect} \equiv \widehat{rst}$	(10)

According to the behavior of the basic processes, the encoding is split into three classes:

- **monochronous**: equivalence encoding.
  As the processes in lines (1), (4), (7), (9) and (10) are built on monochronous operators, their encoding expresses that the referred signals must be *synchronous: their clocks must be equivalent.*
- **selection**: $\wedge$-encoding.
  The selection operator produces less frequent signals: its encoding is achieved through the $\wedge$ operator. Line (3) has been split in two parts by the introduction of the boolean condition of selection Ψ. The encoding of this line expresses that `RST` occurs when the condition Ψ is defined with the value *true* (Ψ is defined each time `ZV` occurs: $\widehat{\psi} \equiv \widehat{zv}$). In line (8), the encoding does not mention selection through a condition since `event OUT` stands for the signal-clock (a signal which carries only the value *true*) of `OUT`;
- **merge**: $\vee$-encoding.
  The default operator produces more frequent signals: its encoding is achieved with the $\vee$ operator. Such an encoding is realized in lines (2), (5) and (6).

The encoding over $\mathcal{B}$ produces an intricate set of control equivalences. In the next subsection, we synthesize a compact and equivalent form of it.

3.2 Control synthesis

From this explicit representation of control, a natural compaction is achieved by the projection of the equations system through the equivalence of characteristic functions. In the **UNFOLD** example, from the equations (1), (4), (7), (9) and (10), we infer the equivalence classes:

$\{\widehat{\psi}, \widehat{v}, \widehat{zv}, \widehat{scalar}, \widehat{out}\}$		$\widehat{\psi}$
$\{\widehat{rst}, \widehat{vect}\}$	which are identified by	$\widehat{rst}$
$\{\widehat{mem}, \widehat{zmem}\}$		$\widehat{mem}$

Then, the equations (2) and (5) are rewritten in $\widehat{\psi} \equiv \widehat{rst} \vee \widehat{\psi}$ and $\widehat{mem} \equiv \widehat{rst} \vee \widehat{\psi}$, thus $\widehat{mem} \equiv \widehat{\psi}$. As none of lines (6) and (8) refutes this result, the equations system of control has a solution: *the control of* **UNFOLD** *is statically consistent.* If C is the set of characteristic functions and Σ is the initial system of control equations over C, an equivalent compact control representation of the **UNFOLD** program is:

$$C/_{\equiv} = \{\widehat{rst}, \widehat{\psi}\} \qquad\qquad \Sigma/_{\equiv} = \{\widehat{rst} \equiv [\psi]\}$$

The projection through $\equiv$ does not delete the equivalence between clocks $\widehat{rst}$ and $[\psi]$ since $[\psi]$ is a basic characteristic function which represents some data selection over the signal Ψ. Incorrect or conditionally correct programs may be detected as well. For instance, the process

```
(| X:= A when (A>0)
 | Y:= X+A
 |)
```

is encoded by

$$\widehat{x} \equiv [a{>}0]$$
$$\widehat{y} \equiv \widehat{x} \equiv \widehat{a}$$

From this encoding, we induced that $\widehat{a} \equiv [a{>}0]$. The solutions[4] of this equivalence stand for: the program is inactive ($\widehat{a} = 0$), or the value of **A** is always positive ($[a{>}0]{=}1$). These solutions express the conditions at which the above process is correct. The reader interested in further verifications is referred to [11].

3.3 Mathematical properties of the control representation

A control is defined by a couple $< C, \Sigma >$ where C is a set of characteristic functions. The control constraints, represented by Σ, are expressed by a set of equivalences over the boolean algebra $\mathcal{B} =< C, \vee, \wedge, \widehat{0}, \widehat{1} >$. As boolean algebras are lattices, an alternative representation of the clock algebra $\mathcal{B}$ is achieved through a partial order:

$$< C, \leq > \qquad \text{with} \qquad \widehat{h} \leq \widehat{k} \Leftrightarrow \widehat{h} \vee \widehat{k} \equiv \widehat{k}$$

In the **UNFOLD** example, we infer $\widehat{rst} \leq \widehat{\psi}$

[4] since $[b] \vee [\neg b] \equiv \widehat{b} \quad \Rightarrow \quad \widehat{b} = 0 \Rightarrow [b] = 0$

From this inequality, we deduce that $\widehat{\psi}$ is the condition which controls the entire activity of the **UNFOLD** program. Besides the detection of control conditions used to infer implementations, this lattice form is used to implement the resolution process in the SIGNAL compiler: this form offers a structured control representation; some algebraic equivalences are simply proved by using geometric properties over a particular tree representation of the lattice [3].

Finally, using a single operation, namely the equivalence projection, the SIGNAL compiler: (a) verifies the static consistency of the control and, (b) synthesizes a minimized control representation used to infer efficient implementations.

4 Synchronous Flows Dependence Graphs

The complete abstract representation of SIGNAL programs is achieved by connecting the algebraic control model with a dependence graph which represents the data relations. This structure mixing a dependence graph with an equational control representation is called *Synchronous Flows Dependence Graph* (SFD graph).

4.1 Example and Definition

To apprehend the requested representation of the data flows, let us consider the basic process of **UNFOLD**: `V := ( 1 when RST )default( ZV + 1 )`

As expressed by the control equations, the control state where $\widehat{\psi} = 0$ and $\widehat{rst} = 1$ is unreachable ($\widehat{rst} \leq \widehat{\psi}$). According to the reachable states of $\widehat{\psi}$ and $\widehat{rst}$, the different data-dependency configurations induced from the above basic process are depicted in Fig. 3.

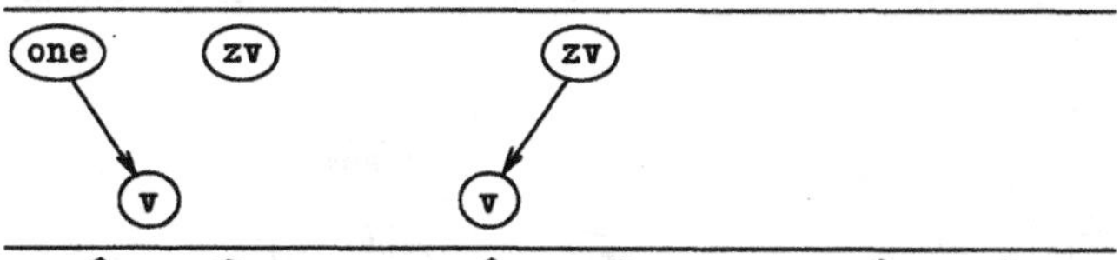

(a) $\widehat{\psi} = 1, \widehat{rst} = 1$ (b) $\widehat{\psi} = 1, \widehat{rst} = 0$ (c) $\widehat{\psi} = 0, \widehat{rst} = 0$

Fig. 3. The data-dependencies according to the control states

As $\widehat{\psi}$ identifies the equivalence class which includes the clocks of **V** and **ZV**, their nodes exist in Fig. 3-a and 3-b. When $\widehat{rst}$ is equal to 1, **V** is defined by **ONE** which is a signal that constantly carries the value 1; otherwise, the value of **V** is defined[5] by the value of **ZV**.

All the data-dependence configurations drawn in Fig. 3 are superimposed to build the SFD graph depicted in Fig. 4. From the dependence graph of an SFD graph that merges all the possible dependence graphs, the dependence configurations are induced from two mappings f_N and f_Γ which respectively label its nodes and its vertices. Note that we have introduced a new clock-label, namely $\widehat{\widehat{rst}}$, which denotes the control state: $\widehat{\psi} = 1, \widehat{rst} = 0$. The definition of $\widehat{\widehat{rst}}$ presented in Fig. 4 is built over the negation of $\widehat{rst}$ which is denoted by $\widehat{1} - \widehat{rst}$.

[5] For presentation reasons, we have substituted **ZV + 1** by **ZV**.

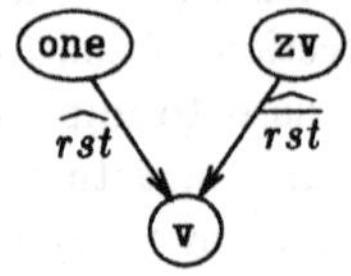

$$f_N(\mathtt{v}) = f_N(\mathtt{zv}) = \widehat{\psi}$$
$$f_N(\mathtt{one}) = \widehat{rst}$$

$$\text{with} \quad \widehat{rst} \equiv [\psi] \text{ and } \widehat{\overline{rst}} \equiv \widehat{\psi} \wedge (\widehat{1} - \widehat{rst}) \equiv \widehat{\psi} - [\psi] \equiv [\neg\psi]$$

Fig. 4. A Synchronous Flows Dependence graph

Formally, a SFD graph is defined by[6]:

$< G, C, \Sigma, f_N, f_\Gamma >$ is a Synchronous Flows Dependence graph (SFD graph) iff:

- *$G =< N, \Gamma, I, O >$ is a dependence graph $< N, \Gamma >$ with communication nodes: the input nodes set I and the output nodes set O are such that $I \subset N, O \subset N$ and $I \cap O = \emptyset$.*
- *$< C, \Sigma >$ is an equational control representation where Σ is a set of constraints over a clock set C;*
- *$f_N : N \longrightarrow C$ is a mapping labeling nodes with clock expressions; it defines their existence condition.*
- *$f_\Gamma : \Gamma \longrightarrow C$ is a mapping labeling edges with clock expressions; it defines their existence condition.*

The SFD graph associated with the **UNFOLD** program is presented in Fig. 5. Square nodes symbolize vertices associated with input and output signals.

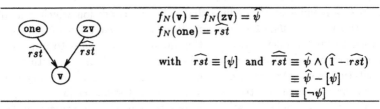

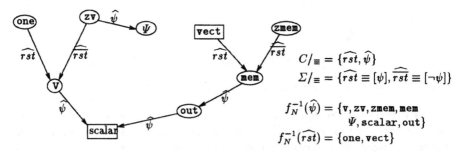

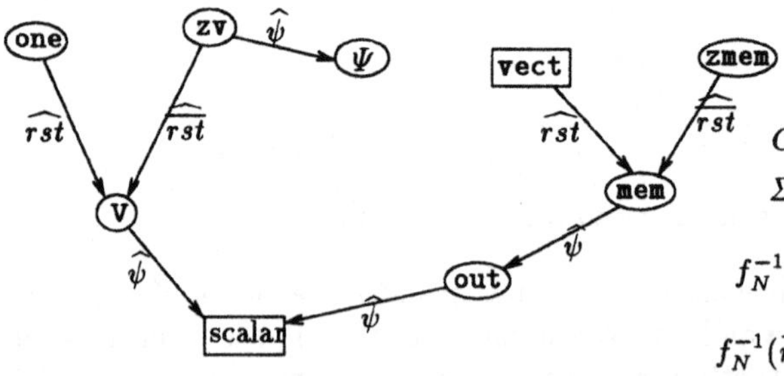

$$C/_{\equiv} = \{\widehat{rst}, \widehat{\psi}\}$$
$$\Sigma/_{\equiv} = \{\widehat{rst} \equiv [\psi], \widehat{\overline{rst}} \equiv [\neg\psi]\}$$

$$f_N^{-1}(\widehat{\psi}) = \{\mathtt{v}, \mathtt{zv}, \mathtt{zmem}, \mathtt{mem}, \Psi, \mathtt{scalar}, \mathtt{out}\}$$
$$f_N^{-1}(\widehat{rst}) = \{\mathtt{one}, \mathtt{vect}\}$$

Fig. 5. The Synchronous Flows Dependence graph of **UNFOLD**

With the two mappings f_N and f_Γ, SFD graphs define a generalization of Directed Acyclic Graphs (DAGs) [1] to represent non purely computational (i.e. monochronous) parts of programs. The dynamic feature of SFD graphs requires

[6] The complete definition of SFD graphs includes another kind of dependencies: the dependencies between instants induced from the shift register operator.

the addition of two constraints which are implicit for DAGs:

1. *an edge cannot exist if one of its extremity node does not exist.*
   This property translated in the clock algebra, the image set of the mappings f_N and f_Γ, is:
$$\forall \mathbf{x}, \mathbf{y} \in N \qquad f_\Gamma(\mathbf{x}, \mathbf{y}) \le f_N(\mathbf{x}) \wedge f_N(\mathbf{y})$$
2. *a cycle of dependencies stands for a deadlock.*
   This property is generalized to SFD graphs by:

   A SFD graph $< G, C, \Sigma, f_N, f_\Gamma >$ *is deadlock free iff, for every cycle* $\mathbf{x1}, \ldots, \mathbf{xn}, \mathbf{x1}$ *in* G,
$$f_\Gamma(\mathbf{x1}, \mathbf{x2}) \wedge f_\Gamma(\mathbf{x2}, \mathbf{x3}) \wedge \ldots \wedge f_\Gamma(\mathbf{xn}, \mathbf{x1}) \equiv \widehat{0}$$

Finally, we have presented: (1) the concept of SFD graphs which, thanks to the equational control modeling, defines an architecture-independent representation and, (2) two validation tools, namely the verification of the control consistency and the deadlock criterion, to achieve an architecture-independent validation of SIGNAL specifications.

4.2 Extension of the SFD graph concept

The SFD graphs presented so far offer a *non redundant abstract representation* of programs. According to the mixed nature of SFD graphs, their structure may evolve into two directions:

- *Enhancement of the control model to enable a finer validation.*
  An extension which has been studied in the framework of the SIGNAL project was to go from an algebra over $\{0, 1\}$ to an algebra over $\{-1, 0, 1\}$ which enables the encoding of the relations among the boolean signals. By this enhancement, the verification of dynamic properties are achieved by means of trajectory studies of the boolean states [10].
- *Transformations of the graph representation to infer implementations.*
  The design of efficient implementations for SIGNAL programs needs to give up with the equational/constraints-oriented representation of control which was one reason of SIGNAL's architecture independence. Considering scalability properties and adequateness to parallel execution schemes, we abandoned the automaton operational representation and we decided upon a data-flow representation of the control. This option may be translated over SFD graphs by adding control nodes and three kinds of dependencies: (a) *activation dependencies* which express the causality relation induced from f_N, (b) *selection dependencies* which make clear the data selections stated by f_Γ and, (c) *clock implementation dependencies* which are induced from an orientation of the equivalences in $\Sigma/_\equiv$.

These two extensions of the SFD graph concept consider two complementary compilation purposes: specification validation and implementation inference. In the next section, we focus on a transverse problem: how introduce modularity in the compilation process ?

5 Abstraction of Synchronous Flows Dependence Graphs

A key concept in software engineering is the concept of abstraction [8] which supplies the sufficient information to compose processes leaving aside any internal feature; it is the key concept for *modularity*. Abstractions often confine process representations to their interface: an abstracted process is usually considered as a black box. In this section, we present the concept of abstraction over SFD graphs which enables to view abstracted processes as "grey boxes".

According to the mixed nature of SFD graphs, abstractions are computed through two mechanisms:

- *A synthesis of the internal dependencies.*
  This synthesis is achieved through the transitive closure of SFD graphs and its projection (sub-graph) upon the input and output nodes. The transitive closure of SFD graphs is simply computed with the two following rules.

$$\text{rule of series} \qquad \mathbf{x} \xrightarrow{\widehat{h}} \mathbf{y} \xrightarrow{\widehat{k}} \mathbf{z} \Rightarrow \mathbf{x} \xrightarrow{\widehat{h} \wedge \widehat{k}} \mathbf{z}$$

$$\text{rule of parallel} \qquad \left.\begin{array}{l} \mathbf{x} \xrightarrow{\widehat{h}} \mathbf{z} \\ \mathbf{x} \xrightarrow{\widehat{k}} \mathbf{z} \end{array}\right\} \Rightarrow \mathbf{x} \xrightarrow{\widehat{h} \vee \widehat{k}} \mathbf{z}$$

- *A projection of the control representation.*
  This control projection synthesizes the relations (equivalence, inclusion) among the clocks labeling the elements of the synthesized graph.

Applied to the SFD graph depicted in Fig. 5, the abstraction in Fig. 6 is induced.

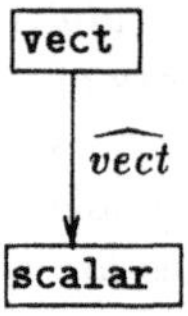

$$C/_{\equiv} = \{\widehat{vect}, \widehat{scalar}\}$$
$$\Sigma/_{\equiv} = \{\widehat{vect} \leq \widehat{scalar}\}$$
$$f_N^{-1}(\widehat{scalar}) = \{\mathbf{scalar}\}$$
$$f_N^{-1}(\widehat{vect}) = \{\mathbf{vect}\}$$

Fig. 6. SFD graph abstraction of **UNFOLD**

As we can notice in Fig. 6, this concept of abstraction provides SFD graphs with a grey box vision since it fully synthesizes the abstract internal behavior which is related to the input and output nodes. By contrast with usual abstract representation, the abstraction of SFD graphs includes an abstraction of the control. For instance, the abstracted control of the **UNFOLD** program which is presented in Fig. 6 expresses that the output **scalar** is more frequent than the input **vect**. Moreover, as abstractions of SFD graphs are SFD graphs, all the tools (validation as well as implementation inference tools) previously defined for SFD graphs are reusable: modularity may be introduced in the whole compilation process.

6 Conclusion

The paper has introduced a new abstract representation called *Synchronous Flows Dependence graph* (SFD graph) and some tools which can be applied to it. SFD graphs constitute a generalization of DAGs: they are made up with a dependence graph connected to an algebraic model of control which makes clear the dynamic evolution of the dependencies according to control states. Three tools are presented in this paper: (a) an algebraic method to verify the control flow consistency, (b) a deadlock detection method which combines graph properties with clock calculus and (c) the notion of abstraction over SFD graphs which provides SFD graphs with grain-size variation capability. The tools (a) and (b) are intended to ensure dependability. The tool (c) may be used to infer parallel implementations onto large-grain architectures by enabling some tuning of the grain of the abstract program representation according to the target architecture.

All these tools have been integrated in a CAD system including a graphic specification interface and a compiler for SIGNAL programs. From this CAD system, the implementation of SIGNAL programs onto distributed architectures is actually available since the SIGNAL compiler is coupled with the SYNDEX system [9]. This coupling is based on a graph representation conceptually very near from SFD graphs; such a graph representation is also going to be shared with LUSTRE [7] and ESTEREL [4].

References

1. A. Aho, R. Sethi and J. Ullman. *Compilers: Principles, Techniques, and Tools.* Addison-Wiley, 1986.
2. G. Berry. Real time programming: special purpose or general purpose languages. In *Information Processing 89*, Elsevier Science Publishers B.V., 1989.
3. L. Besnard. *Compilation de* SIGNAL*: horloges, dépendances, environnement.* PhD thesis, Université de Rennes 1, France, Sept. 1992.
4. F. Boussinot and R. De Simone. The ESTEREL language. *Proceedings of the IEEE*, 79(9):1293–1304, Sept. 1991.
5. R. Cytron, J. Ferrante, B. Rosen, M. Wegman, and F. Zadeck. Efficiently Computing Static Single Assignment Form and the Control Dependence Graph *ACM Trans. on Prog. Language & Systems (TOPLAS)*, 13(4):451–490, Oct. 1991.
6. J. Ferrante, K. Ottenstein and J. Warren. The program dependence graph and its uses in optimization. *ACM TOPLAS*, 9(3):319–349, July 1987.
7. N. Halbwachs, P. Caspi, P. Raymond and D. Pilaud. The synchronous data flow programming language LUSTRE. *Proc. of the IEEE*, 79(9):1305–1321, Sept. 1991.
8. C. W. Krueger. Software reuse. *ACM Comp. Surveys*, 24(2):131–183, June 1992.
9. C. Lavarenne, O. Segrouchni, Y. Sorel and M. Sorine. The SYNDEX software environment for real-time distributed systems design and implementation. In *European Control Conference*, pages 1684–1689, June 1991.
10. M. Le Borgne, A. Benveniste and P. Le Guernic. Dynamical systems over Galois fields and DEDS control problems. In *Proc. of the 30th IEEE conference on Decision and Control*, pages 1505–1510, 1992.
11. P. Le Guernic, T. Gautier, M. Le Borgne and C. Le Maire. Programming real-time applications with SIGNAL. *Proceedings of the IEEE*, 79(9):1321–1336, sept. 1991.
12. K. Pingali, B. Micah, R. Johnson, M. Moudgill and P. Stodghill. Dependence flow graphs: an algebraic approach to program dependencies. In *Proc. of the 18th ACM Symp. on Principles of Programming Languages*, pages 67–78, 1991.

Challenges in developing Useful and Practical Static Analysis for Logic Programs

Peter van Roy

Digital Research Labs
Paris
France

Abstract. What is needed in static analysis for logic programs? In this talk I will give the viewpoint of an implementor who needs information to make things go fast. I'll keep most of the lecture focused on Prolog, with a brief mention of more sophisticated logic languages. I present arguments for three promising approaches. The first point is that for a logic language to go fast, the analysis should in addition to type and mode information also derive information that has no direct logical meaning, but that lives somewhere in the twilight world between logic and assembly code. For example, information about the degree of dereferencing of objects in Prolog. Dereferencing typically takes 10-20The second point is that analysis is only part of the work; it should be done hand in hand with the design of a compiler that can actually use the information. The third point is that the kind of information derived through analysis should be discovered through an iterative process of compiling programs, inspecting and measuring the object code to see where the inefficiencies lie, and improving the analyzer-compiler combination. I will illustrate these three points with examples from Aquarius Prolog and other systems.

Occam's Razor in Metacomputation: the Notion of a Perfect Process Tree

Robert Glück[1] Andrei V. Klimov[2]

Institut für Computersprachen
University of Technology Vienna
A-1040 Vienna, Austria

Keldysh Institute of Applied Mathematics
Russian Academy of Sciences
125047 Moscow, Russia

Abstract. We introduce the notion of a perfect process tree as a model for the full propagation of information in metacomputation. Starting with constant propagation we construct step-by-step the driving mechanism used in supercompilation which ensures the perfect propagation of information. The concept of a simple supercompiler based on perfect driving coupled with a simple folding strategy is explained. As an example we demonstrate that specializing a naive pattern matcher with respect to a fixed pattern obtains the efficiency of a matcher generated by the Knuth, Morris & Pratt algorithm.

1 Introduction

Research in the field of program specialization extends the state-of-the-art in two directions: extending existing methods to new languages and improving the techniques for the specialization of programs. While the first goal can be stated clearly, the second goal is often expressed in rather vague terms such as 'strength' and 'transformation depth'. Often new methods are introduced rather ad hoc and it is hard to see how much has been achieved and what the limitations are.

How should one assess the quality of a program specialization method? Various criteria are conceivable. In this paper we propose the notion of a *perfect process tree*. The goal is to propagate 'enough' information to be able to prune all infeasible program branches at specialization time. Many existing methods, such as partial evaluation, develop imperfect process trees. This should not be taken as a negative statement, but — on the contrary — as a motivation for improving specialization methods further. We present different methods for specializing a simple programming language with tree-structured data, called S-Graph. Starting from constant propagation we develop step-by-step a driving mechanism which ensures the perfect propagation of information along the specialized program branches. The use of perfect driving is shown by introducing a supercompiler with a simple folding strategy. As an example we demonstrate that specializing a naive pattern matcher with respect to a fixed pattern obtains the efficiency of a matcher generated by the Knuth, Morris & Pratt algorithm.

2 Background: Process-Based Transformation

In this section we review Turchin's concept of process-based program transformation. A program $p \in Pgm, p : Data \to Data$, given data $d \in Data$, defines the behavior of a machine: a *computation process*. A computation process is a potentially infinite sequence of states and transitions. A state may contain a program point and a store. Each state and transition in a deterministic computation process is fully defined: $process(p, d) = s_1 \to s_2 \to s_3 \to \ldots$ (This may be defined by some well-understood semantics such as operational or denotational semantics, omit-

---

[1] Supported by the Austrian Science Foundation (FWF) under grant number J0780-PHY.
Current address: DIKU, Dept. of Computer Science, University of Copenhagen, Universitetsparken 1, DK-2100 Copenhagen Ø, Denmark. Email: glueck@diku.dk.

[2] Supported by the Russian Foundation for Fundamental Research under grant number 93-12-628 and in part by the 'Österreichische Forschungsgemeinschaft' under grant number 06/1789.
Email: And.Klimov@refal.msk.su.

ted here). The *set of processes*, $P = \{process(p, d) \mid d \in Data\}$, captures the semantics of a program as a whole. But how can one describe and manipulate the set of processes constructively?

Process Graph. For process-based program transformation one instead uses a *process graph.* A process graph is used to describe and manipulate the set of computation processes. In the following this will be done assuming given a subset of p's initial states (this is the connection to program specialization).

Each node in a process graph represents a *set of states* and is called a *configuration.* Any program graph has a single root node, called *initial configuration*, representing a subset of program p's initial states. A configuration c which branches to two or more configurations in a process graph represents a conditional transition from one set of program states to two or more sets of program states. An edge originating from a branching configuration c is labeled with a test on c. Abstractly this could be thought of as selecting the set of states causing control to follow this edge (a configuration which branches usually corresponds to a test in the program p).

Definition. A process graph g is *correct* for a program p with respect to an initial configuration ci iff
(i) the process graph is *complete*: if program p takes state s into s' in a computation originating from an initial state $si \in ci$, and if s is represented by configuration c, then there is a transition from c to c' in the process graph of p such that c' includes s'.
(ii) the nodes branched to from a branching configuration c are uniquely determined by the tests on c (the configuration c is divided into disjoint sets of states following the corresponding branches).

In general, a program p may have many different correct process graphs. A specific computation process follows a unique *walk* — a sequence of nodes and edges — in the process graph for program p. Because of the two requirements above, any computation process of p corresponds to exactly one walk in a correct process graph for program p (the requirement (i) says there is at least one walk, and (ii) says there is at most one walk). A process graph g for a program p is a *model* of p's computational behavior for a given set of initial states ci. In the following we refer to process graphs when we mean correct process graphs.

Graph Developers. How can one construct a process graph for a program and an initial configuration? Supercompilation [22,24] uses two methods for graph development: *driving* and *folding*.

Driving. This is a general method for constructing a (potentially infinite) *process tree* (a process graph that happens to be a tree) by step-wise exploring all possible computations of a program p starting from an initial configuration ci [20,22,24]. At any point during driving one has a perhaps incomplete process tree and a way to extend the process tree by adding a new node. Driving follows all possible computation processes starting from an initial configuration ci and continues until every leaf of the process tree represents only terminal states. Driving covers the activities of specializing and unfolding in partial evaluation.

Folding. The ultimate goal is to construct a finite process graph for a program p and an initial configuration ci. At any point during driving one may, instead of extending the process graph by driving, try to fold new transitions back into old graph configurations. Folding may include adding a new edge back from a non-terminal configuration N to another configuration M in the process graph, or merging two 'close enough' configurations N and M: given a configuration M with a path to N, one may replace the edges originating from M and create a new edge instead to a generalized configuration M' representing a superset of the states represented by M and N.

Given a finite process graph g that is correct for program p and the set of initial states ci, one may then construct a new program q from g (this is easy to achieve in practice). We will require that g will be correct for q, and q will be functionally equivalent to p with respect to the set of initial states ci. Our aim, of course, is to make q more efficient than the original program p.

3 Perfect Process Graph

How can one assess the 'quality' of a process graph? Clearly, if there is some edge in a process graph which is not used by any computation process, the process graph can't be considered as an 'optimal' model of the program's computational behavior. That is, the process graph contains at least one edge for which no initial state exists to follow it. We say that the more infeasible walks exist in a process tree, the worse is the process graph.

Definition. A walk *w* in a process graph *g* is *feasible* if at least one initial state exists which follows *w*.
Definition. A node *n* in a process graph *g* is *feasible* if it belongs at least to one feasible walk *w* in *g*.
Definition. A process graph is *perfect* if all its walks are feasible.

Infeasible walks not only increases the size of a process graph, but also reduces the efficiency of feasible walks. Consider the last feasible node in an otherwise infeasible walk. Since the node is feasible, at least one feasible walk goes through it. Since the infeasible walk goes through it as well, the node is a branching node: one branch is feasible, another is infeasible. Each branching has several conditions which have to be tested. This is extra work. Thus infeasible branches introduce additional tests and thereby degrade the efficiency of feasible walks. The more interpretive an algorithm is, the less perfect its process graph [23].

Example. Consider the following fragment of a graph (or the program represented by it — we will not distinguish here). The branches `'B` and `'C` are infeasible, and the tests $\texttt{EQA?}_2$ and $\texttt{EQA?}_3$ are redundant. There exists no initial state which follows the branches `'B` and `'C`.

```
(IF (EQA?1 x '5)
    (IF (EQA?2 x '5) 'A 'B)
    (IF (EQA?3 x '5) 'C 'D))
```

Perfect Graph Developers. How can one construct a perfect process graph for a program and a given initial configuration? Unfortunately, no algorithm exists that could transform any program *p* into an equivalent finite, perfect process graph (formally proven in [22]). That is, one can not build a *perfect graph developer*. However, *perfect tree developers* for 'well-formed' languages exist which develop perfect process trees for an arbitrary program *p* and an initial configuration *ci*. This is the case with the programming language presented in this paper. While the problem of perfect graph development cannot be solved in general, perfect tree development may be achieved. This is the main motivation for studying it.

Construction guideline. (1) Start by devising a perfect tree developer; (2) make the corresponding graph developer as 'perfect' as possible, without sacrificing computability and termination. Why do we consider this as essential? Because the first goal may be achieved constructively for 'well-formed' languages, while the second goal can not be achieved in general. Another aspect: one can not expect to make 'clever' folding decisions based on insufficient information obtained by driving. Once a perfect driving mechanism is constructed, it is a solid ground for the further refinement of a graph developer. As a result, the problem of approximation in the development of process graphs is driven into one corner: folding.

4 The Language S-Graph

The choice of the subject language is crucial for writing concise and clear algorithms for program specialization. In order to concentrate on the essence of driving, we limit ourselves to a pure symbol manipulation language, called S-Graph. As the name implies, one can think of S-Graph programs as being textual representations of graphs.

S-Graph is a first-order, functional programming language restricted to tail-recursion. The only data type are well-founded, i.e. non-circular, S-expressions (as known from Lisp). Despite its simplicity the language is complete and universal. The semantics of the language is straightforward. A program is a list of function definitions where each function body is an

```
Prog  ::=  [Def*]
Def   ::=  (DEFINE Fname [Var*] Tree)

Tree  ::=  (LET  Var  Exp  Tree)   |  (CALL Fname [Arg*])
           (IF   Cntr Tree Tree)   |  Exp

Cntr  ::=  (CONS? Arg Var Var)     |  (EQA? Arg Arg)

Exp   ::=  Arg   |   (CONS Exp Exp)
Arg   ::=  Val   |   Var

Val   ::=  (ATOM Atom)
Var   ::=  (VAR  Name)
```

Fig. 1. Syntax of flat S-Graph.

expression built from a few elements: conditionals **IF**, local bindings **LET**, function calls **CALL**, constructors **CONS** and atomic constants (drawn from an infinite set of symbols).

Note the conditional in S-Graph: the test `Cntr` may update the environment. As in supercompilation, we refer to such tests as *contractions* [24]. Two elementary contractions are sufficient for S-expressions:

- `(EQA? x y)` tests the equality of two atoms: `x`'s value and `y`'s value; if the arguments are non-atomic then the test is undefined.
- `(CONS? x h t)` if the value of `x` is a pair `(CONS a b)`, then the test succeeds and the variable `h` is bound to `a` and the variable `t` to `b`; otherwise, the test is false.

The arguments of function calls and contractions are restricted to variables and atomic constants in order to limit the number of places where values may be constructed. Because there are no nested function calls, we call this variant of the language *flat* (i.e. it corresponds to a flow-chart language). This is generalizable to nested function calls at the cost of more complex driving algorithms. In the following we will refer to the flat variant of the language simply as S-Graph.

Example. String pattern matching is a typical problem to which various specialization methods have been applied. The subject program is a naive pattern matcher which checks whether a string `p` (the pattern) occurs within another string `s`. The matcher is fairly simple: it returns `'SUCCESS` if `p` occurs in `s`, `'FAILURE` otherwise. The function `LOOP` compares the pattern with the beginning of the string. If the comparison fails the first element of the string is cut off and the function tries to match the remaining string against the pattern. This strategy is not optimal because the same elements in the string may be tested several times. In case of a mismatch the string is shifted by one and no further information is used for advancing in the string.

Syntactic sugar: we write `'Atom` as shorthand for `(ATOM Atom)`, and lowercase identifiers as shorthand for `(VAR Name)`.

```
(DEFINE MATCH [p s]
  (CALL LOOP [p s p s]))                      ; initialize loop

(DEFINE LOOP [p s pp ss]
  (IF (CONS? p phead ptail)
    (IF (CONS? s shead stail)
      (IF (EQA? phead shead)
        (CALL LOOP [ptail stail pp ss])       ; continue
        (CALL NEXT [pp ss]))                  ; shift string
      'FAILURE)
    'SUCCESS))

(DEFINE NEXT [p s]
  (IF (CONS? s shead stail)
    (CALL LOOP [p stail p stail])             ; restart loop
    'FAILURE))
```

Fig. 2. Naive string matcher in S-Graph.

```
int  :: Tree → Env → Const
cntr :: Cntr → Env → Branch
data Branch  =  TRUE Env | FALSE Env

int (CALL f as) e    =  int t (mkEnv vs as e)
                        where (DEFINE _ vs t) = getDef f

int (LET v x t) e    =  int t (e&[v↦ x/e])

int (IF c t' t") e   =  case cntr c e of
                             TRUE  e' → int t' e'
                             FALSE e" → int t" e"
int x e              =  x/e

cntr (EQA? x y) e    =  case (x/e, y/e) of
                             (ATOM a, ATOM a) → TRUE  e
                             (ATOM _, ATOM _) → FALSE e

cntr (CONS? x h t) e =  case x/e of
                             CONS a b → TRUE (e&[h↦a, t↦b])
                             ATOM _   → FALSE e
```

Fig. 3. Interpretive definition of S-Graph.

Interpretive Definition. The semantics of S-Graph is defined by an interpretive definition (this will be the starting point for defining driving). In order to write the interpreter in a concise way we use some shorthand notations (the syntax is Haskell-like, the semantics is call-by-value):

`[`v_1`↦`c_1`, ... , `v_n`↦`c_n`]` an environment consisting of a list of variables bindings,

`e&[...]` the function `&` updates the environment `e` with the list of variable bindings `[...]`,

`x/e` the function `/` substitutes all variables in the expression `x` by the values given by the bindings in the environment `e`.

The parameter containing the text of the interpreted program is omitted. The function `mkEnv` builds a new environment from a list of variables `vs`, a list of arguments `as` and an environment `e`; the function `getDef` returns the definition of a function given its name. The evaluation of an expression `Exp` does not 'compute' anything, it can only build up a structure. Note that ↦ is a sugared version of a constructor.

State. A computation state in S-Graph is fully defined by the current program point and the current environment. Variables originating from a program are called *program variables* (p-variables) and are bound to constants in the environment. Since we consider only tail-recursive S-Graph programs, states include only one program point `PPoint` (such as `IF`, `CALL`, `LET`).

```
State  ::=  PPoint Env
Env    ::=  [Bind*]

Bind   ::=  Var↦Const
Const  ::=  ATOM Atom  |  CONS Const Const
```

Fig. 4. State in S-Graph.

5 Information Propagation

The main hindrance in removing redundant tests is the lack of sufficient information about unknown values during program specialization. Starting from constant propagation we will develop step-by-step a driving mechanism for S-Graph which ensures the full propagation of information along the specialized program branches. Each step represents a different degree of information propagation.

5.1 Constant Propagation

Constants are the most elementary form of information that can be propagated during program specialization. During specialization we do not deal with precise states, but with configurations representing sets of states. If we do not want to define perfect driving, then we may approximate the sets of states using covering configurations that represent larger sets of states.

Configuration. A simple method for representing sets of states constructively uses *expressions with free variables* [24]. We introduce placeholders, called *configuration variables* (c-variables), which range over arbitrary constants. A p-variable in the environment of a configuration may be bound to a constant or to a c-variable (representing a 'dynamic' values). This is sufficient for constant propagation.

```
Conf    ::=  PPoint Cenv
Cenv    ::=  [Bind*]

Bind    ::=  Var ↦ Cval
Cval    ::=  Const       |  CVAR Name
Const   ::=  ATOM Atom   |  CONS Const Const
```

Fig. 5. Configuration for constant propagation.

Driving. The first version is obtained by extending the S-Graph interpreter (Fig. 3) to propagate constants wherever possible and to produce residual code where the involved constants are 'dynamic' (Fig. 7).

- If the result of evaluating an expression in a **LET** is not a constant then the p-variable is bound to a fresh c-variable (generated by the function **newcvar**).
- If a contraction (**EQA?**, **CONS?**) can not be decided then both branches have to be driven (function **cntr** returns **BOTH** and an environment for each branch).

This implements what is known as *constant propagation*, and corresponds to first-order partial evaluators based on constant propagation (e.g. [12]).

Remark. It was noticed [12] that the test **const?** does not require the values proper and may be approximated in a separate pre-processing phase, called *binding-time analysis*. This granted the first self-application of a partial evaluator.

5.2 Partially Static Structure

A simple extension is the propagation of partially static structures in driving. This corresponds to first-order partial evaluators using partially static structures (e.g. [16,10,2,4]). This extension completes the construction of the function **dev** (in the following we will refine the handling of contractions during driving).

Configuration. The description of a configuration is refined by replacing the definition of **Cval**.

```
Conf    ::=  PPoint Cenv
Cenv    ::=  [Bind*]

Bind    ::=  Var ↦ Cval
Cval    ::=  ATOM Atom   |  CVAR Name   |  CONS Cval Cval
```

Fig. 6. Configuration for partially static structures.

Driving. The propagation of partially static structures is obtained by replacing the **LET** clause in function **dev** (Fig. 7) by

```
dev (LET v x t) e   =   dev t (e&[v ↦ x/e])
```

```
dev    :: Tree → Cenv → Tree
cntr   :: Cntr → Cenv → Branch
const :: Cval → Bool
data Branch  =  TRUE Cenv | FALSE Cenv | BOTH Cntr Cenv Cenv

dev (CALL f as) e  =  dev t (mkEnv vs as e)
                      where (DEFINE _ vs t) = getDef f

dev (LET v x t) e  =  let x' = x/e in
                      if const? x'
                         then dev t (e&[v↦x'])
                         else LET v' x' (dev t (e&[v↦v']))
                              where v' = newcvar

dev (IF c t' t") e =  case cntr c e of
                         TRUE  e'         → dev t' e'
                         FALSE e"         → dev t" e"
                         BOTH  c' e' e"   → IF  c'  (dev t' e')
                                                    (dev t" e")
dev x e            =  x/e

cntr (EQA? x y) e  =
     let x' = x/e; y' = y/e in
     case (x', y') of
          (ATOM a, ATOM a) → TRUE  e
          (ATOM _, ATOM _) → FALSE e
          (CVAR _, CVAR _) → BOTH (EQA? x' y') e e
          (CVAR _, ATOM _) → BOTH (EQA? x' y') e e
          (ATOM _, CVAR _) → BOTH (EQA? x' y') e e

cntr (CONS? x h t) e =
     let x' = x/e in
     case x' of
          CONS a b → TRUE (e&[h↦a, t↦b])
          ATOM _   → FALSE e
          CVAR _   → BOTH (CONS? x' h' t') e' e
                     where h' = newcvar; t' = newcvar
                           e' = e&[h↦h', t↦t']
const? (ATOM _)     =  True
const? (CVAR _)     =  False
const? (CONS a b)   =  and (const? a) (const? b)
```

Fig. 7. Constant propagation in S-Graph.

5.3 Propagation of Contraction Information

Using constant propagation and partially static structures we are able to prune many infeasible branches, but not all (see example in Sect. 3).

Configuration. In addition to the propagation of information by substitution (which we refer to as *positive* information, or *assertions*), we need to propagate the negation of this information (*restrictions*). We refine configurations by adding a list of restrictions on c-variables. A restriction of the form `Rval # Rval` states which values must not be equal. The restriction list may contain zero, one or more restrictions for each c-variable. Otherwise the configuration remains unchanged (Fig. 8). The ↦ and # are sugared versions of constructors.

Assertions. Propagating assertions requires a updating the bindings of p-variables (corresponding to the well-known concept of unification). To capture the information that two unknown values are equal, we exploit the *equality of c-variables*. This is done by adding an extra case for equal c-variables to the `EQA?` clause. This goes beyond constant propagation. For example, the assertion `x='5` is passed into the then-branch simply by replacing the c-variable `cx` by `'5`:

`([x↦cx],[])  (EQA? x '5)` ⇒ *then-branch:* `([x↦'5],[])`

```
Conf   ::=  PPoint Cenv
Cenv   ::=  [Bind*] [Restr*]

Bind   ::=  Var ↦ Cval
Cval   ::=  ATOM Atom   |   CVAR Name   |   CONS Cval Cval

Restr  ::=  Rval # Rval
Rval   ::=  ATOM Atom   |   CVAR Name   |   CONS
```

Fig. 8. Configuration for perfect driving.

Restrictions. Propagating restrictions requires updating a list of restrictions on c-variables. For example, the restriction **x≠'5** is passed into the else-branch by adding a restriction on the c-variable **cx**:

`([x↦cx],[])  (EQA? x '5)` ⇒ *else-branch:* `([x↦cx],[cx # '5])`

The mechanism for checking restrictions is separated into the function **both** which is common for both contractions. If a contraction can not be decided using the list of p-variable bindings, then the list of restrictions is checked whether, possibly, a restriction exists which can be used to decide the contraction. In case such a restriction is found one can cut off the infeasible then-branch. This is done in function **both** by checking whether a substitution in the list of restrictions leads to a contradiction.

Auxiliary functions. To simplify the definition we provide the following three functions for manipulating a configuration environment **e**: the function **&** adds new bindings to **e**, the function **** adds new restrictions to **e**, and the substitution **/** is extended to substitute variables in the configuration environment. In our case these functions may be defined as follows (the function **++** is list append, the function **b2r** converts a **Bind** into a **Restr**):

```
(b,r) & bs   =   ((b++bs), r)
(b,r) / bs   =   ((b/bs),  (r/(b2r bs)))
(b,r) \ bs   =   ( b,      (r++(b2r bs)))
```

During driving, c-variables are generated and may disappear as result of a substitution, leaving 'dangling' restrictions or tautologies, such as **'A # 'B**. They may be cleared out (e.g. after **/**), though this does not interfere with driving.

Correctness and Perfectness. In order to verify S-Graph driving we have to prove that the mechanism is correct and perfect. The correctness of driving with respect to the interpretive definition of S-Graph ensures that the process tree contain at least all necessary (and maybe some infeasible) branches. The perfectness of driving guarantees that the process tree contains no infeasible branches. The existence of a perfectness theorem guarantees that driving propagates all information sufficient for pruning the process tree to its minimal size (omitted due to lack of space). This completes the task of defining perfect driving for S-Graph (Fig. 9).

Remark. In order to keep the presented perfect tree developer as simple as possible and at the same time to preserve the termination properties of the subject programs in the residual programs, we require that subject programs do not go 'wrong', i.e. atomic equality **EQA?** is not applied to non-atomic arguments. This may be guaranteed by adding a **CONS?** test for each non-atomic argument of **EQA?** in the subject programs.

6 Perfect Driving of a Naive Pattern Matcher

By specializing the naive pattern matcher (Fig. 2) with respect to a fixed pattern we show that perfect driving coupled with a simple folding strategy obtains the efficiency of a matcher generated by the Knuth, Morris & Pratt (KMP) algorithm [15]. This effect is achieved without the need for an 'insightful reprogramming' of the naive matcher as necessary for partial evaluation [5,11]. The complexity of the specialized algorithm is $O(n)$, where n is the length of the string. The naive algorithm has complexity $O(m \cdot n)$, where m is the length of the pattern.

```
dev   :: Tree → Cenv → Tree
cntr  :: Cntr → Cenv → Branch
both  :: Cntr → Cenv → Cenv → Bind → Branch
contradict :: Cenv → Bool
data Branch  =  TRUE Cenv | FALSE Cenv | BOTH Cntr Cenv Cenv

dev (CALL f as) e  =  dev t (mkEnv vs as e)
                      where (DEFINE _ vs t) = getDef f

dev (LET v x t) e  =  dev t (e&[v ↦ x/e])

dev (IF c t' t") e =  case cntr c e of
                          TRUE  e'        → dev t' e'
                          FALSE e"        → dev t" e"
                          BOTH  c' e' e"  → IF  c'  (dev t' e')
                                                    (dev t" e")
dev x e            =  x/e

cntr (EQA? x y) e  =
     let x' = x/e; y' = y/e in
     case (x', y') of
          (ATOM a, ATOM a) → TRUE  e
          (ATOM _, ATOM _) → FALSE e
          (CVAR a, CVAR a) → TRUE  e
          (CVAR _, CVAR _) → both (EQA? x' y') e e [x' ↦ y']
          (CVAR _, ATOM _) → both (EQA? x' y') e e [x' ↦ y']
          (ATOM _, CVAR _) → both (EQA? x' y') e e [y' ↦ x']
cntr (CONS? x h t) e  =
     let x' = x/e in
     case x' of
          CONS a b → TRUE (e&[h↦a, t↦b])
          ATOM _   → FALSE e
          CVAR _   → both (CONS? x' h' t') e' e [x' ↦CONS h' t']
                     where h' = newcvar; t' = newcvar
                           e' = e&[h↦h', t↦t']
both c' te fe b  =
     let e' = te/b; e" = fe\b in
     if  contradict e' then FALSE e
                       else BOTH  c' e' e"
contradict (b,r) =
     or (map contradict' r)
     where contradict' (x # x)   =  True
           contradict' (_ # _)   =  False
```

Fig. 9. Perfect driving in S-Graph.

Folding. At any point during driving one has a way to examine a non-terminal configuration and to decide to do one of: (i) fold the current configuration into an existing configuration; (ii) drive the configuration further. Two questions are relevant for folding:

1) Which *program points* do we consider for folding?
2) What is the *criterion* for folding?

It is sufficient to couple perfect driving with *folding of identical configurations* for obtaining efficient matchers from a naive pattern matcher and a given pattern. Driving can be coupled with more sophisticated folding strategies, but this is beyond the scope of this paper (and not needed for the example). Folding of identical configurations answers the questions as follows:

1) Dynamic conditionals are considered for folding.
2) Two configurations represent the same set of states.

The method of dynamic conditionals is a well-known technique in program specialization [22,3]: only those program points are considered for folding which introduce a branching (the conditional can not be decided, it is 'dynamic').

When the descriptions of two configurations are identical (i.e. contain the same bindings and restrictions, modulo variable renaming) they represent the same set of states and one may, instead of continuing driving, add a new transition back from the current configuration into the old configuration.

```
(DEFINE F1 [s]
  (IF (CONS? s shead-1 stail-2)
    (IF (EQA? shead-1 'A)
      (IF (CONS? stail-2 shead-3 stail-4)
        (IF (EQA? shead-3 'A)
          (CALL F5 [stail-4])
          (CALL F1 [stail-4]))
        'FAILURE)
      (CALL F1 [stail-2]))
    'FAILURE))

(DEFINE F5 [stail-4]
  (IF (CONS? stail-4 shead-5 stail-6)
    (IF (EQA? shead-5 'B)
      'SUCCESS
      (IF (EQA? shead-5 'A)
        (CALL F5 [stail-6])
        (CALL F1 [stail-6])))
    'FAILURE))
```

Fig. 10. KMP-like residual program for the pattern **AAB**.

7 Related Work

The principles of driving were first formulated in the early seventies by Turchin [20,21] and further developed in the eighties [22,24]. From its very inception, supercompilation has been tied to a specific programming language, called Refal [24]. Applications of supercompilation include, among others, program specialization, program inversion and theorem proving. Other related aspects have been investigated in [1,7,8,13,14,17,18,26]. The notion of perfect process graphs and perfect driving were introduced in [22,23].

The language S-Graph is closely related to Turchin's Refal graphs [25]. But due to S-Graph's simpler data structure, untyped variables and only two elementary contractions, one may build rather clear and concise driving algorithms. In particular, there is only one way to compose and decompose S-expressions (as opposed to Refal data structures). There is a close relation between driving and the neighborhood analysis for S-Graph [1]. Another 'graph-like' language representing decision trees, was used by Bondorf for the implementation of a self-applicable partial evaluator Treemix [2].

Specializing a naive string matcher is a typical problem to which various methods of program manipulation have been applied. A partial evaluator can achieve the same non-trivial result after identifying static components in the naive matcher and reprogramming the subject program [5,11]. Clearly, doing this by using an "automatic insight" frees the user from performing such subtle tasks. Generalized Partial Computation (GPC), another principle for program specialization based on partial evaluation and theorem proving, achieves the same optimal version [6]. In its essence GPC is related to driving, but differs in the propagation of arbitrary predicates, assuming the use of a theorem prover. Disunification in GPC was considered in [19]. It is not surprising, that the same optimal pattern matcher can be achieved by a Refal supercompiler [9]. Note that we used only a small part of the supercompilation methodology: perfect driving for a language with tree-structured data coupled with a simple folding strategy.

8 Conclusion

We introduced a simple model for assessing the 'quality' of program specialization: the closer a process tree is to a perfect one, the better the method. This enables us to rate various specialization techniques. Although specialization methods vary from language to language, they all have the same goal in common: propagating as much information as possible in order to increase the efficiency of the resulting programs.

We showed that a mechanism for perfect driving can be constructed for a simple language, called S-Graph. On the one hand the propagation of additional information requires extra work during specialization, but on the other hand less time is spent for developing infeasible branches. Most important, the efficiency of the resulting programs may be improved considerably. In particular, perfect driving coupled with a simple folding strategy obtains the efficiency of a matcher generated by the Knuth, Morris & Pratt algorithm without 'insightful reprogrammig' of the naive matcher. This reveals that the power of Turchin's supercompilation method is independent of the language used to express it (i.e. Refal) and that the principles may be applied to other languages. Partial evaluation and supercompilation do not contradict each other and the question of integrating them is on the agenda. How far these principles can be taken, how they can be applied to more realistic languages and what their limitations are will be a task for future research.

Acknowledgments. This work could not have been carried out without the pioneering work of Valentin Turchin and we are very grateful for many stimulating discussions. It is a great pleasure to thank Neil Jones for thorough comments and for clarifying an earlier version of this paper. We greatly appreciate fruitful discussions with the members of the Refal group in Moscow and the TOPPS group at DIKU. Many thanks are due to Sergei Abramov, Anders Bondorf, Ruten Gurin, Jesper Jørgensen, Victor Kistlerov, Arkady Klimov, Alexander Romanenko, Sergei Romanenko and David Sands. Special thanks to Thomas Eisenzopf for implementing the graph developers.

References

1. Abramov S. M., Metacomputation and program testing. In: *1st International Workshop on Automated and Algorithmic Debugging.* (Linköping, Sweden). 121-135, Linköping University 1993.
2. Bondorf A., A self-applicable partial evaluator for term rewriting systems. In: Díaz J., Orejas F. (ed.), *TAPSOFT '89.* (Barcelona, Spain). Lecture Notes in Computer Science, Vol. 352, 81-95, Springer-Verlag 1989.
3. Bondorf A., Danvy O., Automatic autoprojection of recursive equations with global variables and abstract data types. In: *Science of Computer Programming*, 16(2): 151-195, 1991.
4. Consel C., Binding time analysis for higher order untyped functional languages. In: *Proceedings of the 1990 ACM Conference on Lisp and Functional Programming.* (Nice, France). 264-272, ACM Press 1990.
5. Consel C., Danvy O., Partial evaluation of pattern matching in strings. In: *Information Processing Letters*, 30(2): 79-86, 1989.
6. Futamura Y., Nogi K., Takano A., Essence of generalized partial computation. In: *Theoretical Computer Science*, 90(1): 61-79, 1991.
7. Glück R., Towards multiple self-application. In: *Proceedings of the Symposium on Partial Evaluation and Semantics-Based Program Manipulation.* (New Haven, Connecticut). 309-320, ACM Press 1991.
8. Glück R., Projections for knowledge based systems. In: Trappl R. (ed.), *Cybernetics and Systems Research '92.* Vol. 1, 535-542, World Scientific: Singapore 1992.
9. Glück R., Turchin V. F., Application of metasystem transition to function inversion and transformation. In: *Proceedings of the ISSAC '90.* (Tokyo, Japan). 286-287, ACM Press 1990.

10. Jones N. D., Automatic program specialization: a re-examination from basic principles. In: Bjørner D., Ershov A. P., Jones N. D. (ed.), *Partial Evaluation and Mixed Computation.* (Gammel Avernæs, Denmark). 225-282, North-Holland 1988.
11. Jones N. D., Gomard C. K., Sestoft P., *Partial Evaluation and Automatic Program Generation.* Prentice Hall International Series in Computer Science. Prentice Hall: New York, London, Toronto 1993.
12. Jones N. D., Sestoft P., Søndergaard H., Mix: a self-applicable partial evaluator for experiments in compiler generation. In: *Lisp and Symbolic Computation,* 2(1): 9-50, 1989.
13. Klimov And. V., Dynamic specialization in extended functional language with monotone objects. In: *Proceedings of the Symposium on Partial Evaluation and Semantics-Based Program Manipulation.* (Yale University, Connecticut). 199-210, ACM Press 1991.
14. Klimov And. V., Romanenko S. A., A metaevaluator for the language Refal. Basic concepts and examples. Keldysh Institute of Applied Mathematics, Academy of Sciences of the USSR, Moscow. Preprint No. 71, 1987 (in Russian).
15. Knuth D. E., Morris J. H., Pratt V. R., Fast pattern matching in strings. In: *SIAM Journal of Computation,* 6(2): 323-350, 1977.
16. Mogensen T. Æ., Partially static structures in a self-applicable partial evaluator. In: Bjørner D., Ershov A. P., Jones N. D. (ed.), *Partial Evaluation and Mixed Computation.* (Gammel Avernæs, Denmark). 325-347, North-Holland 1988.
17. Romanenko A. Yu., Inversion and metacomputation. In: *Proceedings of the Symposium on Partial Evaluation and Semantics-Based Program Manipulation.* (Yale University, Connecticut). 12-22, ACM Press 1991.
18. Romanenko S. A., Driving for Refal-4 programs. Keldysh Institute of Applied Mathematics, Academy of Sciences of the USSR, Moscow. Preprint No. 211, 1987 (in Russian).
19. Takano A., Generalized partial computation using disunification to solve constraints. In: Rusinowitch M., Rémy J. L. (ed.), *Conditional Term Rewriting Systems. Proceedings.* (Pont-à-Mousson, France). Lecture Notes in Computer Science, Vol. 626, 424-428, Springer-Verlag 1993.
20. Turchin V. F., Equivalent transformations of recursive functions defined in Refal. In: *Teoria Jazykov i Metody Programmirovanija (Proceedings of the Symposium on the Theory of Languages and Programming Methods).* (Kiev-Alushta, USSR). 31-42, 1972 (in Russian).
21. Turchin V. F., Equivalent transformations of Refal programs. In: *Avtomatizirovannaja Sistema upravlenija stroitel'stvom. Trudy CNIPIASS,* 6: 36-68, 1974 (in Russian).
22. Turchin V. F., The language Refal, the theory of compilation and metasystem analysis. Courant Institute of Mathematical Sciences, New York University. Courant Computer Science Report No. 20, 1980.
23. Turchin V. F., Semantic definitions in Refal and automatic production of compilers. In: Jones N. D. (ed.), *Semantics-Directed Compiler Generation.* (Aarhus, Denmark). Lecture Notes in Computer Science, Vol. 94, 441-474, Springer-Verlag 1980.
24. Turchin V. F., The concept of a supercompiler. In: *ACM TOPLAS,* 8(3): 292-325, 1986.
25. Turchin V. F., The algorithm of generalization in the supercompiler. In: Bjørner D., Ershov A. P., Jones N. D. (ed.), *Partial Evaluation and Mixed Computation.* (Gl. Avernæs, Denmark). 341-353, 1988.
26. Turchin V. F., Program transformation with metasystem transitions. In: *Journal of Functional Programming,* 1993 (to appear).

Tupling Functions with Multiple Recursion Parameters

Wei-Ngan CHIN and Siau-Cheng KHOO
Dept of Information Systems & Computer Science
National University of Singapore
(Preliminary Report)

Abstract

Tupling is a transformation tactic to obtain new functions, without redundant calls and/or multiple traversals of common inputs. It achieves this feat by allowing a set (tuple) of function calls to be computed recursively from its previous set. In [Chi93c], a safe (terminating) unfold/fold transformation algorithm was proposed for a class of functions which has a single recursion parameter per function.

In this paper, we propose two new classes of functions with multiple recursion parameters that could also be safely tupled. The first class of functions has a set of *tightly-synchronised* recursion parameters. This class of functions could be used to eliminate multiple traversals due to a common variable being shared by its multiple recursion arguments. The second class of functions has *loosely-synchronised* recursion parameters. The loose-synchronisation property is specified indirectly by the ability to convert (in an effective way) the multiple recursion parameters into a single recursion parameter.

These two new classes of functions help to widen the applicability of the tupling tactic. In particular, they allow us to combine both the tupling and fusion tactics together to achieve new optimisations which were not possible from either tactic individually.

1 Introduction

In [Chi93c], we proposed a safe automated tupling method to help transform functions with redundant calls and/or multiple traversals to equivalent functions without them. A classic application of this transformation is the fibonacci function (shown below) with a time-complexity of $O((1+\frac{\sqrt{5}}{2})^n)$ where n is the initial argument value.

```
dec fib: int → int;
---fib(0)        ⇐ 1;
```

```
---fib(1)        ⇐ 1;
---fib(n+2)      ⇐ fib(n+1)+fib(n);
```

The above program is given in the **Hope** language where the **dec** statement is for declaring the types of functions; and equations of the form, ---LHS ⇐ RHS, for defining functions. To remove the redundant *fib* calls, we need to define a new tuple function, shown below.

```
dec fib_tup: int → (int,int);
---fib_tup(n)    ⇐ (fib(n+1),fib(n));
```

Unfold/fold transformation can then be applied to the above function to obtain a linear recursive function with a time-complexity of $O(n)$. Together with a fold to use *fib_tup* in *fib*, we have eliminated the earlier redundant calls by forcing re-use, instead of re-computation, of the function calls stored in the tuple, as shown below.

```
---fib(0)        ⇐ 1;
---fib(1)        ⇐ 1;
---fib(n+2)      ⇐ (u,v) WHERE (u,v) = fib_tup(n);
---fib_tup(0)    ⇐ (1,1) ;
---fib_tup(n+1)  ⇐ (u+v,u) WHERE (u,v)=fib_tup(n);
```

The most difficult step of this transformation is to find the eureka tuple(s) that would allow each set of function calls to be computed from its previous set down the recursion. In the case of the *fib* function, the appropriate eureka tuple was *(fib(n+1),fib(n))*.

In [Chi93c], we formulated a tupling transformation algorithm which is able to find such eureka tuples automatically. Presently, we have identified a class of functions for which the tupling transformation is terminating and is always able to find the eureka tuples in finite time. This class of functions has only one recursion parameter per function. A recursion parameter of a function is a parameter which is *strictly increasing* or *strictly decreasing* down the recursion. An example of this is the above *fib* function where the sole parameter is a recursion parameter.

However, there are also other functions which have more than one recursion parameters per function. A simple example is the function *zip* below which has two recursion parameters.

```
data list(A) = nil ++ cons(A,list(A)) ;
dec zip: (list(A),list(B)) → list(A,B);
---zip(cons(x,xs),cons(y,ys)) ⇐ cons((x,y),zip(xs,ys));
---zip(xs,ys)                 ⇐ nil;
```

Such a function may appear as an auxiliary call to another function where redundant calls are possible. Alternatively, it may also be used in a situation where the presence of a common variable among its different recursion parameters allows the input to be traversed more than once. An example of such multiple traversals is highlighted by the next function.

```
dec dupl: list(A) → list(A,A);
---dupl(xs)                   ⇐ zip(xs,xs)
```

We call this form of multiple traversals, *intra-call multiple traversals*, because the traversals are performed by the same call *zip(xs,xs)*. This form of *intra-call traversals* could be eliminated by the tupling transformation but the eureka tuples used need only consist of a single function call each.

Another (better known) form of multiple traversals, called *inter-call (multiple) traversals*, involves traversing the same input from different function calls. A classic example of this is illustrated by the function av below where duplicate traversals of the input list, *xs*, could be eliminated by tupling up the two recursive calls, *(sum(xs),length(xs))*, together.

```
dec av, length, sum: list(int) → int;
---av(xs)               ⇐ sum(xs)/length(xs);
---length(nil)          ⇐ 0;
---length(cons(x,xs))   ⇐ 1+length(xs);
---sum(nil)             ⇐ 0;
---sum(cons(x,xs))      ⇐ x+sum(xs);
```

This paper proposes two new classes of functions with multiple recursion parameters that could be safely tupled to eliminate multiple traversals and/or redundant calls. Initially, we review the safe tupling tactic together with the original class of functions, called the **T0** class, (with single recursion parameter) that is guaranteed to have eureka tuples (Section 2). Next, we formulate an extended class of functions, called the **T1** class, where the multiple recursion parameters are *tightly-synchronised* (Section 3). This class of functions can help eliminate intra-call multiple traversals. The third class of functions requires only *loose-synchronisation* of the multiple recursion parameters for successful tupling (Section 4). This class covers more functions than the **T1** class but may not be used to eliminate intra-call multiple traversals. The loose-synchronisation property is specified indirectly through the ability to combine the multiple recursion parameters into a single recursion parameter. The two new classes of functions allow more optimisation to be performed, especially in conjunction with the fusion tactic (Section 5). Nevertheless, some limitations exist for the present proposal. These limitations are outlined together with suggestions for further improvements (Section 6) before we conclude the paper (Section 7).

2 Tupling Tactic and the T0 Class

To find eureka tuples automatically, we have formulated a tupling transformation which searches through a *tree-of-cuts* for matching tuples. (The term *cut* was introduced by Pettorossi in [Pet84] and is treated synonymously to *tuples* in this paper. The original definition of *cut* is used to denote a set of calls in the call dependency graph of a function which when removed will divide the dependency graph into two disjoint halves. Our tupling tactic is structured to obtain such cuts as tuples during transformation.) Presently, this transformation is applicable to mutually recursive functions with a single recursion parameter per function. It repeats the transformation process of *instantiating*, *unfolding* and *splitting* to each cut until it obtains a tree-of-cuts for which each branch is found to match with an earlier cut up the tree. The tupling transformation algorithm is given below as

Algorithm 1. The search (of the transformation) branches out whenever there are (i) different (recursive) instantiations or (ii) distinct recursion arguments among the calls in the cut.

Algorithm 1: Tupling Algorithm

1. Start with an initial function call.
2. From the current tuple, get the next tuple(s) by different minimal *instantiations* (which permit one or more unfolds) to the recursion parameter.
3. Perform *unfolding* (without instantiations) and eliminate duplicate calls.
4. *Split* the function calls into separate tuples according to the different recursion variables. For each tuple, perform:
   (a) Attempt a fold match with the previously constructed tuples up the tree.
   (b) IF successful, we have found an eureka tuple and could terminate for this branch;
   OTHERWISE repeat from (2) with this tuple as the current tuple.

To illustrate this tupling transformation, consider the following set of mutually recursive functions which each has a single recursion parameter (of possibly different types) per function.

```
data weird(A) = empty(A) | pair(list(weird(A)),tree(weird(A)));
data tree(A) = leaf(A) | node(tree(A),tree(A))
--- f(empty(a))        ⇐ ....;
--- f(pair(ws,n))      ⇐ ...[g(ws),h(ws),t(n),s(n)]...;
--- g(nil)             ⇐ ....;
--- g(cons(w,ws))      ⇐ ...[f(w),g(ws)]...;
--- h(nil)             ⇐ ....;
--- h(cons(w,ws))      ⇐ ...[f(w),h(ws)]...;
--- t(leaf(w))         ⇐ ...[f(w)]...;
--- t(node(l,r))       ⇐ ...[t(l),s(r)]...;
--- s(leaf(w))         ⇐ ...[f(w)]..;
--- s(node(l,r))       ⇐ ...[t(l),t(r)]...;
```

When the tupling transformation algorithm is applied to the function call *f(w)*, it results in a tree-of-cuts shown in Figure 1.

Starting with *f(a)* as cut_1, we unfold that call to obtain its subsidiary calls *(g(s),h(s),t(n),s(n))* as cut_2. There are two different recursion arguments in cut_2 which would have to be splitted up into two sub-cuts, cut_{2a} *(g(s),h(s))* and cut_{2b} *(t(n),s(n))*. In the case of cut_{2b}, two different recursive instantiations (followed by unfolding) are possible which result in cut_5 and cut_6. We terminate the branch at cut_5 because it matches with cut_1, and repeat the safe transformation process of *instantiating, unfolding and splitting* for the other branches until they match with some cuts higher up in the tree. Eureka tuples found are *(g(s),h(s))* and *(t(n),s(n))*, while *f(w)* and *t(l)* represent cuts of a single call each (which are allowed to match with

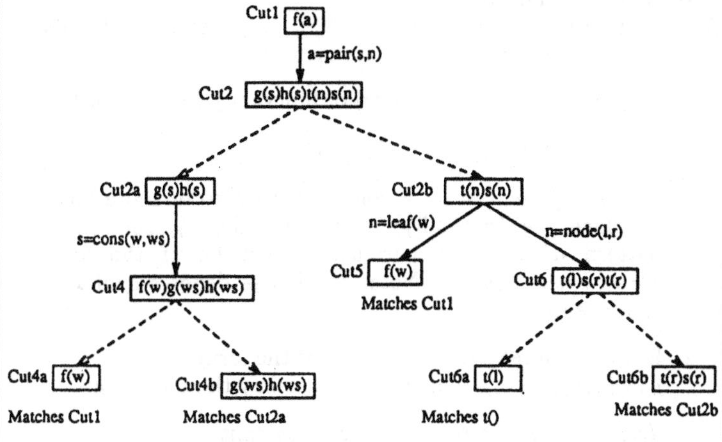

Figure 1: A Tree-of-Cuts for *f(a)*

the original functions rather than be subjected to function re-definitions through further transformations).

These matching tuples enable the tupling transformation to obtain the following transformed program without redundant calls.

```
--- f(empty(a))          ⇐ ....;
--- f(pair(ws,n))        ⇐ ...[G,H,T,S]... WHERE (G,H)=gh_tup(ws), (T,S)=ts_tup(n);
--- gh_tup(nil)          ⇐ (.... , ....);
--- gh_tup(cons(w,ws))   ⇐ (...[F,G]... , ...[F,H]...) WHERE (G,H)=gh_tup(ws), F=f(w);
--- ts_tup(leaf(w))      ⇐ (...[F]... , ...[F]...) WHERE F=f(w);
--- ts_tup(node(l,r))    ⇐ (...[Tl,Sr]... ,...[Tl,Tr]...) WHERE Tl=t(l), (Tr,Sr)=ts_tup(r);
--- t(leaf(w))           ⇐ ...[f(w)]...;
--- t(node(l,r))         ⇐ ...[t(l),s(r)]...;
--- s(leaf(w))           ⇐ ...[f(w)]..;
--- s(node(l,r))         ⇐ ...[t(l),t(r)]...;
```

In general, the above tupling transformation may fail to terminate for some programs. However, we have managed to identify a class of (mutually) recursive functions, called the **T0** class for which it is guaranteed to terminate. This class of functions has a single (strictly decreasing) recursion parameter per function with the other parameters having the non-accumulating property (do not syntactically increase down the recursion). It can be formally defined, as follows:

Definition 2: T0 Class
A set of mutually recursive functions, $f_1, \ldots, f_h$, satisfies the **T0** class if the following conditions are present.

1. Each equation (the s-th one) of function f_i has the form:

   $$--- f_i(p, v_1, \ldots, v_n) \Leftarrow \ldots[C_1, .., C_k]\ldots$$

   where ...[ ]... represents a context with zero or more holes to place the (mutually) recursive calls, $C_1, .., C_k$. The pattern of the first parameter must be of the form $p \equiv v' \mid c_s(v'_1, \ldots, v'_m)$. (Note: symbol $\equiv$ denotes syntactic equivalence.)

2. Each of the recursive call, C_j, is of the form: $f_{i_j}(S_1^j[p], w_1, \ldots, w_a)$. This call must satisfy the following:

   (a) $\forall x \in 1..a.\ w_x \in \{v_1, \ldots, v_n\}$ or a constant.

   (b) $p \equiv c_s(v'_1, \ldots, v'_m) \rightarrow (S_1^j[p] \equiv v'_{j_1}) \wedge (j_1 \in \{1..m\})$.

   (c) $p \equiv v' \rightarrow (S_1^j[p] \equiv v') \wedge (f_i >_{fn} f_{i_j})$

3. The function name ordering ($>_{fn}$) introduced in 2(c) must not be cyclic.

Condition (1) states that each **T0** function has only a single (descending) recursion parameter whose pattern is a simple one (c.f. simple pattern of [Aug85]) with at most a single constructor. Condition (2a) states that the other parameters of the function are non-accumulating (either variables or constants) with no new variables introduced. Condition (2b) ensures that the corresponding recursion argument of each recursive calls ($C_1, .., C_k$) is taken from a variable of the recursion pattern. Conditions (2c) & (3) ensures that each recursion argument will always decrease by at least one constructor when it cycles back to the same function.

All mutually recursive functions (and their auxiliary functions) which satisfy the **T0** form are guaranteed to have eureka tuple(s). As a result, the tupling algorithm is bound to terminate when applied to this class of functions. The proof for this is pretty simple, as outlined below.

<u>Termination Proof</u>
Given a set of **T0** functions, the tupling transformation will only have to deal with finitely many different tuples. Firstly, there is a finite number of function names. Secondly, each cut has only one recursion variable. Also, the number of different variables for the other parameters is finite, as no new variables have been introduced by unfolding. Thus, if there are n different functions and the largest number of parameters for the functions is m and the number of different variables and constants used is s, then the maximum number of distinct function calls which could be obtained is $n \times s^m$. As the number of distinct calls is bounded, the number of different tuples (modulo renaming) encountered will also be bounded (at most $2^{n \times s^m}$). Hence, a re-occurring (matching) tuple is bound to happen after a finite number of steps by the tupling algorithm.

3 Tightly-Synchronised Recursion Parameters

For functions that have multiple recursion parameters, there are two possible types of tupling optimisations based on whether there are identical recursion arguments (e.g. *zip(xs,xs)*) or if there are possibly distinct recursion arguments (e.g. *zip(xs,ys)*) for their calls.

We can perform a better optimisation for function calls with identical arguments, but this class of applicable functions is more restrictive than those where the recursion arguments are not assumed to be identical. Specifically, the class of functions which could be successfully tupled up with identical recursion arguments must have recursion parameters which are tightly-synchronised (in lock-step consumption of their input). For example, the two parameters of *zip* are tightly-synchronised because they each consume a *cons* cell per recursive call.

In contrast, the function *uzip*, shown below, is not tightly-synchronised because the first recursion parameter will consume twice as fast as the second recursion parameter.

```
dec uzip: (list(A),list(B)) → list(A,B);
--- uzip(cons(x,xs),cons(y,ys))  ⇐ cons((x,y),uzip'(xs,ys));
--- uzip(xs,ys)                  ⇐ nil;
--- uzip'(cons(x,xs),ys)         ⇐ uzip(xs,ys));
--- uzip'(xs,ys)                 ⇐ nil;
```

We define a new class of functions, called the **T1** class, with multiple recursion parameters that are tightly-synchronised, as follows.

Definition 3: T1 Class
A set of mutually recursive functions, $f_1,\ldots,f_h$ with r recursion parameters, satisfies the **T1** class if the following conditions are present.

1. Each equation (the s-th one) of function f_i has the form:

   $$\text{---}\ f_i(p_1,..,p_r,v_1,\ldots,v_n) \Leftarrow ...[C_1,..,C_k]...$$

   where ...[ ]... represents a context with zero or more holes to place the (mutually) recursive calls, $C_1,..,C_k$. The patterns of the r recursion parameters must be either: $\forall z \in 1..r.p_z \equiv v'$ or $\forall z \in 1..r.p_z \equiv c_s(v'_1,\ldots,v'_m)$.

2. Each of the recursive call, C_j, is of the form: $f_{i_j}(S^j_1[p_1],..,S^j_1[p_r],w_1,\ldots,w_a)$. This call must satisfy the following:

   (a) $\forall z \in 1..a.\ w_z \in \{v_1,\ldots,v_n\}$ or a constant.

   (b) $\forall z \in 1..r.p_z \equiv c_s(v'_1,\ldots,v'_m)$
   $\rightarrow (S^j_1[p_z] \equiv v'_{j_1}) \wedge (j_1 \in \{1..m\})$.

   (c) $\forall z \in 1..r.p_z \equiv v' \rightarrow (S^j_1[p_z] \equiv v') \wedge (f_i >_{fn} f_{i_j})$

3. The ordering ($>_{fn}$) introduced in 2(c) must not be cyclic.

Condition (1) (and the form of the recursive calls) states that each **T1** function has r recursion parameters which have the same constructor (c_i) for the patterns (in each equation) and the same descending function (i.e. S_i^j) for each of the recursive calls (C_j). In other words, these recursion parameters are identically synchronised for each function call. Condition (2a) states that the other parameters of the function are non-accumulating with no new variables introduced. Condition (2b) ensures that each recursive calls' recursion argument is taken from a variable of its recursion pattern. Conditions (2c) & (3) ensures that each recursion argument will always decrease by at least one constructor when it cycles back to the same function.

This class of functions is a generalisation of the **T0** class (with multiple instead of a single recursion parameter). It could be used by the same safe tupling transformation algorithm to eliminate both intra-call and inter-call multiple traversals and/or redundant calls.

For example, the *zip* function is a member of the **T1** class. Used as the call *zip(xs,xs)* in function *dupl* (of Section 1), the intra-call multiple traversals could be eliminated by transforming *dupl* to:

```
--- dupl(cons(x,xs)) ⇐ cons((x,x),dupl(xs))
--- dupl(xs)         ⇐ nil;
```

The tupling transformation algorithm (Algorithm 1) is terminating for the **T1** class. The proof is given below.

<u>Termination Proof</u>

Given a set of **T1** functions with r recursion parameters, we can show that the tupling transformation need only deal with finitely many different tuples. Assume we start with a call with r recursion arguments (variables), $ra_1, \ldots, ra_r$, some of which may be common. Then, because of the tight-synchronisation property a corresponding pattern of recursion arguments will appear in the sub-sequent recursive calls. Our tupling algorithm will group calls with the same set of r recursion arguments together. Thus, if there are n different functions and the largest number of the other (non-recursion) parameters for the functions is m and the number of different variables and constants used is s, then the maximum number of distinct function calls which could be obtained is $n \times s^m$. As the number of distinct calls is bounded, the number of different tuples (modulo renaming) will also be bounded. Hence, a re-occurring (matching) tuple is bound to happen after a finite number of steps by the tupling algorithm.

4 Loosely-Synchronised Recursion Parameters

If the multiple recursion arguments are not identical (no intra-call traversals required), it is not necessary to have their parameters tightly-synchronised. Instead, a weaker property among the multiple recursion parameters, called *loose-synchronization*, could be used to help remove redundant calls and inter-call multiple traversals.

We specify this loose-synchronization property by the ability to perform a data-type transformation to combine the multiple recursion parameters together into a single recursion parameter. If this is feasible, then we would obtain new functions which satisfy the **T0** class, and hence could be safely tupled.

As an example, consider the earlier *uzip* function which presently does not belong to the **T0** (nor **T1**) class. We could introduce a new (mutually recursive) data-type and a corresponding data conversion function *to_nt* below. (For simplicity, we allow the names of the data constructors to be overloaded. Also, *[A]* is a shorthand notation for *list(A)*.) These will be used later to help combine the two recursion parameters of *uzip*.

```
data nt(A,B) = c1([A],[B]) ++ c2(A,B,[A],[B],nt'(A,B)) ;
data nt'(A,B) = c1([A],[B]) ++ c2(A,[A],[B],nt(A,B)) ;
dec to_nt :: ([A],[B]) → nt(A,B);
dec to_nt' :: ([A],[B]) → nt'(A,B);
--- nuzip(xys)                      ⇐ uzip(xs,ys) st {xys=to_nt(xs,ys)};
--- to_nt(cons(x,xs),cons(y,ys)) ⇐ c2(x,y,xs,ys,to_nt'(xs,ys));
--- to_nt(xs,ys)                    ⇐ c1(xs,ys);
--- to_nt'(cons(x,xs),ys)           ⇐ c2(x,xs,ys,to_nt(xs,ys));
--- to_nt'(xs,ys)                   ⇐ c1(xs,ys);
```

A new *nuzip* function is expressed in terms of the old *uzip* function via a constraint[1] *{xys=to_nt(xs,ys)}* on the new parameter. This function could be systematically transformed to the following **T0** function with a single recursion parameter.

```
--- nuzip(c2(x,y,_,_,xys)) ⇐ cons((x,y),nuzip'(xys)) ;
--- nuzip(xys)              ⇐ nil ;
--- nuzip'(c2(x,_,_,xys))   ⇐ nuzip(xys) ;
--- nuzip'(xys)             ⇐ nil ;
```

Also, the old *uzip* function could be re-defined in terms of the new *nuzip* function, as follows:

```
--- uzip(xs,ys)        ⇐ nuzip(to_nt(xs,ys));
```

This data-type conversion obtains a new *nuzip* function which belongs to the **T0** class and is thus suitable for tupling with other **T0** functions that use similar data structures. (Similar or isomorphic data structures could be identified by using a correspondence/equivalence matching algorithm. One such correspondence algorithm is outlined in the Appendix.) Some readers may notice that this data-type transformation also introduces a new intermediate data structure - the converse of fusion. However, this is not a problem because the safe fusion method of [Chi92] could be applied, at a later stage, to eliminate the need for such intermediate data term.

We call the class of mutually-recursive functions which allow such data-type conversion, the **T2** class. This class of functions can be formally defined, as follows:

---

[1] Such constraints, enclosed by curly braces and specified after **st** keyword, state relationships that are valid for a given expression (or context). They could be used to perform constraint-dependent transformations, for e.g. *if b then* e_1 *else* e_2 **st** $\{b=true\} \Rightarrow e_1$. These constraints are used during transformations but ignored at run-time.

Definition 4: T2 Class
A set of mutually recursive functions, $f_1, \ldots, f_h$ with r recursion parameters, satisfies the T2 class if the following conditions are present.

1. Each equation (the s-th one) of function f_i has the form:

   $$--- f_i(p_1, .., p_r, v_1, \ldots, v_n) \Leftarrow ...[C_1, .., C_k]...$$

   where ...[ ]... represents a context with zero or more holes to place the (mutually) recursive calls, $C_1, .., C_k$. Each pattern of the r recursion parameters is of the form $\forall z \in 1..r. p_z \equiv v' \mid c_{s_z}(v'_1, \ldots, v'_m)$.

2. Each of the recursive call, C_j, is of the form: $f_{i_j}(S^j_1[p_1], .., S^j_r[p_r], w_1, \ldots, w_a)$.
   This call must satisfy the following:

   (a) $\forall x \in 1..a. w_x \in \{v_1, \ldots, v_n\}$ or a constant.

   (b) $\forall z \in 1..r. p_z \equiv c_{s_z}(v'_1, \ldots, v'_m) \rightarrow (S^j_z[p_z] \equiv v'_{j_z}) \wedge (j_z \in \{1..m\})$

   (c) $\forall z \in 1..r. p_z \equiv v' \rightarrow (S^j_z[p_z] \equiv v') \wedge (f_i[z] >_{fn} f_{i_j}[z])$

3. The ordering ($>_{fn}$) introduced in 2(c) must not be cyclic.

4. Also, it must be possible for each function of $f_1, \ldots, f_h$ to have its multiple recursion parameters *efficiently convertible* to a single recursion parameter.

Condition (1) (and the form of the recursive calls) states that each T2 function has r recursion parameters which are possibly distinct patterns that have at most a single constructor each. Notice that no synchronisation is imposed on the recursion parameters because the patterns $(p_1, .., p_r)$ and the descending functions $(S^j_1, .., S^j_r)$ could be different. Condition (2a) states that the other parameters of the function are non-accumulating and no new variables are introduced. Condition (2b) ensures that each recursive calls' recursion argument is taken from a variable of its recursion pattern. Conditions (2c) & (3) ensures that each recursion argument will always decrease by at least one constructor when it cycles back to the same function.

The loose-synchronization property is specified indirectly as Condition (4) which states that it must be possible to convert the multiple recursion parameters into a single recursion parameter in an efficient manner. The idea of *efficient* data type conversion is formalised below.

The r recursion parameters of type, $T_1, \ldots, T_r$, of each function f_i could be combined into a single parameter of type, NT_i, if we could obtain a conversion function, to_nt_i, as follows:

Definition 5: Data-Type Convertibility

1. Each conversion function will be of the type:

   $$\textbf{dec}\ to\_nt_i :: (T_1, \ldots, T_r) \rightarrow NT_i;$$

2. For each equation (the s-th one) of f_i:

   $$\text{---}\ f_i(p_1, .., p_r, v_1, \ldots, v_n) \Leftarrow ...[C_1, .., C_k]...$$

   where the recursive call, C_j, is of the form: $f_{i_j}(S^j_1[p_1], .., S^j_r[p_r], w_1, \ldots, w_a)$. We introduce a conversion equation:

   $$\begin{aligned} &\text{---}\ to\_nt_i(p_1, .., p_r) \\ &\quad \Leftarrow c_s(freevar[p_1, .., p_r] \\ &\qquad , to\_nt_{i_1}(S^1_1[p_1], .., S^1_r[p_r]),\ .., to\_nt_{i_k}(S^k_1[p_1], .., S^k_r[p_r])) \end{aligned}$$

3. For a data converter to be *efficient*, we further require that every pair of recursive calls, C_x and C_y, satisfies:

   (a) The recursion arguments for the two calls: $S^x_1[p_1], .., S^x_r[p_r]$ and $S^y_1[p_1], .., S^y_r[p_r]$, are either *exactly identical* or *completely disjoint.*

   (b) If the arguments are *exactly identical*; we require

      i. $to\_nt_{i_x} = to\_nt_{i_y}$. This equivalence can be proved by a *correspondence algorithm.*

      ii. One of the two calls, either $to\_nt_{i_x}$ or $to\_nt_{i_y}$, could be removed from the RHS of the above conversion equation for to_nt_i.

We place an efficiency restriction on the data conversion in order to avoid duplicating the data traversal in the combined type. This is assured by having the recursion arguments of any two calls to be either exactly identical or totally disjoint. If there is partial overlap, there is a danger that the combined type may contain duplicated data structures. With the above requirements, the data-type conversion could be performed as outlined below:

1. For each function f_i, we introduce a new function:

   $$\text{---}\ f'_i(v_0, v_1, \ldots, v_n) \Leftarrow f_i(v'_1, .., v'_r, v_1, \ldots, v_n)\ \ \textbf{st}\{v_0 = to\_nt_i(v'_1, .., v'_r)\}$$

2. Unfold f_i and simplify, as follows, for each equation:

   $$\begin{aligned} &\text{---}\ f'_i(v_0, v_1, \ldots, v_n) \Leftarrow ...[C_1, .., C_k]...\ \ \textbf{st}\{v_0 = to\_nt_i(p_1, .., p_r)\} \\ &\text{---}\ f'_i(v_0, v_1, \ldots, v_n) \Leftarrow ...[C_1, .., C_k]... \\ &\qquad\qquad \textbf{st}\{v_0 = c_s(...., to\_nt_{i_1}(S^1_1[p_1], .., S^1_r[p_r]), \\ &\qquad\qquad\quad .., to\_nt_{i_k}(S^k_1[p_1], .., S^k_r[p_r]))\} \\ &\text{---}\ f'_i(c_s(...., v'_1, .., v'_k), v_1, \ldots, v_n) \Leftarrow ...[C_1, .., C_k]... \\ &\qquad\qquad \textbf{st}\{v'_1 = to\_nt_{i_1}(S^1_1[p_1], .., S^1_r[p_r]) \\ &\qquad\qquad\quad .....v'_k = to\_nt_{i_k}(S^k_1[p_1], .., S^k_r[p_r])\} \end{aligned}$$

3. Apply fold (which is allowed by the data-convertibility property):

$$---f'_i(c_s(\ldots,v'_1,..,v'_k),v_1,\ldots,v_n) \Leftarrow \ldots[C'_1,..,C'_k]\ldots$$

WHERE $C'_j \equiv f'_{i_j}(v'_j, w_1, \ldots, w_a)$.

This specification is given in the same style as that for the **T0** and **T1** class and is a generalisation of the two former classes. It relaxes the need for the recursion arguments to be tightly-synchronised which is instead substituted by the weaker loose-synchronization property. It is trivial to show that a set of tightly-synchronised recursion parameters could always be data-converted efficiently and hence is a special case of the loose-synchronisation property. (This is because the recursion arguments of the tightly-synchronised parameters are always either exactly identical or completely disjoint as required by the efficient data-conversion technique. In addition, it is trivial to show that the combined types of this class of functions always satisfies the correspondence algorithm.) No new transformation algorithm is needed, as the same safe tupling algorithm for the **T0** class could be used.

5 Synergy with the Fusion Tactic

In this section, we illustrate how the above classes of functions could allow the tupling tactic to be combined synergistically with the fusion tactic to achieve new optimisations not obtainable from either tactic alone. The fusion tactic (also called deforestation[Wad88]) is used to merge nested compositions of functions in order to obtain new functions without unnecessary intermediate data structures. In contrast, tupling is used for eliminating multiple traversals and/or redundant calls. These two tactics have quite distinct aims and are best constructed separately.

However, there are certain programs where the two tactics may be simultaneously applicable. In some cases, only one of the two tactics may be used; so we have to choose carefully the better tactic to apply in order to obtain better optimisation. In other cases, both tactics may be used but we may have to apply them in a suitable order to achieve fuller benefits.

Let us consider a simple example in which both tactics are applicable and see how more optimisations could be achieved than either tactic alone.

Consider a function to zip up two lists (one doubled and the other tripled) as follows:

```
dec main: list(int) → list(int,int);
dec double,triple: list(int) → list(int);
---main(xs)              ⇐ zip(double(xs),triple(xs));
---double(nil)           ⇐ nil;
---double(cons(a,as))    ⇐ cons(2*a,double(as));
---triple(nil)           ⇐ nil;
---triple(cons(a,as))    ⇐ cons(3*a,triple(as));
```

One way of optimising the function *main* is to fuse the expression *zip(double(xs),triple(xs* together; so that the intermediate data structures from *double(xs)* and *triple(xs)* are eliminated. The fusion method does this by defining a new function, shown below, where the two occurrences of *xs* are uniquely renamed. (Without renaming, the fusion method could only be applied to those expressions where multiple occurrences of the same variable are properly synchronised during transformation. This unnecessarily restrict the class of expressions which could be safely fused.)

```
--- zipdt(xs,ys) ⇐ zip(double(xs),triple(ys));
```

The renamed definition (of *zipdt*) could be transformed (with *main*) to:

```
--- main(xs)                      ⇐ zipdt(xs,xs);
--- zipdt(cons(x,xs),cons(y,ys)) ⇐ cons((2*x,3*y),zipdt(xs,ys));
--- zipdt(xs,ys)                  ⇐ nil;
```

The above fusion manages to eliminate the intermediate data structures but not the multiple traversals of variable *xs* (of *main*).

Another way of optimising the function *main* is to tuple up the two recursive calls *double(xs)* and *triple(xs)* using the tuple function:

```
--- dttup(xs) ⇐ (double(xs),triple(xs))
```

The tupled function is then transformed to:

```
--- main(xs)            ⇐ zip(u,v) WHERE (u,v)=dttup(xs);
--- dttup(nil)          ⇐ (nil,nil);
--- dttup(cons(x,xs)) ⇐ (cons(2*x,u),cons(3*x,v))  WHERE (u,v)=dttup(xs);
```

This transformation has managed to eliminate multiple traversals of the variable *xs* but not the intermediate data structures originating from functions *double* and *triple*.

Most of the past transformation techniques for fusion (e.g. [Wad88, Chi92]) and tupling (e.g. [Pet84, Chi93c]) are constructed separately; so that only one of the above two optimisations is possible. However, there are also a handful of techniques (e.g. [Wad84, Wat91, PP91]) which use *integrated*[2] procedures that could handle the above example. However, these integrated procedures tend to have limited fusion and/or tupling capabilities because of the need to cater to the constraints of the two types of transformations.

In [Chi93a], we proposed a modular (as opposed to integrated) combination strategy, called *interleaved bottom-up combination*, which interleaves the two separate tactics on each set of *mutually recursive*[3] functions selected according to the calling hierarchy; starting from the bottom functions until the top function. This combination strategy allows both the fusion and tupling tactics to be improved by harnessing their synergies, and at the same time avoiding their conflicts.

In the case of the above program, the synergy is harnessed by first applying the fusion tactic to *main* to obtain *zipdt*. This is then followed by the tupling tactic which would identify the *zipdt* function as a **T1** class function whose two recursion parameters are tightly-synchronised. Applying tupling to eliminate the intra-call multiple traversals yields the following desired program:

```
--- main(cons(x,xs)) ⇐ cons((2*x,3*x),main(xs));
--- main(xs)          ⇐ nil;
```

[2]typically fusion with integrated tupling capability

[3]c.f. strongly connected sub-set of functions based on the call graph

6 Further Improvements

The present proposals for classes of functions which could be safely tupled are quite easy to check as they are syntactically-based. However, one serious limitation is that simple syntactic changes could make a function unsafe for tupling. To help alleviate this problem, we are recommending the use of (i) pre-processing techniques, and (ii) more advanced analyses.

In [Chi93c], we showed how pre-processing techniques, like pattern-matching compilation[Aug85] and fusion[Chi92], could be used to transform certain non-**T0** functions to their **T0** equivalent. This approach helps to enlarge the class of functions which could be safely tupled.

Another approach is to make use of more advanced analyses in the identification of safe classes of functions. In particular, the present syntactic formulation of tight-synchronisation for the **T1** class is a little restrictive. It requires the multiple recursion parameters to be synchronised for every call, rather than for each cycle of calls back to the same recursive function. As a result, the following alternative definition of *zip* does not belong to the **T1** class.

```
--- zip(cons(x,xs),ys)       ⇐ zip'(xs,ys,x);
--- zip(xs,ys)               ⇐ nil;
--- zip'(xs,cons(y,ys),x)    ⇐ cons((x,y),zip(xs,ys));
--- zip'(xs,ys,x)            ⇐ nil;
```

This is so, even though intra-call multiple traversals could also be eliminated for this alternative definition. Currently, work is in-progress to formulate a parameter (synchronisation) analysis technique for identifying multiple recursion parameters which are tightly-synchronised for each cycle of recursive calls. This will be the subject of a forth-coming paper[Chi93b].

Another limitation of our current proposal is that the same safe tupling algorithm is being used to eliminate intra-call/inter-call multiple traversals and redundant calls for the **T1** class and inter-call multiple traversals and redundant calls for the **T0** and **T2** classes. As a result, the tupling algorithm has to place a combined set of restrictions on the classes of functions which could be safely tupled. However, the elimination of intra-call traversals, inter-call traversals and redundant calls can be viewed as three different types of tupling optimisations which could be separated into three different phases. This modular decomposition could result in fewer restrictions and hence more cases of successful tupling transformations.

For example, the technique of eliminating redundant calls requires that the non-recursion parameters of our functions be non-accumulating. However, this restriction is not required by the technique of eliminating inter-call/intra-call multiple traversals, as illustrated by the following program.

```
--- av(xs)                   ⇐ sumit(xs,0)/lenit(xs,0);
--- lenit(nil,w)             ⇐ w;
--- lenit(cons(x,xs),w)      ⇐ lenit(xs,1+w);
--- sumit(nil,w)             ⇐ w;
--- sumit(cons(x,xs),w)      ⇐ sumit(xs,a+x);
```

Both *sumit* and *lenit* contain accumulating parameters which disqualify them from the **T0** class. However, inter-call multiple traversals could still be eliminated by a variant of tupling algorithm (which performs parameter generalisation) by transforming the above program to:

```
---av(xs)                     ⇐ u/v WHERE (u,v)=avtup(xs,0,0);
---avtup(xs,w,z)              ⇐ (w,z);
---avtup(cons(x,xs),w,z)      ⇐ avtup(xs,x+w,1+z);
```

The proposed extension to decompose the tupling algorithm into three separate phases re-affirms the modular approach we have been adopting for transformation tactics. It is also a topic of our forthcoming paper.

7 Conclusion

Previous work on the tupling method[Pet84, PP91, Chi93c] have concentrated principally on functions with a single recursion parameter per function. This paper contributes to the field of automated tupling transformation by identifying two new classes of functions with multiple recursion parameters which are safe to tuple. The key observation is that ***tightly-synchronised*** recursion parameters help to eliminate intra-call traversals, while ***loosely-synchronised*** recursion parameters is required for eliminating inter-call traversals and/or redundant calls.

One side benefit of having such an extended tupling capability is that it has helped to bring about a better understanding of how fusion and tupling tactics could be combined. In particular, we have managed to combine both the safe fusion and safe tupling tactics in a modular way. Using a careful combination strategy, we have managed to avoid the conflicts which may arise and harness the synergies from the two tactics. The details of this combination is given in a separate paper [Chi93a].

We advocate a modular approach to the constructions of automated transformation methods. We have formulated both the fusion and tupling tactics as separate program transformation methods [Chi92, Chi93c] and made several attempts to improve them separately. The extended classes of functions proposed in this paper have helped to contribute towards a more synergistic combination. Further work could proceed on improving these tactics separately and in combination. Also, we intend to make practical evaluations of these transformation tactics.

8 Acknowledgement

Part of this work was done during the first author's visit to the Dept of Computer Science, Chalmers University of Technology. The author would like to thank Dr Lennart Augustsson, Dr Thomas Johnsson and Prof John Hughes for their help in facilitating the visit. We would also like to acknowledge the encouraging support of this work from Prof Neil Jones and Prof Alberto Pettorossi. Thanks also to the reviewers for useful comments.

References

[Aug85] Lennart Augustsson. Compiling pattern-matching. In *Conference on Functional Programming and Computer Architecture (LNCS 201, ed Jouannaud)*, pages 368–381, Nancy, France, 1985.

[Chi92] Wei-Ngan Chin. Safe fusion of functional expressions. In *ACM Lisp and Functional Programming Conference*, pages 11–20, San Francisco, California, June 1992.

[Chi93a] Wei-Ngan Chin. A modular strategy for combining the fusion and tupling methods. In *Unpublished*, April 1993.

[Chi93b] Wei-Ngan Chin. Synchronisation analysis. In *(in preparation)*, July 1993.

[Chi93c] Wei-Ngan Chin. Towards an automated tupling strategy. In *ACM Symposium on Partial Evaluation and Semantics-Based Program Manipulation*, Copenhagen, Denmark, June 1993.

[Pet84] Alberto Pettorossi. A powerful strategy for deriving programs by transformation. In *ACM Lisp and Functional Programming Conference*, pages 273–281, 1984.

[PP91] M Proietti and A Pettorossi. Unfolding - definition - folding, in this order for avoiding unnecessary variables in logic programs. In *Proc PLILP'91, LNCS 528*, pages 347–358, Passau, Germany, August 1991.

[Wad84] Phil Wadler. Listlessness is better than laziness: Lazy evaluation and garbage collection at compile-time. In *ACM Symposium on Lisp and Functional Programming*, pages 45–52, Austin, Texas, August 1984.

[Wad88] Phil Wadler. Deforestation: Transforming programs to eliminate trees. In *European Symposium on Programming*, pages 344–358, Nancy, France, March 1988.

[Wat91] Richard C Waters. Automatic transformation of series expressions into loops. *ACM Transaction on Programming Languages and Systems*, 13(1):52–98, January 1991.

A Correspondence Algorithm

The correspondence algorithm is used to check if two data conversion functions are equivalent to one another and could be made to generate the same combined type. We outline one such algorithm in this section.

Given two conversion functions, to_nt_x and to_nt_y, which each has a set of equations. For any two equations, say the s-th equation from to_nt_x and the u-th equation from to_nt_y:

$$
\begin{array}{l}
{-}{-}{-}\, to\_nt_x(px_1,..,px_r) \\
\quad \Leftarrow c_s(freevar[px_1,..,px_r], to\_nt_{x_{s1}}(S_1^{s1}[px_1],..,S_r^{s1}[px_r]),\ ..,to\_nt_{x_{sk}}(S_1^{sk}[px_1],..,S_r^{sk}[px_r]))
\end{array}
$$

$$---to\_nt_y(py_1, .., py_r)$$
$$\Leftarrow c_u(freevar[py_1, .., py_r], to\_nt_{y_{u1}}(S_1^{u1}[py_1], .., S_r^{u1}[py_r]), \; .., to\_nt_{x_{uk}}(S_1^{uk}[py_1], .., S_r^{uk}[py_r]))$$

We attempt to make a correspondence between the two equations to see if they can be made to be equivalent by *correspond(s,u)* using the following algorithm.

correspond(s,u) = *CASE compare*($px_1..px_r, py_1..py_r$) *OF*
conflict: *succeed*
overlap: *fail*
equiv: *any two calls from* $to\_nt_{x_{s1}}..to\_nt_{x_{sk}}$ *and* $to\_nt_{y_{u1}}..to\_nt_{y_{uk}}$
must have arguments which are either exactly
identical or completely disjoint
IF there are exactly identical, we must
recursively apply the correspondence
algorithm to the pair of function calls

If all pairs of equations from the two equations succeed in the correspondence test, the two conversion functions to_nt_x and to_nt_y could be made to be equivalent. We simply replace the two functions by a single function to_nt_{xy} which represents a sum (or super-set) of the equations from the two functions.

Avoiding Repeated Tests in Pattern Matching

Peter Thiemann*

Wilhelm-Schickard-Institut, Universität Tübingen, Sand 13, D-72076 Tübingen, Germany

1 Introduction

When programming in functional languages with pattern matching there are often situations where nested patterns are used to look ahead into the argument data structure. What we want is information about the structure below the top level data constructor in order to take the appropriate action. ML has the alias pattern *var* **as** *pattern* as a special syntax for cases where we also need values from the inside of a pattern.

The kind of nested patterns as just mentioned often leads to inefficiencies that are not obvious to the programmer. Consider the function `last` taken literally from Wikstrøm's SML library [11].

```
(* last : 'a list -> 'a *)
fun last []        = raise Last
  | last [x]       = x
  | last (x::xs) = last xs
```

Compilation of pattern matching transforms the definition to

```
fun last L = case L of
                 nil     => raise Last
               | x :: L' => case L' of
                              nil     => x
                            | x'::L'' => last L'
```

Now we can make the following observation. Only the very first invocation of `last` can ever enter the `nil` branch of the first `case` and raise the exception. For all recursive invocations of `last` it is known that the argument is a non-empty list. An implementation of `last` that avoids repeating the test whether the argument list is empty can be given as follows.

```
fun last' x nil = x
  | last' _ (x::xs) = last' x xs

fun last nil = raise Last
  | last (x::xs) = last' x xs
```

The specialized function `last'` could be declared locally to `last`, but it is more advantageous to have `last'` declared globally since it can be used whenever it is known that the argument to `last` is a non-empty list.

* Email address: thiemann@informatik.uni-tuebingen.de

It is the purpose of this paper to give a simple and cheap approximate structure analysis (by abstract interpretation) that uncovers cases of repeated testing and generates specialized versions of the functions involved like `last'` above. Out intention is to use the analysis in a compiler. The techniques employed are connected to sharing analysis and partial evaluation. The analysis is applicable to a first order subset of ML.

It might be argued that such an analysis is applicable only to sloppy programming. However we feel that this is not the case. Consider the following fragment of an ML program to compute the next generation for Conway's game of life.

```
fun next_generation
    (x1::(xs as (x2::x3::_)))
    (y1::(ys as (y2::y3::_)))
    (z1::(zs as (z2::z3::_)))
  = fate y2 x1 x2 x3 y1 y3 z1 z2 z3:: next_generation xs ys zs
  | next_generation _ _ _ = [ 0 ]
```

Out of the nine constructor tests performed per recursive call, the outcome of six tests is known in advance since they have already been performed by the calling function. To expand the code by hand is tedious, error prone, and bad programming style since code for the same task is repeated in several places of the program. Our analysis identifies all of the repeated tests and produces specialized versions of `next_generation` without repeated tests.

The structure of the presentation is as follows. In Section 2 the syntax of a first order ML subset is defined along with an instrumented semantics that can express sharing properties. The next Section 3 defines a special environment structure for use in the abstract semantics. Section 4 introduces an analysis to find candidates for specialization by discovering argument patterns to function calls. The specialization process itself is detailed in Section 5 using arity raising. Finally we discuss related work in Section 6 and conclude in Section 7.

2 Syntax and semantics

We consider a first order ML subset with the syntax given by the grammar in Fig. 1.

The language is given an instrumented strict semantics. The instrumentation is chosen to provide enough detail to express sharing of structured values. Values are considered structured if an implementation allocates them on the heap (*eg.* constructed data, tuples, ...) so that they can be shared. Basic values like integers and nullary constructors are not considered structured. Each node of an object of a constructed data type carries a unique identification in the form of a non-empty sequence of numbers $m_0.m_1 \ldots m_n$, $n \geq 0$. When sharing occurs the object is formally copied but in a manner that shared nodes have a common (non-empty) prefix. Thus, we have unique nodes with unique access paths but are able to express sharing. A strict semantics with a store may be obtained by truncating all identifications to length 1 and considering m_0 as a store address. The strict standard semantics is recovered by projecting out the allocation information of the Mark component. The semantic domains are defined in Figure 2 where $\oplus$, $\otimes$, and $\circ\!\!\rightarrow$ denote coalesced sum, smash product and strict function space construction. $\mathsf{Con}_\perp^{(k)}$ is the flat partial

$$
\begin{aligned}
prg &\rightarrow dec\ exp \\
dec &\rightarrow \mathbf{fun}\ f\ v_1\ \ldots\ v_n = exp\ dec \\
&\mid\ \varepsilon \\
exp &\rightarrow \mathbf{case}\ exp\ \mathbf{of}\ pat_1\ :\ exp_1 \mid \ldots \mid pat_m\ :\ exp_m \\
&\mid\ \mathbf{let}\ v = exp\ \mathbf{in}\ exp' \\
&\mid\ c(exp_1, \ldots, exp_k) \\
&\mid\ f(exp_1, \ldots, exp_n) \\
&\mid\ v \\
pat &\rightarrow c(v_1, \ldots, v_k)
\end{aligned}
$$

where

$v \in \mathsf{Var}$	denumerable set of variables
$c \in \mathsf{Con}$	data constructors with arities $k(c)$
$f \in \mathsf{Fun}$	finite set of function symbols

Fig. 1. Syntax of the first-order language.

$$
\begin{aligned}
\mathsf{Int} &= \{\ldots, -2, -1, 0, 1, 2, \ldots\}_\perp \\
\mathsf{Mark} &= (\mathbb{N}^*)_\perp \\
\mathsf{Val0} &= \mathsf{Int} \oplus \mathsf{Con}_\perp^{(0)} \oplus \underbrace{\mathsf{Con}_\perp^{(k)} \otimes \mathsf{Mark} \otimes \overbrace{\mathsf{Val0} \otimes \ldots \otimes \mathsf{Val0}}^{k}}_{\text{structured values}} \\
\mathsf{Val} &= \mathbb{N}_\perp \otimes \mathsf{Val0} \\
\mathsf{Env} &= \mathsf{Var} \rightarrow \mathsf{Val0} \\
\mathsf{FVal} &= (\mathbb{N}_\perp \otimes \mathsf{Val0} \multimap \mathsf{Val}) \oplus \ldots \oplus (\mathbb{N}_\perp \otimes \overbrace{\mathsf{Val0} \otimes \ldots \otimes \mathsf{Val0}}^{n} \multimap \mathsf{Val}) \\
\mathsf{FEnv} &= \mathsf{Fun} \rightarrow \mathsf{FVal}
\end{aligned}
$$

Fig. 2. Semantic domains.

order constructed from the constructor symbols of arity k. The instrumentation consists of supplying each structured value with a Mark component as discussed above and threading a generator of unique identifications (a natural number) through the whole execution. All functions take an unused identification as an additional argument and return an unused identification as part of the value. The semantic functions ensure that every identification is used at most once in an evaluation. The semantic functions are defined in Figure 3.

3 Representing environments

In our analyses we need a special environment structure which is able to transmit bindings. For example, if we match a list L against the pattern $x :: xs$ during the analysis the environment must keep track of the information that L is no longer a

$\mathcal{E}$: Exp → Mark → FEnv → Env → Val

$$\begin{aligned}
&\mathcal{E}[\![\, v \,]\!] m\psi\rho && = share(m, \rho(v))\\
&\mathcal{E}[\![\, c(e_1,\ldots,e_k) \,]\!] m_0\psi\rho && = \textbf{let } (m_1, w_1) = \mathcal{E}[\![\, e_1 \,]\!] m_0\psi\rho \textbf{ in}\\
& && \quad \ldots\\
& && \quad \textbf{let } (m_k, w_k) = \mathcal{E}[\![\, e_k \,]\!] m_{k-1}\psi\rho \textbf{ in}\\
& && \quad fresh\ (m_k, (c, m_k, w_1, \ldots, w_k))\\
&\mathcal{E}[\![\, \texttt{let } v = e_1 \texttt{ in } e_2 \,]\!] m_0\psi\rho && = \textbf{let } (m_1, w_1) = \mathcal{E}[\![\, e_1 \,]\!] m_0\psi\rho \textbf{ in}\\
& && \quad \mathcal{E}[\![\, e_2 \,]\!] m_1\psi\rho[v \mapsto w_1]\\
&\mathcal{E}[\![\, f(e_1,\ldots,e_n) \,]\!] m_0\psi\rho && = \textbf{let } (m_1, w_1) = \mathcal{E}[\![\, e_1 \,]\!] m_0\psi\rho \textbf{ in}\\
& && \quad \ldots\\
& && \quad \textbf{let } (m_n, w_n) = \mathcal{E}[\![\, e_n \,]\!] m_{n-1}\psi\rho \textbf{ in}\\
& && \quad \psi(f)(m_n, w_1, \ldots, w_n)
\end{aligned}$$

$$\begin{aligned}
&\mathcal{E}[\![\, \texttt{case } e_0 \texttt{ of} \ldots c_j(v_1,\ldots,v_k) : e_j \ldots \,]\!] m_0\psi\rho =\\
&\qquad \textbf{let } (m_1, w) = \mathcal{E}[\![\, e_0 \,]\!] m_0\psi\rho \textbf{ in}\\
&\qquad \textbf{if } w = (c_j, M, w_1, \ldots, w_k)\\
&\qquad \textbf{then } \mathcal{E}[\![\, e_j \,]\!] m_1\psi\rho[v_i \mapsto w_i]\\
&\qquad \textbf{elseif } w = (\ldots) \textbf{ then } \ldots\\
&\qquad \textbf{else } \bot
\end{aligned}$$

$\mathcal{F}$: Dec → FEnv

$$\begin{aligned}
&\mathcal{F}[\![\, \{f(v_1,\ldots,v_{n_f}) = e_f \mid f \in \mathsf{Fun}\} \,]\!] =\\
&\qquad \mathbf{fix}\psi.\psi[f \mapsto \textbf{strict } \lambda(m, y_1, \ldots, y_{n_f}).\mathcal{E}[\![\, e_f \,]\!] m\psi\{v_i \mapsto y_i\} \mid f \in \mathsf{Fun}]
\end{aligned}$$

$\mathcal{P}$: Prg → Val

$$\mathcal{P}[\![\, d\ e \,]\!] = \mathcal{E}[\![\, e \,]\!] 1(\mathcal{F}[\![\, d \,]\!])\bot_{\mathsf{Env}}$$

where $m, m_i, m' \in \mathbb{N}$, $M \in$ Mark, $\psi \in$ FEnv, $\rho \in$ Env. The semantic **let** has a strict interpretation: **let** $v = \bot$ **in** e is equal to $\bot$ even if v does not occur in e. The projection **strict** is defined for domains D_1 and D_2 by

$$\begin{aligned}
&\textbf{strict}: (D_1 \to D_2) \to (D_1 \circ\!\!\to D_2)\\
&\textbf{strict } f\ x = \begin{cases} \bot & \text{if } x = \bot \\ f\ x & \text{otherwise} \end{cases}
\end{aligned}$$

and the auxiliary functions *share* and *fresh* are defined by

$$\begin{aligned}
&fresh \in \mathsf{Val} \circ\!\!\to \mathsf{Val} && share: \mathsf{Val} \circ\!\!\to \mathsf{Val}\\
&fresh\ (m, x) = (m+1, x) && share(m, x) = fresh\ (m, copy\ x)\\
& && \textbf{where } copy\ i = i \qquad\qquad i \in \mathsf{Int}\\
& && \qquad copy\ c = c \qquad\qquad c \in \mathsf{Con}^{(0)}\\
& && \qquad copy\ (c, M, w_1, \ldots, w_k) =\\
& && \qquad\qquad (c, M.m, copy\ w_1, \ldots, copy\ w_k)
\end{aligned}$$

Fig. 3. Instrumented semantic functions.

totally unknown value, but that it is known to be a non-empty list with head x and tail xs. To achieve the transmission of bindings we represent an environment by

1. an equivalence relation on variables,
2. a mapping from equivalence classes of variables to right hand sides.

Right hand sides are defined by the grammar

$$\begin{array}{lll} \mathsf{Rhs} \to & 1 & \text{the completely unknown value} \\ & \mid 0 & \text{the contradictory value} \\ & \mid c(v_1, \ldots, v_k) & \text{some constructor } c \text{ applied to representatives of} \\ & & \text{equivalence classes of variables.} \end{array}$$

Formally we define analysis environments by

$$\mathsf{Env}' = (\mathsf{Var} \to \mathsf{Rhs}) \times \mathcal{P}(\mathsf{Var} \times \mathsf{Var}).$$

Each $\rho = (\rho_1, \rho_2) \in \mathsf{Env}'$ is subject to the conditions

1. if $(v, v') \in \rho_2$ then $\rho_1 v = \rho_1 v'$,
2. if $\rho_1 v = c(v_1, \ldots, v_k)$ then $\{v_1, \ldots, v_k\} \subseteq \mathbf{dom}\ \rho_1$,
3. ρ_2 is an equivalence relation on $\mathbf{dom}\ \rho_1$, the domain of ρ_1.

We denote equivalence classes of ρ_2 by $[v]_{\rho_2}$.

An environment stores annotated values. An annotated value $d \in \mathsf{AVal}$ is a tree whose nodes are decorated with a set of variables and a constructor symbol. If two variables appear at the same node, the variables are considered equivalent or — in other words — they are aliases for each other. Thus we take AVal as the greatest solution (wrt. set inclusion) of the equation

$$\mathsf{AVal} = \mathcal{P}\mathsf{Var} \times (\{0, 1\} + \mathsf{Con} \times \mathsf{AVal}^*)$$

where $\mathcal{P}\mathsf{Var}$ denotes the powerset of Var, * is formation of finite sequences, and $+$ is disjoint union.

Define an ordering $\leq$ on AVal by

$$\begin{array}{c} (S_1, 0) \leq (S_2, x) \Leftrightarrow S_1 \supseteq S_2 \\ (S_1, x) \leq (S_2, 1) \Leftrightarrow S_1 \supseteq S_2 \\ (S_1, c(d_1, \ldots, d_k)) \leq (S_2, c(d'_1, \ldots, d'_k)) \Leftrightarrow S_1 \supseteq S_2 \wedge \forall 1 \leq i \leq k : d_i \leq d'_i \end{array}$$

Proposition 1. (AVal, $\leq$) *forms a lattice.*

The least element of AVal is (Var, 0), the top element is $(\emptyset, 1)$. For example, the greatest lower bound operation $\sqcap$ on AVal is defined as

$$\begin{array}{ll} (S_1, 0) \sqcap (S_2, x) & = (S_1 \cup S_2, 0) \\ (S_1, x) \sqcap (S_2, 1) & = (S_1 \cup S_2, x) \\ (S_1, c(\ldots)) \sqcap (S_2, c'(\ldots)) & = (S_1 \cup S_2, 0) \quad \text{if } c \neq c' \\ (S_1, c(d_1, \ldots, d_k)) \sqcap (S_2, c(d'_1, \ldots, d'_k)) & = (S_1 \cup S_2, c(d_1 \sqcap s'_1, \ldots, d_k \sqcap d'_k)) \end{array}$$

There are two functions that manipulate environments namely *lookup* and *enter* to lookup and enter bindings in an environment. Both functions preserve the conditions 1.–3. above.

An enquiry to the environment yields an annotated value.

$$
\begin{array}{l}
lookup\colon \mathsf{Var} \rightarrow \mathsf{Env}' \rightarrow \mathsf{AVal} \\
lookup\ v\ \rho = ([v]_{\rho_2}, w) \\
\qquad \text{where } (\rho_1, \rho_2) = \rho \\
\qquad\qquad w = 1 \qquad\qquad\qquad\qquad\qquad\qquad\qquad\qquad \text{if } \rho_1 v = 1 \\
\qquad\qquad w = c(lookup\ v_1\ \rho, \ldots, lookup\ v_k\ \rho) \text{ if } \rho_1 v = c(v_1, \ldots, v_k)
\end{array}
$$

Entering an annotated value into an environment does not cause aliasing of previously not aliased variables. Existing equivalence classes are enlarged as well as — possibly — some new classes are added.

$$
\begin{array}{l}
enter\colon \mathsf{Var} \rightarrow \mathsf{AVal} \rightarrow \mathsf{Env}' \rightarrow \mathsf{Env}' \\
enter\ v\ d\ \rho = \text{let } \ (vs, x) = (\{v\}, 1) \sqcap d \\
\qquad\qquad\qquad\qquad (\rho_1, \rho_2) = \rho \\
\qquad\qquad\qquad\qquad \rho_2' = (\rho_2 \cup \{(v, v') \mid v' \in vs\})^* \\
\qquad\qquad\quad \text{in if } x \in \{0, 1\} \text{ then} \\
\qquad\qquad\qquad\qquad (\rho_1[v' \mapsto x \mid v' \in vs]) \\
\qquad\qquad\qquad \text{else} \quad x = c(d_1, \ldots, d_k) \\
\qquad\qquad\qquad\qquad \text{let } \rho_1' = \rho_1[v' \mapsto c(n_1, \ldots, n_k) \mid v' \in vs] \\
\qquad\qquad\qquad\qquad\quad \text{where the } n_i \text{ are fresh variables} \\
\qquad\qquad\qquad\qquad \text{in } enter\ n_1\ d_1\ \ldots (enter\ n_k\ d_k\ (\rho_1', \rho_2')) \ldots
\end{array}
$$

In the second case for *enter* the variables $n_1, \ldots, n_k$ are fresh variables, *i.e.*, they do not appear anywhere else in the environment.

Symbolic evaluation of an expression to an annotated value is defined by the non-standard semantics $\mathcal{E}'$. Its type is

$$\mathcal{E}'\colon \mathsf{Exp} \rightarrow \mathsf{FEnv}' \rightarrow \mathsf{Env}' \rightarrow \mathsf{AVal}$$

so that it takes an expression e, a function environment $\psi \in \mathsf{FEnv}'$, an environment $\rho \in \mathsf{Env}'$, and yields an annotated value AVal that describes the shape of the result of evaluating e with values bound to the variables whose shapes are as described by ρ. A function environment FEnv' is a mapping from function names Fun to functions over annotated values, *i.e.*, $\mathsf{FEnv}' = \mathsf{Fun} \rightarrow \mathsf{AVal}^n \rightarrow \mathsf{AVal}$. The greatest function environment $\psi_0 \in \mathsf{FEnv}'$ is $\psi_0(f)(d_1, \ldots, d_n) = (\emptyset, 1)$ for all functions.

$$
\begin{array}{l}
\mathcal{E}'[\![v]\!]\psi\rho \qquad\qquad\qquad = lookup\ v\ \rho \\
\mathcal{E}'[\![c(e_1, \ldots, e_k)]\!]\psi\rho \quad = (\emptyset, c(\mathcal{E}'[\![e_1]\!]\psi\rho, \ldots, \mathcal{E}'[\![e_k]\!]\psi\rho)) \\
\mathcal{E}'[\![f(e_1, \ldots, e_n)]\!]\psi\rho \quad = \psi(f)(\mathcal{E}'[\![e_1]\!]\psi\rho, \ldots, \mathcal{E}'[\![e_n]\!]\psi\rho) \\
\mathcal{E}'[\![\texttt{let } v = e_1 \texttt{ in } e_2]\!]\psi\rho = \mathcal{E}'[\![e_2]\!]\psi(enter\ v\ (\mathcal{E}'[\![e_1]\!]\psi\rho)\ \rho) \\
\mathcal{E}'[\![\texttt{case } e_0 \texttt{ of} \ldots c_j(v_1, \ldots, v_k) : e_j \ldots]\!]\psi\rho = \\
\quad \text{case } \mathcal{E}'[\![e_0]\!]\psi\rho \text{ of} \\
\quad (vs, c_j(d_1, \ldots, d_k)) : \mathcal{E}'[\![e_j]\!]\psi(enter\ v_1\ d_1 \ldots (enter\ v_k\ d_k\ \rho) \ldots) \\
\quad |(vs, 1) : \bigsqcup_{j=1}^{m} \mathcal{E}'[\![e_j]\!]\psi(enter\ n_0\ c_j(\ldots(\{v_j\}, 1)\ldots))\rho)
\end{array}
$$

Explanation: variables are looked up in the environment. Constructor applications create a new value which is completely unshared at the top, hence the $\emptyset$ at the top node. Function application is handled by a lookup through the function environment ψ. The **let** expression opens a possibility for sharing in the variable v. There are two possibilities at a **case** expression. If the branch which is taken can be predicted by means of $\mathcal{E}'$ the value of the **case** expression is the value of e_j. Otherwise all branches are entered with the environment changed to reflect the supposed structure of $\mathcal{E}'[\![e_0]\!]$ and the least upper bound of the result is taken. Another possiblity at this place would be to safely approximate the outcome of the **case** expression by $(\emptyset, 1)$.

$\mathcal{E}$ is an abstract interpretation in the sense of Cousot and Cousot [4]. It is an abstraction of a concrete semantics that reveals sharing properties of the graph representation of the values. As outlined in previous work the standard semantics can be constructed as an abstraction thereof [9].

4 Finding specializable calls

The analysis function $\mathcal{C}$ finds specializable calls by employing the annotated value semantics of the preceding section to predict the branch taken in a case expression and in order to find approximations to the set of concrete values that are passed as parameters. The type of $\mathcal{C}$ is

$$\mathcal{C}\colon \mathsf{Exp} \rightarrow \mathsf{FEnv}' \rightarrow \mathsf{Env}' \rightarrow \mathcal{P}(\mathsf{Fun} \times \mathsf{AVal}^*)$$

i.e., $\mathcal{C}$ takes an expression $e \in \mathsf{Exp}$ to analyze for calls with partially known arguments, a function environment $\psi \in \mathsf{FEnv}'$, and an environment $\rho \in \mathsf{Env}'$ the analyzed expression e. Its result is a set of function calls coded as tuples consisting of the name of the called function (Fun) and a list of argument shapes as annotated values AVal^*.

$$\begin{array}{ll}
\mathcal{C}[\![x]\!]\psi\rho & = \emptyset \\
\mathcal{C}[\![c(e_1, \ldots, e_k)]\!]\psi\rho & = \bigcup_{i=1}^{k} \mathcal{C}[\![e_i]\!]\psi\rho \\
\mathcal{C}[\![f(e_1, \ldots, e_n)]\!]\psi\rho & = \bigcup_{i=1}^{n} \mathcal{C}[\![e_i]\!]\psi\rho \cup \{(f, \ldots strip(\mathcal{E}'[\![e_i]\!]\psi\rho) \ldots))\} \\
\mathcal{C}[\![\mathtt{let}\ v = e_1\ \mathtt{in}\ e_2]\!]\psi\rho & = \mathcal{C}[\![e_1]\!]\psi\rho \cup \mathcal{C}[\![e_2]\!]\psi(enter\ v\ (\mathcal{E}'[\![e_1]\!]\psi\rho)\ \rho) \\
\multicolumn{2}{l}{\mathcal{C}[\![\mathtt{case}\ e_0\ \mathtt{of} \ldots c_j(v_1, \ldots, v_k) : e_j \ldots]\!]\psi\rho =} \\
\multicolumn{2}{l}{\quad \mathcal{C}[\![e_0]\!]\psi\rho \cup} \\
\multicolumn{2}{l}{\quad \text{case } \mathcal{E}'[\![e_0]\!]\psi\rho \text{ of}} \\
\multicolumn{2}{l}{\qquad (vs, c_j(d_1, \ldots, d_k)) : \mathcal{C}[\![e_j]\!]\psi(enter\ v_1\ d_1 \ldots (enter\ v_k\ d_k\ \rho) \ldots)} \\
\multicolumn{2}{l}{\qquad |(vs, 1) : \bigcup_{j=1}^{m} \mathcal{C}[\![e_j]\!]\psi(enter\ n_0\ c_j(\ldots(\{v_j\}, 1) \ldots)\rho)}
\end{array}$$

Explanation: the equations for variables, constructor applications, and **let**-expressions only serve to collect call patterns from their subexpressions. At a function application the call patterns of the subexpressions are collected and a new call pattern is constructed from the results of the symbolic evaluation of the function arguments. In order to be independant from the variables that are visible at a specific call site, we strip them from the annotated value with the function *strip* described below. At a **case**-expression symbolic evaluation $\mathcal{E}'$ is again used to predict the branch which is taken. If it is possible to predict the branch only the call patterns from that branch are extracted. Otherwise the call patterns are collected from all branches.

$$\begin{array}{ll} \mathit{strip}\colon \mathsf{AVal} \rightarrow \mathsf{AVal} & \\ \mathit{strip}\ (vs, 1) & = (\emptyset, 1) \\ \mathit{strip}\ (vs, c(d_1, \ldots, d_k)) & = (\emptyset, c(\mathit{strip}\ d_1, \ldots, \mathit{strip}\ d_k)) \end{array}$$

The outcome of the call analysis is usable even if we take ψ_0, the greatest function environment, for ψ. So there is no need to do a fixpoint computation at all. However, information may be extracted from comparing the results of adjacent iteration steps. The information can be used to guide an unfolding mechanism [2], which in turn can uncover more specializable calls. Such a procedure can lead to non-termination of the analyzer, a well known phenomenon from partial evaluation.

4.1 Examples

As an example we analyze the set of calls and their associated argument shapes in the body of the function `last`. Initially nothing is known about the parameter L. Thus the initial environment is $\rho_0 = ([L \mapsto 1], \{(L, L)\})$ and $\psi = \psi_0$.

$$\begin{array}{l}
\mathcal{C}[\![\, \texttt{case}\ L\ \texttt{of}\ldots]\!]\psi\ \rho_0\ = \\
\quad \mathcal{C}[\![\, L\,]\!]\psi\ \rho_0 \cup \qquad (*\ d = \mathcal{E}'[\![\, L\,]\!]\psi\rho_0 = 1\ *) \\
\quad \mathcal{C}[\![\, \texttt{raise}\ \ldots]\!]\psi(\mathit{enter}\ y_1\ (\{L\}, \texttt{nil})\ \rho_0) \cup \\
\quad \mathcal{C}[\![\, \texttt{case}\ L'\ \texttt{of}\ldots]\!]\psi(\mathit{enter}\ y_2\ (\{L\}, \texttt{cons}((\{x\},1),(\{L'\},1)))\ \rho_0) \\
\quad (*\ \rho_1 = \mathit{enter}\ldots\rho_0 = [L = y_2 = \texttt{cons}(x, L'), x = 1, L' = 1]\ *) \\
= \emptyset \cup \emptyset \cup \mathcal{C}[\![\, \texttt{case}\ L'\ \texttt{of}\ldots]\!]\psi\rho_1 \\
= \mathcal{C}[\![\, L'\,]\!]\psi\ \rho_1 \cup \\
\quad \mathrm{let}\ d = \mathcal{E}'[\![\, L'\,]\!]\psi\ \rho_1\ \mathrm{in} \qquad (*\ d = (\{L'\},1)\ *) \\
\quad \mathcal{C}[\![\, x\,]\!]\psi\ [y_2 = L = \texttt{cons}(x, L'), x = 1, L' = \texttt{nil}] \\
\quad \cup \mathcal{C}[\![\, \texttt{last}\ L'\,]\!]\psi\ [y_2 = L = \texttt{cons}(x, L'), x = 1, y_3 = L' = \texttt{cons}(x', L''), x' = 1, L'' = 1] \\
= \emptyset \cup \emptyset \cup \mathcal{C}[\![\, L'\,]\!] \ldots \cup \{(f, \mathit{strip}(\mathcal{E}'[\![\, L'\,]\!]\psi\ \rho_2))\} \\
= \{(f, (\emptyset, \texttt{cons}((\emptyset,1),(\emptyset,1))))\}
\end{array}$$

With this information a specialized version of the function `last` can be generated. We apply a technique from partial evaluation called arity raising where one parameter is replaced by many parameters. In the literature arity raising is applied to replacing an argument pair by two single arguments (cf. [8]) whereas we employ a conditional arity raising. Only if it is known that some argument is a constructor term with a certain top constructor we supply the arguments of the constructor in place of the term as arguments to the function.

In our example we have two choices. The argument $L' = \texttt{cons}(x', L'')$ can either be replaced by the constructor arguments x' and L'' or by L' and L''. The first choice is the one shown in the introduction, which is generated almost verbatim by the specializer presented in the next section. The other choice could be even more advantageous, since the corresponding function even avoids accessing the list elements unless it is forced to do so. But more information is required to make that choice.

We are grateful to one of the referees for the following interesting example. Consider a function that merges two ascending lists of numbers.

```
fun merge (xs as xh::xt) (ys as yh::yt) =
        if xh <= yh then xh::merge xt ys else yh::merge xs yt
  | merge ...
```

At either recursive invocation of **merge** that **ys** or **xs**, respectively, are non-empty. Our analysis detects this fact and generates two mutually recursive auxiliary functions which completely avoid the redundant tests. The stripped output of the call analysis $\mathcal{C}$ on the body of merge is

$$\{(\texttt{merge}, 1 \;::(1,1)), (\texttt{merge}, \;::(1,1)\; 1)\}$$

and one of the generated functions is (transcribed in pattern matching notation)

```
fun merge_1_11 (xs as xh::xt) yh yt =
        if xh <= yh then xh::merge_1_11 xt yh yt
                    else yh::merge_11_1 xh xt yt
  | merge_1_11 nil yh yt = yh::yt
```

5 Arity raising and specialization

Suppose we are given a set of function definitions and the outcome of the call analysis $C_f = \mathcal{C}[\![\, e_f \,]\!]\ldots$ on all definitions in $C = \bigcup_{f \in \mathsf{Fun}} C_f$. We will then select a set $C' \subseteq C$ with the requirement that for each $(f, p_1 \ldots p_n) \in C'$ there is some $p_i \neq 1$. The selection for C' must ensure that the specialized functions do not exhibit new call patterns, since new call patterns would cause another specialization phase, which could lead to a non-terminating process. Also if arbitrary call patterns are allowed we will end up in delaying unavoidable data constructions while only creating long argument lists. Only the construction of those poarts of a structure that are certainly decomposed or tested should be avoided or at least delayed. The analyses $\mathcal{T}$ and $\mathcal{R}$ below give information on the tested part of the arguments when given information on the shape of the arguments (a call pattern found by the $\mathcal{C}$-analysis above).

The definitions of $\mathcal{R}^{\langle x_1,\ldots,x_n\rangle}, \mathcal{T}^{\langle x_1,\ldots,x_n\rangle} \colon \mathsf{Exp} \to \mathsf{FEnv}' \to \mathsf{Env}' \to \mathsf{AVal}^n$ are as follows with $\overline{x} = \langle x_1, \ldots, x_n\rangle$ and the operations on AVal pointwise extended to AVal^n.

$$
\begin{array}{ll}
\mathcal{T}^{\overline{x}}[\![\, e \,]\!]\psi\rho & = \langle \ldots, \mathit{lookup}\ x_i\ \rho, \ldots\rangle \sqcap \mathcal{R}^{\overline{x}}[\![\, e \,]\!]\psi\rho \\
\\
\mathcal{R}^{\overline{x}}[\![\, v \,]\!]\psi\rho & = \langle(\emptyset,1),\ldots,(\emptyset,1)\rangle \\
\mathcal{R}^{\overline{x}}[\![\, c(\ldots e_i \ldots) \,]\!]\psi\rho & = \bigsqcap_i \mathcal{R}^{\overline{x}}[\![\, e_i \,]\!]\psi\rho \\
\mathcal{R}^{\overline{x}}[\![\, f(\ldots e_i \ldots) \,]\!]\psi\rho & = \bigsqcap_i \mathcal{R}^{\overline{x}}[\![\, e_i \,]\!]\psi\rho \\
\multicolumn{2}{l}{\mathcal{R}^{\overline{x}}[\![\, \texttt{let}\ v = e_1\ \texttt{in}\ e_2 \,]\!]\psi\rho = \mathcal{R}^{\overline{x}}[\![\, e_1 \,]\!]\psi\rho \sqcap \mathcal{T}^{\overline{x}}[\![\, e_2 \,]\!]\psi(\mathit{enter}\ v\ (\mathcal{E}'[\![\, e_2 \,]\!]\psi\rho)\ \rho} \\
\multicolumn{2}{l}{\mathcal{R}^{\overline{x}}[\![\, \texttt{case}\ e_0\ \texttt{of} \ldots c_j(v_1,\ldots,v_k) : e_j \ldots \,]\!]\psi\rho =} \\
& \text{case } \mathcal{E}'[\![\, e_0 \,]\!]\psi\rho \text{ of} \\
& (vs, c_j(d_1,\ldots,d_k)) : \mathcal{T}^{\overline{x}}[\![\, e_j \,]\!]\psi(\mathit{enter}\ v_1\ d_1 \ldots (\mathit{enter}\ v_k\ d_k\ \rho)\ldots) \\
& |(vs,1) : \bigsqcup_j \mathcal{T}^{\overline{x}}[\![\, e_j \,]\!]\psi(\mathit{enter}\ n_0\ (vs, c_j(\ldots(\{v_j\},1)\ldots))\rho)
\end{array}
$$

Explanation: the function $\mathcal{R}^{\overline{x}}$ only provides the control structure for the analysis. The function $\mathcal{T}^{\overline{x}}$ is called at every update of the environment. It keeps track of bindings of the variables $\overline{x}$ and merges their current values with the recursive result from $\mathcal{R}$.

It remains to extract the tested part of the patterns from the result of $\mathcal{T}$. We define the closure operator *close* to yield an upper approximation to the tested part.

$$
\begin{array}{ll}
\multicolumn{2}{l}{close \colon \mathcal{P}\mathsf{Var} \rightarrow \mathsf{AVal} \rightarrow \mathsf{AVal}} \\
close\ V\ (vs, 1) & = (V \cap vs, 1) \\
close\ V\ (c(d_1, \ldots, d_k)) & = \text{let } d'_i = (vs_1, x_i) = close\ V\ d_i \text{ for } 1 \leq i \leq k \text{ in} \\
& \quad \text{if } \bigcup vs_i = \emptyset \text{ then } (V \cap vs, 1) \\
& \quad \text{else } (V \cap vs, c(d'_1, \ldots, d'_k))
\end{array}
$$

We only create specialized versions for tested part of the call patterns, *i.e.*

$$
\begin{array}{l}
C' = \{(f, p'_1 \ldots p'_n) \mid (f, p_1 \ldots p_n) \in C, \\
\qquad \langle p'_1, \ldots, p'_n \rangle = (strip \circ close\ \mathtt{var}(e_f) \circ \mathcal{T}^{\langle x_1, \ldots, x_n \rangle}[\![\, e_f \,]\!]\psi) \\
\qquad\qquad (enter\ x_1\ p_1 \ldots (enter\ x_n\ p_n\ \bot_{\mathsf{Env'}})) \sqcup \langle p_1, \ldots, p_n \rangle\}
\end{array}
$$

For the call patterns mentioned in C' we generate specialized functions as follows. First the function body, say e_f, is transformed in such a way that each intermediate value is bound to a variable. This is called transformation to sequential form in [5] and can be combined with common subexpression elimination [1]. Sequential form SExp is defined by the grammar

$$
\begin{array}{rl}
s \rightarrow & v \\
\mid & \mathtt{let}\ v = c(v_1, \ldots, v_k)\ \mathtt{in}\ s \\
\mid & \mathtt{let}\ v = f(v_1, \ldots, v_n)\ \mathtt{in}\ s \\
\mid & \mathtt{case}\ v\ \mathtt{of}\ \ldots c_j(v_1, \ldots, v_k) : s_j \ldots
\end{array}
$$

where $v, v_i \in \mathsf{Var}$, $c, c_j \in \mathsf{Con}$, $f \in \mathsf{Fun}$, and $s, s_j \in \mathsf{SExp}$. We will also assume that all variables have unique names.

$\mathcal{S} \colon \mathsf{SExp} \rightarrow \mathsf{FEnv'} \rightarrow \mathsf{Env'} \rightarrow \mathsf{Env'} \rightarrow \mathcal{P}(\mathsf{Fun} \times \mathsf{AVal}^*) \rightarrow \mathsf{SExp}$ is the specialization function. It is applied to the sequentialized expression ($\mathcal{S}$ is described below). In the last step we remove unused variables from the resulting expression.

The arguments of $\mathcal{S}[\![\, e \,]\!]\psi\rho\sigma P$ have the following meaning. The (sequentialized) expression e is the right hand side of a function definition. The function environment $\psi \in \mathsf{FEnv'}$ is needed to predict the outcome of **case** expressions. $\rho \in \mathsf{Env'}$ is the usual environment. $\sigma \in \mathsf{Env'}$ is another environment that keeps track of the arity raising process. If σ is defined on v it means that $\sigma(v)$ is the known part of the value bound to v. Because of our special environment structure we can deduce the variables that are bound to substructures of v's value from the entry for v. The functions that will have specialized versions are described by P as a set of function symbols with (a list of) call patterns.

Since the output of $\mathcal{S}$ is an expression we need to carefully distinguish our meta notation from generated program text. We make the distinction by underlining the generated program text.

$$
\begin{array}{l}
\mathcal{S}[\![\; v \;]\!]\psi\rho\sigma P = \begin{cases} \textit{build } p \text{ if } p \equiv \textit{lookup } v \; \sigma \\ \underline{v} \quad \text{otherwise} \end{cases} \\
\mathcal{S}[\![\; \texttt{let } v = c(v_1,\ldots,v_k) \texttt{ in } s \;]\!]\psi\rho\sigma P = \\
\quad \underline{\texttt{let } v = c(v_1,\ldots,v_k) \texttt{ in}} \; \mathcal{S}[\![\; s \;]\!]\psi(\textit{enter } v \; (\emptyset, c((\{v_1\},1),\ldots,(\{v_k\},1))) \; \rho)\sigma P \\
\mathcal{S}[\![\; \texttt{let } v = f(v_1,\ldots,v_n) \texttt{ in } s \;]\!]\psi\rho\sigma P = \\
\quad \text{choose } (f, p_1 \ldots p_n) \in P \text{ minimal where } \textit{MATCH}(p_i, \textit{lookup } v_i \; \rho) \text{ in} \\
\quad \underline{\texttt{let } v = f(\textit{extract}(p_1,d_1)\underline{,}\ldots\underline{,}\textit{extract}(p_n,d_n)) \texttt{ in}} \; \mathcal{S}[\![\; s \;]\!]\psi(\textit{enter } v \; (\emptyset,1) \; \rho) \; \sigma P \\
\mathcal{S}[\![\; \texttt{case } v \texttt{ of } \ldots c_j(v_1,\ldots,v_k) : s_j \ldots]\!]\psi\rho\sigma P = \\
\quad \text{case } \textit{lookup } v \; \rho \text{ of} \\
\quad (vs, c_j(d_1,\ldots,d_k)) : \mathcal{S}[\![\; s_j \;]\!]\psi(\textit{enter } v_1 \; d_1 \; (\textit{enter} \ldots \rho))\sigma P \\
\mid (vs, 1) : \underline{\texttt{case } v \texttt{ of}} \; \ldots \\
\qquad \underline{c_j(v_1,\ldots,v_k) :} \mathcal{S}[\![\; s_j \;]\!]\psi(\textit{enter } v \; (vs, c_j(\ldots(\{v_j\},1)\ldots))\rho)\sigma P
\end{array}
$$

We have used the auxiliary functions *build*: AVal $\rightarrow$ SExp to build concrete values from annotated values, *MATCH*: AVal $\times$ AVal $\rightarrow$ Boolean to dispatch **case** branches and *extract*: AVal $\times$ AVal $\rightarrow$ Var* to flatten argument expressions. They are defined as follows.

$$
\begin{array}{ll}
\textit{build } (\{v,\ldots\},1) & = \underline{v} \\
\textit{build } (vs, c((vs_1,x_1),\ldots,(vs_k,x_k))) & = \text{let } v_i \in vs_i \quad v \in vs \text{ in} \\
\qquad\qquad \textit{build } (\{v_1\},x_1) \; \ldots \; \textit{build } (\{v_k\},x_k) & \underline{\texttt{let } v = c(v_1,\ldots,v_k) \texttt{ in}} \\
 & \\
\textit{MATCH}((S,1),d) & = \text{true} \\
\textit{MATCH}((S,c(p_1,\ldots,p_k)),(S',c(d_1,\ldots,d_k)) & = \bigwedge_{i=1}^{k} \textit{MATCH}(p_i,d_i) \\
\textit{MATCH}(p,d) & = \text{false} \\
 & \\
\textit{extract}((S,1),(\{v,\ldots\},d)) & = \underline{v} \\
\textit{extract}((S,c(p_1,\ldots,p_k)),(S',c(d_1,\ldots,d_k)) & = \textit{extract}(p_1,d_1)\underline{,}\ldots\underline{,}\textit{extract}(p_k,d_k) \\
\textit{extract}(p,d) & = \text{abort}
\end{array}
$$

Notice that *extract*(p,d) is only called if *MATCH*(p,d) is true. But that means that the abort case will not occur in the evaluation of *extract*.

6 Related work

Wadler (and others subsequently) worked on deforestation [10, 3, 6]. Deforestation is an algorithm to eliminate intermediate trees by symbolic composition. Although a different goal is pursued deforestation also avoids some tests by delaying the construction of results. In contrast, specialization with arity raising delays the construction of values that are passed as parameters.

Romanenko deals with arity raising in the context of partial evaluation and program specialization [8]. He discusses the structure and principles of operation of an arity raiser in the context of a subset of pure Lisp. His arity raiser replaces a pair-valued argument by two single arguments. Here arity raising is conditional, since the top constructor of the argument which has to be decomposed must be known.

7 Conclusion and future work

We have presented an analysis that uncovers redundant tests caused by function declarations with pattern matching. Abstract interpretation yields function calls with pattern arguments and methods known from partial evaluation are employed to generate specialized functions that avoid the redundant tests. The analysis is simple and cheap enough to be incorporated into a compiler. It is shown with several examples that many interesting functions can be improved by the proposed technique.

Although demonstrated here in the context of strict functional languages, avoiding redundant test might prove even more beneficial for non-strict functional languages with lazy evaluation. In fact, all evaluation is driven by pattern matching in implementations like the the STG-machine [7] and avoiding a single constructor test really spares two tests: the test whether the argument closure is evaluated and the dispatch according to the constructor number.

Further directions of work include measurements with an implementation, the extension of the analysis to higher-order programs and the exploration of the connections to fusion and deforestation algorithms.

Acknowledgements The comments of the anonymous referees helped to improve the presentation of the paper. Special thanks to one of the referees for the merge example.

References

1. A. V. Aho, R. Sethi, and J. D. Ullman. *Compilers Principles, Techniques, and Tools.* Addison-Wesley, 1986.
2. R. M. Burstall and J. Darlington. A transformation system for developing recursive programs. *J. ACM*, 24(1):44–67, 1977.
3. W.-N. Chin. Safe fusion of functional expressions. In *Proceedings Conference on Lisp and Functional Programming*, pages 11–20, San Francisco, June 1992.
4. P. Cousot and R. Cousot. Abstract interpretation: A unified lattice model for static analysis of programs by construction or approximation of fixpoints. In *Proc. 4th ACM POPL*. ACM, 1977.
5. C. K. Gomard and P. Sestoft. Globalization and live variables. In *Proc. PEPM '92*, pages 166–177, New Haven, June 1991. ACM. SIGPLAN Notices v26,9.
6. G. W. Hamilton and S. B. Jones. Extending deforestation for first order functional programs. In R. Heldal, C. K. Holst, and P. Wadler, editors, *Proceedings of the 1991 Glasgow Workshop on Functional Programming*, pages 134–145, Portree, Isle of Skye, Aug. 1992. Springer-Verlag, Berlin.
7. S. L. Peyton Jones. Implementing lazy functional languages on stock hardware: the spineless tagless G-machine. *Journal of Functional Programming*, 2(2):127–202, Apr. 1992.
8. S. A. Romanenko. Arity raiser and its use in program specialization. In N. D. Jones, editor, *ESOP 1990*, pages 341–360. Springer Verlag, 1990. LNCS 432.
9. P. Thiemann. A safety analysis for functional programs. In D. Schmidt, editor, *Proc. PEPM '93*, pages 133–144, Copenhagen, Denmark, June 1993. ACM.
10. P. L. Wadler. Deforestation: Transforming programs to eliminate trees. *Theoretical Comput. Sci.*, 73(2):231–248, 1990.
11. Å. Wikström. *Functional Programming Using Standard ML.* Prentice Hall, 1987.

Freeness, Sharing, Linearity and Correctness — All at Once*

M. Bruynooghe ** M. Codish ***

Department of Computer Science
K.U. Leuven, Belgium
email: maurice@cs.kuleuven.ac.be

Abstract. The availability of freeness and sharing information for logic programs has proven useful in a wide variety of applications. However, deriving correct freeness and sharing information turns out to be a complex task. In a recent paper, Codish *et al.* introduce a domain of abstract equation systems and illustrate the systematic derivation of an abstract unification algorithm for sharing and freeness. This paper follows the same approach, and using a more detailed abstraction, develops a more powerful transition system. The resulting algorithm is more prone to efficient implementation as it computes a single abstract solved form which exhibits sharing, freeness, groundness and linearity information.

1 Introduction

The aim of possible sharing analysis of a logic program P is to identify independent variables in a clause of P. A set of variables is said to be *independent* if no computation binds them to terms which contain a common variable. Groundness, linearity and freeness analyses aim to identify program variables which are respectively bound to ground terms, linear terms (a term is linear if no variable occurs in it more than once) and variable terms by all computations of P. The availability of groundness and linearity information is useful for improving the precision of sharing analyses. The availability of sharing and freeness information has proven useful in a wide range of applications including parallelisation of programs, compiler optimisations as well as for improving the precision of other analyses.

We focus here on semantic based analyses such as those specified within the framework of abstract interpretation [5]. In this approach a program analysis is viewed as a non-standard semantics defined over a domain of data-descriptions. Analyses are constructed by replacing the basic operations on data in a suitable concrete semantics with corresponding abstract operations defined on data-descriptions. Formal justification is reduced to proving conditions on the relation between data and data-descriptions and on the elementary operations defined on the data-descriptions. This approach eases both the development and the justification of program analyses. In the case of logic programming languages, proving the correctness of an abstract unification function is the major step in justifying an analysis.

* Funded in part by the ESPRIT project 5246 PRINCE.
** Supported by the Belgian National Fund for Scientific Research.
*** From Oct. 93 at Dept. of Math. & Comp. Sci., Ben Gurion Univ., Beer-Sheba, Israel.

In its short history, the design and formal justification of sharing and freeness analyses for logic programs has proven to be a surprisingly difficult task. The first formally justified abstract unification algorithm for the "pair-sharing" domain proposed by Søndergaard in 1986 [10] was not given until 1991 in [2]. Many of the combined sharing and freeness analyses proposed in the literature have since been found incorrect in various details. In a recent paper [1], Codish *et al.* introduce a novel domain of abstract equation systems and illustrate the derivation of an abstract unification algorithm for sharing and freeness together with its formal justification.

The basic strategy applied in [1] is to systematically mimic each step in the Martelli – Montanari unification algorithm [8]. However, since an abstract equation may describe different concrete equations, to which different concrete rules apply, the resulting abstract algorithm is non-deterministic. The abstract equation is reduced by different abstract rules to mimic each of the corresponding concrete rules. Consequently different abstract solved forms may be obtained, all of which must be considered: a variable is definitely free only if it is free in all solved forms. This makes it doubtful whether it can be the basis for a very efficient analysis. Moreover, it should be enhanced to consider linearity information to improve its precision.

In this paper, we take the systematic development of [2] and [1] one step further. Choosing a different abstraction of equations, which distinguishes between abstract equations and a sharing component, we formalise a transition system which computes a single solved form which captures possible sharing and definite freeness information together with groundness and linearity. In addition to concrete terms, abstract equations also involve abstract variables which are no more than symbols from a designated set. For the sharing component we adopt the domain of Jacobs and Langen [6] which captures possible sharing as well as covering information and provides a good propagation of groundness information. Abstract variables are annotated to capture additional freeness and linearity information.

Here we do not require the abstract unification algorithm to mimic all possible steps in the concrete algorithm. Instead, we exploit the confluence of concrete unification to mimic a particular strategy on the concrete level which is determined by the structure of the equations on the abstract level. Each abstract rewrite rule is associated with an equivalence preserving transformation on concrete equations. Correctness follows by showing that each abstract transition mimics the corresponding transformation. The abstract unification algorithm is deterministic in the sense that at most one rule applies to a given abstract equation in a system. While not confluent, correctness holds for any sequence of selected equations.

We assume the reader is familiar with the basic concepts of abstract interpretation of logic programs and understands that abstract unification is the key step in developing a semantic based analysis of logic programs.

2 Preliminaries

Let Σ and *Var* denote respectively a fixed set of function symbols and an enumerable set of variables. The term algebra over Σ and *Var* is denoted Term. We reserve the symbols T and S to denote elements of Term. Variables are typically denoted U, V, W, X, Y, Z. The predicates *nonvar*(T), *var*(T), *ground*(T) and *linear*(T) denote respectively that T is non-variable, variable, ground and linear. Note that a free variable and a ground term are always linear. The power set of S is denoted $\wp S$.

A (concrete) equation system is a set of equations of the form $T_1 = T_2$. Given an equation system Eqs and an equation e, we let $e ::$ Eqs denote the set $\{e\} \cup$ Eqs. We fix a partial function *mgu* which maps an equation system Eqs to a solved form *mgu*(Eqs). A reference to *mgu*(Eqs) implicitly implies that Eqs is satisfiable. We do not distinguish between equations in solved form and idempotent substitutions as the correspondence between them is well known (see for example [7]). We often view *mgu*(Eqs) as an idempotent substitution and write $eq(\theta)$ to denote the set of equations corresponding to an idempotent substitution θ. Equation systems Eqs_1 and Eqs_2 are said to be *equivalent with respect to a set of variables* V, denoted $\mathsf{Eqs}_1 \approx_V \mathsf{Eqs}_2$, if there exist most general unifiers θ_1 and θ_2 of Eqs_1 and Eqs_2 such that $\theta_1 \lceil V = \theta_2 \lceil V$.

Example 1 Let $\mathsf{Eqs}_1 = \{X = f(Y)\}$, $\mathsf{Eqs}_2 = \{X = f(Z), Y = Z\}$ and $\mathsf{Eqs}_3 = \{X = f(Y), Z = Y\}$. Then $\mathsf{Eqs}_1 \approx_V \mathsf{Eqs}_2$ where $V = \{X, Y\}$. Indeed $\theta_1 \lceil V = \theta_2 \lceil V$ for $\theta_1 = \{X/f(Y)\}$ and $\theta_2 = \{X/f(Y), Z/Y\}$ which are most general unifiers of Eqs_1 and Eqs_2. Also $\mathsf{Eqs}_1 \approx_V \mathsf{Eqs}_3$ because θ_2 is also a most general unifier of Eqs_3.

In addition to concrete terms and variables, we assume a disjoint and enumerable set AVar of abstract variables. Intuitively an abstract variable represents a term from Term. We reserve the symbol A to denote abstract variables. The term algebras over Σ and AVar and over Σ and $Var \cup$ AVar are denoted respectively ATerm (abstract terms) and MTerm (mixed terms). The sets of variables and abstract variables occurring in a syntactic object s are respectively denoted $vars(s)$ and $avars(s)$.

Definition 2 (abstract equation system) *An abstract equation system consists of a pair* $\langle$AEqs$, \Delta\rangle$ *where* AEqs *is a set of abstract equations of the form* $T_1 = T_2$ *or of the form* $T = A$ *and* $\Delta \in \wp\wp\, avars(\mathsf{AEqs})$ *is a sharing component with an associated annotation mapping* $ann_\Delta : avars(\Delta) \rightarrow \{\{f, \ell\}, \{\ell\}, \emptyset\}$.

Notice that for the time being we avoid abstract equations of the forms $A_1 = A_2$, $A = T$ and abstract equations involving mixed terms. While these extensions can easily be given a meaning, they complicate the abstract unification algorithm.

We follow Jacobs and Langen [6] in the representation of the sharing component. Each set $\{A_1, \ldots A_n\}$ indicates that the terms represented by the abstract variables $A_1, \ldots, A_n$ can share one or more variables. Moreover, the annotations on abstract variables enrich the domain with linearity information as captured by the sharing domain of Søndergaard [10] and with freeness information. Let AS $= \langle$AEqs$, \Delta\rangle$ be an abstract equation system. We define the following predicates on the abstract variables occurring in AS:

- $ground_\Delta(A) \Leftrightarrow A \notin avars(\Delta)$; – $free_\Delta(A) \Leftrightarrow ann_\Delta(A) = \{f, \ell\}$;
- $linear_\Delta(A) \Leftrightarrow ann_\Delta(A) = \{\ell\}$; – $share_\Delta(A_1, A_2) \Leftrightarrow \exists S \in \Delta.\ \{A_1, A_2\} \subseteq S$.

Basically, AS describes a concrete equation system Eqs if it is possible to map each of the abstract variables in AEqs to a concrete term and obtain Eqs. However, the mapping is required to preserve the information specified by Δ. We say that a mapping $\alpha : avars(\mathsf{AS}) \rightarrow$ Term is *Δ preserving* if: (1) $ground_\Delta(A) \Rightarrow ground(\alpha(A))$; (2) $linear_\Delta(A) \Rightarrow linear(\alpha(A))$; (3) $free_\Delta(A) \Rightarrow free(\alpha(A))$; and (4) for every $X \in$

Var. $\{A \in avars(\Delta) \mid X \in \alpha(A)\} \in \Delta$. A mapping $\alpha : \mathsf{AVar} \to \mathsf{Term}$ is extended into a mapping $\alpha' : \mathsf{MTerm} \to \mathsf{Term}$ as follows:

$$\alpha'(M) = \begin{cases} M & \text{if } M \in Var \\ \alpha(M) & \text{if } M \in \mathsf{AVar} \\ f(\alpha'(M_1), \ldots, \alpha'(M_n)) & \text{if } M = f(M_1, \ldots, M_n). \end{cases}$$

Further extending α to apply to abstract equation systems is similar.

Definition 3 (description) *An abstract equation system* $\mathsf{AS} = \langle \mathsf{AEqs}, \Delta \rangle$ *describes a concrete system* Eqs *via* α, *denoted* $\mathsf{AS} \propto_\alpha \mathsf{Eqs}$, *if there is a* Δ *preserving mapping* $\alpha : avars(\mathsf{AS}) \to \mathsf{Term}$ *such that* $\alpha(\mathsf{AEqs}) = \mathsf{Eqs}$ *and for every* $A \in \mathsf{AVar}$, $vars(\alpha(A)) \cap vars(\mathsf{AEqs}) = \emptyset$. *We write* $\mathsf{AS} \propto \mathsf{Eqs}$ *to denote that there exists a mapping* α *such that* $\mathsf{AS} \propto_\alpha \mathsf{Eqs}$.

Let $\mathsf{AS} = \langle \mathsf{AEqs}, \Delta \rangle$ be an abstract equation system with associated annotation mapping ann_Δ and let A be an abstract variable occurring in Δ. We annotate the occurrences of A in Δ to indicate the value of $ann_\Delta(A)$: A^f, A^ℓ and A denote respectively that $ann_\Delta(A)$ is $\{f, \ell\}$, $\{\ell\}$ and $\emptyset$. We denote $\Delta(A) = \{S \in \Delta \mid A \in S\}$ and $\bar{\Delta}(A) = \{S \in \Delta \mid A \notin S\}$. Likewise $\bar{\Delta}(A_1, A_2) = \{S \in \Delta \mid A_1 \notin S,\ A_2 \notin S\}$.

Example 4 $\langle \{X = A_1, Y = A_2, U = f(V)\}, \{\{A_1^f, A_2\}\} \rangle$ describes $\{X = Z_1, Y = Z_2, U = f(V)\}$ as well as $\{X = Z_1, Y = f(g(Z_1, Z_1)), U = f(V)\}$ but not $\{X = V, Y = f(V, V), U = f(V)\}$. Denoting $\Delta = \{\{A_1^f, A_2\}\}$, $ann_\Delta(A_1) = \{f, \ell\}$ and $ann_\Delta(A_2) = \emptyset$. In addition, $\Delta(A_1) = \Delta(A_2) = \Delta$ and $\bar{\Delta}(A_1) = \bar{\Delta}(A_2) = \bar{\Delta}(A_1, A_2) = \emptyset$.

3 Abstract unification

A call pattern is a pair $(p(\bar{t}); \mathsf{AS})$ where $p(\bar{t})$ is an atom and $\mathsf{AS} = \langle \mathsf{AEqs}, \Delta \rangle$ is an abstract equation system such that AEqs consists of an equation of the form $X = A$ for each variable X in $p(\bar{t})$. Using abstract equation systems is well suited to describe definite freeness and possible sharing information. A variable X is definitely free if there is an equation $X = A$ and $free_\Delta(A)$. Variables X and Y possibly share if $X = Y$ or if $X = A_1$ and $Y = A_2$ and $share_\Delta(A_1, A_2)$. Given a call pattern $(p(\bar{t}); \langle \mathsf{AEqs}, \Delta \rangle)$ and a renamed clause of the form $p(\bar{s}) \leftarrow body$ we wish to reduce the abstract equation system $\langle \bar{t} = \bar{s} :: \mathsf{AEqs}, \Delta \rangle$ to a *solved form* which describes the result of a corresponding concrete unification. More generally:

Definition 5 (problem specification) *Given an abstract equation system* AS, *derive an abstract equation system* AS′ *in solved form such that* $\mathsf{AS} \propto \mathsf{Eqs} \Rightarrow \mathsf{AS}' \propto \mathsf{Eqs}'$ *and* $\mathsf{Eqs}' \approx_{vars(\mathsf{AS})} mgu(\mathsf{Eqs})$.

An algorithm which satisfies the above problem specification is called an *abstract unification algorithm*. We present an abstract unification algorithm consisting of two parts. The first part is a transition system which is applied to rewrite a given abstract system into a *pseudo solved form* of the form $\langle \{X_i = A_i\}_{i=1}^m :: \mathsf{Eqs}, \Delta \rangle$ where $\{X_1, \ldots, X_m\}$ and $\{A_1, \ldots, A_m\}$ are sets of variables and abstract variables respectively, Eqs is a set of concrete equations in solved form, and the left side of an equation in Eqs is not equal to a variable X_i ($1 \leq i \leq m$). The difference with a standard solved form is that the X_i can occur in the right side of an equation in Eqs. The second part of the algorithm derives from the pseudo solved form a solved form which expresses definite freeness, linearity and groundness information together with possible sharing information.

In the following we introduce a set of rewrite rules which are applied to reduce an abstract equation system to a solved form. Correctness follows because each transition AS $\rightarrow$ AS$'$ is shown to mimic a corresponding equivalence preserving transformation on concrete equation systems. Namely, if AS $\propto$ Eqs and Eqs is satisfiable, then there is a corresponding sequence of concrete transformations Eqs $\rightarrow^*$ Eqs$'$ such that Eqs $\approx_{vars(\mathsf{AS})}$ Eqs$'$ and AS$'$ $\propto$ Eqs$'$. We illustrate the intuition of each rule AS $\rightarrow$ AS$'$ by examples of the form

$$\begin{array}{ccc} \mathsf{AS} & \propto & \mathsf{Eqs} \\ \downarrow & & \wr\wr \\ \mathsf{AS}' & \propto & \mathsf{Eqs}' \end{array}$$

indicating that AS $\propto$ Eqs and that there is a transformation (sequence) of the form Eqs $\rightarrow^*$ Eqs$'$ such that AS$'$ $\propto$ Eqs$'$ and Eqs $\approx_{vars(\mathsf{AS})}$ Eqs$'$. As a convention, the equations chosen for reduction are underlined. Figure 1 illustrates the concrete transformations needed to justify our abstract algorithm. A transformation from Eqs to Eqs$'$ is denoted Eqs $\rightarrow_V$ Eqs$'$ where the V indicates that the transformation preserves equivalence with respect to the variables in $V \subseteq Var$. Clearly, if Eqs $\rightarrow_V$ Eqs$'$ then also Eqs $\rightarrow_{V'}$ Eqs$'$ for any $V' \subseteq V$. When $V = vars(\mathsf{Eqs})$ the subscript V is omitted. Rules 1–4 consist of the rules of the Martelli – Montanari algorithm. Rule 5 takes an equation, *solves* it and applies the result to the rest of the equations. Rule 6 *shuffles* the terms in two equations with a common right side. Rule 7 removes an equation of the form $X = \mathrm{T}$ if X does not occur in Eqs. This rule preserves equivalence with respect to the variables in Eqs. Rule 8 gives a fresh name Z to a variable X in an equation e and introduces a new equation $X = Z$.

Reducing equations of the form $\mathrm{T}_1 = \mathrm{T}_2$

These rules are basically the same as for concrete unification [8].

1. $\langle X = X :: \mathsf{AEqs}, \Delta\rangle \overset{\text{remove}}{\rightarrow} \langle \mathsf{AEqs}, \Delta\rangle$.
2. $\langle X = \mathrm{T} :: \mathsf{AEqs}, \Delta\rangle \overset{\text{substitute}}{\rightarrow} \langle X = \mathrm{T} :: \mathsf{AEqs}[X/\mathrm{T}], \Delta\rangle$ if $X \notin vars(\mathrm{T})$.
3. $\langle f(\mathrm{T}_1, \ldots, \mathrm{T}_n) = X :: \mathsf{AEqs}, \Delta\rangle \overset{\text{switch}}{\rightarrow} \langle X = f(\mathrm{T}_1, \ldots, \mathrm{T}_n) :: \mathsf{AEqs}, \Delta\rangle$.
4. $\langle f(\mathrm{T}_1, \ldots, \mathrm{T}_n) = f(\mathrm{S}_1, \ldots, \mathrm{S}_n) :: \mathsf{AEqs}, \Delta\rangle \overset{\text{peel}}{\rightarrow} \langle \{\mathrm{T}_i = \mathrm{S}_i\}_{i=1}^{n} :: \mathsf{AEqs}, \Delta\rangle$.

Reducing equations of the form $\mathrm{T} = \mathrm{A}$ such that $nonvar(\mathrm{T})$

Let T be a non-variable term such that $vars(\mathrm{T}) = \{X_1, \ldots, X_n\}$ (if $n = 0$ then T is ground). The following set of transitions are applied under the restriction that A *does not occur elsewhere in the abstract system*. If A does occur elsewhere, then a transition which better exploits the structural information in T is applied (see below). We distinguish the following cases:

1. $X = X :: \mathsf{Eqs} \overset{\text{remove}}{\rightarrow} \mathsf{Eqs}$.
2. $f(\mathrm{T}_1,\ldots,\mathrm{T}_n) = X :: \mathsf{Eqs} \overset{\text{switch}}{\rightarrow} X = f(\mathrm{T}_1,\ldots,\mathrm{T}_n) :: \mathsf{Eqs}$.
3. $f(\mathrm{T}_1,\ldots,\mathrm{T}_n) = g(\mathrm{S}_1,\ldots,\mathrm{S}_m) :: \mathsf{Eqs} \overset{\text{peel}}{\rightarrow} \begin{cases} \{\mathrm{T}_i = \mathrm{S}_i\}_{i=1}^n :: \mathsf{Eqs} & \text{if } f/n \equiv g/m \\ \mathit{fail} & \text{otherwise.} \end{cases}$
4. $X = \mathrm{T} :: \mathsf{Eqs} \overset{\text{subst}}{\rightarrow} \begin{cases} X = \mathrm{T} :: \mathsf{Eqs}[X/\mathrm{T}] & \text{if } X \notin \mathit{vars}(\mathrm{T}) \\ \mathit{fail} & \text{otherwise.} \end{cases}$
5. $e :: \mathsf{Eqs} \overset{\text{solve}}{\rightarrow} eq(\theta) :: \mathsf{Eqs}\,\theta$ where $\theta = mgu(e)$.
6. $\mathrm{T}_1 = \mathrm{T}, \mathrm{T}_2 = \mathrm{T} :: \mathsf{Eqs} \overset{\text{shuffle}}{\rightarrow} \mathrm{T}_1 = \mathrm{T}_2, \mathrm{T}_1 = \mathrm{T} :: \mathsf{Eqs}$.
7. $X = \mathrm{T} :: \mathsf{Eqs} \overset{\text{restrict}}{\rightarrow_V} \mathsf{Eqs}$ where $X \notin \mathit{vars}(\mathsf{Eqs})$ and $V \subseteq \mathit{vars}(\mathsf{Eqs})$.
8. $e :: \mathsf{Eqs} \overset{\text{fresh}}{\rightarrow_V} e[X/Z], X = Z :: \mathsf{Eqs}$ where $X \in \mathit{vars}(e)$, Z is a fresh variable, and $V \subseteq \mathit{vars}(e :: \mathsf{Eqs})$.

Fig. 1. Equivalence preserving transformations for equation systems

5. $\langle \mathrm{T} = \mathrm{A} :: \mathsf{AEqs}, \Delta\rangle \overset{\text{fresh,solve\&restrict}}{\rightarrow} \langle X_1 = \mathrm{A}_1, \ldots, X_n = \mathrm{A}_n :: \mathsf{AEqs}, \Delta'\rangle$ where $\mathrm{A}_1,\ldots,\mathrm{A}_n$ are fresh abstract variables, and
   (a) If $\mathit{ground}_\Delta(\mathrm{A})$ then $\Delta' = \Delta$ (note that this implies that $\mathit{ground}_{\Delta'}(\mathrm{A}_i)$ $(1 \le i \le n)$) and for $\mathrm{A}' \in \mathit{avars}(\Delta')$, $\mathit{ann}_{\Delta'}(\mathrm{A}') = \mathit{ann}_\Delta(\mathrm{A}')$;
   (b) Else if $\mathit{free}_\Delta(\mathrm{A})$ then
   * $\Delta' = \bar{\Delta}(\mathrm{A}) \cup \{\, (S \setminus \{\mathrm{A}\}) \cup \{\mathrm{A}_i\} \mid S \in \Delta(\mathrm{A}),\ 1 \le i \le n \,\}$;
   * $\mathit{ann}_{\Delta'}(\mathrm{A}') = $ **if** $\mathrm{A}' \in \{\mathrm{A}_1,\ldots,\mathrm{A}_n\}$ **then** $\{f, \ell\}$
     else **if** $\mathit{share}_\Delta(\mathrm{A},\mathrm{A}')$ **then**
     if $\mathit{linear}(\mathrm{T})$ **then** $\mathit{ann}_\Delta(\mathrm{A}') \setminus \{f\}$
     else $\mathit{ann}_\Delta(\mathrm{A}') \setminus \{f, \ell\}$
     else $\mathit{ann}_\Delta(\mathrm{A}')$
   (c) Else ($\mathit{ann}_\Delta(\mathrm{A}) \subseteq \{\ell\}$)
   * $\Delta' = $ **if** $\mathit{linear}(\mathrm{T})$ **then**
     $\bar{\Delta}(\mathrm{A}) \ \cup\ \{\, (S \setminus \{\mathrm{A}\}) \cup S' \mid S \in \Delta(\mathrm{A}),\ S' \in SS' \,\}$
     else
     $$\bar{\Delta}(\mathrm{A}) \ \cup\ \left\{ (\cup\, SS \setminus \{\mathrm{A}\}) \cup S' \;\middle|\; \begin{array}{l} SS \subseteq \Delta(\mathrm{A}), SS \neq \emptyset, \\ S' \in SS' \end{array} \right\}$$
     where $SS' = $ **if** $\mathit{linear}(\mathrm{A})$ **then** $\{\, \{\mathrm{A}_i\} \mid 1 \le i \le n \,\}$.
     else $\{\, S \subseteq \{\mathrm{A}_1,\ldots,\mathrm{A}_n\} \mid S \neq \emptyset \,\}$
   * $\mathit{ann}_{\Delta'}(\mathrm{A}') = $ **if** $\mathrm{A}' \in \{\mathrm{A}_1,\ldots,\mathrm{A}_n\}$ **then**
     if $\mathit{linear}(\mathrm{A})$ **then** $\{\ell\}$**else** $\emptyset$
     else
     if $\mathit{share}_\Delta(\mathrm{A},\mathrm{A}')$ **then**
     if $\mathit{linear}(\mathrm{T})$ **then** $\mathit{ann}_\Delta(\mathrm{A}') \setminus \{f\}$
     else $\mathit{ann}_\Delta(\mathrm{A}') \setminus \{\ell, f\}$
     else $\mathit{ann}_\Delta(\mathrm{A}')$

Example 6

1. **T is ground**

$$\left\langle \begin{array}{l} \{\underline{a = \mathbf{A}_1}, X = \mathbf{A}_2, Y = \mathbf{A}_3\}, \\ \{\{\mathbf{A}_1, \mathbf{A}_2, \mathbf{A}_3\}, \{\mathbf{A}_3^f\}\} \end{array} \right\rangle \propto \{a = Z_1, X = f(Z_1), Y = Z_1\}$$

$$\downarrow \qquad\qquad \wr\wr$$

$$\langle \{X = \mathbf{A}_2, Y = \mathbf{A}_3\}, \{\{\mathbf{A}_3^\ell\}\} \rangle \propto \{X = f(a), Y = a\}$$

2. **A is free, T is non-linear**

$$\left\langle \begin{array}{l} \{\underline{f(X,X) = \mathbf{A}_1}, Y = \mathbf{A}_2, U = \mathbf{A}_3\}, \\ \{\{\mathbf{A}_1^f, \mathbf{A}_2^\ell, \mathbf{A}_3^f,\}\} \end{array} \right\rangle \propto \{f(X,X) = Z, Y = g(Z), U = Z)\}$$

$$\downarrow \qquad\qquad \wr\wr$$

$$\left\langle \begin{array}{l} \{X = \mathbf{A}_{1,1}, Y = \mathbf{A}_2, U = \mathbf{A}_3\}, \\ \{\{\mathbf{A}_{1,1}^f, \mathbf{A}_2, \mathbf{A}_3\}\} \end{array} \right\rangle \propto \left\{ \begin{array}{l} X = Z_1, Y = g(f(Z_1, Z_1)), \\ U = f(Z_1, Z_1) \end{array} \right\}$$

3. **A is linear, T is non-linear (observe that the new abstract variables are linear and both linearity and freeness are lost in all abstract variables which possibly share with $\mathbf{A}_1$)**

$$\left\langle \begin{array}{l} \{\underline{f(g(X,X),X) = \mathbf{A}_1}, V = \mathbf{A}_3, U = \mathbf{A}_2\}, \\ \{\{\mathbf{A}_1^\ell, \mathbf{A}_2^f\}, \{\mathbf{A}_1^\ell, \mathbf{A}_3^f\}\} \end{array} \right\rangle \propto \left\{ \begin{array}{l} f(g(X,X),X) = f(Z_1, h(Z_2)), \\ V = Z_2, U = Z_1 \end{array} \right\}$$

$$\downarrow \qquad\qquad \wr\wr$$

$$\left\langle \begin{array}{l} \{X = \mathbf{A}_{1,1}, V = \mathbf{A}_3, U = \mathbf{A}_2\}, \\ \{\{\mathbf{A}_{1,1}^\ell, \mathbf{A}_2\}, \{\mathbf{A}_{1,1}^\ell, \mathbf{A}_3\}, \{\mathbf{A}_{1,1}^\ell, \mathbf{A}_2, \mathbf{A}_3\}\} \end{array} \right\rangle \propto \left\{ \begin{array}{l} X = h(Z_2), V = Z_2, \\ U = g(h(Z_2), h(Z_2)) \end{array} \right\}$$

4. **A is 'any', T is non-linear**

$$\left\langle \begin{array}{l} \{\underline{f(X,X) = \mathbf{A}_1}, U = \mathbf{A}_2, V = \mathbf{A}_3\}, \\ \{\{\mathbf{A}_1, \mathbf{A}_2^f\}, \{\mathbf{A}_1, \mathbf{A}_3^f,\}\} \end{array} \right\rangle \propto \left\{ \begin{array}{l} f(X,X) = f(Z_1, h(Z_2, Z_2)), \\ U = Z_1, V = Z_2) \end{array} \right\}$$

$$\downarrow \qquad\qquad \wr\wr$$

$$\left\langle \begin{array}{l} \{X = \mathbf{A}_{1,1}, U = \mathbf{A}_2, V = \mathbf{A}_3\}, \\ \{\{\mathbf{A}_{1,1}, \mathbf{A}_2\}, \{\mathbf{A}_{1,1}, \mathbf{A}_3\}, \{\mathbf{A}_{1,1}, \mathbf{A}_2, \mathbf{A}_3\}\} \end{array} \right\rangle \propto \left\{ \begin{array}{l} X = h(Z_2, Z_2), \\ U = h(Z_2, Z_2), V = Z_2 \end{array} \right\}$$

5. **A is 'any', T is linear**

$$\left\langle \begin{array}{l} \{\underline{f(X,Y) = \mathbf{A}_1}, U = \mathbf{A}_2\}, \\ \{\{\mathbf{A}_1, \mathbf{A}_2^f\}\} \end{array} \right\rangle \propto \left\{ \begin{array}{l} f(X,Y) = f(g(Z), g(Z)), \\ U = Z \end{array} \right\}$$

$$\downarrow \qquad\qquad \wr\wr$$

$$\left\langle \begin{array}{l} \{X = \mathbf{A}_{1,1}, Y = \mathbf{A}_{1,2}, U = \mathbf{A}_2\}, \\ \{\{\mathbf{A}_{1,1}, \mathbf{A}_2^\ell\}, \{\mathbf{A}_{1,2}, \mathbf{A}_2^\ell\}, \{\mathbf{A}_{1,1}, \mathbf{A}_{1,2}, \mathbf{A}_2^\ell\}\} \end{array} \right\rangle \propto \{X = g(Z), Y = g(Z), U = Z\}$$

Reducing equations of the form $X = \mathbf{A}$

Equations of the form $X = \mathbf{A}$ are maintained in the pseudo solved form as long as X does not appear elsewhere as a left hand side. The following rule is applied to reduce the number of occurrences of a variable X occurring in the left side of an equation. The abstract variables participating in the reduction must have single occurrences in the equations of the system.

6. $\langle X = \mathbf{A}_1, X = \mathbf{A}_2 :: \mathsf{AEqs}, \Delta\rangle \stackrel{\textbf{shuffle,solve\&restrict}}{\longrightarrow} \langle X = \mathbf{A}_1 :: \mathsf{AEqs}, \Delta'\rangle$ where
   - $\Delta' =$ if $ground_\Delta(\mathbf{A}_1) \vee ground_\Delta(\mathbf{A}_2)$ then $\bar{\Delta}(\mathbf{A}_1, \mathbf{A}_2)$
     else

$$\bar{\Delta}(\mathbf{A}_1, \mathbf{A}_2) \cup \left\{ (S_{\mathbf{A}_1} \cup S_{\mathbf{A}_2}) \setminus \{\mathbf{A}_2\} \;\middle|\; \begin{array}{l} i, j \in \{1, 2\},\ i \neq j, \\ \text{if } \ linear_\Delta(\mathbf{A}_i) \wedge \\ \qquad\qquad \neg share_\Delta(\mathbf{A}_i, \mathbf{A}_j) \\ \text{then } \ S_{\mathbf{A}_j} \in \Delta(\mathbf{A}_j) \\ \text{else } \ S_{\mathbf{A}_j} = \cup\, SS \text{ where} \\ \qquad SS \subseteq \Delta(\mathbf{A}_j), SS \neq \emptyset \end{array} \right\}$$

   - for $\mathbf{A}' \in avars(\Delta')$:
     $ann_{\Delta'}(\mathbf{A}') =$
       if $\mathbf{A}' = \mathbf{A}_1$ then
         if $free_\Delta(\mathbf{A}_1) \wedge free_\Delta(\mathbf{A}_2)$ then $\{f, \ell\}$
         else if $linear_\Delta(\mathbf{A}_1) \wedge linear_\Delta(\mathbf{A}_2) \wedge \neg share_\Delta(\mathbf{A}_1, \mathbf{A}_2)$ then $\{\ell\}$
         else $\emptyset$
       else if
         $(\neg share_\Delta(\mathbf{A}_1, \mathbf{A}') \wedge \neg share_\Delta(\mathbf{A}_2, \mathbf{A}')) \vee$
         $(free_\Delta(\mathbf{A}_1) \wedge free_\Delta(\mathbf{A}_2) \wedge$
             $(free_\Delta(\mathbf{A}') \vee \neg share_\Delta(\mathbf{A}_1, \mathbf{A}') \vee \neg share_\Delta(\mathbf{A}_2, \mathbf{A}'))) \vee$
         $(free_\Delta(\mathbf{A}_2) \wedge \neg share_\Delta(\mathbf{A}_2, \mathbf{A}')) \vee (free_\Delta(\mathbf{A}_1) \wedge \neg share_\Delta(\mathbf{A}_1, \mathbf{A}'))$
           then $ann_\Delta(\mathbf{A}')$
       else if
         $(linear_\Delta(\mathbf{A}_2) \wedge \neg share_\Delta(\mathbf{A}_2, \mathbf{A}')) \vee (linear_\Delta(\mathbf{A}_1) \wedge \neg share_\Delta(\mathbf{A}_1, \mathbf{A}')) \vee$
         $(free_\Delta(\mathbf{A}') \wedge (free_\Delta(\mathbf{A}_2) \wedge linear_\Delta(\mathbf{A}_1)) \vee$
           $(free_\Delta(\mathbf{A}_1) \wedge linear_\Delta(\mathbf{A}_2)))$ then $ann_\Delta(\mathbf{A}') \setminus \{f\}$
       else $\emptyset$

Example 7

$$\left\langle \left\{ \begin{array}{l} \underline{X = \mathbf{A}_1}, \underline{X = \mathbf{A}_2}, \\ Y_1 = \mathbf{A}_3, Y_2 = \mathbf{A}_4, \\ U_1 = \mathbf{A}_5, U_2 = \mathbf{A}_6 \end{array} \right\}, \left\{ \begin{array}{l} \{\mathbf{A}_1, \mathbf{A}_3^f\}, \{\mathbf{A}_1, \mathbf{A}_4^\ell\}, \\ \{\mathbf{A}_2^\ell, \mathbf{A}_5^f\}, \{\mathbf{A}_2^\ell, \mathbf{A}_6^\ell\} \end{array} \right\} \right\rangle \propto \left\{ \begin{array}{l} X = f(g(Z_1, Z_1), Z_2), \\ X = f(Z_3, h(Z_4)), \\ Y_1 = Z_2, Y_2 = h(Z_1), \\ U_1 = Z_3, U_2 = h(Z_4) \end{array} \right\}$$

$$\downarrow \qquad\qquad\qquad\qquad\qquad\qquad \parallel$$

$$\left\langle \left\{ \begin{array}{l} X = \mathbf{A}_1, \\ Y_1 = \mathbf{A}_3, Y_2 = \mathbf{A}_4, \\ U_1 = \mathbf{A}_5, U_2 = \mathbf{A}_6 \end{array} \right\}, \left\{ \begin{array}{l} \{\mathbf{A}_1, \mathbf{A}_3^\ell, \mathbf{A}_5\}, \\ \{\mathbf{A}_1, \mathbf{A}_3^\ell, \mathbf{A}_6\}, \\ \{\mathbf{A}_1, \mathbf{A}_3^\ell, \mathbf{A}_5, \mathbf{A}_6\}, \\ \{\mathbf{A}_1, \mathbf{A}_4^\ell, \mathbf{A}_5\}, \\ \{\mathbf{A}_1, \mathbf{A}_4^\ell, \mathbf{A}_6\}, \\ \{\mathbf{A}_1, \mathbf{A}_4^\ell, \mathbf{A}_5, \mathbf{A}_6\} \end{array} \right\} \right\rangle \propto \left\{ \begin{array}{l} X = f(g(Z_1, Z_1), h(Z_4)), \\ Y_1 = h(Z_4), Y_2 = h(Z_1), \\ U_1 = g(Z_1, Z_1), U_2 = h(Z_4) \end{array} \right\}$$

While linearity is preserved for $\mathbf{A}_3$ and $\mathbf{A}_4$, it is lost for $\mathbf{A}_5$ and $\mathbf{A}_6$. Taking $f(g(Z_1, Z_2), Z_1)$ for $\mathbf{A}_1$ in the original concrete equation illustrates the need for $\{\mathbf{A}_1, \mathbf{A}_4^\ell, \mathbf{A}_5, \mathbf{A}_6\}$ in the transformed sharing component.

Reducing equations of the form $\mathbf{T} = \mathbf{A}$ (multiple occurrences of A)

The previous set of rules did not apply to the case in which the abstract variable occurring in an abstract equation system has multiple occurrences. The following rule reduces the number of occurrences of an abstract variable:

7. $\langle \mathbf{T}_1 = \mathbf{A}, \mathbf{T}_2 = \mathbf{A} :: \mathsf{AEqs}, \Delta \rangle \overset{\text{shuffle}}{\rightarrow} \langle \mathbf{T}_1 = \mathbf{T}_2, \mathbf{T}_1 = \mathbf{A} :: \mathsf{AEqs}, \Delta \rangle$.

Example 8

$$\begin{array}{ccc}
\left\langle \left\{ \begin{array}{l} \underline{f(a,X) = \mathbf{A}_1}, U = \mathbf{A}_2, \\ \underline{f(Y,b) = \mathbf{A}_1}, V = \mathbf{A}_3 \end{array} \right\}, \left\{ \begin{array}{l} \{\mathbf{A}_1, \mathbf{A}_2^f\}, \\ \{\mathbf{A}_1, \mathbf{A}_3^f\} \end{array} \right\} \right\rangle & \propto & \left\{ \begin{array}{l} f(a,X) = f(Z_1,Z_2), U = Z_1, \\ f(Y,b) = f(Z_1,Z_2), V = Z_2 \end{array} \right\} \\
\downarrow & & \wr\wr \\
\left\langle \left\{ \begin{array}{l} f(a,X) = f(Y,b), U = \mathbf{A}_2, \\ f(a,X) = \mathbf{A}_1, V = \mathbf{A}_3 \end{array} \right\}, \left\{ \begin{array}{l} \{\mathbf{A}_1, \mathbf{A}_2^f\}, \\ \{\mathbf{A}_1, \mathbf{A}_3^f\} \end{array} \right\} \right\rangle & \propto & \left\{ \begin{array}{l} f(a,X) = f(Y,b), U = Z_1, \\ f(a,X) = f(Z_1,Z_2), V = Z_2 \end{array} \right\}
\end{array}$$

Psuedo solved form

Repeated application of rules 1 – 7 provides an abstract equation system of the form $\langle \{X_i = \mathbf{A}_i\}_{i=1}^m :: \mathsf{Eqs}, \Delta \rangle$ where $\{X_1, \ldots, X_m\}$ and $\{\mathbf{A}_1, \ldots, \mathbf{A}_m\}$ are sets of variables and abstract variables respectively, Eqs is a set of <u>concrete</u> equations in solved form, and the left side of an equation in Eqs is not equal to a variable X_i $(1 \leq i \leq m)$. An abstract equation system of this form is said to be in *pseudo solved form*.

Reducing the pseudo solved form

The following rule is applied to reduce an abstract system in pseudo solved form to an abstract system in *solved form*. Namely, an abstract system which describes only concrete systems which are in solved form.

8. $\langle \{X_i = \mathbf{A}_i\}_{i=1}^m :: \mathsf{Eqs}, \Delta \rangle \overset{\text{abstract-subst}}{\rightarrow} \langle \{X_i = \mathbf{A}_i\}_{i=1}^m :: \mathsf{Eqs}\, \sigma, \Delta \rangle$
   where $\sigma = \{X_1/\mathbf{A}_1, \ldots, X_m/\mathbf{A}_m\}$

Strictly speaking, the result of this transition is not an abstract equation system as it may potentially involve equations with mixed terms. However, the definition of description is applicable. Moreover the following rules remove mixed terms.

Example 9

$$\begin{array}{ccc}
\langle \{ \underline{X = \mathbf{A}_1}, Y = g(X,U,X) \}, \{ \{\mathbf{A}_1^f\} \} \rangle & \propto & \{ X = f(Z_1), Y = g(X,U,X) \} \\
\downarrow & & \wr\wr \\
\langle \{ X = \mathbf{A}_1, Y = g(\mathbf{A}_1,U,\mathbf{A}_1) \}, \{ \{\mathbf{A}_1^f\} \} \rangle & \propto & \{ X = f(Z_1), Y = g(f(Z_1),U,f(Z_1)) \}
\end{array}$$

Abstracting the solved form

Recall that a mixed term is a term which involves variables as well as abstract variables. The following transition is applied to remove variables occurring in mixed terms.

9. $\langle \mathsf{AEqs}, \Delta \rangle \overset{\text{remove-var}}{\rightarrow} \langle X = \mathbf{A} :: \mathsf{AEqs}[X/\mathbf{A}], \Delta \cup \{\{\mathbf{A}^f\}\} \rangle$
   if X occurs in a mixed term (which is not a term) in some equation of AEqs and $\mathbf{A}$ is a fresh abstract variable.

Repeated application of Rule 9 replaces all variables in mixed terms by abstract variables hence transforming mixed terms to abstract terms. From here on, we assume without loss of generality that mixed terms do not occur in abstract equation systems.

Example 10

$$\left\langle \begin{Bmatrix} X = \mathrm{A}_1, \underline{Y = g(\mathrm{A}_1, U, \mathrm{A}_1)} \}, \\ \{\mathrm{A}_1^\ell\} \end{Bmatrix} \right\rangle \propto \begin{Bmatrix} X = f(Z_1), \\ Y = g(f(Z_1), U, f(Z_1)) \end{Bmatrix}$$

$$\downarrow \qquad\qquad\qquad \wr\wr$$

$$\left\langle \begin{Bmatrix} U = \mathrm{A}_2, X = \mathrm{A}_1, \underline{Y = g(\mathrm{A}_1, \mathrm{A}_2, \mathrm{A}_1)} \}, \\ \{\mathrm{A}_1^\ell\}, \{\mathrm{A}_2^f\} \end{Bmatrix} \right\rangle \propto \begin{Bmatrix} U = Z_2, X = f(Z_1), \\ Y = g(f(Z_1), Z_2, f(Z_1)) \end{Bmatrix}$$

Let $\mathcal{T}$ be an abstract term occurring in an abstract equation system $\langle \mathsf{AEqs}, \Delta \rangle$. We denote: $free_\Delta(\mathcal{T})$, if $\mathcal{T} = \mathrm{A}$ and $free_\Delta(\mathrm{A})$; and $linear_\Delta(\mathcal{T})$, if $\forall \mathrm{A}, \mathrm{A}' \in avars(\mathcal{T})$, (i) $linear_\Delta(\mathrm{A})$, (ii) if A occurs more than once in $\mathcal{T}$ then $ground_\Delta(\mathrm{A})$, and (iii) $\neg share_\Delta(\mathrm{A}, \mathrm{A}')$. An abstract system involving abstract terms is abstracted using the following rule

10. $\langle \mathsf{AEqs}, \Delta \rangle \overset{\text{abstract}}{\rightarrow} \langle \mathsf{AEqs}', \Delta' \rangle$
    where $\{\mathcal{T}_1, \ldots, \mathcal{T}_n\}$ is the set of non variable abstract terms occurring (on the right sides of the equations) in AEqs $\mathrm{A}_1, \ldots, \mathrm{A}_n$ are fresh abstract variables and
    - AEqs' is obtained by replacing each $\mathcal{T}_i$ in AEqs by the corresponding A_i;
    - $\Delta' = \{ S \cup \{ \mathrm{A}_i \mid avars(\mathcal{T}_i) \cap S \neq \emptyset,\ 1 \le i \le n \} \mid S \in \Delta \}$; and
    - $ann_{\Delta'}(\mathrm{A}) =$ **if** $\mathrm{A} \in \{\mathrm{A}_1, \ldots, \mathrm{A}_n\}$ **then**
      if $free_\Delta(\mathcal{T}_i)$ **then** $\{f, \ell\}$
      else if $linear_\Delta(\mathcal{T}_i)$ **then** $\{\ell\}$
      else $\emptyset$
      else $ann_\Delta(\mathrm{A})$

Example 11

$$\left\langle \begin{Bmatrix} U = \mathrm{A}_2, X = \mathrm{A}_1, \underline{Y = g(\mathrm{A}_1, \mathrm{A}_2, \mathrm{A}_1)} \}, \\ \{\mathrm{A}_1^\ell\}, \{\mathrm{A}_2^f\} \end{Bmatrix} \right\rangle \propto \begin{Bmatrix} U = Z_2, X = f(Z_1), \\ Y = g(f(Z_1), Z_2, f(Z_1)) \end{Bmatrix}$$

$$\downarrow \qquad\qquad\qquad \wr\wr$$

$$\left\langle \begin{Bmatrix} U = \mathrm{A}_2, X = \mathrm{A}_1, Y = \mathrm{A}_3 \}, \\ \{\mathrm{A}_1^\ell, \mathrm{A}_3\}, \{\mathrm{A}_2^f, \mathrm{A}_3\} \end{Bmatrix} \right\rangle \propto \begin{Bmatrix} U = Z_2, X = f(Z_1), \\ Y = g(f(Z_1), Z_2, f(Z_1)) \end{Bmatrix}$$

4 Examples

The following examples are adapted from [9].

Example 12

$$\left\langle \begin{matrix} \left\{ \begin{matrix} X_1 = \mathrm{A}_1, X_2 = \mathrm{A}_2, X_3 = \mathrm{A}_3, X_4 = \mathrm{A}_4, X_5 = \mathrm{A}_5, X_6 = \mathrm{A}_6, \underline{f(X_1, X_2) = Y_1}, \\ \underline{f(X_3, X_4) = Y_1}, \underline{X_3 = a}, \underline{X_5 = Y_2}, \underline{X_6 = Y_2}, \underline{X_6 = f(Y_1, Y_3)} \end{matrix} \right\}, \\ \{\{\mathrm{A}_1^f, \mathrm{A}_2\}, \{\mathrm{A}_2\}, \{\mathrm{A}_3^f\}, \{\mathrm{A}_5^f\}, \{\mathrm{A}_6^f\}\} \end{matrix} \right\rangle \rightarrow^*$$

[rules 1–4; the sharing component is not effected.]

$$\left\langle \begin{matrix} \left\{ \begin{matrix} X_1 = a, X_3 = a, X_4 = X_2, X_5 = f(f(a, X_2), Y_3), X_6 = f(f(a, X_2), Y_3), \\ Y_1 = f(a, X_2), Y_2 = f(f(a, X_2), Y_3), \underline{a = \mathrm{A}_1}, \underline{a = \mathrm{A}_3}, X_2 = \mathrm{A}_4, X_2 = \mathrm{A}_2, \\ f(f(a, X_2), Y_3) = \mathrm{A}_5, f(f(a, X_2), Y_3) = \mathrm{A}_6 \end{matrix} \right\}, \\ \{\{\mathrm{A}_1^f, \mathrm{A}_2\}, \{\mathrm{A}_2\}, \{\mathrm{A}_3^f\}, \{\mathrm{A}_5^f\}, \{\mathrm{A}_6^f\}\} \end{matrix} \right\rangle \rightarrow^*$$

[rule 5; A_1 and A_3 become ground.]

$$\left\langle \begin{array}{l} \left\{ \begin{array}{l} X_1 = a, X_3 = a, X_4 = X_2, X_5 = f(f(a, X_2), Y_3), X_6 = f(f(a, X_2), Y_3), \\ Y_1 = f(a, X_2), Y_2 = f(f(a, X_2), Y_3), \underline{X_2 = \mathbf{A}_2}, \underline{X_2 = \mathbf{A}_4}, \\ f(f(a, X_2), Y_3) = \mathbf{A}_5, f(f(a, X_2), Y_3) = \mathbf{A}_6 \end{array} \right\}, \\ \{\{\mathbf{A}_2\}, \{\mathbf{A}_5^f\}, \{\mathbf{A}_6^f\}\} \end{array} \right\rangle \rightarrow$$

[rule 6; $\mathbf{A}_2$ becomes ground.]

$$\left\langle \begin{array}{l} \left\{ \begin{array}{l} X_1 = a, X_3 = a, X_4 = X_2, X_5 = f(f(a, X_2), Y_3), X_6 = f(f(a, X_2), Y_3), \\ Y_1 = f(a, X_2), Y_2 = f(f(a, X_2), Y_3), \\ X_2 = \mathbf{A}_4, \underline{f(f(a, X_2), Y_3) = \mathbf{A}_5}, \underline{f(f(a, X_2), Y_3) = \mathbf{A}_6} \end{array} \right\}, \\ \{\{\mathbf{A}_5^f\}, \{\mathbf{A}_6^f\}\} \end{array} \right\rangle \rightarrow^*$$

[rules 5 and 6; $\mathbf{A}_{5,1}$ and $\mathbf{A}_{6,1}$ remain free.]

$$\left\langle \begin{array}{l} \left\{ \begin{array}{l} X_1 = a, X_3 = a, X_4 = X_2, X_5 = f(f(a, X_2), Y_3), X_6 = f(f(a, X_2), Y_3), \\ Y_1 = f(a, X_2), Y_2 = f(f(a, X_2), Y_3), \underline{X_2 = \mathbf{A}_4}, \underline{X_2 = \mathbf{A}_{5,1}}, Y_3 = \mathbf{A}_{5,2} \end{array} \right\}, \\ \{\{\mathbf{A}_{5,1}^f\}, \{\mathbf{A}_{5,2}^f\}\} \end{array} \right\rangle \rightarrow$$

[rule 6; $\mathbf{A}_{5,1}$ becomes ground.]

$$\left\langle \begin{array}{l} \left\{ \begin{array}{l} X_1 = a, X_3 = a, X_4 = X_2, X_5 = f(f(a, X_2), Y_3), X_6 = f(f(a, X_2), Y_3), \\ Y_1 = f(a, X_2), Y_2 = f(f(a, X_2), Y_3), \underline{X_2 = \mathbf{A}_4}, \underline{Y_3 = \mathbf{A}_{5,2}} \end{array} \right\}, \\ \{\{\mathbf{A}_{5,2}^f\}\} \end{array} \right\rangle \rightarrow^*$$

[pseudo solved form.] [rule 8.]

$$\left\langle \begin{array}{l} \left\{ \begin{array}{l} X_1 = a, X_3 = a, X_4 = \mathbf{A}_4, \underline{X_5 = f(f(a, \mathbf{A}_4), \mathbf{A}_{5,2})}, \underline{X_6 = f(f(a, \mathbf{A}_4,), \mathbf{A}_{5,2})}, \\ \underline{Y_1 = f(a, \mathbf{A}_4)}, \underline{Y_2 = f(f(a, \mathbf{A}_4), \mathbf{A}_{5,2})}, X_2 = \mathbf{A}_4, Y_3 = \mathbf{A}_{5,2} \end{array} \right\}, \\ \{\{\mathbf{A}_{5,2}^f\}\} \end{array} \right\rangle \rightarrow$$

[solved form (mixed terms).] [rule 10.]

$$\langle \{ X_1 = a, X_3 = a, X_4 = \mathbf{A}_4, X_5 = \mathbf{A}_7, X_6 = \mathbf{A}_7, Y_1 = \mathbf{A}_8, Y_2 = \mathbf{A}_7, X_2 = \mathbf{A}_4, Y_3 = \mathbf{A}_{5,2} \}, \{\{\mathbf{A}_{5,2}^f, \mathbf{A}_7^f\}\} \rangle$$

[solved form (no mixed terms).]

This shows that X_1 and X_3 are ground (and equal), that X_2 and X_4 are ground (and equal), that Y_1 is ground , that X_5, X_6 and Y_2 are not free (and equal), that Y_3 is free and that X_5, X_6, and Y_2 are linear terms which can share Y_3.

Example 13

$$\langle \left\{ \begin{array}{l} \underline{X_1 = \mathbf{A}_1}, X_2 = \mathbf{A}_2, X_3 = \mathbf{A}_3, \\ X_4 = \mathbf{A}_4, \underline{X_1 = \mathbf{A}_5}, X_2 = \mathbf{A}_6 \end{array} \right\}, \{\{\mathbf{A}_1^f\}, \{\mathbf{A}_3^f\}, \{\mathbf{A}_2^f, \mathbf{A}_4^f\}, \{\mathbf{A}_5\}, \{\mathbf{A}_6\}\} \rangle \stackrel{6}{\rightarrow}$$

$$\langle \left\{ \begin{array}{l} X_1 = \mathbf{A}_1, \underline{X_2 = \mathbf{A}_2}, X_3 = \mathbf{A}_3, \\ X_4 = \mathbf{A}_4, \underline{X_2 = \mathbf{A}_6} \end{array} \right\}, \{\{\mathbf{A}_1\}, \{\mathbf{A}_3^f\}, \{\mathbf{A}_2^f, \mathbf{A}_4^f\}, \{\mathbf{A}_2\}, \{\mathbf{A}_6\}\} \rangle \stackrel{6}{\rightarrow}$$

$$\langle \{ X_1 = \mathbf{A}_1, X_2 = \mathbf{A}_2, X_3 = \mathbf{A}_3, X_4 = \mathbf{A}_4 \}, \{\{\mathbf{A}_1\}, \{\mathbf{A}_3^f\}, \{\mathbf{A}_2, \mathbf{A}_4\}\} \rangle$$

This correctly shows that only X_3 remains free and that X_2 and X_4 can be non-linear.

5 Conclusion

We have presented a powerful abstract unification algorithm for deriving sharing and freeness information together with groundness and linearity. The algorithm appears to be at least as precise as other previously proposed algorithms such as [1, 3, 4, 9, 11]. The algorithm is formalised as a transition system which reduces a set of abstract equations to an abstract solved form. In this approach each transition can be analysed and justified seperately. A formal proof of correctness, an implementation of the algorithm and an experimental evaluation of its precision are underway.

Acknowledgements We acknowledge the comments of M. García de la Banda, Anne Mulkers and the anonymous referees of a previous version of this paper. We thank Joost for typing the first draft.

References

1. M. Codish, D. Dams, G. File, M. Bruynooghe. Freeness Analysis for Logic Programs - And Correctness? *Proc. of Tenth Int. Conf. on Logic Programming*, Budapest, 1993.
2. M. Codish, D. Dams, and E. Yardeni. Derivation and safety of an abstract algorithm for groundness and aliasing analysis. In K. Furukawa, editor, *Proc. Eighth Int. Conf. on Logic Programming*, pages 79- 93. MIT Press, 1991.
3. M. Codish, A. Mulkers, M. Bruynooghe, M. García de la Banda and M. Hermenegildo. Improving abstract interpretations by combining domains. In *Proc. ACM Symposium on Partial Evaluation and Semantics Based Program Manipulation*. 1993.
4. A. Cortesi and G. Filé. Abstract interpretation of logic programs: an abstract domain for groundness, sharing, freeness and compoundness analysis. In P. Hudak and N. Jones, editors, *Proc. ACM Symposium on Partial Evaluation and Semantics Based Program Manipulation*. SIGPLAN NOTICES vol. 26, n.11, 1991.
5. P. Cousot and R. Cousot. Abstract interpretation: a unified lattice model for static analysis of programs by construction or approximation of fixpoints. In *Proc. Fourth ACM symp. on Principles of Programming Languages*, pages 238–252, Los Angeles, California, 1977.
6. D. Jacobs and A. Langen. Static analysis of logic programs for independent and-parallelism. *Journal of Logic Programming*, 13(2 and 3):291–314, July 1992.
7. J.-L. Lassez, M.J. Maher, and K. Marriott. Unification revisited. In J. Minker, editor, *Foundations of Deductive Databases and Logic Programming*. Morgan Kauffmann, 1987.
8. A. Martelli and U. Montanari. An efficient unification algorithm. *ACM Transactions on Programming Languages and Systems*, 4(2):258–282, April 1982.
9. K. Muthukumar and M. Hermenegildo. Combined determination of sharing and freeness of program variables through abstract interpretation. In K. Furukawa, editor, *Proc. Eighth International Conference on Logic Programming*, pages 49–63. MIT Press, 1991.
10. H. Søndergaard. An application of abstract interpretation of logic programs: occur check reduction. In B. Robinet and R. Wilhelm, editors, *ESOP'86 Proc. European Symposium on Programming*, LNCS 213, pages 327–338. Springer-Verlag, 1986.
11. R. Sundararajan and J. Conery. An abstract interpretation scheme for groundness, freeness, and sharing analysis of logic programs. *Proc. Twelfth FST & TCS Conf.*, New Delhi, Dec. 1992.

Synthesis of directionality information for functional logic programs

Johan Boye *Jukka Paakki* * *Jan Małuszyński*

Department of Computer and Information Science
Linköping University
S-581 83 Linköping, Sweden
E-mail: { johbo, jukpa, janma}@ida.liu.se

Abstract. Many functional logic programming languages are based on reduction of functional expressions. This feature is also provided by many Prolog systems that offer the facility of calling external functions written in non-logic programming languages. A basic requirement is usually that the arguments of the functions must be ground at invocation time, otherwise an error is reported, or the call is *delayed* until the arguments are sufficiently instantiated. The drawback of the latter method is twofold: (1) the arguments might never be instantiated, and (2) the dynamic checks made by the delaying mechanism are expensive. This paper presents a method, which for a given program identifies a class of atomic goals for which (1) will not occur. Moreover, we describe a method for transforming a program into an equivalent program, for which dynamic delays are avoided. The static analysis is based on the concept of *dependency graphs* over an automatically annotated program, a technique originally introduced in connection of attribute grammars.

1 Introduction

Many logic programming systems are enriched with mechanisms for expressing functional computations. For instance, most Prolog systems have facilities for invocation of built-in arithmetics and procedures written in non-logic programming languages (like C). This is very useful, or even necessary, for writing realistic programs. However, the use of the extensions requires special care, since an external procedure can only be executed if its arguments are ground.

The usual solution to this problem is to perform a dynamic groundness test at invocation time. If the arguments of the call are ground the procedure is executed, otherwise two solutions are possible. The first solution, used by Prolog arithmetic, is to abort the execution and report a runtime error. The other, used e.g. in [1, 11]), is to *delay* (to freeze) the call until the arguments become sufficiently instantiated.

Both solutions have drawbacks. Aborting the execution causes incompleteness with respect to the declarative semantics. Introducing delays solves the problem of immediate abort, but makes the analysis of execution even more complicated. A delayed call can be seen as a constraint, whose satisfiability is being checked only when the

* On leave from the Department of Computer Science, University of Jyväskylä, Finland.

arguments of the call become ground. The computation may succeed without grounding the arguments, thus leaving possibly unsatisfiable constraints, or it may loop even if the accumulated constraints are unsatisfiable. Another drawback is the cost of the dynamic check performed and the cost of freezing and unfreezing of the calls.

To summarize, two questions addressed in this paper are of particular importance:

1. *Operational completeness*: A program is operationally complete iff no delayed call remains non-ground on success of the computation. Generally, operational completeness depends on the initial goal. We propose a method that guarantees operational completeness (if possible), if the indicated arguments of the initial goal are ground.
2. *Delay-freeness*: For some programs, all invocations may be ground under the standard (Prolog) execution strategy, so that no dynamic delay is needed. We present a method that transforms the program into an equivalent one, which is delay-free provided that the initial goal satisfies the operational completeness requirement.

The programs considered in this paper are collections of definite clauses, which may contain calls to external functions. The semantics of the language is based on the assumption that any ground call evaluates to a ground constructor term. Under this assumption the declarative semantics of the language is constructed as for equational logic programs (for more details see e.g. [10]). The operational semantics is an extension of SLD-resolution, where term unification is enriched with evaluation of ground calls. Non-ground calls selected for unification are delayed and retained in form of constraints until their arguments become ground (for a formal definition of this kind of resolution, see [2]).

Before describing our method, we first present an example with complex data dependencies. The example will be used throughout the paper.

Example 1. We consider a small and simplified part of a typesetting program, which typesets text tables. The input consists of a description of the table as a list of lists, for instance:

```
[[This, is, some, text], [Another, line, of, text]]
```

The produced output consists of a list of commands for a typesetting device:

```
[[put(1,1,This), put(1,8,is), put(1,12,some), put(1,16,text)],
 [put(2,1,Another), put(2,8,line), put(2,12,of), put(2,16,text)]]
```

where the two first arguments to put represent the line and the indentation on the line. In this case, the output list of typesetting commands represents the table:

This	is	some	text
Another	line	of	text

Note that every column is supposed to have the width of the longest word in the column. We now describe our program. First we consider the predicate `typesetrow/6`, which typesets one row of the table.

```
(C1) typesetrow(_, _, [], [], [], []).

(C2) typesetrow(Line, Ind, [Text|Ts], [MaxWid|Ms], [size(Text)|Ss],
                [put(Line, Ind, Text)|Insts]) :-
        typesetrow(Line, Ind+MaxWid, Ts, Ms, Ss, Insts).
```

Here Ind+MaxWid and size(Text) are functional expressions, the latter returning the number of characters in Text. The arguments represent (from left to right) the current line, the current indentation on the line, the description of one row of the table (for instance [This, is, some, text]), the width of the widest element in each column, the number of characters in each element of the row, and the output list of typesetting instructions.

typesetrow/6 is called from typesettab/6:

```
(C3) typesettab(_, _, [], X, X, []).

(C4) typesettab(Line,Ind,[Row|Rows],MaxWidths,MaxSoFar,[InstRow|Insts]) :-
        typesetrow(Line, Ind, Row, MaxWidths, Widths, InstRow),
        compute_max(Widths, MaxSoFar, NewMaxSoFar),
        typesettab(Line+1, Ind, Rows, MaxWidths, NewMaxSoFar, Insts).
```

Here Line+1 is a functional expression. The arguments represent (from left to right) the current line, the current indentation on the line, the description of the whole table, the width of the widest element in each column, the width of the widest element in each column in the rows processed so far, and the output list of typesetting instructions (for simplicity the output list is not flattened).

Here compute_max is a predicate that, given two lists of integers $[i_1, \ldots, i_n]$ and $[j_1, \ldots, j_n]$, returns the list $[max(i_1, j_1), \ldots, max(i_n, j_n)]$ (we omit the definition of compute_max).

Note that the maximum width of each column cannot be computed until the whole table has been processed. This means that in the second clause of typesetrow, the value for MaxWid in the functional expression Ind+MaxWid will not be computed when execution reaches this point. Because of the non-trivial right-to-left dataflow in the program, it seems like we are obliged to dynamically delay the evaluation of Ind+MaxWid. However, we will show that this program can be transformed to avoid all the dynamic delays. □

Another way to avoid dynamic delays for the program above would be to apply a *multi-pass* execution scheme [12].

2 Preliminaries

In what follows, we let P be a program. We let the clauses of P be numbered $C_1, C_2, \ldots$, and the atoms of every clause be numbered $0, 1, \ldots$, so that the 0:th atom is the head, the 1st atom is the leftmost atom in the body and so forth. The function symbols of P are divided into two disjoint categories: the *constructors* and the *defined symbols*, where the latter are associated with external functions. Terms whose principal functor is a defined symbol are called *functional terms*.

Let q be a predicate in P. We let the argument positions of q be numbered $1, 2, \ldots$, and denote the k:th argument position in q with q_k. Let $\mathcal{A}rgpos(q)$ be the set of argument positions in q, and let $\mathcal{A}rgpos(P) = \bigcup_{q \text{ in } P} \mathcal{A}rgpos(q)$.

Let C_i be a clause in P of the form $a_0 :- a_1, \ldots, a_n$. We can now unambiguously refer to the k:th argument position in a_j with the tuple (C_i, j, q, k), where q is the predicate symbol of a_j. We call such a tuple a *(program) position*. Let $\mathcal{P}os(P)$ denote the set of positions in P, and $\mathcal{P}os(C_i)$ the set of positions in the clause C_i. The letters γ and β, possibly with subscripts, will denote positions. We will not make a distinction between positions and terms occurring at positions; we may e.g. apply a substitution to a position, e.g. write $\gamma\theta$ instead of $t\theta$, where t is the term occurring at γ.

We write $C_1 \mapsto C_2$ if the clause C_2 can be called from C_1, i.e. there is an atom a in C_1 such that unification of a and the head of C_2 (with variables renamed) does not fail[2]. The relation $\mapsto$ is called the *static call graph*. We write $\mapsto^*$ for the reflexive and transitive closure of $\mapsto$.

3 Static analysis

In this section we present a groundness analysis technique for functional logic programs, inspired by attribute grammar theory (see e.g. [6, 9]). Some of the concepts have been originally presented in [7]. A basic idea is that some of the predicate arguments in P are *annotated*, either as *inherited* ($\downarrow$) or *synthesized* ($\uparrow$), that is: there is a function (or *annotation*) $\mu : \mathcal{A}rgpos(P) \rightarrow \{\downarrow, \uparrow, \Box\}$, where $\Box$ is read "unannotated". An annotation is *partial* if some positions are unannotated. The intuitive meaning of the annotation in this context is: Whenever a predicate is called with ground inherited arguments, the synthesized arguments will be ground on success. An annotation is called *correct* for a given program iff this property holds.

Another important concept is the notion of *input* and *output* argument of a clause C_i: If $\mu(q_k) =\downarrow$ and a_j is the head atom of C_i, or if $\mu(q_k) =\uparrow$ and a_j is a body atom in C_i, we call (C_i, j, q, k) an *input* position. If $\mu(q_k) =\uparrow$ and a_j is the head atom in C_i, or if $\mu(q_k) =\downarrow$ and a_j is a body atom in C_i, we call (C_i, j, q, k) an *output* position. The intuitive explanation for these names is that data is brought *in* to a clause through the input positions, and sent *out* through the output positions.

Let $\mathcal{I}(C_i)$ and $\mathcal{O}(C_i)$ denote the input and output positions of C_i, respectively. Let $\mathcal{I}(P) = \bigcup_{C_i \in P} \mathcal{I}(C_i)$ and $\mathcal{O}(P) = \bigcup_{C_i \in P} \mathcal{O}(C_i)$.

In section 3.1 we state conditions for an annotation to be correct, and in section 3.2 we give a method to synthesize a correct annotation. The subject is more extensively addressed in [4], where also proofs of the propositions are given.

3.1 Dependency graphs

In a logic program, information is passed in two ways: either *within* a clause (between two positions sharing a variable), or *between* two clauses (through unification). If an

[2] This means that unification of a and the head of C_2 either succeeds or suspends (freezes).

annotation μ for the program is known, we further know in what *direction* information is passed: from input positions to output positions within a clause, and from output positions to input positions at unification. To reflect this dataflow, we introduce the notions of *local dependency graph* $\leadsto_C$ for each clause C, and *transition graph* $\leadsto_{C,D}$ for each pair of clauses C and D. These graphs will then be used for static groundness analysis of the program. Throughout this section, we assume that the program P has an annotation μ.

Definition 1. **[Local dependency graph]** For each clause C, the *local dependency graph* $\leadsto_C \subseteq \mathcal{I}(C) \times \mathcal{O}(C)$, is defined as follows:

$$\gamma \leadsto_C \beta \quad \text{iff} \quad \gamma \text{ and } \beta \text{ have at least one common variable.}$$

Definition 2. **[Transition graph]** Let C and D be two clauses, b_0 the head atom in D, and a_j a body atom in C such that unification of a_j and b_0 (with variables renamed) does not fail. The *transition graph* $\leadsto_{C,D}$ on $\mathcal{O}(C \cup D) \times \mathcal{I}(C \cup D)$ is defined as follows:

$$\gamma \leadsto_{C,D} \beta \quad \text{iff} \quad \begin{cases} \gamma = (C, j, q, k) \\ \beta = (D, 0, q, k) \\ \mu(q_k) = \downarrow \end{cases} \quad \text{or} \quad \begin{cases} \gamma = (D, 0, q, k) \\ \beta = (C, j, q, k) \\ \mu(q_k) = \uparrow \end{cases}$$

Definition 3. **[Program dependency graph]** The *program dependency graph* $\leadsto_P$ is defined as follows:

$$\leadsto_P = \bigcup_{C \in P} \leadsto_C \;\cup\; \bigcup_{C,D \in P} \leadsto_{C,D}$$

We let $\leadsto_P^*$ denote the transitive and reflexive closure of $\leadsto_P$. Intuitively, $\leadsto_P$ models the data flow for each possible execution of P. Therefore, it can be used for statically analyzing the operational behavior of the program.

Example 2. A part of the $\leadsto_P$ graph for the typesetting program is shown in figure 1. We assume the annotation **typesetrow**: $\downarrow\downarrow\downarrow\downarrow\uparrow\uparrow$ and **typesettab**: $\downarrow\downarrow\downarrow\uparrow\downarrow\uparrow$. For reasons of space we have only included (parts of) the clauses C_2 and C_4, abbreviated the predicate names, and only included the first, second and fourth argument of the predicates. If $\gamma \leadsto_P \beta$ and $\beta \leadsto_P \gamma$ (stemming from recursion between two atoms in the program), the graph contains a double-arrowed edge. □

The $\leadsto_P$ graph can be used to compute groundness information about P. For each functional position γ, we are interested in finding the first point in the program (with respect to the standard computation order) where all the variables occurring in γ are guaranteed to have a ground instantiation. Suppose γ is contained in the atom a_j in the clause $C : a_0 :- a_1, \ldots, a_n$. We can distinguish four cases:

(1) γ is always ground when execution reaches a_j.
(2) γ is not necessarily ground when execution reaches a_j, but is always ground when a_k has been refuted ($j \leq k \leq n$). In this case a *local* transformation of C can be performed; the function call in γ can be moved to the point after a_k.

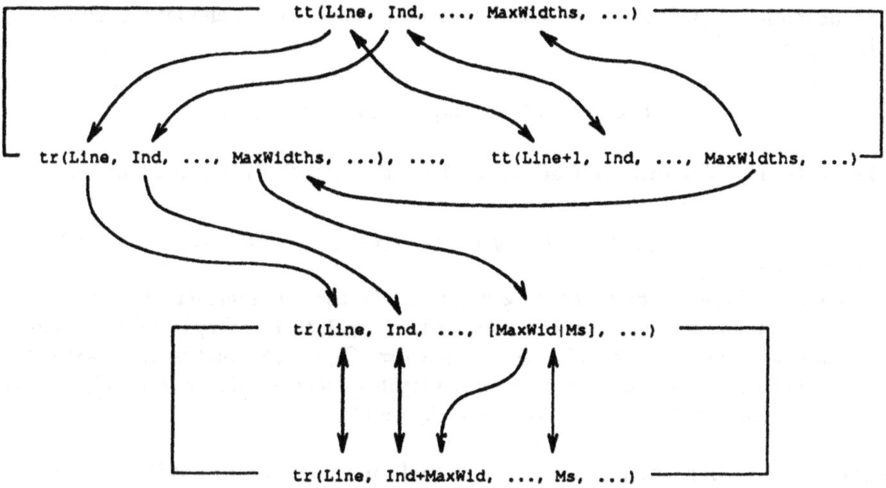

Fig. 1. A part of a $\leadsto_P$ graph for the typesetting program

(3) The variables of γ are always ground when some atom b in some clause D has been refuted ($D \neq C$). In this case a *global* transformation of P, affecting several clauses, can be performed.

(4) None of the three cases above applies.

Using dependency analysis over the $\leadsto_P$ graph, we can state sufficient conditions for cases (1) – (3) above. We first give a basic definition:

Definition 4. [Simple position] A position $\gamma \in \mathcal{O}(P)$ is *simple* if for all output positions β in every clause C holds:

$$\beta \leadsto_P^* \gamma \implies \text{every variable in } \beta \text{ occurs at some input position in } C$$

Note that if γ is simple, and if $\beta \in \mathcal{O}(P)$ and $\beta \leadsto_P^* \gamma$, then β is also simple. If every $\beta \in \mathcal{O}(P)$ is simple, we say that the annotation is simple.

It is known that P is operationally complete if P can be given a simple and *non-circular* annotation, such that function calls occur at output positions only [2]. Intuitively, if the annotation is simple and non-circular, equations of the form $X = f(X)$ will never have to be solved during unification. Throughout this section, we assume all annotations to be non-circular.

We next define a sufficient condition for case (1) above. The intuition behind the *L-annotated* condition is that dependencies that are entirely *left-to-right* allow for immediate evaluation of function calls during computation. This concept is analogous to "L-attributed grammars" that can be evaluated in a single preorded traversal over the input (see e.g. [6]).

Definition 5. Let D and C be two clauses such that $D \mapsto^* C$, and let $\gamma \in \mathcal{O}(C)$. $\leadsto_\gamma$ is defined by:

$$\beta_1 \leadsto_\gamma \beta_2 \quad \text{iff} \quad (\beta_1 \leadsto_D \beta_2 \quad \text{and} \quad \beta_2 \leadsto_P^* \gamma)$$

Definition 6. **[L-annotated position]** A position $\gamma \in \mathcal{O}(P)$ is *L-annotated* if:

$$(D, i, p, k) \leadsto_\gamma (D, j, q, l) \implies (i < j \quad \text{or} \quad i = j = 0)$$

Example 3. Consider the typesetting program. We use the abbreviated names *tr* for **typesetrow**, and *tt* for **typesettab**. The position $(C_2, 1, tr, 1)$ is simple and L-annotated, as can easily be seen in figure 1. The position $\gamma = (C_2, 1, tr, 2)$ (that is, **Ind+MaxWid**) is simple but not L-annotated, since there is a right-to-left dependency from $(C_4, 3, tt, 4)$ to $(C_4, 1, tr, 4)$, and $(C_4, 3, tt, 4) \leadsto_P^* \gamma$ (see figure 1). □

The following proposition states that for simple and L-annotated positions, condition (1) indeed holds:

Proposition 7. Let C be the clause $a_0 :- a_1, \ldots, a_m$, and let γ be a simple and L-annotated position in the atom a_j. If a_j is the current atom and θ is the current substitution, then $\gamma\theta$ is ground.

Thus if γ contains a function call, this call can always be immediately evaluated.
To state a sufficient condition for (2), we need the following definition:

Definition 8. **[(Locally) R-annotated position]** A position $\gamma \in \mathcal{O}(C)$ is *R-annotated* if it is not L-annotated. γ is *locally R-annotated* if it is R-annotated, and for all $\beta \in \mathcal{O}(D)$ such that $\beta \leadsto_P^* \gamma$, $D \mapsto^* C$ and $D \neq C$, β is L-annotated. γ is *non-locally R-annotated* if γ is R-annotated but not locally R-annotated. □

Example 4. Consider the typesetting program. The position $(C_4, 1, tr, 4)$ is locally R-annotated, because of the right-to-left dependency from $(C_4, 3, tt, 4)$. As a consequence of this, $(C_2, 1, tr, 2)$ is non-locally R-annotated (see figure 1). □

If γ is simple and locally R-annotated, we can find an atom in the same clause after which the functional expression can be evaluated:

Proposition 9. Let C be the clause $a_0 :- a_1, \ldots, a_m$, and let γ be a simple and locally R-annotated position in a_j. Let a_k be the rightmost atom in C that contains an input position γ' such that $\gamma' \leadsto_C \gamma$. Suppose C has been called and $a_1, \ldots, a_k$ have been refuted, yielding a current substitution θ. Then $\gamma\theta$ is ground.

Thus if γ contains a function call, it can be evaluated after a_k has been refuted.
Case (3) above, requiring a non-trivial global transformation of the program, will be discussed in Chapter 4.

3.2 Fixpoint computation of annotations

In this section we present an algorithm that for a given functional logic program P generates an annotation μ. The algorithm will also extract, for every predicate p, the positions that must be ground if p is called in an initial goal.

Recall the requirements for safe functional evaluation as expressed by propositions 7 and 9: The annotation should be *simple*. Moreover, function calls should appear in *output* positions only. There may be many annotations satisfying the requirements above; thus our algorithm is non-deterministic. It may also be the case that there is no such annotation; then our algorithm fails. Our intention is to annotate as few positions as possible, in order to restrict the use of predicates as little as possible. [4] includes an exhaustive deterministic version of the algorithm that also constructs a program dependency graph when annotating the program.

The starting point for the algorithm is the minimal annotation that makes all functional positions into output ones. This annotation will be called the *initial* annotation of the program.

Example 5. Consider the typesetting program which has three function calls: `size(Text)` in the head of C_2, `Ind+MaxWid` in the body of C_2, and `Line+1` in the body of C_4. In order to make all these into output positions, we must assume the annotation $\mu(tr_5) = \uparrow, \mu(tr_2) = \downarrow, \mu(tt_1) = \downarrow$, which is the initial annotation of the program. □

A variable X is *uncovered* in a clause C by a given annotation iff X occurs in an output position in C, but X does not occur in an input position in C. X is *covered* if it is not uncovered. In example 5, the variable `Text` is uncovered in clause C_2 by μ, while the variable `Line` in clause C_4 is covered by μ.

A necessary and sufficient condition for an annotation to be simple is that every variable is covered in every clause. We now consider the question how to extend a given partial annotation μ to a simple annotation. The first step is to identify uncovered variables in the clauses. Let γ be an output position in the clause C, and let X be an uncovered variable in γ. If X does not appear in any unannotated position of C then μ cannot be extended to a simple annotation. Otherwise, we can non-deterministically choose one of the unannotated positions β that contains X, and define it to be an input position, thus extending the annotation of the corresponding predicate. This corresponds to inducing a data flow from β into γ and a local dependency edge $\beta \leadsto_C \gamma$.

Note that if there are no uncovered variables in the program, the annotation must be simple. The above operation (i.e. extending the annotation) can be defined as a monotone operator whose fixpoints represent simple annotations.

We let an annotation μ be represented by a set $S \subset Argpos(P) \times \{\downarrow, \uparrow\}$, so that $(p_i, \downarrow) \in S$ iff $\mu(p_i) = \downarrow$, and $(p_i, \uparrow) \in S$ iff $\mu(p_i) = \uparrow$. If $\mu(p_i) = \square$ then there is no pair containing p_i in S. We call S the *annotation set* corresponding to μ.

Note that the intersection of two annotation sets S_1 and S_2 is an annotation set. However, $S_1 \cup S_2$ may be *contradictory* in the sense that it contains both $(p_i, \downarrow)$ and $(p_i, \uparrow)$ for some p_i. In that case, we define $S_1 \cup S_2$ to be $\top$.

Let S_P be the set of all (non-contradictory) annotation sets for some program P. Then $S_P \cup \top$ is a complete lattice under the ordering $\sqsubseteq$, defined as:

1. $S_1 \sqsubseteq S_2$ if $S_1 \subseteq S_2$
2. $S \sqsubseteq \top$ for all $S \in \mathcal{S}_P$

Let $d \in \{\downarrow, \uparrow\}$, and let $Outpos(p_i, d)$ be a function returning the set

$$\{(C, j, p, i) \in \mathcal{P}os(P) | (C, j, p, i) \in \mathcal{O}(P) \text{ iff } \mu(p_i) = d\}$$

That is, $Outpos(p_i, d)$ returns the set of positions that become output positions as a result of annotating p_i with d. For example, in the typesetting program we have $Outpos(tr_2, \downarrow) = \{(C_2, 1, tr, 2), (C_4, 1, tr, 2)\}$.
We extend $Outpos$ to annotation sets as follows:

$$Outpos(S) = \bigcup_{(p_i, d) \in S} Outpos(p_i, d)$$

Let S be an annotation set, let $\gamma \in \mathcal{O}(C)$, and let X be an uncovered variable in γ. Let $pick(S, \gamma, X)$ be a function returning $\{\beta\}$, where β is a non-deterministically selected unannotated position in C in which X occurs. If no such position β exists then $pick(S, \gamma, X) = \top$ (undefined). If X is a covered variable, then $pick(S, \gamma, X) = \emptyset$.
We extend $pick$ to positions as follows:

$$pick(S, \gamma) = \bigcup_{X \in \gamma} pick(S, \gamma, X)$$

We also extend $pick$ to sets of positions Γ as follows:

$$pick(S, \Gamma) = \bigcup_{\gamma \in \Gamma} pick(S, \gamma)$$

Again, $pick(S, \Gamma) = \top$ if we get a contradictory annotation when making all positions in $pick(S, \Gamma)$ into input positions.

Suppose $\beta = (C, j, p, i)$. Let $annotate(\beta)$ be a function that returns (p_i, d), where $d \in \{\downarrow, \uparrow\}$ is chosen so that β becomes an input position. That is, $d = \downarrow$ if β is in the head, and $d = \uparrow$ if β is in the body.

We extend $annotate$ to sets of positions Γ as follows:

$$annotate(\Gamma) = \bigcup_{\beta \in \Gamma} annotate(\beta)$$

We are now ready to define our monotone operator Ψ as follows. Let S be an annotation set. Then

$$\Psi(S) = S \cup annotate(pick(S, Outpos(S)))$$

We assume that $pick$, $annotate$ and Ψ are strict, i.e. they return $\top$ if any argument is $\top$.

Proposition 10. Every simple annotation is a fixpoint of Ψ. Every fixpoint of Ψ is either $\top$ or a simple annotation.

Let S be an initial annotation. Then the limit element of the sequence $S, \Psi(S), \Psi(\Psi(S)), \ldots$ is a fixpoint to Ψ. That is, starting from the initial annotation we incrementally extend it by selecting clause-wise local dependencies, until a simple annotation has been reached.

Recall that a main assumption is that the annotation is non-circular. This property is decidable [9], but the general circularity test is exponential. However, the circularity problem can be tackled by techniques that are well-known within attribute grammars, by giving sufficient conditions for non-circularity. From the program dependency graph $\leadsto_P$, we construct a clause dependency graph $\leadsto_{C^\bullet}$ for each clause C. Intuitively, $\leadsto_{C^\bullet}$ characterizes all the possible dataflow paths in any sub-proof tree T whose root is labeled with the head of C.

Definition 11. **[Clause dependency graph]** Let $\leadsto_P$ be a program dependency graph and C a clause in P. The ***clause dependency graph*** $\leadsto_{C^\bullet}$ is defined as follows:

- $\beta \leadsto_{C^\bullet} \gamma$ if $\beta \leadsto_C \gamma$.
- for $\gamma \in \mathcal{O}(C)$ and $\beta \in \mathcal{I}(C)$, where γ and β are in the same *body* atom of C, $\gamma \leadsto_{C^\bullet} \beta$ if $\gamma \leadsto_P^* \beta$.

If the clause dependency graph $\leadsto_{C^\bullet}$ is acyclic for each clause C, the annotation for P is ***absolutely non-circular***. This definition corresponds to the definition of absolutely non-circular attribute grammars (see e.g. [6]). Absolute non-circularity is a sufficient condition for non-circularity, which is important to ensure operational completeness, as mentioned previously.

Example 6. Consider again the typesetting program. As shown in example 5, the initial annotation can be represented by the set

$$S_1 = \{(tr_5, \uparrow), (tr_2, \downarrow), (tt_1, \downarrow)\}$$

Outpos(S_1) is the set of positions containing the function calls `size(Text)`, `Ind+MaxWid` and `Line+1`, plus the second argument of tr in C_4. Let us consider `Ind+MaxWid` (in the body of C_2). The variable `Ind` is already covered, since it occurs in an input position (the second argument of the head). The variable `MaxWid` is uncovered, but it occurs at an unannotated position (the fourth argument of the head). We make this into an input position, which means we have to annotate tr_4 as $\downarrow$.

When analyzing the other positions in ***Outpos***(S_1), we obtain:

$$\Psi(S_1) = S_2 = S_1 \cup \{(tr_3, \downarrow), (tr_4, \downarrow), (tt_2, \downarrow)\}$$

We now have no uncovered variables in C_2, but in C_4 the variables `Row` and `MaxWidths` (in the third and fourth argument of tr) are uncovered.

Below we present the remaining iterations without comments. The non-deterministic choices are underlined:

$$\Psi(S_2) = S_3 = S_2 \cup \{(tt_3, \downarrow), \underline{(tt_4, \uparrow)}\}$$
$$\Psi(S_3) = S_4 = S_3 \cup \{(tt_5, \downarrow)\}$$
$$\Psi(S_4) = S_5 = S_4 \cup \{(computemax_3, \uparrow)\}$$
$$\Psi(S_5) = S_6 = S_5 \cup \emptyset$$

We have reached a fixpoint. S_6 now represents the simple annotation tr : $\square\downarrow\downarrow\downarrow\uparrow\square$ and tt :$\downarrow\downarrow\downarrow\uparrow\downarrow\square$. The program dependency graph for this annotation is illustrated in example 2. Notice that the algorithm produces an annotation which is only partial, as opposed to the total annotation assumed in example 2. □

The annotation in the previous example can be shown to be non-circular. We can draw the conclusion that every initial query with the predicate tr must have the second, third and fourth arguments ground. Every initial query with the predicate tt must have the first, second, third and fifth arguments ground. If this is the case, no unsolved equations will remain at the end of computation. Note that the method does not restrict the use of the other arguments.

The transition graphs are uniquely determined by the annotation. When constructing the local dependency graphs we may have choices, if a variable in an output position can be allocated to several input positions. In such a case a good heuristics is to add edges going from left to right (if possible), since we are interested in having as many L-annotated positions as possible to avoid transformations. Another optimization is to take only one local dependency for each variable in an output position; notice that this is sufficient since all the candidates have the same final value under the semantics of (functional) logic programming.

4 Program transformations

The information included in the $\leadsto_P$ graph can be used to transform P into an equivalent program in which no dynamic delays are needed. The details of the method are presented in [3].

As discussed in section 3.1, we can immediately evaluate function calls occurring at L-annotated (and simple) positions; thus no transformation is necessary. Function calls occurring at locally R-annotated positions can be moved locally within the clause.

Also at *non*-locally R-annotated (simple) positions, we can avoid dynamic delays by transforming the program. The space is too limited to describe this transformation in its full generality, but we will illustrate it by means of the typesetting example.

Recall that `Ind+MaxWid` in clause C_2 is non-locally R-annotated, as seen in example 4. Intuitively, this is because `MaxWid` does not become ground until the last atom in C_4 has been refuted. We now move `Ind+MaxWid` to the point immediately after the last atom in the clause C_4. This is not straightforward, since the variables occurring in `Ind+MaxWid` are not visible in C_4. Therefore we add an extra argument to the head atom in C_2 and to the calling atom in C_4, so that the variables in `Ind+MaxWid` are communicated from C_2 to C_4, and the result of calling `Ind+MaxWid` is brought back from C_4 to C_2.

Example 7. Using the transformations outlined above, the typesetting program would be transformed into:

(C_1) `typesetrow(_, _, [], [], [], [], true).`

(C_2) `typesetrow(Line, Ind, [Text|Ts], [MaxWid|Ms], [ZO|Ss],`

```
            [put(Line, Ind, Text)|Insts],
            (NewVar = Ind+MaxWid, Evals)) :-
        Z0 = size(Text),
        typesetrow(Line, NewVar, Ts, Ms, Ss, Insts, Evals).
```

(C_3) `typesettab(_, _, [], X, X, []).`

(C_4)
```
typesettab(Line,Ind,[Row|Rows],MaxWidths,MaxSoFar,[InstRow|Insts]) :-
        typesetrow(Line,Ind,Row,MaxWidths,Widths,InstRow,[],Evals),
        compute_max(Widths, MaxSoFar, NewMaxSoFar),
        Z0 = Line+1,
        typesettab(Z0, Ind, Rows, MaxWidths, NewMaxSoFar, Insts),
        Evals.
```

□

The transformed program is delay-free. To give an idea of the effects of the transformations, we analyzed two compiled versions of the typesetting program with a table of 10×10, 20×20 and 30×30 elements. The "naïve" version uses dynamic delays. The transformed program is about ten times faster (the time unit is milliseconds).

	10×10	20×20	30×30
Naïve	110	450	1000
Transformed	10	50	110

5 Discussion

We have presented a technique for static groundness analysis of functional logic programs. It is assumed that the operational semantics of the language requires that functional expressions are evaluated before unification with another term, but evaluation can only performed if the functional expression is ground. If the functional expression is non-ground, the unification is (***dynamically***) ***delayed*** until the arguments have been instantiated to ground terms. Under this assumption, two problems arise:

1. Given a program P and an initial goal, will any delayed unifications remain unresolved after computation?
2. For every function call $f(X)$ in P, find a point in P where X always will be bound to a ground term, and thus $f(X)$ can be evaluated.

Problem 1 is important for completeness, and problem 2 for efficiency. Our analysis method solves the two problems in a uniform way, using the notion of ***dependency graph***. The method applies techniques developed for attribute grammars [6, 9].

Another approach to solving problem 1, based on abstract interpretation, was presented by Hanus [8]. In contrast to the abstract interpretation technique, our method does not require information on the form of the goal. This information is instead inferred by an algorithm generating the ***annotations*** of the program predicates. Our algorithm is nondeterministic, and in the general case derives different allowed forms of goals. If the type of goal is given a priori, the same algorithm can be used for analysis. In the latter case the computation will converge faster.

Another difference to the abstract interpretation method of Hanus is that our groundness analysis is guided by the dependency relation. Thus it may be the case that certain positions of the program need not be involved in the analysis (as illustrated by the typesetting example). The directionality restrictions on the goal obtained by this kind of analysis may be quite limited, since they concern only the positions on which the functional calls depend. Thus, multidirectional use of the program may still be possible.

The concept of dependency-based analysis is used in a growing number of papers for solving different problems. We believe that dependency-based analysis can be linked to Deransart's annotation proof method for logic programs [5]. Furthermore, the relation between dependency-based analysis and abstract interpretation needs to be clarified. Future work includes investigations of these relations, as well as the development of a formal framework for dependency-based analysis. Finally, an implementation of the framework is currently in progress, based on an exhaustive version of the annotation inference algorithm [4].

References

1. H. Aït-Kaci. An overview of LIFE. In Schmidt, Stogny (eds.) *Next generation information system technology*, pp. 42–58, LNCS 504, Springer-Verlag, 1990.
2. J. Boye. S-SLD-resolution - an operational semantics for logic programs with external procedures. In *Programming language implementation and logic programming*, pp. 383–393, LNCS 528, Springer-Verlag, 1991.
3. J. Boye. Avoiding dynamic delays in functional logic programs. In *Programming language implementation and logic programming*, Springer-Verlag, 1993.
4. J. Boye, J. Paakki and J. Małuszyński. *Dependency-based groundness analysis of functional logic programs*. Research report LiTH-IDA-R-93-20, Department of computer and information science, Linköping university, 1993.
5. P. Deransart. *Proof methods of declarative properties of logic programs*. Report 1248, INRIA Rocquencourt, 1990.
6. P. Deransart, M. Jourdan and B. Lorho. *Attribute grammars — Definitions, systems and bibliography*. LNCS 323, Springer-Verlag, 1988.
7. P. Deransart and J. Małuszyński. Relating logic programs and attribute grammars. *Journal of logic programming*, 2(2), pp. 119-156, 1985.
8. M. Hanus. On the completeness of residuation. In *Proc. of the joint international conference and symposium on logic programming*, pp. 192–206, The MIT Press, 1992.
9. D. Knuth. Semantics of context-free languages. *Mathematical systems theory*, 2, pp. 127–145, 1968.
10. J. Małuszyński, S. Bonnier, J. Boye, F. Kluźniak, A. Kågedal and U. Nilsson. Logic programs with external procedures. In Apt, de Bakker, Rutten (eds.) *Logic programming languages: constraints, functions and objects*. The MIT Press, 1993.
11. L. Naish. Adding equations to NU-Prolog. In *Programming language implementation and logic programming*, pp. 15–26, LNCS 528, Springer-Verlag, 1991.
12. J. Paakki. *Multi-pass evaluation of functional logic programs*. Research report LiTH-IDA-R-93-02, Department of computer and information science, Linköping university, 1993.

Abstract Rewriting

Didier Bert[1], Rachid Echahed[1], Bjarte M. Østvold[2]

[1] IMAG-LGI, BP 53 X, 38041 Grenoble cedex, France
Email: {bert,echahed}@imag.fr
[2] Division of Computer Systems and Telematics
Norwegian Institute of Technology
N-7034 Trondheim, Norway
Email: bjartem@idt.unit.no

Abstract. We introduce the notion of abstract term rewriting system, R^a, corresponding to a constructor-based term rewriting system R. R^a is aimed to determine the set of possible constructors of a given term, using abstract rules in R^a. A characterization of an abstract term rewriting system as a fixed point is given. Among the possible applications of the introduced concepts, we quote: E-unification, proofs by consistency, type checking etc.

1 Introduction

Abstract interpretation is a nice theory that allows to extract relevant information from programs without considering all the details given by the standard semantics. This theory has been applied successfully to several areas. In this paper, we apply it to term rewriting systems [11]. Our goal is to determine what kind of normal form can be expected from a given term without performing rewritings. For example, consider the following rewrite system which defines the append(+) operator on sequences:

$$R = \{\text{nil} + x \to x,\ \ \text{cons}(a, u) + v \to \text{cons}(a, u + v)\}$$

Given the terms $t_1 = \text{nil} + \text{nil}$, $t_2 = x + \text{cons}(a, u)$ and $t_3 = x + (y + z)$. The normal form of t_1 is clearly nil. The case of t_2 is less obvious, but it could be interesting to show that its normal form will be headed by the constructor cons, and also that the normal form of t_3 will be headed by a constructor in the set $\{\text{nil}, \text{cons}\}$.

The original motivation for this work is the improvement of the operational semantics of logic and functional languages such as [8], [2], [12], [9] and [1]. The semantics of these languages is mainly based on E-unification algorithms using the narrowing relation [10]. Actually, the process of E-unification can be improved if we are able to determine whether two terms cannot be E-unified without carrying out the unification. For example, the following E-unification problem

$$x + (y + z) = \text{nil}$$

modulo the system R given above, has one solution which assigns nil to the three variables. What we want is to find a method of pruning the unnecessary branches from the search tree developed by E-unification algorithms. Here this would mean avoiding to use the cons-rule in the unification process.

The notion of an abstract domain constructed to facilitate the analysis of some properties in another (concrete) domain has been discussed in [3] with relevance to logic programming. In this paper, we consider algebraic specifications $SP = (\Sigma, R)$, where Σ is a many-sorted first order signature and R is a term rewriting system. For such specifications, we introduce the notion of abstract specifications $SP^a = (\Sigma^a, R^a)$ consisting of an abstract signature and an abstract term rewriting system. An abstract specification is used to determine the possible constructors of terms constructed over a given signature. It is computed as a fixed point of a transformation.

Overview: First we list some basic concepts in Section 2, then in Section 3 we define the notions of abstract signature, abstract term rewriting systems and abstract specifications and prove the soundness of these notions. In Section 4 we provide a way to compute an abstract specification as a least fixed point.

2 Preliminaries

We start by giving some basic definitions needed for the concepts to be introduced in the next sections. Concepts not defined here can be found for example in [5], [11] or [7].

A *signature* is a pair $\Sigma = (S, \Omega)$ where S is a set of sort names, and Ω is a family of sets of operator names indexed by $S^* \times S$. f in $\Omega_{u,s}$ is said to have *arity* u, *sort* s, and *rank* u,s; we may write $f : u \rightarrow s$ to indicate this.

Let t be a term. *Var(t)* denotes the set of variables in t. A term t is said to be *ground* if $\text{Var}(t) = \emptyset$. Let $\Sigma = (S, \Omega)$ be a signature and X an S-indexed set of variables such that $\Omega \cap X = \emptyset$. We denote by $T_\Omega(X)$ the free Σ-algebra over X, also called the *term algebra*. When X is empty, T_Ω denotes the initial Σ-algebra.

A *substitution* σ is a mapping $\sigma : X \rightarrow T_\Omega(X)$. We also denote by σ the unique extension of the substitution to $T_\Omega(X)$. We denote by $\text{dom}(\sigma) = \{x \in X | \sigma(x) \neq x\}$ the domain of the substitution σ. A *ground substitution* σ, $\sigma : X \rightarrow T_\Omega$ is a substitution such that $\sigma(x)$ is a ground term for all x in $\text{dom}(\sigma)$. GS is the set of all ground substitutions.

The set of occurrences of a term t is denoted $O(t)$. The subterm of t at an occurrence p is denoted $t|_p$. $t[p \leftarrow s]$ denotes t with the subterm at occurrence p replaced by the term s.

A *rewrite rule* consists of two terms noted $l \rightarrow r$, indicating that l can be replaced with r when the rule is applied. l and r are terms of the same sort, i.e. $l, r \in T_\Omega(X)_s$ for $s \in S$ and X a set of variables. Variables in rules are universally quantified.

A *term rewriting system*, or *TRS* for short, over a signature Σ is a finite set of rewrite rules $\{l_i \to r_i | i = 1, \ldots, n\}$ where $l_i, r_i \in T_\Omega(X)_s$ for some $s \in S$ and $\mathrm{Var}(l_i) \supseteq \mathrm{Var}(r_i)$. We denote by $|R|$ the number of rewrite rules in the TRS R. A term t rewrites to a term t', written $t \to_R t'$, if $t|_u = \sigma(l)$ and $t' = t[u \leftarrow \sigma(r)]$ for some rewrite rule $l \to r \in R, u \in O(t)$ and substitution σ. We denote by $\xrightarrow{*}_R$ the transitive and reflexive closure of $\to_R$. $\xleftrightarrow{*}_R$ denotes the symmetric closure of $\xrightarrow{*}_R$. A TRS is said to be *canonical* iff

1. $\to_R$ is Noetherian (there is no infinite derivation $t \to_R t_1 \to_R \cdots$)
2. $\to_R$ is confluent (for all t_1, t_2, t_3, $t_1 \xrightarrow{*}_R t_2$ and $t_1 \xrightarrow{*}_R t_3 \Rightarrow \exists t_4 : t_2 \xrightarrow{*}_R t_4$ and $t_3 \xrightarrow{*}_R t_4$

Given a term $t \in T_\Omega(X)$ and a TRS R. If $t \xrightarrow{*}_R t'$ and t' cannot be rewritten, we say that t' is a *normal form* of t. This is denoted $t\downarrow_R$.

A *specification* is a pair $SP = (\Sigma, R)$ where Σ is a signature and R a TRS over Σ.

Definition 1 (Constructor-based specification). A specification $SP = (\Sigma, R)$ where $\Sigma = (S, \Omega)$ is said to be *constructor-based* iff

1. R is canonical
2. Ω is split into two disjoint sets, $\Omega = C \cup D$; C is called the set of constructors and D the set of completely defined operators
3. $\forall t \in T_{\Omega_s}, \exists t' \in T_{C_s} \mid t \xleftrightarrow{*}_R t'$
4. $\forall t, t' \in T_{C_s}, t \xleftrightarrow{*}_R t' \Leftrightarrow t = t'$
5. The left-hand sides of the rewrite rules in R are of the form $d(t_1, \ldots, t_n)$ where $d \in D$ and $t_i \in T_{C_{s_i}}(X)$, i = 1, ..., n.

3 Abstract Specifications

The purpose of this section is to introduce the notion of an abstract specification corresponding to a given constructor-based specification. Assume that *SP* is a constructor-based specification. Let t be a term constructed over *SP*. We know per definition of constructor-based specifications that any ground instance of t can be rewritten into a constructor term t' (i.e. $t' \in T_C$). Let t' be of the form $c(t_1, \ldots, t_n)$, our goal is to determine the *set of constructors* c such that there exists a ground instance of t that rewrites into $c(t_1, \ldots, t_n)$. For ground terms this set contains only one constructor.

Definition 2 (Constructor set). Let $SP = (\Sigma, R)$ be a constructor-based specification and t a term in $T_\Omega(X)$. The *constructor set* of t is denoted c-set(t) and defined by

$$\text{c-set}(t) = \{c \in C \mid \exists \sigma \in GS, \exists t_1, \ldots, t_n \in T_\Omega, \sigma(t)\downarrow_R = c(t_1, \ldots, t_n), n \geq 0\}$$

Example 1. c-set(nil+ nil) = {nil}
c-set(x + cons(a, u)) = {cons}
c-set(x + (y + z)) = {nil, cons}

Unfortunately, computing the constructor set of a term can be quite expensive and generally not possible using ordinary rewriting. Our aim in this paper is to provide a way to compute efficiently such constructor sets. For that, we construct an abstract specification, SP^a, corresponding to a specification SP. An abstract specification consists of an abstract signature and an abstract term rewrite system.

In following, we define the notion of abstract signature and observe that the term algebra of this signature is ordered. We prove that this is in fact a complete lattice. Then the abstraction of terms is defined, to prepare the definition of abstract TRSs, and finally that of abstract specifications. The properties of abstract specifications are so that, instead of rewriting a term t using its (concrete) TRS, we abstract the term and normalize it with the abstract TRS. This yields an approximation of the constructor set of t, c-set(t).

Throughout this section the same example will be elaborated on to illustrate the concepts introduced.

Example 2. Consider a constructor-based specification of sequences of natural numbers $SP = (\Sigma, R), \Sigma = (S, C \cup D), S = \{\text{seq}, \text{nat}\}, C = C_{\text{seq}} \cup C_{\text{nat}}, D = D_{\text{seq}} \cup D_{\text{nat}}, R = R_{\text{seq}} \cup R_{\text{nat}}$ and a set of variables $X = X_{\text{seq}} \cup X_{\text{nat}}$. Furthermore

$$\begin{array}{ll}
C_{\text{seq}} = \{\text{nil}, \text{cons}\} & X_{\text{seq}} = \{a : \text{nat};\ s, u : \text{seq}\} \\
\text{nil} : \to \text{seq} & R_{\text{seq}} = \{\ \text{nil} + s \to s, \\
\text{cons} : \text{nat} \times \text{seq} \to \text{seq} & \qquad \text{cons}(a, s) + u \to \text{cons}(a, s + u)\} \\
D_{\text{seq}} = \{+\} & \\
+ : \text{seq} \times \text{seq} \to \text{seq} &
\end{array}$$

The parts of SP concerning the natural numbers are assumed to be already known.

Definition 3 (Abstract signature). Given a constructor-based specification $SP = (\Sigma, R)$ with a signature $\Sigma = (S, C \cup D)$. A signature $\Sigma^a = (S^a, C^a \cup D^a)$ is called an *abstract signature* for Σ iff $\forall s \in S$

1. $s^a \in S^a$

2. $\forall c \in C_s$, $c^a \in C_s^a$, $c^a :\to s^a$

3. $\bot_s \in C_s^a$, $\bot_s :\to s^a$

4. $\sqcup_s \in C_s^a$, $\sqcup_s : s^a \times s^a \to s^a$
   $\sqcup_s$ is idempotent, commutative and associative with identity $\bot_s$.

5. $\forall d \in D_s$, $d : s_1 \times \cdots \times s_n \to s$, $n \geq 1$, $d^a \in D_s^a$, $d^a : s_1^a \times \cdots \times s_n^a \to s^a$

Notation: In the sequel we use $\sqcup_s$ as an n-ary operator ($\forall n$) and write $\sqcup_s(x_1, \ldots, x_n)$ or $\sqcup_s\{x_1, \ldots, x_n\}$ and $\sqcup_s\emptyset = \bot_s$. Let $\{c_1^a, \ldots, c_n^a\}$ be the set $C_s^a \setminus \{\sqcup_s, \bot_s\}$ then we write $\top_s$ for $\sqcup_s(c_1^a, \ldots, c_n^a)$.

An abstract signature $\Sigma^a = (S^a, C^a \cup D^a)$ is a signature where all constructors are constants but one which can be understood as the "union".

Example 3. Let us return to the specification given above. As in the definitions we have just seen, the abstract signature has its sort set S^a, its constructors C^a and its operations D^a. Then we have: $\Sigma^a = (S^a, C^a \cup D^a)$, $S^a = \{\text{seq}^a, \text{nat}^a\}$, $C^a = C^a_{\text{seq}} \cup C^a_{\text{nat}}$, $D^a = D^a_{\text{seq}} \cup D^a_{\text{nat}}$ where

$$
\begin{array}{ll}
C^a_{\text{seq}} = \{\text{nil}^a, \text{cons}^a, \sqcup_{\text{seq}}, \bot_{\text{seq}}\} & D^a_{\text{seq}} = \{+^a\} \\
\text{nil}^a :\to \text{seq}^a & +^a : \text{seq}^a \times \text{seq}^a \to \text{seq}^a \\
\text{cons}^a :\to \text{seq}^a & \\
\bot_{\text{seq}} :\to \text{seq}^a & \\
\sqcup_{\text{seq}} : \text{seq}^a \times \text{seq}^a \to \text{seq}^a & \\
\top_{\text{seq}} = \sqcup_{\text{seq}}(\text{nil}^a, \text{cons}^a) &
\end{array}
$$

In the rest of the paper we write T_{C^a, s^a} for the carriers of the quotient algebra generated from C^a modulo the properties of $\sqcup_s$.

Notice that for each abstract sort s^a the term algebra T_{C^a, s^a} consists of elements t such that t is either a constant or made up of constants and the constructor symbol $\sqcup_s$. Informally, any constant c^a in T_{C^a, s^a} abstracts the ground terms in $T_{\Omega, s}$ that normalize to a term headed by c. $\sqcup_s(c_1^a, c_2^a)$ abstracts the union of the abstractions c_1^a and c_2^a. $\bot_s$ abstracts no term.

We define below a partial order on the term algebra T_{Ω^a, s^a} as follows:

Definition 4 (Term order $\leq_s$). $\forall s \in S$:

$$
\begin{array}{rl}
\bot_s \leq_s t & \text{if } t \in T_{\Omega^a, s^a} \\
t \leq_s t & \text{if } t \in T_{\Omega^a, s^a} \\
\sqcup_s(c_1^a, \ldots, c_n^a) \leq_s \sqcup_s(c_1^{a\prime}, \ldots, c_m^{a\prime}) & \text{if } \{c_1^a, \ldots, c_n^a\} \subseteq \{c_1^{a\prime}, \ldots, c_m^{a\prime}\} \\
& \quad \text{where } c_i^a, c_i^{a\prime} \in C_s^a \\
d^a(t_1, \ldots, t_n) \leq_s d^{a\prime}(t_1', \ldots, t_m') & \text{if } d^a = d^{a\prime} (\text{so } n = m) \\
& \quad \wedge\ t_i \leq_{s_i} t_i' \text{ for } i = 1, \ldots, n, \quad \text{where } t_i, t_i' \in T_{\Omega^a}, d^a, d^{a\prime} \in D_s^a
\end{array}
$$

Example 4. We show how some terms constructed over Σ^a are ordered:

$\perp_{seq} \leq_{seq} \text{cons}^a$	$\text{nil}^a +^a \perp_{seq} \leq_{seq} \text{nil}^a +^a \text{cons}^a$
$\text{nil}^a \leq_{seq} \top_{seq}$	nil^a and cons^a are not comparable.
$\text{cons}^a \leq_{seq} \text{cons}^a$	

Proposition 5. *$\forall s \in S$, $(T_{C^a, s^a}, \leq_s)$ is a finite complete lattice.*

Proof. Follows from the fact that $\forall s \in S$, $(T_{C^a, s^a}, \leq_s)$ is isomorphic to $(\mathcal{P}(T_{C^a, s^a}), \subseteq)$ (the power set of T_{C^a, s^a} and set inclusion) and that T_{C^a, s^a} is finite. □

The next two definitions are given to facilitate the introduction of the notion of abstract TRS (Definition 7).

Definition 6 (Term abstraction α). $\alpha : T_\Omega(X) \mapsto T_{\Omega^a}$

$$\begin{aligned} \alpha(x) &= \top_s \text{ if } x \in X_s \\ \alpha(c) &= c^a \text{ if } c \in C \\ \alpha(c(t_1, \ldots, t_m)) &= c^a \text{ if } c \in C \\ \alpha(d) &= d^a \text{ if } d \in D \\ \alpha(d(t_1, \ldots, t_m)) &= d^a(\alpha(t_1), \ldots, \alpha(t_m)) \text{ if } d \in D \end{aligned}$$

The function α maps every term t to an abstract term t^a. Particularly, the reader may notice that terms headed by a constructor, such as $c(t_1, \ldots, t_m)$, are abstracted by the abstract term constant, c^a, whereas the variables are abstracted by $\top$.

Example 5. Σ is the signature of *SP*. The abstract signature corresponding to Σ is Σ^a. Let t be a term constructed over $T_\Omega(X)$, $X = \{x : \text{seq}\}$, $t = \text{cons}(5, \text{cons}(2, \text{nil})) + (\text{nil} + x)$. Using the definition above we can now calculate the abstraction of t, $t^a = \alpha(t)$, using functional notation as in the definition above:

$$\begin{aligned} t^a &= \alpha(t) \\ &= \alpha(+(\text{cons}(5, \text{cons}(2, \text{nil})), +(\text{nil}, x))) \\ &= +^a(\alpha(\text{cons}(5, \text{cons}(2, \text{nil}))), \alpha(+(\text{nil}, x))) \\ &= +^a(\text{cons}^a, +^a(\alpha(\text{nil}), \alpha(x))) \\ &= +^a(\text{cons}^a, +^a(\text{nil}^a, \top_{seq})) \end{aligned}$$

In order to compute the constructor set of a term t, c-set(t), we reduce the problem into the normalization of $\alpha(t)$ with respect to a new term rewriting system (over Σ^a) we call α-abstract TRS (Definition 11). Below we start by defining the notion of abstract TRS.

Definition 7 (Abstract TRS). Let SP be a constructor-based specification $SP = (\Sigma, R)$, $\Sigma = (S, C \cup D)$. An *abstract TRS* R^a for R is defined by:

$\forall d \in D,\ d : s_1 \times \cdots \times s_m \to s,\ \forall c_i^a \in T_{C^a, s_i^a} \setminus \{\bot_{s_i}\},\ i = 1, \ldots, m:$

$$d^a(c_1^a, \ldots, c_m^a) \to r^a \in R^a$$

where $r^a \in T_{C^a, s^a}$

and also $\forall d \in D,\ d : s_1 \times \cdots \times s_m \to s,\ x_1^a, \ldots, x_m^a \in X^a, \forall i \in \{1, \ldots, m\}$:

$$d^a(x_1^a, \ldots, x_{i-1}^a, \bot_{s_i}, x_{i+1}^a, \ldots, x_m^a) \to r^a \in R^a$$

where $r^a \in T_{C^a, s^a}$

such that $\forall l^a \to r^a, l^{a\prime} \to r^{a\prime} \in R^a, l^a \leq_s l^{a\prime} \Rightarrow r^a \leq_s r^{a\prime}$.

In the definition above, we have only fixed the left hand-sides of the abstract TRS. These left hand-sides are intended to cover the domain of every abstract defined operator, d^a. Of course one may fix these left hand-sides differently, provided that the d^a's are completely defined.

Example 6. $R_1^a = \{l_i \to \mathrm{nil} \mid i = 1, \ldots, n\}$
$R_2^a = \{l_i \to \top_{\mathrm{seq}} \mid i = 1, \ldots, j-1, j+1, \ldots, n\} \cup \{l_j \to \mathrm{nil}\}$
$R_3^a = \{l_i \to \top_{\mathrm{seq}} \mid i = 1, \ldots, n\}$

Definition 8 (Order on abstract TRSs $\leq_{\mathrm{TRS}}$). Let R and R' be two abstract TRSs for a same specification, $R = \{l_i \to r_i \mid i = 1, \ldots, n\}$, $R' = \{l'_i \to r'_i \mid i = 1, \ldots, n\}$, $n = |R| = |R'|$.

$$R \leq_{\mathrm{TRS}} R' \Leftrightarrow l_i = l'_i \wedge r_i \leq_s r'_i \text{ for } i = 1, \ldots, n$$

Example 7. From the preceding example:

$$R_1^a \leq_{\mathrm{TRS}} R_2^a \leq_{\mathrm{TRS}} R_3^a$$

Proposition 9. *Given two abstract TRSs R and R', $R = \{l_i \to r_i \mid i = 1, \ldots, n\}$, $R' = \{l_i \to r'_i \mid i = 1, \ldots, n\}$ such that $R \leq_{\mathrm{TRS}} R'$. Then*

$$l_i \leq_s l_j \Rightarrow r_i \leq_s r'_j \textit{ for } i, j = 1, \ldots, n.$$

Proof. Follows from Definition 7 and Definition 8 and the transitivity of $\leq_s$. □

Proposition 10. *Given two terms $t, t' \in T_{\Omega^a, s^a}$, and R, R' two abstract TRSs, $R = \{l_i \to r_i \mid i = 1, \ldots, n\}$, $R' = \{l'_i \to r'_i \mid i = 1, \ldots, n\}$ such that $R \leq_{\mathrm{TRS}} R'$ then*

$$t \leq_s t' \Rightarrow t{\downarrow_R} \leq_s t'{\downarrow_{R'}}$$

Proof. Since t and t' are comparable abstract terms they must have the same number of possible rewriting positions, and R, R' being comparable abstract rewriting systems (having the same left-hand sides), we know that t and t' will normalize in the same number of steps. We use structural induction:

$t = \bot_s$. Trivial.

$t \in T_{C^a, s^a}$. t, t' are already normalized

$t = d^a(t_1, \ldots, t_n), t' = d^a(t_1', \ldots, t_n')$. $t_i \leq_s t_i' \Rightarrow t_i{\downarrow_R} \leq_s t_i'{\downarrow_{R'}}$ by the induction hypothesis.

Then by definition of the term order $\leq_s$ we have $d^a(t_1{\downarrow_R}, \ldots, t_n{\downarrow_R}) \leq_s d^a(t_1'{\downarrow_{R'}}, \ldots, t_n'{\downarrow_{R'}})$. Thus, by Proposition 9 we have $t{\downarrow_R} \leq_s t'{\downarrow_{R'}}$. □

We define below the best abstract TRS (w.r.t. the abstraction α) that may be used to compute the constructor sets.

Definition 11 (α-abstract TRS). Let SP be a constructor-based specification $SP = (\Sigma, R)$, $\Sigma = (S, C \cup D)$. The *α-abstract TRS* for R w.r.t. α, denoted by R^a_α, is defined by:

$\forall d \in D,\ d : s_1 \times \cdots \times s_m \to s,\ \forall c_i^a \in T_{C^a, s_i^a} \setminus \{\bot_{s_i}\},\ i = 1, \ldots, m:$

$$d^a(c_1^a, \ldots, c_m^a) \to \sqcup_s\{\alpha(t{\downarrow_R}) \mid t \in T_\Omega \ \wedge\ \alpha(t) \leq_s d^a(c_1^a, \ldots, c_m^a)\} \in R^a_\alpha$$

and also $\forall d \in D,\ d : s_1 \times \cdots \times s_m \to s,\ x_1^a, \ldots, x_m^a \in X^a, \forall i \in \{1, \ldots, m\}$:

$$d^a(x_1^a, \ldots, x_{i-1}^a, \bot_{s_i}, x_{i+1}^a, \ldots, x_m^a) \to \bot_s \in R^a_\alpha$$

Example 8. We give an example of an α-abstract TRS, and show how it can be used. The α-abstract TRS for SP is $R^a_\alpha = R^a_{\mathrm{seq}\alpha} + R^a_{\mathrm{nat}\alpha}$ where $x^a \in X^a_{\mathrm{seq}}$:

$$\begin{aligned}
R^a_{\mathrm{seq}\alpha} = \{\ & \mathrm{nil}^a +^a \mathrm{nil}^a && \to \mathrm{nil}^a, \\
& \mathrm{nil}^a +^a \mathrm{cons}^a && \to \mathrm{cons}^a, \\
& \mathrm{nil}^a +^a \top_{\mathrm{seq}} && \to \top_{\mathrm{seq}}, \\
& \mathrm{cons}^a +^a \mathrm{nil}^a && \to \mathrm{cons}^a, \\
& \mathrm{cons}^a +^a \mathrm{cons}^a && \to \mathrm{cons}^a, \\
& \mathrm{cons}^a +^a \top_{\mathrm{seq}} && \to \mathrm{cons}^a, \\
& \top_{\mathrm{seq}} +^a \mathrm{nil}^a && \to \top_{\mathrm{seq}}, \\
& \top_{\mathrm{seq}} +^a \mathrm{cons}^a && \to \mathrm{cons}^a, \\
& \top_{\mathrm{seq}} +^a \top_{\mathrm{seq}} && \to \top_{\mathrm{seq}}, \\
& x^a +^a \bot_{\mathrm{seq}} && \to \bot_{\mathrm{seq}}, \\
& \bot_{\mathrm{seq}} +^a x^a && \to \bot_{\mathrm{seq}} \ \}
\end{aligned}$$

Clearly the α-abstract TRSs are terminating and confluent. Let $t = x + (y + \mathrm{cons}(a, u))$. The abstraction of t, $\alpha(t) = t^a = \top_{\mathrm{seq}} + (\top_{\mathrm{seq}} + \mathrm{cons}^a)$ normalizes to cons^a; indeed we have the following derivation: $t^a \to_{R^a_\alpha} \top_{\mathrm{seq}} + \mathrm{cons}^a \to_{R^a_\alpha} \mathrm{cons}^a$. Thus the constructor set of t is $\{\mathrm{cons}\}$.

Definition 12 (Abstract specification). Let *SP* be a constructor-based specification $SP = (\Sigma, R)$. A specification $SP^a = (\Sigma^a, R^a)$ is an *abstract specification* for *SP* iff

1. Σ^a is an abstract signature for Σ
2. R^a is an abstract TRS for R

The abstract specification $SP^a_\alpha = (\Sigma^a, R^a_\alpha)$ where R^a_α is the α-abstracted TRS for R, is called the *α-abstract specification* of *SP*.

Example 9. The TRS $R^a_{\alpha\ seq}$ and the signature Σ^a defined for *SP* above form an α-abstract specification.

From the definition of an α-abstract specification, it is easy to derive the following proposition:

Proposition 13. (Compatibility of the order w.r.t the α-abstraction) *Let $SP = (\Sigma, R)$ be a constructor based-specification, let $SP^a_\alpha = (\Sigma^a, R^a_\alpha)$ be its α-abstraction and let $t_i \in T_{C_{s_i}}, i = 1, \ldots, m$ be ground terms normalized by R, then $\forall d \in D$, $d : s_1 \times \cdots \times s_m \to s$:*

$$\alpha(d(t_1, \ldots, t_m)\downarrow_R) \leq_s \alpha(d(t_1, \ldots, t_m))\downarrow_{R^a_\alpha}$$

Theorem 14. (Soundness of the α-abstraction) *Given a constructor-based specification $SP = (\Sigma, R)$, and its α-abstract specification $SP^a_\alpha = (\Sigma^a, R^a_\alpha)$. Then $\forall s \in S$, $\forall t \in T_\Omega(X)_s$, $\forall \sigma \in GS$:*

$$\alpha(\sigma(t)\downarrow_R) \leq_s \alpha(t)\downarrow_{R^a_\alpha}$$

Proof. Hints: the proof is done by induction on the structure of the term t.

1. For the basis cases $t = x$ where $x \in X_s$, $t = c$, $t = c(t_1, \ldots, t_m)$, where $c \in C$, the proof is straightforward.
2. We detail the key steps of the proof for the case $t = d(t_1, \ldots, t_m)$ where $d \in D$:
   By induction hypothesis, we assume:

   $$\forall t_i \in T_\Omega(X)_{s_i}, \forall \sigma \in GS \Rightarrow \alpha(\sigma(t_i)\downarrow_R) \leq_{s_i} \alpha(t_i)\downarrow_{R^a_\alpha}\ i = 1, \ldots, m$$

   The first part of the inequality, i.e. the exact abstraction of $\sigma(t)\downarrow_R$ is:

   $$\begin{aligned}\alpha(\sigma(t)\downarrow_R) &= \alpha(\sigma(d(t_1, \ldots, t_m))\downarrow_R)\\ &= \alpha(d(\sigma(t_1)\downarrow_R, \ldots, \sigma(t_m)\downarrow_R)\downarrow_R)\end{aligned}$$

The second part of the inequality in the conjecture, i.e. the abstraction by R^a_α, is:

$$\begin{aligned}\alpha(t)\downarrow_{R^a_\alpha} &= \alpha(d(t_1,\ldots,t_m))\downarrow_{R^a_\alpha}\\ &= d^a(\alpha(t_1)\downarrow_{R^a_\alpha},\ldots,\alpha(t_m)\downarrow_{R^a_\alpha})\downarrow_{R^a_\alpha}\end{aligned}$$

By the proposition 13, we obtain:

$$\alpha(d(\sigma(t_1)\downarrow_R,\ldots,\sigma(t_m)\downarrow_R)\downarrow_R) \leq_s d^a(\alpha(\sigma(t_1)\downarrow_R),\ldots,\alpha(\sigma(t_m)\downarrow_R))\downarrow_{R^a_\alpha}$$

By induction hypothesis, by congruence of the order on the terms and by the compatibility of the order with respect to the rewriting in the case where $R =_{TRS} R'$ (Proposition 10):

$$d^a(\alpha(\sigma(t_1)\downarrow_R),\ldots,\alpha(\sigma(t_m)\downarrow_R))\downarrow_{R^a_\alpha} \leq_s d^a(\alpha(t_1)\downarrow_{R^a_\alpha},\ldots,\alpha(t_m)\downarrow_{R^a_\alpha})\downarrow_{R^a_\alpha}$$

Hence by transitivity of the order, the theorem holds.

□

4 Approximating Abstract Specifications

Given a specification *SP*, the corresponding α-abstract specification $SP^a_\alpha = (\Sigma^a, R^a_\alpha)$ together with its signature and term rewriting system has been defined in the previous section. Computing SP^a_α is not an easy task in general as the right-hand sides are infinite unions. In this section, we provide a way to compute an approximation of the right-hand sides of the α-abstract term rewriting system R^a_α (Note that the left-hand sides can be obtained directly from Definition 11). We do this by finding the least fixed point of a transformation on abstract TRSs. The basic idea is to gather progressively the information of abstract terms.

In order to define the transformation we need a way of abstracting rewrite rules in R. This requires a technical definition that introduces the notion of *rule abstraction*. The abstraction of a rewrite rule is the same as the abstraction of the terms on the left- and right-hand sides, except for the treatment of variables: Variables in the left-hand side are turned into abstract variables unless they are hidden by constructors. Variables in the right-hand side are turned into abstract variables *if* they also occur in the abstracted left-hand side.

Definition 15 (Rule abstraction α). Let $l \to r$ be a rule in R. Its abstraction, noted $\alpha(l \to r)$ is defined by:

$$\alpha(l \to r) = \alpha^l(l) \to \alpha^r[\alpha^l(l)](r)$$

where

$$\begin{aligned}
\alpha^l(x) &= x^a \text{ if } x \in X_s \\
\alpha^l(c) &= c^a \text{ if } c \in C \\
\alpha^l(c(t_1,\ldots,t_m)) &= c^a \text{ if } c \in C \\
\alpha^l(d(t_1,\ldots,t_m)) &= d^a(\alpha^l(t_1),\ldots,\alpha^l(t_m)) \text{ if } d \in D
\end{aligned}$$

and

$$\begin{aligned}
\alpha^r[l^a](x) &= x^a \text{ if } x^a \in \mathrm{Var}(l^a) \\
\alpha^r[l^a](x) &= \top_s \text{ if } x \notin \mathrm{Var}(l^a) \\
\alpha^r[l^a](c) &= c^a \text{ if } c \in C \\
\alpha^r[l^a](c(t_1,\ldots,t_m)) &= c^a \text{ if } c \in C \\
\alpha^r[l^a](d(t_1,\ldots,t_m)) &= d^a(\alpha^r[l^a](t_1),\ldots,\alpha^r[l^a](t_m)) \text{ if } d \in D
\end{aligned}$$

Example 10. $d(c(x),y)) \to d(x,y)$ is a rule in R, x and y are variables of sort s, c is a constructor in C_s and d an operator in D_s.

$$\begin{aligned}
\alpha(d(c(x),y) \to d(x,y)) &= \alpha^l(d(c(x),y)) \to \alpha^r[l^a](d(x,y)) \\
&= d^a(\alpha^l(c(x)),\alpha^l(y)) \to d^a(\alpha^r[l^a](x),\alpha^r[l^a](y)) \\
&= d^a(c^a,y^a) \to d^a(\top_s,y^a)
\end{aligned}$$

where we use l^a as a short-hand for the abstracted left-hand side.

To define the transformation on the TRSs we need the notion of matching substitution that matches one abstract term onto another. As in ordinary TRSs, we choose the most "general" matching substitution.

Example 11. Let $\sigma(f^a(c^a,y)) \leq_s f(\top_s,\top_s)$. There are at least two possibilities for σ: $\sigma = \{y \to c^a\}$, or $\sigma = \{y \to \top_s\}$. The last possibility is the most general since it gives the largest term less than $f(\top_s,\top_s)$.

In the definition below, we introduce a transformation on abstract TRSs denoted Φ_R. Our interest is to compute the least fixed point of this transformation by successive iterations. We will note by R^a_{k+1} the application of the transformation Φ_R on R^a_k (i.e. $\Phi_R(R^a_k) = R^a_{k+1}$).

Definition 16 (Φ_R). Given a constructor-based specification $SP = (\Sigma, R)$, $\Sigma = (S, C \cup D)$, n is the number of left-hand sides in the abstract TRS. The transformation on abstract rewrite systems Φ_R is defined as follows :

$$\Phi_R : (l_1^a \to T_{C^a,s_1^a}) \times \cdots \times (l_n^a \to T_{C^a,s_n^a}) \mapsto (l_1^a \to T_{C^a,s_1^a}) \times \cdots \times (l_n^a \to T_{C^a,s_n^a})$$

$$\begin{aligned}
\Phi_R(R^a_k) &= R^a_{k+1} \\
\Phi_R(\{l_i^a \to r_{ik}^a \mid i = 1,\ldots,n\}) &= \{l_i^a \to r_{i(k+1)}^a \mid i = 1,\ldots,n\}
\end{aligned}$$

where

$$r^a_{i(k+1)} = \sqcup_{s_i}\{\sigma(r^a_j)\downarrow_{R^a_k} | l_j \to r_j \in R, \alpha(l_j \to r_j) = l^a_j \to r^a_j, \sigma(l^a_j) \leq_{s_i} l^a_i\}$$

Note that Φ_R only changes the right-hand sides.

Proposition 17. *Φ_R is continuous*

Proof. Since we are dealing with a finite lattice, we only have to prove Φ_R to be monotonic.

Let $R^a = \{l^a_i \to r^a_i \mid i = 1,\ldots,n\}$ and $R^{a\prime} = \{l^a_i \to r^{a\prime}_i \mid i = 1,\ldots,n\}$, $R^a \leq_{\text{TRS}} R^{a\prime}$. Then

$$\begin{aligned}\Phi_R \text{ monotonic} &\Leftrightarrow \Phi_R(R^a) \leq_{\text{TRS}} \Phi_R(R^{a\prime}) \\ &\Leftrightarrow \sigma(r^a_j)\downarrow_{R^a} \leq_{s_i} \sigma(r^{a\prime}_j)\downarrow_{R^{a\prime}} \\ &\quad \forall l_j \to r_j \in R, \alpha(l_j \to r_j) = l^a_j \to r^a_j, \sigma(l^a_j) \leq_{s_i} l^a_i \\ &\quad \text{for } i = 1,\ldots,n.\end{aligned}$$

The latter is a special case of Proposition 10. □

From the proposition above, Φ_R admits a least fixed point that may be computed iteratively starting from the bottom, say $\{l^a_i \to \bot_{s_i} \mid i = 1,\ldots,n\}$. This computation always terminates because the considered lattice is finite. We denote by R^a_c the least fixed point of Φ_R. The subscript c in R^a_c stands for *computed abstract TRS.*

Example 12. Given the following system based on the natural numbers:

$$R = \{f(0) \to 0,\ f(\text{succ}(x)) \to f(f(x))\}$$

where 0 and succ are constructors and f a defined operator. We obtain the computed abstract TRS by computing the least fixed point as described above:

R^a_0		R^a_1		R^a_2		$R^a_3 = R^a_c$	
$f^a(\bot_{\text{nat}})$	$\to \bot_{\text{nat}}$	$f^a(\bot_{\text{nat}})$	$\to \bot_{\text{nat}}$	$f^a(\bot_{\text{nat}})$	$\to \bot_{\text{nat}}$	$f^a(\bot_{\text{nat}})$	$\to \bot_{\text{nat}}$
$f^a(0^a)$	$\to \bot_{\text{nat}}$	$f^a(0^a)$	$\to 0^a$	$f^a(0^a)$	$\to 0^a$	$f^a(0^a)$	$\to 0^a$
$f^a(\text{succ}^a)$	$\to \bot_{\text{nat}}$	$f^a(\text{succ}^a)$	$\to \bot_{\text{nat}}$	$f^a(\text{succ}^a)$	$\to 0^a$	$f^a(\text{succ}^a)$	$\to 0^a$
$f^a(\top_{\text{nat}})$	$\to \bot_{\text{nat}}$	$f^a(\top_{\text{nat}})$	$\to 0^a$	$f^a(\top_{\text{nat}})$	$\to 0^a$	$f^a(\top_{\text{nat}})$	$\to 0^a$

In this case, four iterations were needed to compute the fixed point.

Theorem 18. *Given a constructor-based specification $SP = (\Sigma, R)$, and its α-abstract specification $SP^a_\alpha = (\Sigma^a, R^a_\alpha)$. Let SP^a_c be the computed abstract specification (Σ^a, R^a_c) where R^a_c is the least fixed point of Φ_R. Then, $R^a_\alpha \leq_{\text{TRS}} R^a_c$.*

Proof. (Sketch) Let $l^a \to r^a \in R^a_\alpha$ and $l^a \to r^a_c \in R^a_c$. Let us prove that $r^a \leq_s r^a_c$. Since $l^a \to r^a \in R^a_\alpha$, by definition of R^a_α, for every term $t = f(t_1, \ldots, t_m) \in T_\Omega$ with $\alpha(t) \leq_s l^a$, $f \in D$, we have (1) $f(t_1, \ldots, t_m) \xrightarrow{*}_R t{\downarrow_R}$ with $\alpha(t{\downarrow_R}) \leq_s r^a$. Let n be the maximal length of (1) ($n = 0$ is impossible). Let us prove by induction on n that $\alpha(t{\downarrow_R}) \leq_s r^a_c$. Thus $r^a \leq_s r^a_c$ (since r^a is the "union" ($\sqcup$) of such $\alpha(t{\downarrow_R})$).

Case $n = 1$:

$$f(t_1, \ldots, t_m) \to_{[g \to d]} c_1(\ldots)$$

This means that there exists a matching substitution θ such that (2) $\theta(g) = f(t_1, \ldots, t_m)$. Let $g^a \to d^a = \alpha(g \to d)$. Then, there exists, from (1) and (2), σ such that $\sigma(g^a) \leq_s l^a$. Then by definition of Φ_R and R^a_c being a fixed point, we have: $c^a_1 = \alpha(t{\downarrow_R}) \leq_s r^a_c$.

Induction hypothesis: If $t \xrightarrow{n} t{\downarrow_R}$, with $t = h(t_1, \ldots, t_m), h \in D, \alpha(t) \leq_s l^a, l^a \to r^a \in R^a_\alpha$ and $l^a \to r^a_c \in R^a_c$, then $\alpha(t{\downarrow_R}) \leq_s r^a_c$.

Induction step: Let $t \xrightarrow{n+1} t{\downarrow_R}$, then $t \to t' \xrightarrow{n} t{\downarrow_R}$. Let $t = f(t_1, \ldots, t_m)$ such that $\alpha(t) \leq_s l^a$. There are two possibilities for t'.

1. $t' = c_1(\ldots), c_1 \in C$
2. $t' = h(u_1, \ldots, u_n), h \in D$

Case 1: Similar to the base case $n = 1$.

Case 2: We have

$$f(t_1, \ldots, t_m) \to_{[g \to d]} h(u_1, \ldots, u_n) \xrightarrow{n} t{\downarrow_R}$$

Let $l^{a\prime} = h^a(\alpha(u_1{\downarrow_R}), \ldots, \alpha(u_n{\downarrow_R}))$ and $l^{a\prime} \to r^{a\prime}_c$ be in R^a_c so that $\alpha(h(u_1{\downarrow_R}, \ldots, u_n{\downarrow_R})) \leq_s l^{a\prime}$. We have $l^{a\prime} \to w^a \in R^a_\alpha$ with $\alpha(t{\downarrow_R}) \leq_s w^a$ (I). By the induction hypothesis $w^a \leq_s r^{a\prime}_c$ (II). Let $g^a \to d^a = \alpha(g \to d)$. As in case 1, there exists a matching substitution σ such that $\sigma(g^a) \leq_s l^a$. By the definition of Φ_R and R^a_c being a fixed point of Φ_R we have $r^{a\prime}_c \leq_s r^a_c$ (III). From (I), (II) and (III) we have $\alpha(t{\downarrow_R}) \leq_s r^a_c$. □

5 Conclusion

We have developed a method of finding possible head constructors of terms. To do this, we have introduced the concept abstract specification corresponding to a given constructor-based specification. Terms are abstracted and the computation is done using the abstract specification. Our computation have been proved sound. This theory can easily be rephrased within the framework of abstract interpretation [4] with minor changes.

Since abstract specifications cannot be computed effectively from the definition, we have provided a way of approximating them. This is done by computing a least-fixed point of a transformation on abstract rewrite rules. Soundness of the approximation have been proved.

Our work can easily be applied to improve E-unification: Indeed, if the greatest upper bound of $\alpha(t)\downarrow_{R^a_\alpha}$ and $\alpha(t')\downarrow_{R^a_\alpha}$ is $\bot_s$ then the terms t and t' are not E-unifiable. In this areas, other improvements to the technique of narrowing have been made. The authors of [6] have an idea close to ours. Conditions on the applications of the rewrite rules are used to prune the search tree. The conditions are determined in advance by looking at the function symbols on top of each left- and right-hand side of the rules, and determining which function symbols can be obtained from which. Our method is more precise and thus allows us to handle cases where their method fails.

Several limitations have been introduced in the framework at hand:

1. The definition of a constructor-based specification, Definition 1, could be weakened to accept limited rewrite rules between constructors.
2. The interpretation domain T_{C^a} could be generalized to deal with finer interpretations. As defined now, the approximated abstract specification sometimes gives a too loose estimation for the constructor sets. This can be seen from the following example

$$R = \{f(c_1) \rightarrow f(c_2(c_1)),\ f(c_2(x)) \rightarrow x\}$$

where $S = \{s\}$, $f \in D$ and $c_1, c_2 \in C$, $c_1 :\rightarrow s$, $c_2 : s \rightarrow s$. By using the fixed point of Φ_R, i.e. R^a_c, we will not realize that $f^a(c_1^a) = c_1^a$. To overcome this problem, we need more fine-grained abstract constructors, i.e. taking into account their parameters, like $c_2^a(c_1^a)$ and generally $c_2^a(c_2^a(\ldots c_2^a(c_1^a)\ldots))$ depending on the shape of the rewrite rules in R.

References

1. Didier Bert and Rachid Echahed. Design and implementation of a generic, logic and functional programming language. Number 213 in Lecture Notes in Computer Science, pages 119–132. Springer-Verlag, 1986.
2. P.G. Bosco, E. Giovannetti, G. Levi, and C. Moiso, C.and Palamidessi. A complete semantic characterization of K-LEAF, a logic language with partial functions. In *Proceedings of the 4th IEEE International Symposium on Logic Programming*, pages 318–327, San Francisco, 1987.
3. Patrick Cousot and Radhia Cousot. Abstract interpretation and application to logic programs. *Journal of Logic Programming*, 13(1, 2, 3 and 4):103–179, 1992. Also appeared as Technical Report LIENS-92-12, École normale supérieure, Paris.

4. Patrick Cousot and Radhia Cousot. Abstract interpretation frameworks. Technical Report LIX-RR-92-05, École polytecnique, 1992.

5. N. Dershowitz and J. Jouannaud. Rewrite systems. In J. van Leeuwen, editor, *Handbook of Theoretical Computer Science B: Formal Methods and Semantics*, chapter 6, pages 243–320. North Holland, Amsterdam, 1990.

6. Nachum Dershowitz and G. Sivakumar. Solving goals in equational languages. Number 308 in Lecture Notes in Computer Science, pages 45–55. Springer-Verlag, July 1987.

7. Harmut Ehrig and Bernd Mahr. *Fundamentals of Algebraic Specification 1: Equations and Initial Semantics*. EATCS Monographs on Theoretical Computer Science. Springer-Verlag, 1985.

8. L. Fribourg. Slog: A logic programming language interpreter based on clausal superposition and rewriting. In *Proc. IEEE International Symposium on Logic Programming*, pages 172–184, Boston, 1985.

9. M. Hanus. Compiling logic programs with equality. In *Proceedings of the 2nd International Workshop on Programming Language Implementation and Logic Programming*, number 456 in Lecture Notes in Computer Science, pages 387–401. Springer-Verlag, 1990.

10. J.-M. Hullot. Canonical forms and unification. In *Proc. 5th Conference on Automated Deduction*, number 87 in Lecture Notes in Computer Science, pages 318–334. Springer-Verlag, 1980.

11. J. W. Klop. Term Rewriting Systems. In S. Abramsky, D. Gabbay, and T. Maibaum, editors, *Handbook of Logic in Computer Science, Vol. II*, pages 1–112. Oxford University Press, 1992. Previous version: Term rewriting systems, Technical Report CS-R9073, Stichting Mathematisch Centrum, Amsterdam, 1990.

12. J. J. Moreno-Navarro and M. Rodríguez-Artalejo. Logic programming with functions and predicates: The language BABEL. *Journal of Logic Programming*, 12:191–223, 1992.

Reflections on Program Optimization

Paul Hudak

Department of Computer Science
Yale University

Abstract. Modern program optimization techniques that rely on sophisticated program analyses can result in enormous improvements in program performance. The cost associated with such an effort is usually measured in terms of compiler speed and complexity. However, there are at least two other, perhaps more severe, costs to be reckoned with: First, program performance can become very difficult to reason about (the programmer needs to understand the inner workings of the compiler). Second, programs can lose portability (a large enough quantitative difference amounts to a qualitative difference). In this talk I will attempt to classify the kinds of languages, language features, optimizations, etc. that are particularly susceptible to these problems, and discuss ways whereby we might alleviate the problems.

Finiteness Conditions for Strictness Analysis

Flemming Nielson, Hanne Riis Nielson
Computer Science Department, Aarhus University
Ny Munkegade, DK-8000 Aarhus C, Denmark

e-mail: {fnielson,hrnielson}@daimi.aau.dk

Abstract

We give upper bounds on the number of times the fixed point operator needs to be unfolded for strictness analysis of functional languages with lists. This extends previous work both in the syntax-directed nature of the approach and in the ability to deal with Wadler's method for analysing lists. Limitations of the method are indicated.

1 Introduction

Strictness analysis for functional programs by means of abstract interpretation is a very powerful technique: both in terms of the accuracy of the results produced and in the applicability to various language constructs. The main disadvantage of the method is that the computational cost may be too high for many applications and as a result the method is not usually incorporated in a compiler.

Rather than resorting to cruder methods, e.g. based on variations of type analysis, we believe that it is possible to identify certain programs where the cost may be analysed in advance and determined not to be excessive. This would allow the compiler to perform the abstract interpretation in those instances where the cost is not prohibitive. The notion of cost we will be taking throughout this paper is the number of iterations needed to reach the fixed point.

In [6] we developed first results along this line. Section 2 contains a brief review of the main results of [6] but with a change of emphasis that is more suited to a structural approach (for functional programs). Section 3 then develops our main results for simple strictness analysis and in Section 4 we add the analysis of lists using Wadler's "inverse cons" method. Finally, Section 5 contains the conclusion. We refer to [9] for some of the proofs.

2 Boundedness

The abstract interpretation of a recursive program gives rise to a functional

$$H : (A \to B) \to (A \to B)$$

Typically, and as we shall assume throughout, A and B are finite complete lattices: this means that all subsets Y of A (resp. B) have least upper bounds denoted $\bigsqcup Y$ (or $y_1 \sqcup \cdots \sqcup y_n$ if $Y = \{y_1, \cdots, y_n\}$). Furthermore all functions will be monotone: for H this means that if $h_1 \sqsubseteq h_2$ then $H(h_1) \sqsubseteq H(h_2)$ for all $h_1, h_2 \in A \to B$. The least fixed point of H is given by

$$\text{FIX } H = \bigsqcup \{H^i \bot \mid i \geq 0\}$$

where $\bot$ is the least element of $A \to B$. Clearly if $H^{k+1}\bot = H^k\bot$ then FIX $H = H^k\bot$ because of the monotonicity of H. By the finiteness of A and B there will always be some (perhaps large) k such that this holds.

The notion of k-boundedness is of interest when the functional H is additionally additive: this is the case when $H(h_1 \sqcup h_2) = H(h_1) \sqcup H(h_2)$ for all $h_1, h_2 \in A \to B$. It is helpful to write

$$H^{[k]}h = \bigsqcup \{H^i h \mid 0 \leq i < k\}$$

and motivated by [4] we say that H is *k-bounded* if

$$H^k h \sqsubseteq H^{[k]} h \quad \text{for all} \quad h \in A \to B$$

We shall write

$$H \in \mathcal{A}(k)$$

to mean that H is additive and k-bounded.

Proposition 2.1 When $H \in \mathcal{A}(k)$, i.e. H is k-bounded and additive, we have FIX $H = H^{[k]}\bot = H^{k-1}\bot = H^k\bot$.

Proof: This is a revised version of [6, Lemma 11]; some key facts (necessary for the subsequent proofs) are presented in Appendix A of [9]. □

Types:	$[\![\texttt{num}]\!]$	$=$	$\mathbf{2}$
	$[\![\texttt{bool}]\!]$	$=$	$\mathbf{2}$
	$[\![t_1 \times t_2]\!]$	$=$	$[\![t_1]\!] \times [\![t_2]\!]$
	$[\![t_1 \to t_2]\!]$	$=$	$[\![t_1]\!] \to [\![t_2]\!]$
Expressions:	$[\![c]\!]\rho$	$=$	$\hat{c}$
	$[\![x]\!]\rho$	$=$	$\rho\ x$
	$[\![\texttt{fst}\ e]\!]\rho$	$=$	$\mathit{fst}([\![e]\!]\rho)$
	$[\![\texttt{snd}\ e]\!]\rho$	$=$	$\mathit{snd}([\![e]\!]\rho)$
	$[\![(e_1, e_2)]\!]\rho$	$=$	$([\![e_1]\!]\rho, [\![e_2]\!]\rho)$
	$[\![\texttt{lam}\ x.e]\!]\rho$	$=$	$\lambda a.[\![e]\!](\rho[x \mapsto a])$
	$[\![e_1\ e_2]\!]\rho$	$=$	$[\![e_1]\!]\rho([\![e_2]\!]\rho)$
	$[\![\texttt{if}\ e\ \texttt{then}\ e_1\ \texttt{else}\ e_2]\!]\rho$	$=$	$[\![e]\!]\rho \rhd ([\![e_1]\!]\rho \sqcup [\![e_2]\!]\rho)$
	$[\![\texttt{fix}\ e]\!]\rho$	$=$	$\mathrm{FIX}\ ([\![e]\!]\rho)$

Table 1: Strictness Analysis

3 Strictness Analysis

To motivate the form of the functionals considered we begin with a brief review of strictness analysis. To this end consider a simply typed λ-calculus with constants, a conditional and a fixed point construct. The types are

$$t ::= \texttt{num} \mid \texttt{bool} \mid t_1 \times t_2 \mid t_1 \to t_2$$

and the expressions are

$$\begin{array}{rcl} e & ::= & c \mid x \mid \texttt{fst}\ e \mid \texttt{snd}\ e \mid (e_1, e_2) \\ & \mid & \texttt{lam}\ x.e \mid e_1\ e_2 \\ & \mid & \texttt{if}\ e\ \texttt{then}\ e_1\ \texttt{else}\ e_2 \mid \mathrm{FIX}\ e \end{array}$$

The expressions are assumed to be well-typed but it is outside the scope of this paper to present the formal machinery for enforcing this.

The strictness analysis is specified in Table 1. In the *type part* we write $\mathbf{2}$ for the complete lattice $(\{0, 1\}, \sqsubseteq)$ where $0 \sqsubseteq 1$. We write $D_1 \times D_2$ for the cartesian product of D_1 and D_2, and we write $D_1 \to D_2$ for the complete lattice of monotone functions from D_1 to D_2 ordered pointwise.

The *expression part* of the analysis associates a property $\hat{c}$ with each constant c. To specify the analysis of expressions with free variables we use an environment

ρ mapping variables to properties. The analysis of the conditional uses the operator $\triangleright$ defined by

$$d_0 \triangleright d = \begin{cases} \bot & \text{if } d_0 = 0 \\ d & \text{if } d_0 = 1 \end{cases}$$

where $\bot$ is the least element of the lattice that d belongs to and where d_0 belongs to **2**. This is then lifted pointwise to functions

$$(h_0 \triangleright h) = \lambda d.\ (h_0\ d) \triangleright (h\ d).$$

A Structural Approach to Boundedness

Given a functional H as might arise from the above strictness analysis the aim now is to find sufficient conditions for H to be additive and k-bounded for some hopefully low value of k. We begin with a simple fact and a brief review of the main results from [6]; then we move on to a more general treatment of the operators $\sqcup$ and $\triangleright$.

Fact 3.1 $Id = \lambda h.h \in \mathcal{A}(1)$, $\lambda h.g \in \mathcal{A}(2)$ and $\lambda h.\bot \in \mathcal{A}(1)$.

The monotone length $len_m(h)$ of a function $h \in A \to B$ is given by

$$len_m(h) = max\{l_m(h,a) | a \in A\}$$

where $l_m(h,a) = min\{i | h^i(a) \in \{a, h(a), \cdots, h^{i-1}(a)\}\downarrow, i > 0\}$. Here we write $Y\downarrow$ for the down-closure of Y, i.e. the set $\{d | \exists y \in Y : d \sqsubseteq y\}$.

Lemma 3.2 $\lambda h.\ g_1 \circ h \circ g_2 \in \mathcal{A}(len_m(g_1) \cdot len_m(g_2))$ if g_1 is additive.

Proof: This is essentially [6, Lemma 25]. □

Corollary 3.3 $\lambda h.\ h \circ g \in \mathcal{A}(len_m(g))$ and if g is additive then $\lambda h.\ g \circ h \in \mathcal{A}(len_m(g))$.

Proof: When id is the identity function we have $len_m(id) = 1$. □

We now extend the development of [6] by considering the least upper bound operator.

Lemma 3.4 $H_1 \sqcup H_2 \in \mathcal{A}(k_1 + k_2 - 1)$ if $H_1 \in \mathcal{A}(k_1)$, $H_2 \in \mathcal{A}(k_2)$ and if H_1 and H_2 commute (i.e. $H_1 \circ H_2 = H_2 \circ H_1$) and B is not trivial.

Proof: See Appendix B of [9]. □

Corollary 3.5 $H \sqcup Id \in \mathcal{A}(k)$ if $H \in \mathcal{A}(k)$ and B is not trivial.

Lemma 3.6 $H_1 \sqcup H_2 \in \mathcal{A}(k+1)$ if $H_1 \in \mathcal{A}(k)$ and $H_2 = \lambda h.g$ (for some $g \in A \rightarrow B$).

Proof: See Appendix B of [9]. □

Remark This shows that if $H = \lambda h.\ g \sqcup (G\ h)$ and $G \in \mathcal{A}(k)$ then $H \in \mathcal{A}(k+1)$ so that FIX $H = H^k \bot$ (as opposed to $H^{k-1}\bot$). Since functionals of the form H typically arise for iterative programs this explains the naturality of the definition of k-boundedness in the setting of [4]; in our setting it might have been more natural to redefine k-boundedness of H to mean $H^{k+1} \sqsubseteq H^{[k+1]}$. □

We next turn to the $\rhd$ operator.

Fact 3.7 We have the following properties of $\rhd$:

- $h_0 \rhd (h_1 \sqcup h_2) = (h_0 \rhd h_1) \sqcup (h_0 \rhd h_2)$.
- $(h_1 \rhd h_2) \circ h_3 = (h_1 \circ h_3) \rhd (h_2 \circ h_3)$.
- $h_1 \rhd (h_2 \rhd h_3) = (h_1 \sqcap h_2) \rhd h_3$.

Lemma 3.8 $\lambda h.\ g \rhd (H\ h) \in \mathcal{A}(k)$ if $H \in \mathcal{A}(k)$ and if there exists a (monotone) functional $\delta H \in (A \rightarrow \mathbf{2}) \rightarrow (A \rightarrow \mathbf{2})$ such that $H(h_1 \rhd h_2) = (\delta H(h_1)) \rhd H(h_2)$ for $h_1, h_2 \in A \rightarrow B$.

Proof: See Appendix B of [9]. □

Fact 3.9 $\delta(\lambda h.\ h \circ g_2) = \lambda h.\ h \circ g_2$ and if g_1 is strict then $\delta(\lambda h.\ g_1 \circ h \circ g_2) = \lambda h.\ h \circ g_2$.

Example 3.10 As an example of a tail-recursive program we consider the *factorial program with an accumulator.* It can be written as

$$\text{FIX }(\texttt{lam } fac.\ \texttt{lam } xa.\ \texttt{if } (=0)(\texttt{fst } xa)\ \texttt{then snd } xa$$
$$\texttt{else } fac((-1)(\texttt{fst } xa), *\ xa))$$

Here $(=0)$ tests for equality with 0, $*$ is the multiplication operator and (-1) subtracts one from its argument. The strictness analysis will therefore give rise to a functional H of the form

$$H\ h = g_0 \rhd (g_1 \sqcup h \circ g_2)$$

which may be rewritten to

$$H\ h = (g_0 \rhd g_1) \sqcup (g_0 \rhd (h \circ g_2))$$

using Fact 3.7. The functions g_0, g_1 and g_2 are given by

$$\begin{aligned} g_0 &= \mathit{fst} \\ g_1 &= \mathit{snd} \\ g_2 &= \mathit{tuple}(\mathtt{fst}, \hat{*}) \end{aligned}$$

where $\mathit{tuple}(h_1, h_2)x = (h_1(x), h_2(x))$ and $\hat{*}(x_1, x_2) = x_1 \sqcap x_2$. Since g_2 is reductive (i.e. $g_2 \sqsubseteq \mathit{id}$) it follows that $\mathit{len}_m(g_2) = 1$. By Corollary 3.3, Lemma 3.8, Fact 3.9, and Lemma 3.6 the functional H is 2-bounded and by Proposition 2.1 the first unfolding will give the fixed point.

Lemma 3.11 Let $H : (A \to B) \to (A \to B)$ be defined by

$$H\ h = g \circ \mathit{tuple}(h \circ g_1, g_2)$$

where $g : B \times B \to B$, $g_1 : A \to A$ and $g_2 : A \to B$. Assume that

- g is *associative*, i.e. $g(g(b_1, b_2), b_3) = g(b_1, g(b_2, b_3))$ for all $b_1, b_2, b_3 \in B$,
- g is strict and additive *in its left argument*, i.e. $g(\bot, b) = \bot$ and $g(b_1 \sqcup b_2, b) = g(b_1, b) \sqcup g(b_2, b)$ for all $b, b_1, b_2 \in B$, and
- g has a *right identity* b_0, i.e. $g(b, b_0) = b$ for all $b \in B$, and
- $k = \mathit{len}_m(\mathit{tuple}(g_1 \circ \mathit{fst}, g \circ \mathit{tuple}(g_2 \circ \mathit{fst}, \mathit{snd})))$.

Then $H \in \mathcal{A}(k)$ and $\delta H = \lambda h.\ h \circ g_1$.

Proof: See Appendix B of [9]. This result was stated but not proved in [6]. □

One undesirable feature of the above lemma is that we need to take the length of a composite function. However, the lemma suffices for treating a non-accumulator version of factorial.

Example 3.12 The usual *factorial program* can be written as

$$\text{FIX}\ (\mathtt{lam}\ \mathit{fac}.\ \mathtt{lam}\ x.\ \mathtt{if}\ (=0)(x)\ \mathtt{then}\ 1\ \mathtt{else}\ *(\mathit{fac}((-1)x), x))$$

The strictness analysis will therefore give rise to a functional H of the form

$$H\ h = g_0 \ \triangleright\ (g_1 \ \sqcup\ g \circ \mathit{tuple}(h \circ g_2, g_3))$$

which may be rewritten to

$$H\ h = (g_0 \triangleright g_1) \sqcup (g_0 \ \triangleright\ g \circ \mathit{tuple}(h \circ g_2, g_3))$$

using Fact 3.7. The functions are $g_0 = \lambda x.x$, $g_1 = \lambda x.\mathit{1}$, $g_2 = \lambda x.x$, $g_3 = \lambda x.x$ and $g = \lambda(x_1, x_2).x_1 \sqcap x_2$. The function $\mathit{tuple}(g_2 \circ \mathit{fst}, g \circ \mathit{tuple}(g_3 \circ \mathit{fst}, \mathit{snd}))$ then amounts to the function called g_2 in Example 3.10.

4 Strictness Analysis for Lists

We shall now extend the typed λ-calculus with lists:

$$t ::= \cdots \mid t\ \mathtt{list}$$

The syntax of expressions is extended with constructs for building lists and for taking them apart:

$$e ::= \cdots \mid \mathtt{nil} \mid \mathtt{cons}\ e_1\ e_2 \mid \mathtt{case}\ e\ \mathtt{of\ nil} : e_1 \,\|\, \mathtt{cons}\ x_1\ x_2 : e_2$$

We shall follow [10] and construct the lattice of properties for lists by a double lifting of the lattice of the element type: if D is the lattice of properties for the elements of the list then $(D_\bot)_\bot$ will be the lattice of properties of the lists. The least element of $(D_\bot)_\bot$ is denoted *0*, the second least element *1* and the remaining elements are denoted $d\epsilon$ where d is an element of D. We write $\top$ for the largest element of D. The idea then is that

- *0*: denotes the undefined list,
- *1*: denotes additionally all infinite lists and all partial lists ending in the undefined list,
- $d\epsilon$: denotes additionally all finite lists where the meet of the elements satisfies property d (for d not being $\top$)[1], and
- $\top\epsilon$: denotes all lists.

The strictness analysis of Table 1 is now extended with the clauses of Table 2. For **nil** we observe that the only property describing the empty list is $\top\epsilon$. For **cons** e_1 e_2 we combine the property of the head with the property of the tail using a greatest lower bound operation. For the **case** construct we want to "reverse" this construction. To this end we use two auxiliary operations

$$\mathit{isnil} : (D_\bot)_\bot \to \mathbf{2}$$

$$\mathit{split} : (D_\bot)_\bot \to \mathcal{P}(D \times (D_\bot)_\bot)$$

Here $\mathcal{P}(D)$ is the *lower powerdomain* of D. When D is a finite complete lattice one may take $\mathcal{P}(D)$ to have as elements those non-empty subsets Y of D that satisfy $Y = Y\!\downarrow$ (i.e. Y is downward closed); the partial order is subset inclusion. Then $\mathcal{P}(D)$ will also be a finite complete lattice with least element $\{\bot\}$ and

[1] When the lattice D of properties for the elements is actually a chain this condition may be expressed in the following more intuitive way: $d\epsilon$ denotes additionally all finite lists where at least one element satisfies property d (for d not being $\top$). We refer to [8, Chapter 7] for a more thorough discussion of this.

Types:	$[\![t\ \mathtt{list}]\!]$	$= ([\![t]\!]_\perp)_\perp$
Expressions:	$[\![\mathtt{nil}]\!]\rho$	$= \top\epsilon$
	$[\![\mathtt{cons}\ e_1\ e_2]\!]\rho$	$= ([\![e_1]\!]\rho)\epsilon \sqcap ([\![e_2]\!]\rho)$
$[\![\mathtt{case}\ e\ \mathtt{of}\ \mathtt{nil} : e_1 \,\|$		
	$\mathtt{cons}\ x_1\ x_2 : e_2]\!]\rho$	$= (isnil([\![e]\!]\rho) \rhd [\![e_1]\!]\rho) \sqcup$ $\bigsqcup (\mathcal{P}(\lambda(a_1,a_2).[\![e_2]\!]\rho[x_1 \mapsto a_1][x_2 \mapsto a_2])$ $(split([\![e]\!]\rho)))$

Table 2: Strictness analysis for lists

greatest element D. We may now define the functions *isnil* and *split* by

$$isnil\ d = \begin{cases} 0 & \text{if } d \neq \top\epsilon \\ 1 & \text{if } d = \top\epsilon \end{cases}$$

$$split\ d = \{(d_1, d_2) | d_1\epsilon \sqcap d_2 \sqsubseteq d\}$$

Thus *isnil* d will return *1* if d is a property of the empty list and *split* d will return (the downward closed set of) all possible pairs of properties that the head and the tail of the list could have had. In the case where $D = \mathbf{2}$ we can tabulate *isnil* and *split* as follows:

	0	*1*	*0*ϵ	*1*ϵ
isnil	*0*	*0*	*0*	*1*
split	$\{(1,0)\}\downarrow$	$\{(1,1)\}\downarrow$	$\{(0,1\epsilon),\ (1,0\epsilon)\}\downarrow$	$\{(1,1\epsilon)\}\downarrow$

In the definition of $[\![\mathtt{case}\ e\ \mathtt{of}\ \mathtt{nil} : e_1 \,\|\, \mathtt{cons}\ x_1\ x_2 : e_2]\!]\rho$ we first determine the property of the list $[\![e]\!]\rho$. If it could possibly be a property of the empty list we must have a contribution from $[\![e_1]\!]\rho$; this is expressed using the $\rhd$ operator. Whether or not this is the case the property of the list is split into a set of properties of the head and the tail and we must have a contribution from $[\![e_2]\!]\rho$ for each of these possibilities. This is expressed using the operator

$$\mathcal{P} : (D_1 \to D_2) \to (\mathcal{P}(D_1) \to \mathcal{P}(D_2))$$

which extends its first argument pointwise to operate on elements in the power domain: for $Y \in \mathcal{P}(D_1)$ we have

$$\mathcal{P}(h)(Y) = \{h(d) \mid d \in Y\}\downarrow .$$

In other words $\mathcal{P}$ is extended to a functor. Finally, all contributions are combined by taking least upper bounds.

Boundedness Results for Lists

To obtain k-boundedness results for functionals arising from the analysis of lists we begin with a characterization of the $\mathcal{P}$ operator. For this it is helpful to write $\{\!\!\{\ \}\!\!\} = \lambda d.(\{d\}\downarrow)$.

Fact 4.1

- $\bigsqcup \circ \mathcal{P}(h_1 \sqcup h_2) = (\bigsqcup \circ \mathcal{P}(h_1)) \sqcup (\bigsqcup \circ \mathcal{P}(h_2))$
- $\mathcal{P}(h) \circ \{\!\!\{\ \}\!\!\} = \{\!\!\{\ \}\!\!\} \circ h$
- $\bigsqcup \circ \{\!\!\{\ \}\!\!\} = id$
- $\mathcal{P}(h_1 \circ h_2) = \mathcal{P}(h_1) \circ \mathcal{P}(h_2)$
- $\bigsqcup \circ \mathcal{P}(\bigsqcup) = \bigsqcup \circ \bigcup$
- $\bigcup \circ \mathcal{P}(\mathcal{P}(h)) = \mathcal{P}(h) \circ \bigcup$
- $\mathcal{P}(\mathcal{P}(h)) \circ \mathcal{P}(\{\!\!\{\ \}\!\!\}) = \mathcal{P}(\{\!\!\{\ \}\!\!\}) \circ \mathcal{P}(h)$
- $\bigcup \circ \mathcal{P}(\bigcup) \circ \mathcal{P}(\mathcal{P}(h)) = \bigcup \circ \mathcal{P}(h) \circ \bigcup$

Proof: Most of these results are straightforward. Some of them are treated in greater detail in [2]. □

Instead of using the measure len_m of Section 3 we shall be able to obtain better results by following [6] and defining

$$len_{sa}(h) = max\{l_{sa}(h, Y) \mid Y \in \mathcal{P}(A)\}$$

where $l_{sa}(h, Y) = min\{i \mid h^i(Y) \sqsubseteq \bigsqcup\{Y, h(Y), \cdots, h^{i-1}(Y)\}, i > 0\}$.

Fact 4.2 $1 \leq len_{sa}(h) \leq len_m(h)$ for all functions h.

Lemma 4.3 $\lambda h. \bigsqcup \circ \mathcal{P}(h \circ g_1) \circ g_0 \in \mathcal{A}(k)$ for $k = len_{sa}(\mathcal{P}(g_1) \circ \bigcup \circ \mathcal{P}(g_0))$.

Proof: See Appendix C of [9]. □

Example 4.4 The *length function* computing the length of a list can be written as

FIX(`lam` *length*. `lam` *xs*. `case` *xs* `of` `nil` : 0 ▌ `cons` *y ys* : (+ 1) (*length ys*))

The overall type of this program is (t_α `list`) → `num`. In the analysis we shall follow the approach of [1] and interpret the type t_α by the domain **2**.

The strictness analysis gives rise to a functional H of the form

$$H\ h = ((isnil \circ g_0) \rhd g_1) \sqcup (\bigsqcup \circ \mathcal{P}(h \circ g_2) \circ split \circ g_0)$$

where

$$g_0 = id$$

$$g_1 = \lambda xs.1$$

$$g_2 = snd.$$

Now consider

$$k = len_{sa}(g') \text{ where } g' = \mathcal{P}(snd) \circ \bigcup \circ \mathcal{P}(split) \circ \mathcal{P}(id)$$

One can show that g' is idempotent ($g' = g' \circ g'$) and this means that $len_{sa}(g') = 2$. It follows from Lemmas 4.3 and 3.6 that H is 3-bounded and hence by Proposition 2.1 only 2 iterations are needed to compute the fixed point. A simple calculation shows that indeed two iterations are needed.

Example 4.5 As an example of a tail recursive program we shall consider the function `foldl` with type $(t_\alpha \to t_\beta \to t_\alpha) \to t_\alpha \times (t_\beta\ \texttt{list}) \to t_\alpha$. It can be written as

$$\texttt{lam}\ f.\ \text{FIX}(\texttt{lam}\ fld.\ \texttt{lam}\ ax.\ \texttt{case snd}\ ax\ \texttt{of nil} : \texttt{fst}\ ax \ \Big|$$

$$\texttt{cons}\ y\ ys : fld\ ((f\ (\texttt{fst}\ ax)\ y),\ ys))$$

Interpreting the types t_α and t_β as **2** one can show that the strictness analysis gives rise to a functional H_g defined by

$$H_g\ h = ((isnil \circ g_0) \rhd g_1) \sqcup (\bigsqcup \circ \mathcal{P}(h \circ g_2) \circ pack \circ tuple(g_1, split \circ g_0))$$

where

$$pack = \lambda(x, \{y_1, \cdots, y_n\}).\ \{(x, y_1), \cdots, (x, y_n)\}\!\downarrow$$

$$g_0 = snd$$

$$g_1 = fst$$

$$g_2 = tuple(g \circ tuple(id, fst \circ snd), snd \circ snd).$$

and g is the analysis (in uncurried form) of the parameter f. Thus we have to determine

$$k_g = len_{sa}(g') \text{ where } g' = \mathcal{P}(g_2) \circ \bigcup \circ \mathcal{P}(pack \circ tuple(g_1, split \circ g_0))$$

The value obtained for k_g will depend on the properties of g but one can show that in all cases $k_g \le 3$. Hence H_g is 4-bounded and at most 3 iterations will be needed.

5 Conclusion

The computation of fixed points plays an important role in abstract interpretation and hence also for strictness analysis by means of abstract interpretation. One major problem is that the number of unfoldings needed for the fixed point operator may be very high. Nothing can be done about this in general, but the results of this paper may be used in a compiler when detecting the situations in which strictness analysis by abstract interpretation will not be prohibitively expensive.

In [3] the concatenation function on lists is defined as **`foldr append nil`** and is shown to give a function that is particularly bad to analyse. Our results do not directly improve upon this, but it is instructive to note that the results of Example 4.5 may be of use: if by program transformation we are able to translate the definition using **`foldr`** into one that uses **`foldl`** then the required number of iterations will be very low. Again one might expect such program transformations to be part of the compiler's repertoire for improving the performance of the program.

As [3] points out the costs involved in tabulating each iteration may also be very high. An idea to overcome this is to note that we need only know the value of FIX H for those arguments that come up in the "recursive calls" for the argument in which we are interested. Thus one might use "minimal function graphs" to keep track of the arguments needed and then it will only be necessary to tabulate the value of $H^k\bot$ on arguments in this set[2]. In general this set will not be a singleton as this is only the case for analysis functions that turn out to be additive [5] and this is not so for strictness analysis.

Acknowledgement

This research was partially supported by the DART-project (funded by the Danish Research Councils).

References

[1] S.Abramsky: Strictness Analysis and Polymorphic Invariance, *Programs as Data Objects*, Springer Lecture Notes in Computer Science **217** 1–23, 1986.

[2] G.L.Burn, C.Hankin, S.Abramsky: Strictness Analysis for Higher-Order Functions, *Science of Computer Programming* **7**, 1986.

[2] Similarly, if we instead test for stabilization then it suffices to test for stabilization for elements in this set.

[3] S.Hunt, C.Hankin: Fixed Points and Frontiers: a New Perspective, *Journal of Functional Programming* **1**, 1991.

[4] T.J.Marlowe, B.G.Ryder: Properties of Data Flow Frameworks - a Unified Model, *Acta Informatica* **28**, 1990.

[5] H.R.Nielson, F.Nielson: Bounded Fixed Point Iteration, *Proceedings of the ACM Sympoisium on Principles of Programming Languages*, 1992. An expanded version appeared in *Journal of Logic and Computation* **2** *4*, 1992.

[6] F.Nielson, H.R.Nielson: Finiteness Conditions for Fixed Point Iteration (Extended Abstract), *Proceedings of the ACM Symposium on LISP and Functional Programming*, 1992. An extended version appeared as [7].

[7] F.Nielson, H.R.Nielson: Finiteness Conditions for Fixed Point Iteration, Technical Report DAIMI PB-384, Aarhus University, Denmark, 1992. An extended abstract appeared as [6].

[8] F.Nielson, H.R.Nielson: *Two-Level Functional Languages*, Cambridge Tracts in Theoretical Computer Science **34**, Cambridge University Press, 1992.

[9] F.Nielson, H.R.Nielson: Finiteness Conditions for Strictness Analysis, Technical Report DAIMI PB-447, Aarhus University, Denmark, 1993.

[10] P.Wadler: Strictness Analysis on Non-Flat Domains (by Abstract Interpretation over Finite Domains), *Abstract Interpretation of Declarative Languages*, S.Abramsky and C.Hankin (eds.), Ellis Horwood, 1987.

Strictness Properties of Lazy Algebraic Datatypes

P. N. Benton
University of Cambridge*

Abstract

A new construction of a finite set of strictness properties for any lazy algebraic datatype is presented. The construction is based on the categorical view of the solutions to the recursive domain equations associated with such types as initial algebras. We then show how the initial algebra induction principle can be used to reason about the entailment relation on the chosen collection of properties. We examine the lattice of properties given by our construction for the type *nlist* of lazy lists of natural numbers and give proof rules which extend the conjunctive strictness logic of [2] to a language including the type *nlist*.

1 Introduction

This paper concerns the problem of extending an ideal-based strictness analysis for a PCF-like language (e.g. the abstract interpretation of [4] or the strictness logic of [2, 6]) to a language which includes lazy algebraic datatypes, such as lazy lists or trees.

We start by giving a brief overview of ideal-based strictness analysis, using the language of strictness logic[1]. A more comprehensive account can be found in [1].

At each type σ of our language Λ_T we define a propositional theory $\mathcal{L}_\sigma = (L_\sigma, \leq_\sigma)$ where L_σ is a set of propositions and $\leq_\sigma \subseteq L_\sigma \times L_\sigma$ is the (finitely axiomatised) entailment relation. Each proposition ϕ^σ is interpreted as a non-empty Scott-closed subset (i.e. an *ideal*) $[\![\phi^\sigma]\!]$ of the domain D_σ which interprets the type σ in the standard denotational semantics for Λ_T. For $d \in D_\sigma$, $\phi^\sigma \in \mathcal{L}_\sigma$ write $d \models \phi^\sigma$ for $d \in [\![\phi^\sigma]\!]$. We require soundness of $\mathcal{L}_\sigma$ with respect to its intended interpretation, so $\phi \leq \psi$ implies that $[\![\phi]\!] \subseteq [\![\psi]\!]$, and we can sometimes get the converse (completeness) too. For decidability, we require that the Lindenbaum algebra $\mathcal{LA}_\sigma$ of the theory $\mathcal{L}_\sigma$ be finite. We shall assume that $\mathcal{L}_\sigma$ contains at least the propositions $\mathbf{t}^\sigma$ (with $[\![\mathbf{t}^\sigma]\!] = D_\sigma$)

*Author's address: University of Cambridge, Computer Laboratory, New Museums Site, Pembroke Street, Cambridge CB2 3QG, UK. Email: Nick.Benton@cl.cam.ac.uk. Research supported by the Cambridge Philosophical Society and a SERC Fellowship.

[1]Most of the present work can, however, be easily reinterpreted in terms of a more traditional abstract interpretation.

and $\mathbf{f}^\sigma$ (with $[\![\mathbf{f}^\sigma]\!] = \{\bot_{D_\sigma}\}$), and that the logic contains conjunction (interpeted as intersection). We can also define a lattice A_σ to be the set $\{[\![\phi^\sigma]\!] \mid \phi^\sigma \in \mathcal{L}_\sigma\}$ ordered by inclusion. The map $abs_\sigma\colon D_\sigma \to A_\sigma$ is given by $abs_\sigma(d) = \bigcap\{I \in A_\sigma \mid d \in I\}$. Note that if $\mathcal{L}_\sigma$ is complete, then $\mathcal{L}A_\sigma$ and A_σ will be isomorphic, but this will not always be the case.

We then give a program logic for deducing judgements of the form $\Gamma \vdash t\colon \phi^\tau$ where t is a language term of type τ and $\Gamma = \{x_i^{\sigma_i}\colon \psi_i^{\sigma_i}\}$ is a finite set of assumptions. The program logic should be sound in the sense that if $\Gamma \vdash t\colon \phi^\tau$ is derivable then for any environment ρ for which $\rho \models \Gamma$ (in the obvious pointwise sense) we have $[\![t]\!]\rho \models \phi^\tau$.

In extending such an analysis to a language with an algebraic datatype a, we first have to pick a set L_a of propositions ϕ^a representing ideals $[\![\phi^a]\!]$ of the domain D_a. We then need inference rules for the relation $\leq_a$ and program logic rules for the constructors and destructors associated with the type a.

Deciding which ideals of D_a we wish to reason about is a rather difficult problem. The collection which we pick should have the following characteristics:

1. It should be finite.
2. It should not be too big. This is because a large collection of properties will lead to an impractically slow analysis system.
3. It should contain as many 'useful' (in terms of optimisation-enabling) properties as possible. This plainly pulls against the previous requirement.
4. It should also contain sufficient points to enable us to deduce useful properties of real programs. Even if, for example, we were only interested in the optimisations which can be performed as a result of simple strictness, an analysis which only made use of the two-point lattice at every type would be extremely weak.
5. It should be closed under intersection, so that each domain element has a 'best' abstraction.
6. There should be some procedure by which the lattice of properties is derived from the type declaration.
7. The compiler should be able automatically to calculate a representation of the lattice of properties from the type declaration.
8. The ordering on the representation should be sound with respect to the inclusion ordering on the interpretations of representatives, and as complete as is practical.
9. The compiler should be able to synthesize proof rules or abstract semantic equations for the constructors and destructors of the type a.

For particular algebraic types, various *ad hoc* solutions to the problem have been suggested, the best known of which is probably Wadler's four point abstract domain for lazy lists of elements of a flat domain [9]. So far, however, there has been no general construction which meets all the above criteria.

2 Recursive Domain Equations

Before we can describe our approach to the problem of constructing lattices of strictness properties for algebraic datatypes, we need to recall how domains for such datatypes are constructed in the standard semantics as the solutions to recursive domain equations. Full details may be found in, for example, [8, 1].

Write $\mathcal{D}om$ for the category of pointed ω-cpo's with continuous maps as morphisms, $\mathcal{D}om_S$ for the subcategory of $\mathcal{D}om$ with only strict maps as morphisms, and $\mathcal{D}om_E$ for the subcategory of $\mathcal{D}om_S$ with only embeddings as morphisms. Although, as we are working with a non-strict language, we shall ultimately want to think of the domains which we construct as living in $\mathcal{D}om$, it will turn out that the category in which they have the properties which we shall use is $\mathcal{D}om_S$. Thus we shall treat the basic domain constructions as functors on $\mathcal{D}om_S$.

Each of the type constructors $+, \times, \rightarrow$ corresponds to a locally continuous functor T from $(\mathcal{D}om_S{}^{op})^m \times \mathcal{D}om_S{}^n$ to $\mathcal{D}om_S$ (in particular, $+$ is interpreted using the *separated* sum functor). Such a functor gives rise to an ω-continuous functor $T^E\colon \mathcal{D}om_E{}^{m+n} \rightarrow \mathcal{D}om_E$. By composing these functors, an arbitrary (not necessarily algebraic) recursive type definition defines an ω-continuous functor $F\colon \mathcal{D}om_E \rightarrow \mathcal{D}om_E$. The domain which interprets the recusive type is then the colimit $\underrightarrow{\lim}\Delta$ of the ω-diagram Δ in $\mathcal{D}om_E$, where

$$\Delta = 1 \xrightarrow{\;!\;} F(1) \xrightarrow{F(!)} F^2(1) \xrightarrow{F^2(!)} \cdots$$

We will write Fix_F for $\underrightarrow{\lim}\Delta$, which comes with an isomorphism $\eta_F\colon F(\mathsf{Fix}_F) \rightarrow \mathsf{Fix}_F$.

Recall that if $F : \mathcal{C} \rightarrow \mathcal{C}$ is an endofunctor on a category $\mathcal{C}$, then an F-*algebra* consists of a pair (A, α) where A is an object of $\mathcal{C}$ and $\alpha\colon FA \rightarrow A$. The collection of F-algebras are the objects of a category $F - \mathcal{A}lg$ in which a morphism from (A, α) to (B, β) is a morphism $f\colon A \rightarrow B$ in $\mathcal{C}$ such that

$$\begin{array}{ccc} FA & \xrightarrow{Ff} & FB \\ {\scriptstyle\alpha}\downarrow & & \downarrow{\scriptstyle\beta} \\ A & \xrightarrow[f]{} & B \end{array}$$

commutes. Such an f is called an F-*homomorphism.*

Now it is the case that for an arbitrary ω-continuous functor $F\colon \mathcal{D}om_E \rightarrow \mathcal{D}om_E$, the pair (Fix_F, η_F) is the initial F-algebra. In the case of an algebraic datatype definition (one in which the name of the type being defined does not appear within the scope of a function space constructor), the functor F arises as T^E, where $T\colon \mathcal{D}om_S \rightarrow \mathcal{D}om_S$ is a locally continuous functor. In this case, the pair $(\mathsf{Fix}_{T^E}, \eta_{T^E})$ is the initial T-algebra. Since in the algebraic case T^E is just the restriction of T, we shall henceforth drop the distinction between T and T^E whenever it seems convenient.

Homomorphisms from the initial T-algebra capture a kind of primitive recursion over lazy algebraic datatypes. In the case of lazy lists, this gives the familiar reduce or fold function.

3 The Construction

We were careful in the introduction to draw a distinction between A_σ (the lattice of properties) and $\mathcal{L}A_\sigma$ (the lattice of representatives for those properties). We shall start by giving a construction of A_a and then address the question of how this may be axiomatised in the theory $\mathcal{L}_a$.

A Scott-closed subset of a domain D is precisely the kernel $f^{-1}(\bot)$ of a continuous map $f: D \to \mathcal{O}$, where $\mathcal{O}$ is the two-point domain. An ideal is the kernel of a *strict* map into $\mathcal{O}$. We can therefore rephrase our problem as being that of finding a good set of strict maps from D_a into $\mathcal{O}$. Our construction will define such a collection of maps using homomorphisms from an initial algebra.

The first step is to generalise the idea of going from the domain of lists of natural numbers to the domain of lists of strictness properties of natural numbers. This latter domain is, of course, infinite and hence unsuited to our purposes (it contains points which represent properties such as 'has a $\bot$ in every prime-numbered position'). We shall then cut this down to a small finite set of properties.

For concreteness, let us assume that we are given the declaration of the type a in sum-of-products form:

$$a \;=\; \mathsf{C}_1 \text{ of } \delta_{1,0} \times \ldots \times \delta_{1,m_1-1} \mid \ldots \mid \mathsf{C}_n \text{ of } \delta_{n,0} \times \ldots \times \delta_{n,m_n-1};$$

where the type expressions δ are defined by the grammar

$$\delta ::= \kappa \mid a$$

$$\kappa ::= \iota \mid (\kappa \to \kappa) \mid (\kappa \times \kappa)$$

and the types of Λ_T are given by

$$\sigma ::= \iota \mid (\sigma \to \sigma) \mid (\sigma \times \sigma) \mid a$$

(Note that whilst m_i may be 0, n is always at least 1.)

The functor $T: \mathcal{D}om_S \to \mathcal{D}om_S$ associated with such a type declaration is then

$$T(X) = \sum_{i=1}^{n} \prod_{j=0}^{m_i-1} D_{i,j}(X)$$

where

$$D_{i,j}(X) = \begin{cases} D_\kappa & \text{if } \delta_{i,j} = \kappa \\ X & \text{if } \delta_{i,j} = a \end{cases}$$

Now let $\widehat{T}: \mathcal{D}om_S \to \mathcal{D}om_S$ be given by

$$\widehat{T}(X) = \sum_{i=1}^{n} \prod_{j=0}^{m_i-1} \widehat{D}_{i,j}(X)$$

where

$$\widehat{D}_{i,j}(X) = \begin{cases} A_\kappa & \text{if } \delta_{i,j} = \kappa \\ X & \text{if } \delta_{i,j} = a \end{cases}$$

Intuitively, $\mathsf{Fix}_{\widehat{T}}$ is then the appropriate generalisation of the idea of the domain of lists of strictness properties mentioned above. We now wish to give a formal definition of the obvious abstraction map from Fix_T to $\mathsf{Fix}_{\widehat{T}}$. Firstly, note that for any domain X, there is a strict map $\mu_X : T(X) \to \widehat{T}(X)$ given by

$$\mu_X = \sum_{i=1}^{n} \prod_{j=0}^{m_i-1} f_{i,j}(X)$$

where $f_{i,j}(X) : D_{i,j}(X) \to \widehat{D}_{i,j}(X)$ is the strict map given by

$$f_{i,j}(X) = \begin{cases} abs_\kappa & \text{if } \delta_{i,j} = \kappa \\ id_X & \text{if } \delta_{i,j} = a \end{cases}$$

$\eta_{\widehat{T}} \circ \mu_{\mathsf{Fix}_{\widehat{T}}}$ makes $\mathsf{Fix}_{\widehat{T}}$ into a T-algebra, so by initiality there is a unique $h : \mathsf{Fix}_T \to \mathsf{Fix}_{\widehat{T}}$ such that $h \circ \eta_T = \eta_{\widehat{T}} \circ \mu_{\mathsf{Fix}_{\widehat{T}}} \circ T(h)$ and this is the map we want.

The second step in the construction uses the fact that $(\mathsf{Fix}_{\widehat{T}}, \eta_{\widehat{T}})$ is the initial $\widehat{T}$-algebra. This means that, given any strict map $g : \widehat{T}(\mathcal{O}) \to \mathcal{O}$, there is a unique strict map $g^* : \mathsf{Fix}_{\widehat{T}} \to \mathcal{O}$ such that

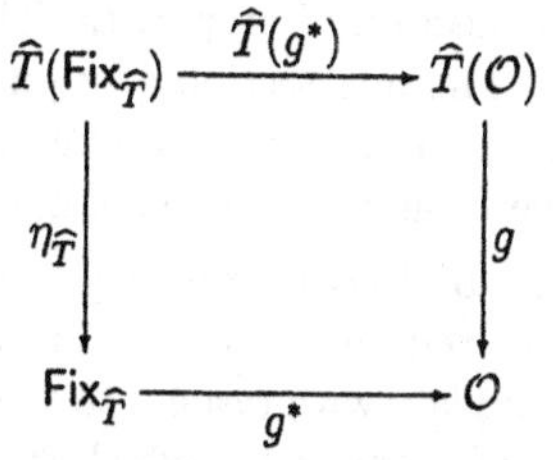

commutes. Because $\widehat{T}(\mathcal{O})$ is constructed from finite sums and products of finite domains, it will itself always be a finite domain. Thus there will only be a finite number of maps $g : \widehat{T}(\mathcal{O}) \to \mathcal{O}$. Each one of these gives rise to an ideal of Fix_T, viz.

$$K_g = (g^* \circ h)^{-1}(\bot)$$

and it is the collection of all these K_g which we propose as a good set of basic strictness properties of the type a. We shall also find it helpful to define $J_g \subseteq \mathsf{Fix}_{\widehat{T}}$ to be $(g^*)^{-1}(\bot)$.

Let us see how this works out in the familiar case of lists of natural numbers. A_ι is the two-point domain, which we will write as $\mathbf{2}$. This is, of course, isomorphic to $\mathcal{O}$, but this is just coincidental. There are twelve strict monotone maps g from $1+\mathbf{2}\times\mathcal{O}$ into $\mathcal{O}$, each of which can be described by giving a pair, the first component of which is the image of the point $inl(*)$ and the second component of which is the image of the point $inr(x, y)$ for $x \in \mathbf{2}$, $y \in \mathcal{O}$. A little calculation then gives the informal interpretation of each K_g as shown in Figure 1 (we write K_n for K_{g_n}).

This collection of properties includes Wadler's four points: his $\bot$, ∞, $\bot\in$ and $\top\in$ are our K_{12}, K_6, K_8 and K_1 respectively. Burn's A^{hs} domain [3] consists of our K_{12}, K_4 and K_1. Ernoult and Mycroft's set of 'uniform ideals' [5] consists of our K_1, K_2, K_6, K_8, K_9, K_{10} and K_{12}. Note also that our twelve maps only give rise to ten distinct properties, as K_1, K_5 and K_7 are all the whole of the domain D_{nlist}.

n	$g_n(inl(*))$	$g_n(inr(x,y))$	K_n
1	$\perp$	$\perp$	All lists.
2	$\top$	$\perp$	All non-empty lists.
3	$\perp$	x	The empty list. Lists with $\perp$ as the first element.
4	$\top$	x	Non-empty lists with $\perp$ as the first element.
5	$\perp$	y	All lists.
6	$\top$	y	All infinite and partial lists.
7	$\perp$	$x \sqcap y$	All lists.
8	$\top$	$x \sqcap y$	Infinite and partial lists. Lists containing a $\perp$ elt.
9	$\perp$	$x \sqcup y$	The empty list.Lists whose elements are all $\perp$.
10	$\top$	$x \sqcup y$	Partial and infinite lists all of whose elt.s are $\perp$.
11	$\perp$	$\top$	The empty list.
12	$\top$	$\top$	Just the completely undefined list $\perp$.

Figure 1: Basic Strictness Properties of *nlist*.

These ten properties are all intuitively compelling: this seems to be the 'right' construction. These ten points alone, however, do not quite satisfy all the criteria we laid down earlier for a good collection of properties. This is because the collection is not closed under intersection. The intersection of K_8 and K_9 is the set of non-empty lists all of whose elements are $\perp$, and this is not one of our properties. This is not a serious problem—we just have to add intersections in explicitly[2].

Another of our criteria for a good collection of properties was that we should be able to calculate an entailment relation on a set of representations of the properties which was sound and fairly complete with respect to the real inclusion ordering on the properties. Defining L_a, a set of propositions which represent the ideals produced by our construction is slightly messy, but not difficult. We represent each K_g by giving a syntactic representation of g. This is done by giving the maximal elements of the kernel of g. More formally, we add the following to the formation rules given in [2]:

Define $P_{i,j}$ to be L_κ if $\delta_{i,j} = \kappa$ and $\mathcal{O}$ if $\delta_{i,j} = a$. Now define the set Q_i by

$$\frac{\phi_0 \in P_{i,0} \quad \dots \quad \phi_{m_i-1} \in P_{i,m_i-1}}{\phi_0 \times \cdots \times \phi_{m_i-1} \in Q_i}$$

and then define the actual propositions in L_a by

$$\frac{S_1 \subseteq^{\text{fin}} Q_1 \quad \dots \quad S_n \subseteq^{\text{fin}} Q_n}{S_1 + \cdots + S_n \in L_a}$$

This means that a typical element of L_a will look like

$$\phi^a = \bigwedge_{k=0}^{l-1} \sum_{i=1}^{n} S_i^k$$

[2]We might also want to add unions, if we were trying to extend a disjunctive strictness analysis [1] to algebraic types.

For example, a proposition representing K_1 is $\{1\} + \{\mathbf{t}^\iota \times \top\}$, whilst one representing K_8 is $\{\} + \{\mathbf{f}^\iota \times \top, \mathbf{t}^\iota \times \bot\}$.

The problem of defining the entailment relation on this set of propositions is more interesting. We approach it by considering reasoning principles which allow us to deduce that one property is contained within another. Note that we already have one simple principle for deducing inclusions between properties, namely that if $g \sqsubseteq g'$ then $g^* \sqsubseteq g'^*$ and hence $K_{g'} \subseteq K_g$. This is not, however, sufficient to deduce all the inclusions which we should like. In the case of *nlist*, for example, we want to be able to deduce that $K_1 \subseteq K_5$, but it is not the case that $g_5 \sqsubseteq g_1$.

Fortunately, initiality offers a solution to this problem too. We can make use of a general induction principle for initial T-algebras which is due to Lehmann, Smyth and Plotkin [7].

Proposition 3.1 (Initial T-Algebra Induction Principle) *If $T : \mathcal{C} \to \mathcal{C}$ is a functor, (A, α) is the initial T-algebra and $m : B \to A$ is a mono in $\mathcal{C}$ which extends to a T-homomorphism $(B, \beta) \to (A, \alpha)$, then m is an isomorphism.* □

Corollary 3.2 *If $T : \mathcal{D}om_S \to \mathcal{D}om_S$ is a functor, (D, α) is the initial T-algebra and P is a subdomain of D with inclusion map $i : P \to D$ then the following induction principle is valid:*

$$\frac{\forall x \in TP.(\alpha \circ Ti)(x) \in P}{\forall y \in D. y \in P}$$

□

And using this, we can get a simple condition on the maps g which is sufficient for J_g to be the whole of $\mathsf{Fix}_{\widehat{T}}$ and hence for K_g to be the whole of Fix_T.

Remark 3.3 A more categorical definition of J_g would have been by the pullback square

$$\begin{array}{ccc} J_g & \xrightarrow{\;j\;} & \mathsf{Fix}_{\widehat{T}} \\ {\scriptstyle !}\downarrow & \lrcorner & \downarrow{\scriptstyle g^*} \\ 1 & \xrightarrow[\;!\;]{} & \mathcal{O} \end{array}$$

where j is the inclusion map. Note that J_g is a subdomain of $\mathsf{Fix}_{\widehat{T}}$, and not just a subset.

Proposition 3.4 *If the following diagram commutes:*

$$\begin{array}{ccc} \widehat{T}(1) & \xrightarrow{\;\widehat{T}(!)\;} & \widehat{T}(\mathcal{O}) \\ {\scriptstyle !}\downarrow & & \downarrow{\scriptstyle g} \\ 1 & \xrightarrow[\;!\;]{} & \mathcal{O} \end{array}$$

then J_g is the whole of $\mathsf{Fix}_{\widehat{T}}$.

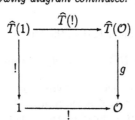

Proof. Consider the following:

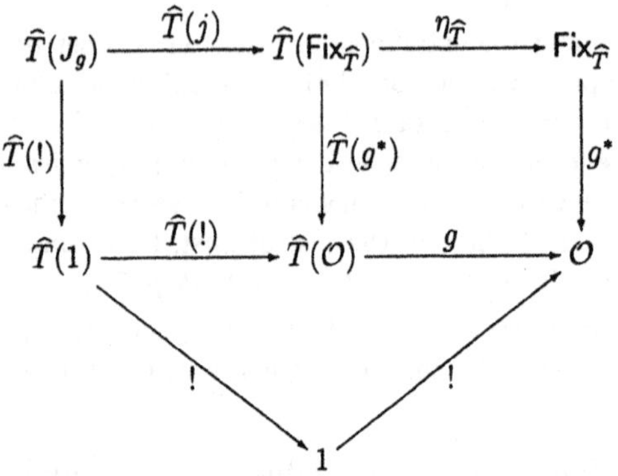

The square on the left commutes because it is $\widehat{T}$ applied to the pullback square in the remark above. The square on the right commutes because it is the definition of g^*, and the large triangle on the bottom commutes by assumption. Hence the outside path commutes, and since the composite $! \circ \widehat{T}(!) : \widehat{T}(J_g) \to 1$ on the left must be equal to $! : \widehat{T}(J_g) \to 1$, we have that

$$\forall x \in \widehat{T}(J_g).\, (\eta_{\widehat{T}} \circ \widehat{T}j)(x) \in J_g$$

so that by Corollary 3.2 we are done. □

Checking the condition of Proposition 3.4 is a simple, finite computation which could be incorporated into a mechanizable formal system for reasoning about strictness properties. Let us see how it works out in the case of *nlist*. In this case, the condition on g is that the following pair of equations hold:

$$g(inl(*)) = \bot$$

$$\forall x \in \mathbf{2}.\, g(inr(x, \bot)) = \bot$$

and by monotonicity, the second of these reduces to checking $g(inr(\top, \bot)) = \bot$. These two conditions pick out g_1, g_5 and g_7, which are precisely those g_n for which K_n is the whole of the domain.

But we need more than a rule for determining when some K_g is the whole of Fix_T. We also want a rule for deducing more general inclusions between intersections of the K_g. In the case of *nlist*, for example, we should like some way of deducing that $K_{11} \cap K_{10} \subseteq K_{12}$ and that $K_8 \cap K_3 \subseteq K_4$. The initial algebra induction principle can give us this too.

If A and B are ideals of a domain D then the set

$$A \Rightarrow B \stackrel{\text{def}}{=} \{d \in D \mid d \in A \Rightarrow d \in B\}$$

is a subdomain of D, since it clearly contains $\bot_D$ and if $\langle d_n \rangle$ is a chain in $A \Rightarrow B$ then if $\bigsqcup d_n \in A$ we must have $d_n \in A$ for all n by down-closure of A. Hence $d_n \in B$ for all n and so $\bigsqcup d_n \in B$ as B is closed under sups of chains. Obviously, if $A \Rightarrow B$ is the whole of D then $A \subseteq B$.

Since the intersection of a set of ideals is an ideal, this means by Corollary 3.2 that to show that $J_{m_1} \cap \cdots \cap J_{m_k} \subseteq J_n$ (and hence that $K_{m_1} \cap \cdots \cap K_{m_k} \subseteq K_n$), it suffices to show

$$\forall l \in \hat{T}(J_{m_1} \cap \cdots \cap J_{m_k} \Rightarrow J_n).\, (\eta_{\hat{T}} \circ \hat{T}i)(l) \in J_{m_1} \cap \cdots \cap J_{m_k} \Rightarrow J_n$$

where $i : (J_{m_1} \cap \cdots \cap J_{m_k} \Rightarrow J_n) \to \mathsf{Fix}_{\hat{T}}$ is the inclusion map. I do not yet have a restatement of this condition in such a pleasant form as the condition of Proposition 3.4, but it is relatively easy to unwind in the special case of *nlist* to obtain

Proposition 3.5 *If the following two conditions hold*

1. *If* $\forall i.\, g_{m_i}(inl(*)) = \bot$ *then* $g_n(inl(*)) = \bot$
2. *For all* $b_1, \ldots, b_k, b \in \mathcal{O}$ *such that if* $\forall i.\, b_i = \bot$ *then* $b = \bot$ *we have that* $\forall x \in \mathbf{2}$ *if* $\forall i.\, g_{m_i}(inr(x, b_i)) = \bot$ *then* $g_n(inr(x, b)) = \bot$

then $K_{m_1} \cap \cdots \cap K_{m_k} \subseteq K_n$. □

Interestingly, this does not subsume Proposition 3.4, since Proposition 3.5 cannot be used to deduce $K_1 \subseteq K_7$. The conditions of Proposition 3.5 are finitely checkable, and it can be seen that this will remain true of the corresponding conditions for any algebraic type.

Using Propositions 3.4 and 3.5, we discover that only two more points need to be added the properties shown in Figure 1 to obtain a set which is closed under intersection. These are $K_4 \cap K_6$, with the informal interpretation of 'partial and infinite lists with $\bot$ as the first element', and $K_4 \cap K_9$ which corresponds to 'non-empty lists all of whose elements are $\bot$'. For *nlist*, we thus get the lattice of properties shown in Figure 2. This figure was deduced with the aid of a short computer program to check the conditions of Proposition 3.5. Burn's A^{rp} abstract domain for lists [3] contains our K_1, K_4, K_6, $K_4 \cap K_6$, K_8 and K_{12}.

Although the initial algebra induction principle is undoubtedly the correct way to reason about inclusions between properties, there is still a problem. We need to be able to express this reasoning as a set of syntactic proof rules for deducing entailments between propositions. At present I do not have a satisfactory way of doing this. The difficulty is that a generalised form of Proposition 3.5 is inherently second-order as it involves quantification over properties (the '$\forall x \in \mathbf{2}$' in the second clause). Thus a naive proof rule would involve quantification over propositions. This is unpleasant for a couple of reasons. Firstly, the theories associated with non-algebraic types are all first-order. Secondly, there will in general be an infinite number of propositions to quantify over. Although this problem is in principle avoidable (as the Lindenbaum algebras are all finite), it leads to a very complicated rule and means that one has to calculate explicitly the whole of $\mathcal{LA}_\sigma$ to be able to reason about entailments at any algebraic type which involves σ. This is completely impractical for any non-trivial σ. I believe that it is possible to reduce the quantification to a manageable finite set of propositions, but have not yet succeeded in doing so. Proof rules which capture the content of Proposition 3.4 and the naive principle $g \sqsubseteq g' \Rightarrow K_{g'} \subseteq K_g$ can, however, be given fairly easily in terms of our representation.

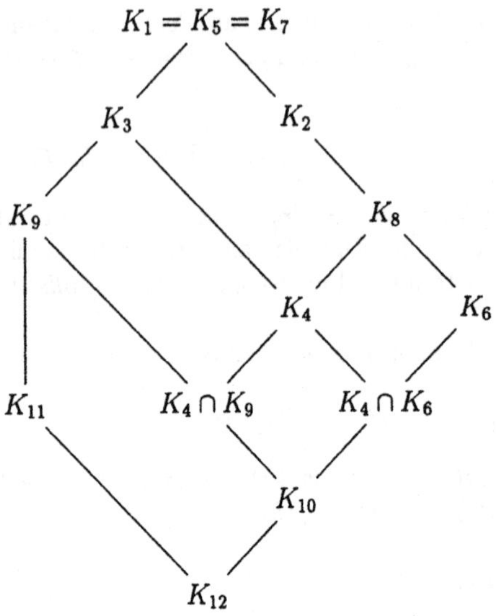

Figure 2: The Lattice of Strictness Properties of *nlist*

The final requirement of a collection of properties was that the compiler be able to synthesize program logic rules for the constructors and destructors of the algebraic type. This is fairly straightforward in terms of syntax of propositions which was given earlier, though the generality of the rules makes them look somewhat intimidating at first sight. For $p = \psi_0 \times \cdots \times \psi_{m_i-1} \in Q_i$ and $\phi \in L_a$, define $p[\phi/\perp] \in L_{\delta_{i,0}} \times \cdots \times L_{\delta_{i,m_i-1}}$ to be $(\psi'_0, \ldots, \psi'_{m_i-1})$ where

$$\psi'_j = \begin{cases} \psi_j & \text{if } \delta_{i,j} = \kappa \\ \phi & \text{if } \delta_{i,j} = a \text{ and } \psi_j = \perp \\ \mathsf{t}^a & \text{otherwise} \end{cases}$$

The program logic proof rule for constructors is then

$$\frac{\exists p \in S_i.\forall j. \quad \Gamma \vdash t_j : \pi_j(p[\sum_{i=1}^{n} S_i/\perp])}{\Gamma \vdash \mathsf{C}_i(t_0, \ldots, t_{m_i-1}) : \sum_{i=1}^{n} S_i}$$

The rule for destructors is

$$\frac{\Gamma \vdash t : \bigwedge_{k=0}^{l-1} \sum_{i=1}^{n} S_i^k \qquad \begin{array}{l} \forall i.\forall \langle p_0, \ldots, p_{l-1}\rangle \in \prod_{k=0}^{l-1} S_i^k. \\ \Gamma, x_{i,0} : \bigwedge_{k=0}^{l-1} \phi_0^k, \ldots, x_{i,m_i-1} : \bigwedge_{k=0}^{l-1} \phi_{m_i-1}^k \vdash u_i : \psi \end{array}}{\begin{array}{ll} \Gamma \vdash \mathsf{case}\ t\ \mathsf{of}\ \ \mathsf{C}_1(x_{1,0}, \ldots, x_{1,m_1-1}) \Rightarrow u_1 & : \psi \\ \qquad\qquad\quad \vdots & \\ \qquad\qquad\quad \mathsf{C}_n(x_{n,0}, \ldots, x_{n,m_n-1}) \Rightarrow u_n & \end{array}}$$

$$\Gamma \vdash \mathsf{Nil} : K_{11} \qquad \frac{\Gamma \vdash u : \mathbf{f} \qquad g(\bot, \top) = \bot}{\Gamma \vdash \mathsf{Cons}(u, l) : K_g}\,[\text{Cons1}]$$

$$\frac{\Gamma, x : \mathbf{t}, xs : K_8 \vdash v : \phi \qquad \Gamma, x : \mathbf{f}, xs : K_1 \vdash v : \phi \qquad \Gamma \vdash l : K_8}{\Gamma \vdash \mathsf{nlistcase}\ l\ \mathsf{of}\ \mathsf{Nil} \Rightarrow u \mid \mathsf{Cons}(x, xs) \Rightarrow v\ : \phi}\,[\text{nlistcase8}]$$

$$\frac{\Gamma, x : \mathbf{f}, xs : K_6 \vdash v : \phi \qquad \Gamma \vdash l : K_4 \cap K_6}{\Gamma \vdash \mathsf{nlistcase}\ l\ \mathsf{of}\ \mathsf{Nil} \Rightarrow u \mid \mathsf{Cons}(x, xs) \Rightarrow v\ : \phi}\,[\text{nlistcase46}]$$

Figure 3: Sample Proof Rules for *nlist*

where ϕ_j^k is an abbreviation for

$$\pi_j(p_k[\sum_{i=1}^{n} S_i^k/\bot])$$

Although these rules may look complicated, in the case of *nlist* they specialise to give a small set of very simple and natural proof rules. Some examples of these are shown in Figure 3, in which an attempt to improve readability has been made by replacing syntactic propositions with the names of the properties which they represent.

4 Conclusions and Further Work

We have presented a construction of a finite lattice of strictness properties (ideals) of any lazy algebraic datatype. This improves on previous work in that it is a general mathematical construction, rather than an *ad hoc* collection of useful-looking points for one particular type. For the particular case of lazy lists of elements of a flat domain our construction gives a set which is remarkably close to being the union of all the sets of properties which have been suggested in the literature. In this case, one's intuition should be that we are choosing as basic properties the kernels of all the evaluators (in the sense of Burn [3]) which can be written in terms of the **reduce** function. We also defined a uniform syntactic representation for these properties.

We then showed how the initial algebra induction principle could be used to reason about the inclusion ordering on (intersections of) our properties, though we do not yet have satisfactory proof rules which capture this reasoning.

We then gave general program logic proof rules which allow properties to be assigned to terms, and showed how these specialised to give derived rules for the case of lazy lists.

There is considerable scope for further work on this construction. The most immediate problem is to formulate good proof rules for the theory $\mathcal{L}_a$. Until this has been done, we have not completely succeeded in extending strictness logic to arbitrary algebraic types, although for any fixed algebraic type we do now at least have a framework for constructing the appropriate theories by hand calculation.

A natural extension of the current work is to investigate a disjunctive logic of strictness properties for algebraic types. Whilst this would simplify some aspects of the logic (for example, the sets S_i of propositions could be replaced by a single proposition), disjunctive strictness analysis introduces a number of further complications. See [1] for further information. We should also look at how well the construction works for more complicated algebraic types. Finally, we have not addressed the question of implementations – it remains to be seen whether a practical analysis system can be based on these ideas.

References

[1] P. N. Benton. *Strictness Analysis of Lazy Functional Programs.* PhD thesis, Computer Laboratory, University of Cambridge, December 1992.

[2] P. N. Benton. Strictness logic and polymorphic invariance. In A. Nerode and M. Taitslin, editors, *Proceedings of the Second International Symposium on Logical Foundations of Computer Science, Tver, Russia*, volume 620 of *Lecture Notes in Computer Science*, pages 33–44. Springer-Verlag, July 1992.

[3] G. L. Burn. *Lazy Functional Languages: Abstract Interpretation and Compilation.* Research Monographs in Parallel and Distributed Computing. MIT Press, Cambridge, Mass., 1991.

[4] G. L. Burn, C. L. Hankin, and S. Abramsky. The theory and practice of strictness analysis for higher-order functions. *Science of Computer Programming*, 7:249–278, 1986.

[5] C. Ernoult and A. Mycroft. Uniform ideals and strictness analysis. In *Proceedings of ICALP 91*. Springer-Verlag, 1991.

[6] T. P. Jensen. Strictness analysis in logical form. In *Proceedings of the 1991 Conference on Functional Programming Languages and Computer Architecture*, 1991.

[7] D. Lehmann and M. Smyth. Algebraic specification of data types: A synthetic approach. *Math. Systems Theory*, 14, 1981.

[8] M. B. Smyth and G. D. Plotkin. The category-theoretic solution of recursive domain equations. *SIAM Journal of Computing*, 11, 1982.

[9] P. Wadler. Strictness analysis on non-flat domains (by abstract interpretation over finite domains). In S. Abramsky and C. L. Hankin, editors, *Abstract Interpretation of Declarative Languages*, chapter 12, pages 266–275. Ellis Horwood Ltd., 1987.

Minimal Thunkification

Torben Amtoft * **
internet: tamtoft@daimi.aau.dk

Computer Science Department, Aarhus University
Ny Munkegade, DK-8000 Århus C, Denmark

Abstract. By "thunkifying" the arguments to function applications and "dethunkifying" variables one can translate a λ-expression e into a λ-expression e', such that call-by-value evaluation of e' gives the same result as call-by-name evaluation of e. By using the result of a strictness analysis, some of these thunkifications can be avoided. In this paper we present a type system for strictness analysis; present a translation algorithm which exploits the strictness proof tree; and give a combined proof of the correctness of the analysis/translation.

1 Introduction

We shall consider the following problem: given λ-expression e, find a λ-expression e' such that e when evaluated using a call-by-name strategy yields the same result as e' when evaluated using a call-by-value strategy. The reason why this is interesting is that it is more convenient [Hug89] to program in a lazy language than in an eager (the former also enjoys the nice property of referential transparency); and that CBV traditionally is considered more efficient than CBN.

The standard technique to solve the problem is to introduce "thunks" everywhere (thus simulating how one would naively implement call-by-name), as done e.g. in [DH92]. That is, we have the following translation T:

- An abstraction $\lambda x.e$ translates into $\lambda x.T(e)$;
- An application $e_1 e_2$ translates into $T(e_1)(\lambda x.T(e_2))$ (where x is a fresh variable) – that is, the evaluation of the argument is suspended ("thunkified");
- A variable x translates into $(x\ d)$ (where d is a "dummy" argument) – since x will become bound to a suspension x must be "dethunkified".

Clearly, this is far from optimal since many expressions may become thunkified only to become dethunkified soon after. This kind of observation motivated Mycroft [Myc80] to introduce *strictness analysis* by means of abstract interpretation: if $e_1^\#$ is the denotation of e_1 in the abstract domain, and if $e_1^\#(\bot) = \bot$, then it is safe to omit thunkification of the argument to e_1. A thunkification algorithm exploiting strictness information is presented in [DH93].

* Supported by the DART-project funded by the Danish Research Council.
** The work reported here evolved from numerous discussions with Hanne Riis Nielson and Flemming Nielson. Also thanks to Jens Palsberg for useful feedback.

Strictness analysis for higher-order functions is treated in [BHA86] and proved correct in the following sense: if $e_1^\#$ is the abstract denotation of e_1, and if $e_1^\#(\perp) = \perp$ (in the abstract domain), then $e_1(\perp) = \perp$ (in the concrete domain) – that is, e_1 will not terminate if its argument does not terminate. However, no attention is given to proving the correctness of a translation using this information.

This is a quite general phenomenon, cf. the claims made in [Wan93]:

> The goal of flow analysis is to annotate a program with certain propositions about the behavior of that program. One can then apply optimizations to the program that are justified by those propositions. However, it has proven remarkably difficult to specify the semantics of those propositions in a way that justifies the resulting optimizations.

The main contribution of this paper is to give a combined proof of the correctness of a strictness analysis and of the resulting transformation. This can be seen as following the trend of [Wan93] who proves the combined correctness of a binding time analysis and a partial evaluation based on the result of this analysis. Also something similar can be found in [Lan92] where the correctness of a code generation exploiting strictness information is proved.

The strictness analysis to be used in this paper will be formulated in terms of inference rules for a type system, where functions arrows have been annotated: $\rightarrow_0$ denoting that a function is strict and $\rightarrow_1$ denoting that we do not know anything for sure. This is inspired by the method of Wright [Wri91] – in [Wri92] he proves the correctness of his *analysis* (by means of a model for the λ-calculus), but does not consider any transformation based on the result of the analysis.

Other type-based approaches to strictness analysis includes [KM89], where the base types (not the arrows) are annotated with strictness information. An attempt to clarify the relation between strictness analysis based on abstract interpretation resp. type inference is presented in [Jen91] – however, the relationship is in no way fully understood. Neither is the relative power of the various approaches in the literature, and accordingly the strength of our analysis will not be compared formally with other analyses.

An Overview of the Paper

In Sect. 2 we present the syntax and semantics of the language to be considered, in particular we give an inference system for assigning (ordinary) types to expressions. In Sect. 3 we present an inference system for *strictness* types, such that any expression which can be given an (ordinary) type also can be given a strictness type. Section 4 gives a translation algorithm (which exploits the proof tree generated by the strictness analysis). In Sect. 5 we formulate predicates expressing the correctness of the translation/analysis, and we briefly outline a correctness proof – for a full proof, see [Amt93].

2 The λ-Calculus with Constants

Expressions. An expression is either a variable x; a constant c; an abstraction $\lambda x.e$; an application $e_1 e_2$; an unbounded recursive definition $\mathsf{rec}\ f\ e$; a bounded recursive definition $\mathsf{rec}_n\ f\ e$ (with $n \geq 0$) or a conditional $\mathsf{if}\ e_1\ e_2\ e_3$. The set of free variables in e will be denoted $\mathsf{FV}(e)$.

Of course, the user will only write programs with unbounded recursion – bounded recursion is introduced as an auxiliary device for proving the correctness of the translation (cf. Theorem 6 and Theorem 7).

The reason for not making if a constant (thereby making it possible to dispense with the conditional) is that if is a *non-strict* constant and hence requires special treatment.

Types. The set of (ordinary) types will be denoted $\mathcal{T}$; such a type is either a base type (Int, Bool, Unit etc.) or a function type $t_1 \rightarrow t_2$. **Base** will denote some base type.

An *iterated base type* is either **Base** or of form **Base**$\rightarrow t$, where t is an iterated base type. We shall assume that there exists a function Ct which assigns iterated base types to all constants.

In Fig. 1 we present a type inference system, where inferences are of form $\Gamma \vdash e : t$. Here Γ is an environment assigning types to (a superset of) the free variables of e. For closed expressions q it makes sense to say that q is of type t, since if $\Gamma \vdash q : t$ then also $\Gamma' \vdash q : t$ for any Γ'.

$$\Gamma \vdash c : Ct(c) \qquad\qquad \Gamma \vdash x : \Gamma(x)$$

$$\frac{\Gamma \cup \{x := t_1\} \vdash e : t}{\Gamma \vdash \lambda x.e : t_1 \rightarrow t} \qquad\qquad \frac{\Gamma \vdash e_1 : t_2 \rightarrow t_1,\ \Gamma \vdash e_2 : t_2}{\Gamma \vdash e_1 e_2 : t_1}$$

$$\frac{\Gamma \vdash e_1 : \mathsf{Bool},\ \Gamma \vdash e_2 : t,\ \Gamma \vdash e_3 : t}{\Gamma \vdash (\mathsf{if}\ e_1\ e_2\ e_3) : t}$$

$$\frac{\Gamma \cup \{f := t\} \vdash e : t}{\Gamma \vdash (\mathsf{rec}\ f\ e) : t} \qquad\qquad \frac{\Gamma \cup \{f := t\} \vdash e : t}{\Gamma \vdash (\mathsf{rec}_n\ f\ e) : t}$$

Fig. 1. An inference system for (ordinary) types.

Semantics. We say that an expression is in weak head normal form (WHNF) if it is either a constant c or of form $\lambda x.e$. As no constructors are present in the language, this choice of normal form will be suitable for CBV as well as for CBN.

We define a SOS for call-by-name (Fig. 2) and a SOS for call-by-value (Fig. 3), with inferences of form $q \Rightarrow_N q'$ resp. $q \Rightarrow_V q'$. Here q and q' are *closed* expressions. We assume the existence of a function Applycon such that for two constants c_1 and c_2, $\mathsf{Applycon}(c_1, c_2)$ *either* yields another constant c such that if $Ct(c_1) = \mathsf{Base} \to t$, $Ct(c_2) = \mathsf{Base}$ then $Ct(c) = t$ *or* the expression $c_1 c_2$ itself (to model errors). For instance, $\mathsf{Applycon}(+, 4)$ could be the constant $+_4$, where $\mathsf{Applycon}(+_4, 3)$ is the constant 7. To model that division by zero is illegal we let e.g. $\mathsf{Applycon}(/_7, 0) = (/_7, 0)$.

$$(\lambda x.e)q \Rightarrow_N e[q/x] \qquad \frac{q_1 \Rightarrow_N q_1'}{q_1 q_2 \Rightarrow_N q_1' q_2}$$

$$c_1 c_2 \Rightarrow_N \mathsf{Applycon}(c_1, c_2) \qquad \frac{q_2 \Rightarrow_N q_2'}{c q_2 \Rightarrow_N c q_2'}$$

$$\mathsf{if}\ \mathsf{True}\ q_2\ q_3 \Rightarrow_N q_2 \qquad \mathsf{if}\ \mathsf{False}\ q_2\ q_3 \Rightarrow_N q_3$$

$$\frac{q_1 \Rightarrow_N q_1'}{\mathsf{if}\ q_1\ q_2\ q_3 \Rightarrow_N \mathsf{if}\ q_1'\ q_2\ q_3} \qquad \mathsf{rec}\ f\ e \Rightarrow_N e[(\mathsf{rec}\ f\ e)/f]$$

$$\mathsf{rec}_0\ f\ e \Rightarrow_N \mathsf{rec}_0\ f\ e \qquad \mathsf{rec}_{n+1}\ f\ e \Rightarrow_N e[(\mathsf{rec}_n\ f\ e)/f]$$

Fig. 2. A SOS for CBN.

$$(\lambda x.e)q \Rightarrow_V e[q/x],\ \text{if } q \text{ in } \mathsf{WHNF} \qquad \frac{q_1 \Rightarrow_V q_1'}{q_1 q_2 \Rightarrow_V q_1' q_2}$$

$$c_1 c_2 \Rightarrow_V \mathsf{Applycon}(c_1, c_2) \qquad \frac{q_2 \Rightarrow_V q_2'}{q_1 q_2 \Rightarrow_V q_1 q_2'},\ \text{if } q_1 \text{ in } \mathsf{WHNF}$$

$$\mathsf{if}\ \mathsf{True}\ q_2\ q_3 \Rightarrow_V q_2 \qquad \mathsf{if}\ \mathsf{False}\ q_2\ q_3 \Rightarrow_V q_3$$

$$\frac{q_1 \Rightarrow_V q_1'}{\mathsf{if}\ q_1\ q_2\ q_3 \Rightarrow_V \mathsf{if}\ q_1'\ q_2\ q_3} \qquad \mathsf{rec}\ f\ e \Rightarrow_V e[(\mathsf{rec}\ f\ e)/f]$$

$$\mathsf{rec}_0\ f\ e \Rightarrow_V \mathsf{rec}_0\ f\ e \qquad \mathsf{rec}_{n+1}\ f\ e \Rightarrow_V e[(\mathsf{rec}_n\ f\ e)/f]$$

Fig. 3. A SOS for CBV.

We have the following (standard) result (which exploits that all constants are of iterated base type, as otherwise $c(\lambda x.e)$ might be well-typed but stuck – we also need the extra assumption that if $Ct(c) = \mathsf{Bool}$ then $c = \mathsf{True}$ or $c = \mathsf{False}$).

Fact 1. *Suppose (with q closed) $\Gamma \vdash q : t$. Then either q is in* WHNF, *or there exists unique q' such that $q \Rightarrow_N q'$ and such that $\Gamma \vdash q' : t$.*
Similarly for $\Rightarrow_V$.

We will introduce a "canonical" looping term Ω, defined by $\Omega = \mathsf{rec}\ f\ f$. There exists no q in WHNF such that $\Omega \Rightarrow_N^* q$ (or $\Omega \Rightarrow_V^* q$), but for all types t (and all Γ) we have $\Gamma \vdash \Omega : t$.

Thunkification and Dethunkification. We shall use the following notation: if t is a type in $\mathcal{T}$, $[t]$ is a shorthand for $\mathsf{Unit} \rightarrow t$.

If e is an expression, let $\underline{e}$ be a shorthand for $\lambda x.e$, where x is a fresh variable.

If e is an expression, let $\mathcal{D}(e)$ be a shorthand for $e\ d$, where d is a dummy constant of type Unit.

Fact 2. *If $\Gamma \vdash e : t$, then $\Gamma \vdash \underline{e} : [t]$. If $\Gamma \vdash e : [t]$, then $\Gamma \vdash \mathcal{D}(e) : t$.*
For all e, $\mathcal{D}(\underline{e}) \Rightarrow_N e$ and $\mathcal{D}(\underline{e}) \Rightarrow_V e$.

3 Strictness Types

The set of strictness types, $\mathcal{T}_{\mathsf{sa}}$, is defined as follows: a strictness type t is either a base type Base or a *strict* function type $t_1 \rightarrow_0 t_2$ (denoting that we *know* that the function is strict) or a *general* function type $t_1 \rightarrow_1 t_2$ (denoting that we do not know whether the function is strict).

We shall impose an ordering $\leq$ on strictness types, defined by stipulating that $t_1 \rightarrow_b t_2 \leq t_1' \rightarrow_{b'} t_2'$ iff $t_1' \leq t_1$, $b \leq b'$ and $t_2 \leq t_2'$, and by stipulating that $\mathsf{Int} \leq \mathsf{Int}$ etc. $t \leq t'$ means that t is more informative than t'; for instance it is more informative to know that a function is of type $\mathsf{Int} \rightarrow_0 \mathsf{Int}$ than to know that it is of type $\mathsf{Int} \rightarrow_1 \mathsf{Int}$.

We define two kinds of mappings from $\mathcal{T}_{\mathsf{sa}}$ into $\mathcal{T}$, E and Z, with the following intended meaning: if e can be assigned strictness type t and (the CBN-term) e translates into an equivalent CBV-term e', then e has type $\mathsf{E}(t)$ and e' has type $Z(t)$. E simply removes annotations from arrows, while Z in addition thunkifies arguments to non-strict functions. That is, we have

- $\mathsf{E}(\mathsf{Base}) = \mathsf{Base}$, $\mathsf{E}(t_1 \rightarrow_0 t_2) = \mathsf{E}(t_1) \rightarrow \mathsf{E}(t_2)$, $\mathsf{E}(t_1 \rightarrow_1 t_2) = \mathsf{E}(t_1) \rightarrow \mathsf{E}(t_2)$.
- $Z(\mathsf{Base}) = \mathsf{Base}$, $Z(t_1 \rightarrow_0 t_2) = Z(t_1) \rightarrow Z(t_2)$, $Z(t_1 \rightarrow_1 t_2) = [Z(t_1)] \rightarrow Z(t_2)$.

A *strict iterated base type* is either Base or of form $\mathsf{Base} \rightarrow_0 t$, where t is a strict iterated base type. Ct can be uniquely extended into $C\mathcal{T}_{\mathsf{sa}}$, a mapping from constants to strictness types, by demanding that with $t = C\mathcal{T}_{\mathsf{sa}}(c)$, t must be a strict iterated base type with $\mathsf{E}(t) = Ct(c)$ (recall that the non-strict constant if has been given a special status).

In Fig. 4 we present an inference system for strictness types. An inference is now of the form $\Gamma, T \vdash_{\mathsf{sa}} e : t, W$. Here

- Γ is an environment assigning strictness types to variables;
- e is an expression such that if $x \in \mathsf{FV}(e)$ then $\Gamma(x)$ is defined;
- t is a strictness type;
- W is a subset of $\mathsf{FV}(e)$. It might be helpful to think of W as variables which are needed in order to evaluate e to "head normal form".
- T is a subset of the domain of Γ, denoting those variables which have been bound by non-strict λ-abstractions in the given context (T is used for recording purposes only).

The first inference rule is non-structural and expresses the ability to forget information: if an expression has type t and needs the variables in W, it also has a more imprecise type and will also need a subset of W. The application of this rule might for instance be needed in order to assign the same type to the two branches in a conditional. The two rules for abstractions (among other things) say that if x is among the variables needed by e then $\lambda x.e$ can be assigned a strict type ($\rightarrow_0$), otherwise not. The two rules for applications (among other things) say that if e_1 is strict then the variables needed by e_2 will also be needed by $e_1 e_2$.

We have $\Gamma, T \vdash_{\mathsf{sa}} \Omega : t, \emptyset$ for all strictness types t. An expression which can be assigned a strictness type can also be assigned an ordinary type:

Fact 3. *Suppose* $\Gamma, T \vdash_{sa} e : t, W$. *Then* $\mathsf{E}(\Gamma) \vdash e : \mathsf{E}(t)$.

Conversely, an expression which can be assigned an ordinary type can also be assigned at least one strictness type:

Fact 4. *Suppose* $\Gamma \vdash e : t$. *Suppose* Γ' *is such that* $\mathsf{E}(\Gamma') = \Gamma$, *and such that for all* x *all arrows in* $\Gamma'(x)$ *are annotated 1. Then (for all* T*) there exists* t' *and* W, *with* $\mathsf{E}(t') = t$, *such that* $\Gamma', T \vdash_{sa} e : t', W$.

Proof. An easy induction; choose $W = \emptyset$ and t' as t with all $\rightarrow$'s replaced by $\rightarrow_1$. We use that $CT_{\mathsf{sa}}(c)$ is a strict iterated base type and hence is least among all types t with $\mathsf{E}(t) = \mathsf{E}(CT_{\mathsf{sa}}(c))$. □

The type system is rather similar to the one of Wright [Wri91] where function arrows are marked by boolean expressions – a major difference is that he imposes a "substitution ordering" (which hence is monotone in both "arrow positions") among types.

Wrt. other approaches, the following two examples will briefly hint at the relative strength of our type system – recall that the main point of this paper is *not* to present a superior strictness analysis!

Example 1. Consider the function f defined by $\mathsf{rec}\ f\ \lambda x.\lambda y.\lambda z.e$ where $e = \mathsf{if}\,(z = 0)\ (x + y)\ (f\ y\ x\ (z - 1))$. f is strict in all its arguments, but this cannot be inferred by the type system from [KM89] (due to the lack of conjunction types). In our system, however, we have

$$\emptyset, \emptyset \vdash_{\mathsf{sa}} \mathsf{rec}\ f\ \lambda x.\lambda y.\lambda z.e : \mathsf{Int} \rightarrow_0 \mathsf{Int} \rightarrow_0 \mathsf{Int} \rightarrow_0 \mathsf{Int}, \emptyset$$

$$\frac{\Gamma, T \vdash_{\mathrm{sa}} e : t, W}{\Gamma, T \vdash_{\mathrm{sa}} e : t', W'} \text{ if } t \leq t', W' \subseteq W$$

$$\Gamma, T \vdash_{\mathrm{sa}} c : CT_{\mathrm{sa}}(c), \emptyset$$

$$\Gamma, T \vdash_{\mathrm{sa}} x : \Gamma(x), \{x\}$$

$$\frac{\Gamma \cup \{x := t_1\}, T \vdash_{\mathrm{sa}} e : t, W \cup \{x\}}{\Gamma, T \vdash_{\mathrm{sa}} \lambda x.e : t_1 \rightarrow_0 t, W} \text{ if } x \notin T$$

$$\frac{\Gamma \cup \{x := t_1\}, T \cup \{x\} \vdash_{\mathrm{sa}} e : t, W}{\Gamma, T \vdash_{\mathrm{sa}} \lambda x.e : t_1 \rightarrow_1 t, W} \text{ if } x \notin W$$

$$\frac{\Gamma, T \vdash_{\mathrm{sa}} e_1 : t_2 \rightarrow_0 t_1, W_1 \quad \Gamma, T \vdash_{\mathrm{sa}} e_2 : t_2, W_2}{\Gamma, T \vdash_{\mathrm{sa}} e_1 e_2 : t_1, W_1 \cup W_2}$$

$$\frac{\Gamma, T \vdash_{\mathrm{sa}} e_1 : t_2 \rightarrow_1 t_1, W_1 \quad \Gamma, T \vdash_{\mathrm{sa}} e_2 : t_2, W_2}{\Gamma, T \vdash_{\mathrm{sa}} e_1 e_2 : t_1, W_1}$$

$$\frac{\Gamma, T \vdash_{\mathrm{sa}} e_1 : \mathsf{Bool}, W_1 \quad \Gamma, T \vdash_{\mathrm{sa}} e_2 : t, W_2 \quad \Gamma, T \vdash_{\mathrm{sa}} e_3 : t, W_3}{\Gamma, T \vdash_{\mathrm{sa}} (\mathsf{if}\ e_1\ e_2\ e_3) : t, W_1 \cup (W_2 \cap W_3)}$$

$$\frac{\Gamma \cup \{f := t\}, T \vdash_{\mathrm{sa}} e : t, W}{\Gamma, T \vdash_{\mathrm{sa}} (\mathsf{rec}\ f\ e) : t, W} \text{ if } f \notin W, f \notin T$$

$$\frac{\Gamma \cup \{f := t\}, T \vdash_{\mathrm{sa}} e : t, W}{\Gamma, T \vdash_{\mathrm{sa}} (\mathsf{rec}_n\ f\ e) : t, W} \text{ if } f \notin W, f \notin T$$

Fig. 4. An inference system for strictness types.

This is because we – with $\Gamma_1 = \{f := \mathsf{Int} \rightarrow_0 \mathsf{Int} \rightarrow_0 \mathsf{Int} \rightarrow_0 \mathsf{Int}\}$ – have

$$\Gamma_1, \emptyset \vdash_{\mathrm{sa}} \lambda x.\lambda y.\lambda z.e : \mathsf{Int} \rightarrow_0 \mathsf{Int} \rightarrow_0 \mathsf{Int} \rightarrow_0 \mathsf{Int}, \emptyset$$

which again is because we – with $\Gamma_2 = \Gamma_1 \cup \{x := \mathsf{Int}, y := \mathsf{Int}, z := \mathsf{Int}\}$ – have

$$\Gamma_2, \emptyset \vdash_{\mathrm{sa}} \mathsf{if}\ (z = 0)\ (x + y)\ (f\ y\ x\ (z - 1)) : \mathsf{Int}, \{x, y, z\}$$

This follows from the fact that $\Gamma_2, \emptyset \vdash_{\mathrm{sa}} (z = 0) : \mathsf{Bool}, \{z\}$ and $\Gamma_2, \emptyset \vdash_{\mathrm{sa}} (x + y) : \mathsf{Int}, \{x, y\}$ and

$$\Gamma_2, \emptyset \vdash_{\mathrm{sa}} (f\ y\ x\ (z - 1)) : \mathsf{Int}, \{x, y, z\}$$

The latter follows since e.g. $\Gamma_2, \emptyset \vdash_{\mathrm{sa}} (f\ y) : \mathsf{Int} \rightarrow_0 \mathsf{Int} \rightarrow_0 \mathsf{Int}, \{y\}$.

Example 2. Our analysis is not very good at handling recursive definitions with free variables. To see this, consider the function g given by

$$\lambda y.\mathsf{rec}\ f\ \lambda x.\mathsf{if}\ (x = 0)\ y\ (f\ (x - 1))$$

Clearly ge_1e_2 will loop if e_1 loops, so the analysis *ought* to conclude that g has strictness type $\mathsf{Int}\rightarrow_0\mathsf{Int}\rightarrow_0\mathsf{Int}$. However, we can do no better than inferring that g has strictness type $\mathsf{Int}\rightarrow_1\mathsf{Int}\rightarrow_0\mathsf{Int}$ – this is because it is impossible to deduce $\ldots\vdash_{\mathsf{sa}}(\mathsf{rec}\ f\ \ldots) : \ldots, \{y\}$ which in turn is because it is impossible to deduce $\ldots\vdash_{\mathsf{sa}}(\mathsf{if}\ (x=0)\ y\ (f\ (x-1))) : \ldots, \{x,y\}$. The reason for this is that we cannot record in $\Gamma(f)$ that f needs y.

In order to repair on that, function arrows should be annotated not only with 0/1 but also with which free variables are needed – at the cost of complicating the theory significantly.

Inferring Strictness Types

First notice that no "least typing property" holds: the expression $\lambda f.f$ has type $(\mathsf{Int}\rightarrow_0\mathsf{Int})\rightarrow_0(\mathsf{Int}\rightarrow_0\mathsf{Int})$ and type $(\mathsf{Int}\rightarrow_1\mathsf{Int})\rightarrow_0(\mathsf{Int}\rightarrow_1\mathsf{Int})$ but *not* type $(\mathsf{Int}\rightarrow_1\mathsf{Int})\rightarrow_0(\mathsf{Int}\rightarrow_0\mathsf{Int})$.

On the other hand, it is possible to develop a type inference algorithm which for each assignment to the arrows occurring in *contravariant* position finds a *least* assignment to the arrows in *covariant* position. The algorithm works by solving constraints "on the fly" and is fully described in [Amt93]; below we shall give a brief outline:

The first step is to reformulate the inference system from Fig. 4 by employing the notion of *strictness variables*, ranging over 0,1. A *pre-strictness type* is now a strictness type where the 0/1's have been replaced by strictness variables. Then judgements take the form $\Gamma \vdash e : t, W, C$ with t a pre-strictness type, with Γ mapping (program) variables into pre-strictness types, with e an expression, with W a mapping from (program) variables into strictness variables, and with C a set of *constraints* among the strictness variables.

The crucial point is that given a proof tree one can *normalize* the constraints by traversing the tree from leaves to root. Employing the convention that $\mathbf{b}^+$ denotes the strictness variables occurring in covariant position in the actual judgement, that $\mathbf{b}^-$ denotes the strictness variables occurring in contravariant position in the actual judgement and that $\mathbf{b}_0$ denotes the strictness variables *not* occurring in the actual judgement but "higher up in the proof tree", a normalized set of constraints consists of

- A constraint of form $\mathbf{b}^+ \geq g(\mathbf{b}^-)$, with g a monotone function from $\{0,1\}^n$ into $\{0,1\}^m$ for appropriate n,m. Hence we see that for each choice of assignment to $\mathbf{b}^-$ there exists a least assignment to $\mathbf{b}^+$.
- A constraint of form $\mathbf{b}_0 \gg g_0(\mathbf{b}^-)$, with g_0 a monotone function. The interpretation of the strange symbol $\gg$ is that by replacing it by "=" one surely gets a solution to the inference system in Fig. 4; and all solutions to this inference system satisfy the constraint resulting from replacing $\gg$ by $\geq$.

4 An Algorithm for Thunkification

4.1 The Mapping $C_t^{t'}$

The first step will be, for types t and t' such that $t \leq t'$, to define a mapping $C_t^{t'}$ from expressions into expressions. The translation is motivated by the desire that if e has type $Z(t)$, then $C_t^{t'}(e)$ has type $Z(t')$.

Example 3. Suppose $t = \mathsf{Int} \rightarrow_0 \mathsf{Int}$ and $t' = \mathsf{Int} \rightarrow_1 \mathsf{Int}$, and suppose e has type $\mathsf{Int} \rightarrow \mathsf{Int}$. $C_t^{t'}$ then has to translate e into something of type $[\mathsf{Int}] \rightarrow \mathsf{Int}$ – it is easily seen that $\lambda x.e\ \mathcal{D}(x)$ (with x fresh) will do the job.

$C_t^{t'}$ is defined as follows (inductively in the "size" of t and t'):

1. If $t = t'$, then $C_t^{t'}(e) = e$.
2. If $t = t_1 \rightarrow_0 t_2$ and $t' = t'_1 \rightarrow_0 t'_2$ (with $t'_1 \leq t_1$, $t_2 \leq t'_2$), then (where x is a "fresh" variable)
$$C_t^{t'}(e) = \lambda x.C_{t_2}^{t'_2}(e\ C_{t'_1}^{t_1}(x))$$
3. If $t = t_1 \rightarrow_1 t_2$ and $t' = t'_1 \rightarrow_1 t'_2$ (with $t'_1 \leq t_1$, $t_2 \leq t'_2$), then (where x is a "fresh" variable)
$$C_t^{t'}(e) = \lambda x.C_{t_2}^{t'_2}(e\ \underline{C_{t'_1}^{t_1}(\mathcal{D}(x))})$$
4. If $t = t_1 \rightarrow_0 t_2$ and $t' = t'_1 \rightarrow_1 t'_2$ (with $t'_1 \leq t_1$, $t_2 \leq t'_2$), then (where x is a "fresh" variable)
$$C_t^{t'}(e) = \lambda x.C_{t_2}^{t'_2}(e\ C_{t'_1}^{t_1}(\mathcal{D}(x)))$$

4.2 The Translation from CBN to CBV

Given an expression e, and a proof of $\Gamma, T \vdash_{\mathsf{sa}} e : t, W$. We now present an algorithm for transforming e into an expression e', with the aim that the "CBV-semantics" of e' should equal the "CBN-semantics" of e.

The translation is defined inductively in the proof tree – several cases:

- Suppose $\Gamma, T \vdash_{\mathsf{sa}} e : t', W'$ because $\Gamma, T \vdash_{\mathsf{sa}} e : t, W$ and $t \leq t'$, $W' \subseteq W$. Suppose e (by the latter proof tree) transforms into e'. Then e (by the former proof tree) transforms into $C_t^{t'}(e')$.
- Suppose $e = c$, and $\Gamma, T \vdash_{\mathsf{sa}} e : CT_{\mathsf{sa}}(c), \emptyset$. Then we let $e' = c$.
- Suppose $e = x$, and $\Gamma, T \vdash_{\mathsf{sa}} e : \Gamma(x), \{x\}$. Two cases:
  - If $x \in T$, we let $e' = \mathcal{D}(x)$ (as x will be bound to a thunkified argument).
  - If $x \notin T$, we let $e' = x$.
- Suppose $e = \lambda x.e_1$, and suppose e_1 (using the relevant proof tree) translates into e'_1. Then e translates into $\lambda x.e'_1$.
- Suppose $e = e_1 e_2$, and suppose e_1 and e_2 (using the relevant proof trees) translate into e'_1 resp. e'_2. Two cases:
  - If e_1 is of type $t_2 \rightarrow_0 t_1$, e translates into $e'_1 e'_2$.
  - If e_1 is of type $t_2 \rightarrow_1 t_1$, e translates into $e'_1 \underline{e'_2}$.

- Suppose $e = \text{if } e_1\ e_2\ e_3$, and suppose e_1, e_2 and e_3 (using the relevant proof trees) translate into e'_1, e'_2 resp. e'_3. Then e translates into $\text{if } e'_1\ e'_2\ e'_3$.
- Suppose $e = \text{rec } f\ e_1$ (resp. $\text{rec}_n\ f\ e_1$), and suppose e_1 (using the relevant proof tree) translates into e'_1. Then e translates into $\text{rec } f\ e'_1$ (resp. $\text{rec}_n\ f\ e'_1$).

This is similar to the translation produced by the thunkification algorithm from [DH93].

Example 4. Consider the expression $twice = \lambda f.\lambda x.f(fx)$. $twice$ has strictness type $(\mathsf{Int}\rightarrow_1\mathsf{Int})\rightarrow_0(\mathsf{Int}\rightarrow_1\mathsf{Int})$ because

$$\{f := \mathsf{Int}\rightarrow_1\mathsf{Int}\}, \emptyset \vdash_{\mathrm{sa}} \lambda x.f(fx) : \mathsf{Int}\rightarrow_1\mathsf{Int}, \{f\} \text{ and}$$

$$\{f := \mathsf{Int}\rightarrow_1\mathsf{Int}, x := \mathsf{Int}\}, \{x\} \vdash_{\mathrm{sa}} f(fx) : \mathsf{Int}, \{f\} \text{ etc.}$$

Accordingly, $twice$ translates into the term

$$\lambda f.\lambda x.f\underline{\underline{f\mathcal{D}(x)}}$$

of type $([\mathsf{Int}]\rightarrow\mathsf{Int})\rightarrow([\mathsf{Int}]\rightarrow\mathsf{Int})$. We see that there is room for some (peephole) optimization here, as $\underline{\mathcal{D}(x)}$ could be replaced by x.

Notice that $twice$ also has strictness type $(\mathsf{Int}\rightarrow_0\mathsf{Int})\rightarrow_0(\mathsf{Int}\rightarrow_0\mathsf{Int})$. Using the corresponding proof tree, $twice$ just translates into itself.

5 Correctness Predicates

We now embark on expressing the *correctness* of the translation – something not addressed in [DH93]. As a first step, we consider closed expressions only – to this end we define a predicate $\sim_t$, indexed over strictness types, such that $q \sim_t q'$ is defined whenever q is a closed expression of type $\mathsf{E}(t)$, and q' is a closed expression of type $Z(t)$. $\sim_t$ is defined inductively on t:

- $q \sim_{\mathsf{Base}} q'$ holds iff for all constants c we have $q \Rightarrow_N^* c$ iff $q' \Rightarrow_V^* c$ (in particular, q loops by CBN iff q' loops by CBV).
- $q_1 \sim_{t_1\rightarrow_0 t_2} q'_1$ holds iff for all q_2, q'_2 such that $q_2 \sim_{t_1} q'_2$ we have $q_1 q_2 \sim_{t_2} q'_1 q'_2$.
- $q_1 \sim_{t_1\rightarrow_1 t_2} q'_1$ holds iff for all q_2, q'_2 such that $q_2 \sim_{t_1} q'_2$ we have $q_1 q_2 \sim_{t_2} q'_1 \underline{q'_2}$.

This very much resembles a logical relation, but notice the difference between $\sim_{t_1\rightarrow_0 t_2}$ and $\sim_{t_1\rightarrow_1 t_2}$. Thus the predicate closely reflects how expressions are to be translated, cf. the claim in [Wan93]:

> This work suggests that the proposition associated with a flow analysis can simply be that "the optimization works".

Now we are ready to consider arbitrary (non-closed) expressions. The main correctness predicate takes the form $e\ \mathsf{COR}(t, W, \Gamma, T)\ e'$, where e and e' are expressions, t belongs to $\mathcal{T}_{\mathrm{sa}}$, Γ maps variables into $\mathcal{T}_{\mathrm{sa}}$, and W and T are sets of variables. We shall need an auxiliary function Z_T, mapping from $\mathcal{T}_{\mathrm{sa}}$-environments into $\mathcal{T}$-environments: $Z_T(\Gamma)(x) = Z(\Gamma(x))$ for $x \notin T$;
and $Z_T(\Gamma)(x) = [Z(\Gamma(x))]$ for $x \in T$.

Definition 5. e $\mathsf{COR}(t, W, \Gamma, T)$ e' holds iff (with $\{x_1 \dots x_n\}$ being the domain of Γ)

1. $\Gamma, T \vdash_{\mathsf{sa}} e : t, W$.
2. $Z_T(\Gamma) \vdash e' : Z(t)$.
3. $\mathsf{FV}(e) = \mathsf{FV}(e')$.
4. Let closed terms q_i, q_i' ($i \in \{1 \dots n\}$) be such that $q_i \sim_{\Gamma(x_i)} q_i'$. Then

   $$e[\{q_1 \dots q_n\}/\{x_1 \dots x_n\}] \sim_t e'[\{Q_1' \dots Q_n'\}/\{x_1 \dots x_n\}]$$

   where Q_i' is defined as follows: if $x_i \in T$ then $Q_i' = \underline{q_i'}$ else $Q_i' = q_i'$. Moreover, suppose that i is such that $x_i \in W$ and $q_i \sim_{\Gamma(i)} \Omega$. Then

   $$e[\{q_1 \dots q_n\}/\{x_1 \dots x_n\}] \sim_t \Omega$$

The first part of 4 resembles the standard way of extending relations from closed terms to open terms; the second part of 4 expresses that the variables in W are "needed".

5.1 Correctness Theorems

We have the following theorem, to be proved in [Amt93]:

Theorem 6. *Suppose $\Gamma, T \vdash_{sa} e : t, W$, suppose e contains no unbounded recursion (i.e. only* rec_n *'s and no* rec *'s) and suppose e (by means of the corresponding proof tree) translates into e'. Then e* $\mathsf{COR}(t, W, \Gamma, T)$ *e'.*

The restriction to bounded recursion is motivated by the SOS-rule $\mathsf{rec}\ f\ e \Rightarrow_N e[(\mathsf{rec}\ f\ e)/f]$, as we want to (inductively) use properties of the latter rec to prove properties of the former rec.

The proof of Theorem 6 proceeds roughly speaking as follows:

1. A number of properties of $\sim_t$ are proved (by induction on t). For instance, we have that if $q \Rightarrow_N q_1$ and $q \sim_t q'$ then also $q_1 \sim_t q'$.
2. Some properties of $C_t^{t'}$ are formulated and proved – for instance that if $q \sim_t q'$ then $q \sim_{t'} C_t^{t'}(q')$.
3. Finally, we are able to prove Theorem 6 by induction in the proof tree.

By means of Theorem 6 we can prove what we are really looking for:

Theorem 7. *Suppose q is a closed expression (which may contain unbounded recursion) such that $\emptyset, \emptyset \vdash_{sa} q$:* $\mathsf{Base}, \emptyset$. *Let q' be the translation of q, using the algorithm in Sect. 4. Now for all constants (of base type) c, $q \Rightarrow_N^* c$ iff $q' \Rightarrow_V^* c$.*

Proof. First some notation: given n, let q_n be the result of substituting rec_n for all occurrences of rec. It is easy to see that q_n translates into q_n'.

First (the "only if" part) suppose $q \Rightarrow_N^* c$. It is easy to see that there exists n such that $q_n \Rightarrow_N^* c$. Since q_n and q_n' does not contain unbounded recursion, Theorem 6 tells us that q_n $\mathsf{COR}(\mathsf{Base}, \emptyset, \emptyset, \emptyset)$ q_n'. This implies that $q_n \sim_{\mathsf{Base}} q_n'$, so $q_n' \Rightarrow_V^* c$. But then it is immediate that $q' \Rightarrow_V^* c$.

The "if" part is analogous. □

6 Concluding Remarks

We have presented a type system for strictness analysis, presented an algorithm which translates a CBN-term into an equivalent CBV-term and finally given a proof of the correctness of the analysis/translation.

It may be of interest to investigate closer the power of our strictness analysis, relative to other approaches. And in order to avoid the kind of superfluous dethunkification/thunkification we encountered in Example 4, one may consider keeping track of context – somewhat similar to what is done in [NN90].

References

[Amt93] Torben Amtoft. Strictness types: An inference algorithm and an application. Technical Report PB-448, DAIMI, University of Aarhus, Denmark, 1993.

[BHA86] Geoffrey L. Burn, Chris Hankin, and Samson Abramsky. Strictness analysis for higher-order functions. *Science of Computer Programming*, 7:249–278, 1986.

[DH92] Olivier Danvy and John Hatcliff. Thunks (continued). In M. Billaud et al., editor, *Analyse statique, Bordeaux 92 (WSA '92)*, pages 3–11, September 1992.

[DH93] Olivier Danvy and John Hatcliff. CPS transformation after strictness analysis. *ACM Letters on Programming Languages and Systems*, 1(3), 1993.

[Hug89] John Hughes. Why functional programming matters. *Computer Journal*, 32(2):98–107, 1989.

[Jen91] Thomas P. Jensen. Strictness analysis in logical form. In John Hughes, editor, *International Conference on Functional Programming Languages and Computer Architecture*, pages 352–366. Springer Verlag, LNCS 523, August 1991.

[KM89] Tsung-Min Kuo and Prateek Mishra. Strictness analysis: A new perspective based on type inference. In *International Conference on Functional Programming Languages and Computer Architecture*, pages 260–272. ACM Press, September 1989.

[Lan92] Torben Poort Lange. The correctness of an optimized code generation. Technical Report PB-427, DAIMI, University of Aarhus, Denmark, November 1992. Also in the proceedings of PEPM '93, Copenhagen, ACM press.

[Myc80] Alan Mycroft. The theory of transforming call-by-need to call-by-value. In B. Robinet, editor, *International Symposium on Programming, Paris*, pages 269–281. Springer Verlag, LNCS 83, April 1980.

[NN90] Hanne Riis Nielson and Flemming Nielson. Context information for lazy code generation. In *ACM Conference on Lisp and Functional Programming*, pages 251–263. ACM Press, June 1990.

[Wan93] Mitchell Wand. Specifying the correctness of binding-time analysis. In *ACM Symposium on Principles of Programming Languages*, pages 137–143. ACM Press, January 1993.

[Wri91] David A. Wright. A new technique for strictness analysis. In *TAPSOFT 91*, pages 235–258. Springer Verlag, LNCS 494, April 1991.

[Wri92] David A. Wright. An intensional type discipline. *Australian Computer Science Communications*, 14, January 1992.

An Efficient Abductive Reasoning System Based on Program Analysis

Shohei Kato Hirohisa Seki Hidenori Itoh

Department of AI and Computer Science
Nagoya Institute of Technology
Gokiso, Showa-ku, Nagoya 466, Japan
E-mail:{ shohei@juno.elcom, seki@ics, itoh@juno.elcom}.nitech.ac.jp

1 Introduction

Static analysis has recently attracted much attention in logic programming (for example, [Deb92]). In this paper, we consider an application of static analysis to first-order Horn clause abductive reasoning. Abductive reasoning is now one of the major research issues in AI (e.g., [Poo88]), and has many interesting application areas such as diagnosis, scheduling and design. It is, however, known to be computationally very expensive for large problems [SL90], thus will require sophisticated heuristic search strategies based on static analysis.

Abductive reasoning is logically formulated as follows: Given a set of axioms F, and a conjunction of atoms O (an observation, or a goal), find a set of atoms h (the hypotheses, or a solution) such that $h \cup F \models O$ and $h \cup F$ is consistent. Once abductive reasoning is logically so defined, it is quite natural that those query processing techniques studied in logic programming and deductive databases are applicable to abductive reasoning. In fact, there are several work done along this line (for instance, [Sti91] and [OI92]), where magic sets [BMSU86] and other query processing strategies are utilized so as to make abductive reasoning both *less redundant* (i.e., avoiding duplicate proofs of the repeated subgoals) and *goal-directed* (i.e., focusing on only relevant subgoals necessary to solve a given goal).

There is, however, an important difference between query processing in deductive databases and abductive reasoning. Consistency conditions a derived solution should satisfy are usually given in the form of negative clauses (i.e., headless clauses). Checking the consistency of solutions wrt negative clauses then becomes a global one, thus losing the goal-directedness. The problem of consistency checking in abductive reasoning is essential, but little work has been done on this problem. One exception is the work by [OI92], where they proposed a procedure to detect only negative clauses relevant to a given goal. Since their procedure uses very primitive information on the consistency checking, it achieves only restricted benefits. This paper extends the previous work; we propose a framework of static analysis for abductive reasoning with consistency checking, to analyze the logical dependency between a goal and each relevant negative clause, thereby pruning unnecessary search involving the consistency checking.

We then present an implemented abductive reasoning system based on the magic sets transformation [BMSU86]. Its computation incorporates the results obtained from the static analysis so that the bottom-up (forward-reasoning) evaluation of the magic sets transformed rules can be controlled to avoid unnecessary work.

The organization of the paper is as follows. In Section 2, we give a brief description of our framework of abductive reasoning, and discuss related work and the problems. Section 3 describes our method of the static analysis for abductive reasoning. In Section 4, we explain our analysis-based abductive reasoning system based on a modified version of the magic sets. Section 5 shows some empirical results of our proposed method.

2 Abductive Reasoning

2.1 Problem Definition

This section describes our framework of abductive reasoning based on [Poo88].

Definition 1. Suppose that a set of first-order Horn clauses F, called *facts*, and a set of atoms (unit clauses) H, called the set of *possible hypotheses*, are given. Suppose further that an existentially quantified conjunction O of atoms, called *an observation* or simply a *goal*, is given. Then, an *explanation* of O from $F \cup H$ is a set h of instances of elements of H such that

$$F \cup h \vdash O \qquad (O \text{ can be proved from } F \cup h) \qquad \text{(AR 1)}$$
$$F \cup h \not\vdash \Box \qquad (F \cup h \text{ is consistent}) \qquad \text{(AR 2)}$$

□

Abductive reasoning is now defined to be a task of finding an explanation h of O from $F \cup H$. In this framework, F is assumed to be consistent and treated as always true.

Definition 2. A headless clause in F is called a *negative clause*. A negative clause is denoted by $false \leftarrow A_1, \cdots, A_n$, where A_i $(1 \leq i \leq n;\ n \geq 1)$ is an atom and $false$ (possibly with subscripts) designates falsity. Each of the negative clauses in F is called a *consistency condition*. □

Example 1.
The following example is a slightly modified version of the one taken from [OI91] (see Figure 1). The intended meaning of those clauses in Figure 1 is as follows. We consider a planning problem to check whether a person X from department $s1$ can have a meeting (resp., discussion) at room (resp., lounge) Z with a person Y from department $s2$, denoted by $m(X,Y,Z)$ (resp., $d(X,Y,Z)$).

Facts: $m(X,Y,Z)$ (resp., $d(X,Y,Z)$) holds if both X and Y can be assumed to be available, denoted by $hp(X,s1), hp(Y,s2)$, and room (resp., lounge) Z is vacant (resp., quiet), denoted by $v(Z)$ (resp., $q(Z)$) (see 1 & 2).
$v(Z)$ (resp., $q(Z)$) holds if Z is a room (resp., lounge) and Z can be assumed to be vacant (resp., quiet), denoted by $hv(Z)$ (resp., $hq(Z)$) (see 3 & 4).

$a(Z)$ holds if Z is a room and can be assumed to be vacant, or if Z is a lounge and can be assumed to be quiet (see 5 & 6).
We know that there exists two rooms (resp., four lounges) and that, among them, room 101 (resp., lounge 204) is known to be unavailable, denoted by $na(101)$ (resp., $na(204)$). By $nhp(X, D)$, we mean that person X from department D is known to be unavailable for both a meeting and a discussion.
(*Hypotheses:*) By $hp(X, Y)$, we mean that person X from department Y is assumed to be available for a meeting or a discussion. Similarly, $hv(Z)$ (resp., $hq(Z)$) means that room (resp., lounge) Z is assumed to be vacant (resp., quiet).
(*Consistency Conditions:*) If both $hp(X, D)$ and $nhp(X, D)$ hold, then it is inconsistent. Similarly, it is inconsistent if both $a(Z)$ and $na(Z)$ hold (see 7 & 8).

Facts	*Hypotheses*
1: m(X,Y,Z) ← hp(X,s1),hp(Y,s2),v(Z).	hp(b,s1). hp(c,s1). hp(e,s2). hp(f,s2).
2: d(X,Y,Z) ← hp(X,s1),hp(Y,s2),q(Z).	hv(Z).
3: v(Z) ← r(Z),hv(Z).	hq(Z).
4: q(Z) ← l(Z),hq(Z).	
5: a(Z) ← r(Z),hv(Z).	*Consistency Conditions*
6: a(Z) ← l(Z),hq(Z).	7: $false_7$ ← hp(X,D),nhp(X,D).
r(101). r(102).	8: $false_8$ ← a(Z),na(Z).
l(201). l(202). l(203). l(204).	
na(101). na(204).	

Fig. 1. An Example : P_{ex}

Let P_{ex} be the set of all the Horn clauses in Figure 1. Suppose that an observation (or a goal) "$m(b, Y, Z)$" is given. □

Any first-order proof procedure works as an abductive reasoning system if it distinguishes hypotheses from facts, satisfying the conditions given in Definition 1.

Example 2. Figure 2 shows SLD-trees [Llo84] for $P_{ex} \cup \{\leftarrow m(b, Y, Z)\}$ and SLD-trees for $P_{ex} \cup \{\leftarrow false_i\}$ ($i = 7, 8$). In those trees, when a subgoal $\leftarrow Q_1, \cdots, Q_{i-1}, Q_i, Q_{i+1}, \cdots, Q_n$ is resolved upon Q_i with a hypothesis using mgu θ, we denote its resolvent by $\leftarrow (Q_1, \cdots, Q_{i-1}, \mathsf{M}Q_i, Q_{i+1}, \cdots, Q_n)\theta$, unless $\mathsf{M}Q_i\theta$ already exists among $(Q_1, \cdots, Q_{i-1})\theta$; otherwise, its resolvent is denoted by $\leftarrow (Q_1, \cdots, Q_{i-1}, Q_{i+1}, \cdots, Q_n)\theta$. $\mathsf{M}Q_i\theta$, called an *assumed atom*, means that $Q_i\theta$ is assumed to be true.

It follows from the leftmost branch of SLD-tree for $P_{ex} \cup \{\leftarrow m(b, Y, Z)\}$ that $m(b, e, 101)$ could have an explanation $O = \{hp(b, s1), hp(e, s2), hv(101)\}$

unless assuming O causes inconsistency. ¿From SLD-tree for $P_{ex} \cup \{\leftarrow false_8\}$, however, it follows that it causes inconsistency to assume that either $hv(101)$ or $hq(204)$ is true. On the other hand, we know that $m(b, e, 102)$, for example, has an explanation, since we can safely assume that $hp(b, s1)$, $hp(e, s2)$ and $hv(102)$ are true. □

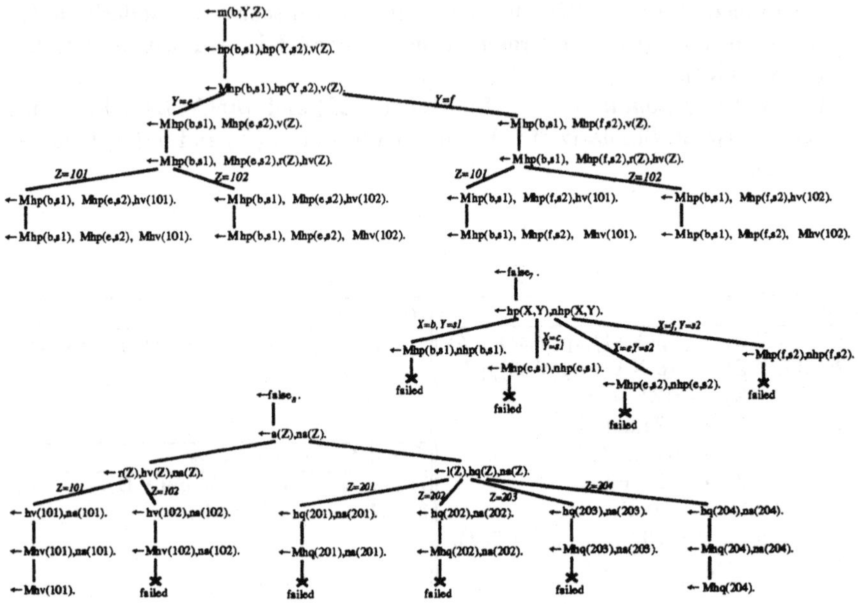

Fig. 2. An Example of Abductive Reasoning for P_{ex}

Throughout the paper, we assume for simplicity that the selection rule in an SLD-derivation always selects the leftmost atom if it is not of the form MQ" for some atom Q; otherwise, it is simply skipped and selects, if possible, the next leftmost non-assumed one. Moreover, we assume that each not-unit clause in facts is assigned a natural number, called a *clause number*, as its identifier.

2.2 Related Work and Problems

Standard approach for implementing abductive reasoning is based on either a topdown proof procedure (e.g., [NM91], [KI91]) or a bottom-up computation method such as the magic sets (e.g., [Sti91], [OI92]), where such a proof procedure should allow some atoms to be assumed instead of proved, obtaining a set of instances of the possible hypotheses. The set of instances of the possible hypotheses so computed should be then checked wrt given consistency conditions. Evaluating consistency conditions similarly to a given goal is, however, not always efficient and sometimes causes redundant work. In Figure 2, for example, the computation of the subtree with a goal "$\leftarrow l(Z), hq(Z), na(Z)$" as its root in SLD-tree for $P_{ex} \cup \{\leftarrow \ false_8\}$, is irrelevant to goal $\leftarrow m(b, Y, Z)$, since, although the subtree shows that assuming $hq(204)$ causes inconsistency, the set of possible hypotheses obtained from the given goal does not contain $hq(204)$ at all. Moreover, computing SLD-tree $P_{ex} \cup \{\leftarrow \ false_7\}$ can be avoided, since it gives no restriction on assuming hypotheses.

The problem of consistency checking in abductive reasoning is essential, but little work has been done on this problem. Ohta and Inoue [OI92] proposed a procedure which detects only negative clauses relevant to a given goal, thereby avoiding consistency checking for goal $\leftarrow \ false_7$ in the above example. Their procedure, however, uses very primitive information on the consistency checking, therefore still losing the goal-directedness, in that it exhaustively explores the search space of an unnecessary consistency condition; for example, all the branches of SLD-tree for $P_{ex} \cup \{\leftarrow \ false_8\}$ are computed in their procedure.

In this paper, we extend the previous work and propose a more refined procedure based on a static analysis which infers a hypotheses-dependency relation between a given goal and each of negative clauses, thereby making it possible to restore the goal-directedness of evaluating consistency conditions.

3 Pruning Search by Program Analysis

We now describe our static analysis to detect irrelevant computation for a given goal when evaluating consistency conditions. In this section, we explain our static analysis method in terms of SLD-resolution for the simplicity of explanation, and then give a description of our actual implementation which is a bottom-up reasoning system based on the magic sets.

The idea of our static analysis is quite simple. It consists of the following two phases:

Phase 1 *(Hypotheses dependency analysis):* We analyze on which hypotheses an explanation of a given observation depends, and also analyze on which hypotheses each consistency condition depends. We do this ***hypotheses dependency analysis*** approximately, by considering a suitably abstracted version of given facts, hypotheses and an observation.

Phase 2 *(Detection of irrelevant computations):* We then detect irrelevant computations in checking consistency conditions from the above-mentioned results of the hypotheses dependency analysis.

3.1 Hypotheses Dependency Analysis

In the hypotheses dependency analysis, we consider as an approximation of actually given facts, hypotheses and an observation their propositional version, simply by ignoring their argument information. It should be noted that the precision of our analysis will increase if more precise argument information is taken into consideration with price paid for sacrificing the efficiency of the analysis. For an expression E (i.e., either an atom, a clause or a set of clauses), we denote its abstracted (i.e., propositional) version by $\bar{E}$.

Example 3. Figure 3 shows an abstracted version, $\bar{P}_{ex}$ of P_{ex} given in Example 1, where each abstracted clause is given the same clause number as before. □

Facts

```
1:  m ← hp,hp,v.
2:  d ← hp,hp,q.
3:  v ← r,hv.
4:  q ← l,hq.
5:  a ← r,hv.
6:  a ← l,hq.
        r.
        na.
        l.
```

Hypotheses

```
hp.
hv.
hq.
```

Consistency Conditions

```
7:  false_7 ← hp,nhp.
8:  false_8 ← a,na.
```

Fig. 3. Abstracted Program $\bar{P}_{ex}$ of P_{ex}

Let P be given facts and hypotheses, and O be an observation. We then consider SLD-tree for $\bar{P} \cup \{\leftarrow \bar{O}\}$ and the ones for $\bar{P} \cup \{\leftarrow \mathit{false}\}$, together with the history information of input (non-unit) clauses necessary to construct SLD-derivations. The history information is denoted by list $[n_1, \cdots, n_k]$ $(k \geq 0)$, where n_i $(i \geq 0)$ is a clause number and we call it a ***history list***. The construction of a history list is done in an obvious way; that is, a root node in an SLD-tree is associated with a nil-list as its history list, and, when a subgoal with its history list L is resolved using an input (non-unit) clause with clause number n, the history list of its resolvent is L with n inserted into its end.

For example, Figure 4 shows the abstracted version of those SLD-trees in Figure 2 with history lists.

3.2 Detection of Irrelevant Computations

We call the set of hypotheses (without M-operators), H_O (resp., $\bar{H}_{\bar{O}}$), occurring in a successful leaf in SLD-tree for $P \cup \{\leftarrow O\}$ (resp., $\bar{P} \cup \{\leftarrow \bar{O}\}$) a set of *candidate hypotheses* for O in P (resp., $\bar{O}$ in $\bar{P}$). For example, $\{hp(b, s1), hp(e, s2), hv(101)\}$ in Figure 2 is a set of candidate hypotheses for $m(b, Y, Z)$ in P_{ex}, and $\{hp, hv\}$ in Figure 4 is a set of candidate hypotheses for m in $\bar{P}_{ex}$.

Moreover, let $\bar{H}_{false}$ be a set of hypotheses (without M-operators), occurring in a successful leaf, if any, in SLD-tree for $\bar{P} \cup \{\leftarrow \mathit{false}\}$. Then, we call

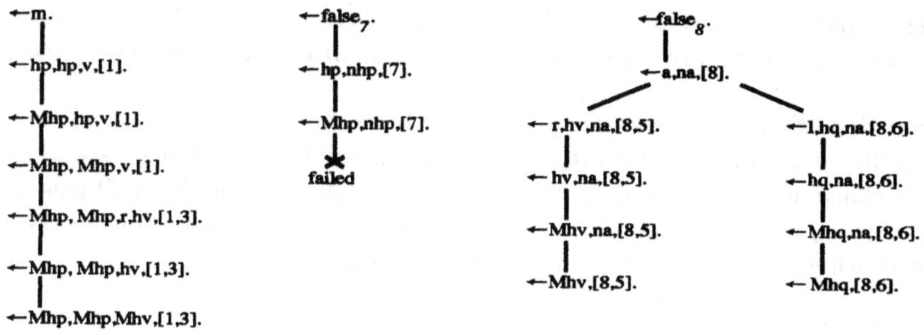

Fig. 4. Abstracted *SLD*-Trees corresponding to those in Figure 2

$(\bar{H}_{\bar{O}}, \bar{H}_{false})$ an *incompatible pair* for $\bar{O}$ in $\bar{P}$ if $\bar{H}_{false}$ is a subset of $\bar{H}_{\bar{O}}$. Such $\bar{H}_{false}$ is said to be a *set of incompatible hypotheses for* $\bar{H}_{\bar{O}}$.

Then, it is easy to see that the following proposition holds:

Proposition 3.
Let P be given facts and hypotheses, and O be an observation. Suppose that a set, H_O, of candidate hypotheses for O in P does not satisfy the condition (AR2). Then, in an SLD-tree for $P \cup \{\leftarrow false\}$, there exists a successful leaf with H_{false} as the set of hypotheses occurring in it such that $(\bar{H}_{\bar{O}}, \bar{H}_{false})$ is an incompatible pair for $\bar{O}$ in $\bar{P}$. □

In other words, the above proposition implies that we can safely do without constructing any SLD-derivation of $P \cup \{\leftarrow false\}$ whose successful leaf gives a set of hypotheses H_{false}, if $\bar{H}_{false}$ is not a set of incompatible hypotheses for $\bar{H}_{\bar{O}}$. In particular, if each successful SLD-derivation of $\bar{P} \cup \{\leftarrow false\}$ satisfies such a condition, then we can do without the whole computation for the consistency condition. Therefore, our method covers the previous work by [OI92] as a special case.

Example 4. In Figure 4, the right branch in the SLD-tree for $\bar{P}_{ex} \cup \{\leftarrow false_8\}$ gives a successful leaf with a set of hypotheses $\{hq\}$. A set of candidate hypotheses for m in $\bar{P}_{ex}$ is $\{hp, hv\}$. Since $(\{hp, hv\}, \{hq\})$ is not an incompatible pair, we can safely eliminate the computation of this branch, thereby pruning the search space.

Moreover, from an SLD-tree for $\bar{P}_{ex} \cup \{\leftarrow false_7\}$, it follows that we can safely do without the entire SLD-refutation of $P_{ex} \cup \{\leftarrow false_7\}$. □

In a nutshell, we know from the hypotheses dependency analysis which branches in the abstracted version of an SLD-tree for $\bar{P} \cup \{\leftarrow false\}$ should be computed. At the same time, we know a history list associated with each of such branches. In actual first-order abductive reasoning, we use those history lists to control the search space of constructing an SLD-tree for $P \cup \{\leftarrow \; false\}$.

Example 5. Figure 5 shows an pruned SLD-tree for $P_{ex} \cup \{\leftarrow \; false_8\}$, constructing only an SLD-derivation whose (non-unit) input clauses are those with clause numbers 8 and 5, in this order. Recall that, in the SLD-tree for $\bar{P}_{ex} \cup \{\leftarrow \; false_8\}$ in Figure 4, the history list associated with the successful leaf which gives a *set of incompatible hypotheses* is [8, 5]. □

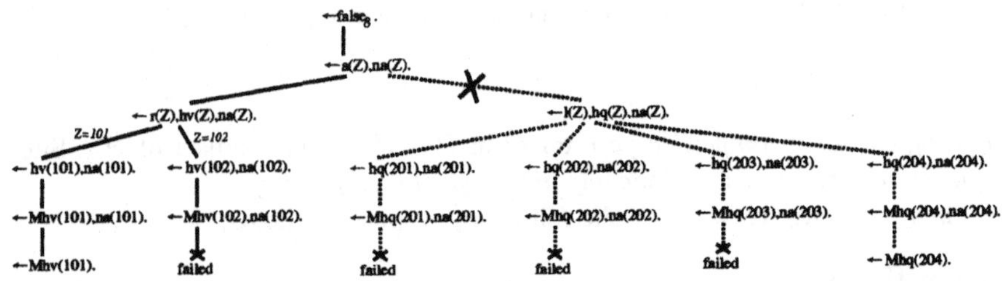

Fig. 5. Pruning SLD-tree for $P_{ex} \cup \{\leftarrow \; false_8\}$

4 Magic Sets Implementation of Analysis-based Abductive Reasoning

The section describes an implementation method of our hypotheses dependency analysis and the actual first-order abductive reasoning based on the analysis. Instead of a topdown proof procedure such as SLD-resolution described in the previous sections, we use a forward reasoning system based on the magic sets [BMSU86], since it is amenable to set-oriented computations, which is commonly preferred for large data-intensive applications. In the magic sets, a given Horn program is transformed into the set of rules whose bottom-up evaluation will simulate the topdown evaluation of the original program. However, we should modify the original magic sets method suitably so as to do the static analysis and the actual abductive reasoning. For the lack of space, we explain our method with the running examples and assume some familiarity the magic sets.

4.1 Hypotheses Dependency Analysis by Magic Sets

We first show how the hypotheses dependency analysis can be performed by a modified version of the magic sets.

Facts		*Hypotheses*	
magic_m,hp,hp → magic_v.	(1.1)	hp. hv. hq.	
magic_m,hp,hp → $cont_{11}$({hp}).	(1.2)		
$cont_{11}$(H),v(Hv,L) → m(H∪Hv,[1|L]).	(1.3)	*Consistency Conditions*	
		$magic\_false_7$,hp,nhp →	
magic_d,hp,hp → magic_q.	(2.1)	false_p({hp},[7]).	(7.1)
magic_d,hp,hp → $cont_{21}$({hp}).	(2.2)	$magic\_false_8$ → magic_a.	(8.1)
$cont_{21}$(H),q(Hq,L) → d(H∪Hq,[2|L]).	(2.3)	$magic\_false_8$ → $cont_{81}$({ }).	(8.2)
		$cont_{81}$(H),a(Hs,L),na →	
magic_v,r,hv → v({hv},[3]).	(3.1)	$false_8$(H∪Hq,[8|L]).	(8.3)
magic_q,l,hq → q({hq},[4]).	(4.1)	*Goals*	
magic_a,r,hv → a({hv},[5]).	(5.1)	→ magic_m.	(9)
magic_a,l,hq → a({hq},[6]).	(6.1)	→ $magic\_false_7$.	(10)
r. na. l.		→ $magic\_false_8$.	(11)

Fig. 6. Magic Sets Transformed Rules $\overline{P}_{ex}^{magic}$ of $\overline{P}_{ex}$

Example 6.
Figure 6 shows the magic sets based transformed rules $\bar{P}_{ex}^{magic}$ of $\bar{P}_{ex}$ in Figure 4, together with unit clauses (9), (10) and (11) corresponding to goals $\leftarrow m$, $\leftarrow false_7$ and $\leftarrow false_8$, respectively. The translation of $\bar{P}_{ex}$ into $\bar{P}_{ex}^{magic}$ is almost similar to the original magic sets, except that we take into consideration the information of both hypotheses and input clause numbers used during the topdown computation in $\bar{P}_{ex}$. For instance, clause $C_1 = m \leftarrow hp, hp, v$ with clause number 1 in $\bar{P}_{ex}$, is translated into three rules (1.1), (1.2) and (1.3), whose bottom-up evaluation simulates the backward reasoning of C_1. That is, rules (1.1) and (1.2) say that, when a goal m is given (this is expressed by *magic_m*) and hypotheses hp, hp are assumed, we try to solve a query v (expressed by *magic_v*), together with continuation information expressed by $cont_{11}(\{hp\})$. The argument of a *cont*-predicate is used for storing a set of assumed hypotheses. Rules (1.3) says that, if a solution of v is obtained together with $cont_{11}(\{hp\})$, a solution of m is also obtained, where the first (resp., second) argument of v means a set of assumed hypotheses (resp., a history list) necessary to infer it, and the same applies to m. Therefore, the forward reasoning of these three rules (1.1), (1.2) and (1.3) exactly corresponds to the backward reasoning of C_1.

The bottom-up computation of $\bar{P}_{ex}^{magic}$ computes the fixpoint $T^{\uparrow\omega}(\bar{P}_{ex}^{magic})$, which satisfies the following:

$$T^{\uparrow\omega}(\bar{P}_{ex}^{magic}) \supseteq \{m(\{hp, hv\}, [1,3]), false_8(\{hv\}, [8,5]), false_8(\{hq\}, [8,6])\}$$

The first argument of $m(\{hp, hv\}, [1,3])$, for example, shows an abstracted explanation of m, while its second argument means its history list. This results are exactly the same as those derived from SLD-derivation of $\bar{P}_{ex} \cup \{\leftarrow m\}$ in Figure 4. □

4.2 Abductive Reasoning based on the Constrained Magic Sets

We now exemplify how the actual first-order abductive reasoning can be performed also by a modified version of the magic sets. The differences between our transformation here and the original magic sets are as follows:

- The translation of rules should take notice of computing not only computed answer substitutions but also a set of hypotheses assumed necessary to prove a given query.
- The bottom-up computation of magic-sets transformed rules are controlled in terms of history lists, so as to prune irrelevant search space.

Example 7.
Figure 7 shows the magic sets based transformed rules P_{ex}^{magic} of P_{ex} in Figure 1, together with unit clauses (9) and (11) corresponding to goals $\leftarrow m(b, Y, Z)$ and $\leftarrow false_8$, respectively. The fourth argument of $magic\_m(X, Y, Z, Path)$, for example, is used to store the information of a history list, thereby controlling the bottom-up computation as intended. The results of the bottom-up computation of $P_{ex}^{magic} \cup \{(11)\}$ are exactly the same as those derived from SLD-tree for $P_{ex} \cup \{\leftarrow false_8\}$ in Figure 2 with the irrelevant computations pruned. □

5 Some Empirical Results

We have made some experiments of our abductive reasoning system based on the static analysis. Figure 8 shows the empirical results on Example 1, by changing the number of unit clauses in Facts (the number is denoted by k in the figure). The solid lines in the figure show the runtime by our method, while the broken lines are those by the previous method by [OI92]. Our experimental system is written in SICStus Prolog and all runtimes are actual execution times on a Sun-4/75. In this particular example, the results indicate that our static analysis-based abductive reasoning system is about 50% ~ 20% faster than the previous method, depending on given queries. It should be also noted that the overhead of our static analysis of hypotheses dependency is less than 1% of the total runtimes of abductive reasoning when a given database becomes large, thus negligible in comparison with the actual runtimes.

6 Concluding Remarks

This paper proposed a first-order abductive reasoning system based on a static analysis. We utilized the static analysis to analyze the logical dependency between a given goal and each of related consistency conditions, thereby pruning the search involving consistency checking unnecessary wrt a given goal.

We then implemented our abductive reasoning system, based on the magic sets transformation. The original magic sets method was extended to do abductive reasoning efficiently, taking into account the results obtained from the

Facts

$$magic\_m(X,Y,Z,Path), hp(X,s1), hp(Y,s2), Path=[1|Ps] \rightarrow magic\_v(Z,Ps). \quad (1.1)$$

$$magic\_m(X,Y,Z,Path), hp(X,s1), hp(Y,s2), Path=[1|Ps] \rightarrow cont_{11}([X,Y,Z],\{hp(X,s1),hp(Y,s2)\},Ps). \quad (1.2)$$

$$cont_{11}([X,Y,Z],H,Ps), v(Z,Hv,P), Ps=P \rightarrow m(X,Y,Z,H\cup Hv,[1|Ps]). \quad (1.3)$$

$$magic\_d(X,Y,Z,Path), hp(X,s1), hp(Y,s2), Path=[2|Ps] \rightarrow magic\_q(Z,Ps). \quad (2.1)$$

$$magic\_d(X,Y,Z,Path), hp(X,s1), hp(Y,s2), Path=[2|Ps] \rightarrow cont_{21}([X,Y,Z],\{hp(X,s1),hp(Y,s2)\},Ps). \quad (2.2)$$

$$cont_{21}([X,Y,Z],H,Ps), q(Z,Hq,P), Ps=P \rightarrow d(X,Y,Z,H\cup Hq,[2|Ps]). \quad (2.3)$$

$$magic\_v(Z,Path), r(Z), hv(Z), Path=[3|Ps] \rightarrow v(Z,\{hv(Z)\},[3]). \quad (3.1)$$

$$magic\_q(Z,Path), l(Z), hq(Z), Path=[4|Ps] \rightarrow q(Z,\{hq(Z)\},[4]). \quad (4.1)$$

$$magic\_a(Z,Path), r(Z), hv(Z), Path=[5|Ps] \rightarrow a(Z,\{hv(Z)\},[5]). \quad (5.1)$$

$$magic\_a(Z,Path), l(Z), hq(Z), Path=[6|Ps] \rightarrow a(Z,\{hq(Z)\},[6]). \quad (6.1)$$

r(101). r(102). l(201). l(202). l(203). l(204). na(101). na(204).

Hypotheses

hp(b,s1). hp(c,s1). hp(e,s2). hp(f,s2). hv(Z). hq(Z).

Consistency Conditions

$$magic\_false_7([\,],Path), hp(X,Y), nhp(X,Y), Path=[7|Ps] \rightarrow false_7([\,],\{hp(X,Y)\},[7]). \quad (7.1)$$

$$magic\_false_8([\,],Path), Path=[8|Ps] \rightarrow magic\_a(Z,Ps). \quad (8.1)$$

$$magic\_false_8([\,],Path), Path=[8|Ps] \rightarrow cont_{81},([\,],\{\,\},Ps). \quad (8.2)$$

$$cont_{81}([\,],\{\,\},Ps), a(Z,Ha,P), na(Z), Ps=p \rightarrow false_8([\,],Ha,[8|Ps]) \quad (8.3)$$

Goals

$$\rightarrow magic\_m(b,Y,Z,[1,3]). \quad (9)$$

$$\rightarrow magic\_false_8([\,],[8,5]). \quad (11)$$

Fig. 7. Magic Sets Transformed Rules P_{ex}^{magic} of P_{ex}

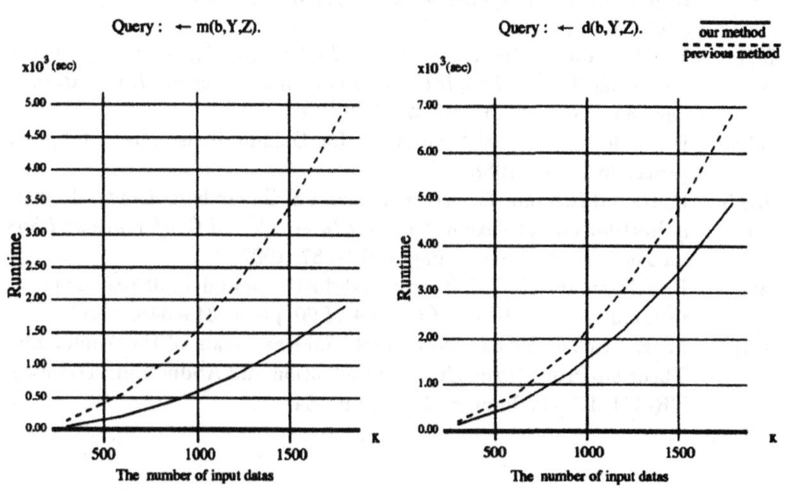

Fig. 8. Empirical Results

static analysis. Our proposed implementation based on the magic sets would be interesting also from the viewpoint of deductive databases, since it gives a way of controlling bottom-up computation (e.g., [RSS92]).

In this paper, we restricted ourselves to non-recursive Horn programs. When facts are recursively defined, we can no longer use history lists, since they will become infinite structures in general. In such cases, as is usual with the abstract interpretation, we have to consider suitably abstracted finite structures instead of the history lists to ensure the termination of the analysis, possibly sacrificing the precision of the analysis. This problem will be discussed in more detail in the forthcoming paper.

Acknowledgments

We are grateful for the members of ICOT working group on Abductive Reasoning for their valuable discussions. We also thank the anonymous referees for their helpful comments.

References

[BMSU86] F. Bancilhon, D. Maier, U. Sagiv, and J. D. Ullman. *Magic Sets and Other Strange Ways to Implement Logic Programs.* In *Proc. of Principles of Database Systems*, pages 1–15, 1986.

[Deb92] S. Debray, editor. *Special Issue:Abstract Interpretation (J. of Logic Programming, Vol. 13, No. 2 & 3).* North-Holland, 1992.

[KI91] A. Kondo and M. Ishizuka. An Efficient Hypothetical Reasoning System for Predicate-logic Knowledge-base. In *Proc. IEEE, Int'l Conf. on Tools for AI, San Jose*, pages 60–67, 1991.

[Llo84] J.W. Lloyd. *Foundations of Logic Programming.* Springer, 1984. Second, extended edition, 1987.

[NM91] H. T. Ng and R. J. Moony. A Efficient First-Order Horn-Clause Abduction Sysem Based on the ATMS. In *Proc. of the AAAI-91*, pages 494–499, 1991.

[OI91] Y. Ohta and K. Inoue. An Efficient Inference Method for Forward-chaining Hypothetical Reasoning with the ATMS. *J. of ISAI*, 7(2):247–259, march 1991. (in japanese).

[OI92] Y. Ohta and K. Inoue. *A Forward-Chaining Hypothetical Reasoner Based on Upside-Down Meta-Interpretation.* In *Proc. of the International Conference on FGCS '92*, pages 522–529, 1992.

[Poo88] D. Poole. A Logical Framework for Default Reasoning. *Artificial Intelligence*, 36:27–47, 1988.

[RSS92] R. Ramakrishnan, D. Srivastava, and S. Sudarshan. Controlling the search in bottom-up evaluation. In *Joint International Conference and Symposium on Logic Programming*, pages 273–287, 1992.

[SL90] B. Selman and H. J. Levesque. Abductive and default reasoning: A computational core. In *Proc. of the AAAI-90*, pages 343–348, 1990.

[Sti91] M. E. Stickel. Upside-Down Meta-Interpretation of the Model Elimination Theorem-Prover Procedure for Deduction and Abduction. Technical Report TR-664, ICOT, January 1991. TR-664.

A Congruence for Gamma Programs

Lindsay Errington*, Chris Hankin** and Thomas Jensen***

Department of Computing
Imperial College of Science, Technology and Medicine
180 Queen's Gate,London SW7 2BZ, UK
e-mail: {le,clh,tpj}@doc.ic.ac.uk

Abstract. This paper defines a congruence relation on Gamma programs. Based on this congruence relation, laws for transforming programs are derived. We define an axiomatic semantics for Gamma based on Brookes' transition assertions. The definition of the congruence is in terms of provable satisfiability of such assertions. We consider the relationship between our congruence and other orderings that have been proposed in the literature.

1 Introduction

In this paper we study the problem of transforming programs expressed in the Gamma programming formalism. We aim at defining a relation between Gamma programs that captures when one program mimics another program. This relation allows us to decide when we can safely replace one program by another *i.e.*, it gives us a means of expressing the correctness of program transformations.

Gamma operates with a single data structure, the multiset, and computation proceeds by rewriting multisets of data. Gamma has proved successful in expressing a variety of algorithms including sorting and graph algorithms. The basic operation in Gamma is the rewrite operation, written $(R(\overline{x}), A(\overline{x}))$. Here $R(\overline{x})$ is a predicate, called the reaction condition, and $A(\overline{x})$ a function, called the action. A rewrite takes place if there is a vector $\overline{x}$ of elements from the multiset that satisfies the reaction condition. In that case the elements in $\overline{x}$ are removed from the multiset and the elements $A(\overline{x})$ added to the multiset. This process continues until no vector of elements satisfies the reaction condition. Thus, the operation $(x > 1, x - 1)$ would rewrite the multiset $\{5, 0\}$ to $\{1, 0\}$ by the computation

$$\{5,0\}\stackrel{4/5}{\rightarrow}\{4,0\}\stackrel{3/4}{\rightarrow}\{3,0\}\stackrel{2/3}{\rightarrow}\{2,0\}\stackrel{1/2}{\rightarrow}\{1,0\}$$

* Funded by NSERC of Canada.

** Partially funded by ESPRIT WG 6345 (SemaGraph) and WG 6809 (Semantique).

*** Funded by DIKU, University of Copenhagen.

where we have annotated the arrows with the substitution taking place. The computation terminates with $\{1,0\}$ since neither 1 nor 0 satisfy the reaction condition.

More complex Gamma programs can be built by combining rewrite operations using the operators for sequential and parallel composition, denoted by $\circ$ and $+$. The sequential composition $C_2 \circ C_1$ will execute C_1 until it can no longer react in which case C_2 takes over and executes until it can no longer react. The parallel composition $C_1 + C_2$ will continue executing as long as one of C_1 and C_2 can execute. If only C_1, say, can react we let C_1 perform a rewrite and then return to check which of the C_i can react next. In case both of C_1 and C_2 can react one of them is chosen in a random fashion. This non-deterministic aspect of Gamma means that the program

$$(x > 1, 1) + (x > 1, 0)$$

can produce either $\{1\}$ or $\{0\}$ from the multiset $\{5\}$, depending on which of the summands is allowed to react. Notice also how parts of a program can switch between being active and inactive during a computation. The program

$$(\mathsf{even}(x), x - 1) + (\mathsf{odd}(x), x + 1)$$

will never terminate when applied to a non-empty multiset since each summand produces an element that will activate the other.

The main goal of this paper is to define a notion of program refinement for Gamma programs. More formally, we want to define a relation, $\sqsubseteq$, such that $C_1 \sqsubseteq C_2$ if C_1's behaviour would be an acceptable behaviour for C_2. This means that it would be correct to replace C_2 by C_1 in an application. We shall define the relation $\sqsubseteq$ in such a way that it becomes a congruence relation, which means that if $C_1 \sqsubseteq C_2$ holds then we can automatically deduce that C_1 can replace C_2 in any context $K[\,]$, *i.e.*, $K[C_1] \sqsubseteq K[C_2]$.

The paper is organised as follows. In the next section we review the syntax and semantics of Gamma. Section 3 presents an assertion language for Gamma based on Brookes' language. In Section 4 we present a sound proof system for determining whether a program satisfies an assertion. The new congruence relation is presented in Section 5 and we compare it to the relational ordering of [HLS92] and the congruence of [San93a] in Section 6. We conclude in Section 7.

2 The Syntax and Semantics of Gamma

In this paper we consider the version of Gamma defined by Hankin et.al. in [HLS92] which includes operators for sequential and parallel composition. Before giving the syntax, we introduce the following classes and associated meta-variables:

$$\begin{array}{llr} M \in \mathbf{M} & = \mathcal{M}\,\mathbf{D} & \textit{non-empty finite multisets over } \mathbf{D} \\ \overline{x} \in \mathbf{T} & = \sum_{n<\omega} \mathbf{D}^n & \textit{tuples of length } n \geq 0 \\ R \in \mathbf{R} & = \mathbf{T} \to \{\mathbf{true}, \mathbf{false}\} & \textit{reaction conditions} \\ A \in \mathbf{Act} & = \mathbf{T} \to \mathbf{T} & \textit{actions} \end{array}$$

The syntax of Gamma programs is defined as follows:

$$\begin{array}{llr} \mathbf{C} \ni C ::= & (R, A) & \textit{rewrite rule} \\ \mid & C_1 + C_2 & \textit{parallel composition} \\ \mid & C_1 \circ C_2 & \textit{sequential composition} \end{array}$$

The underlying domain, $\mathbf{D}$, will be left unspecified. When presenting a Gamma program, we will use the syntax $\overline{x} \to A(\overline{x}) \Leftarrow R(\overline{x})$ as an alternative to (R, A).

Before defining the semantics, we introduce further classes:

$$\begin{array}{llr} \alpha \in \mathbf{Lab} & = \mathbf{Act} \cup \{\delta\} & \textit{labels} \\ (C, M) \in \mathbf{Conf} & = (\mathbf{C} \cup \{\mathbf{nil}\}) \times \mathbf{M} & \textit{configurations} \end{array}$$

We now give the operational semantics of Gamma using the labelled transition system $(\mathbf{C}, \mathbf{Lab}, \{\xrightarrow{\alpha} : \alpha \in \mathbf{Lab}\})$ where for each $\alpha \in \mathbf{Lab}$, $\xrightarrow{\alpha} \subseteq \mathbf{Conf} \times \mathbf{Conf}$ is a transition relation, written $(C_1, M_1) \xrightarrow{\alpha} (C_2, M_2)$. The family of relations is the least satisfying the rules given in figure 1. Each transition is labelled with a pair $\overline{y}/\overline{x}$ except in those instances where a program rewrites without affecting the multiset whereupon the transition is labelled with δ. A label $\overline{y}/\overline{x}$ corresponds to a rewrite on a multiset in which $\overline{y}$ replaces $\overline{x}$. We use the symbol $\uplus$ to represent multiset union.

$$\frac{R(\overline{x})}{((R, A), M \uplus \overline{x}) \xrightarrow{A(\overline{x})/\overline{x}} ((R, A), M \uplus A(\overline{x}))} \qquad \frac{\neg \exists \overline{x} \subseteq M . R(\overline{x})}{((R, A), M) \xrightarrow{\delta} (\mathbf{nil}, M)}$$

$$\frac{(C_1, M) \xrightarrow{\alpha} (C_1', M')}{(C_1 + C_2, M) \xrightarrow{\alpha} (C_1' + C_2, M')} \qquad \frac{(C_2, M) \xrightarrow{\alpha} (C_2', M')}{(C_1 + C_2, M) \xrightarrow{\alpha} (C_1 + C_2', M')}$$

$$\frac{(C_1, M) \xrightarrow{\delta} (C_1', M) \qquad (C_2, M) \xrightarrow{\delta} (C_2', M)}{(C_1 + C_2, M) \xrightarrow{\delta} (\mathbf{nil}, M)}$$

$$\frac{(C_2, M) \xrightarrow{\alpha} (C_2', M')}{(C_1 \circ C_2, M) \xrightarrow{\alpha} (C_1 \circ C_2', M')} \qquad \frac{(C_2, M) \xrightarrow{\delta} (\mathbf{nil}, M) \qquad (C_1, M) \xrightarrow{\alpha} (C_1', M')}{(C_1 \circ C_2, M) \xrightarrow{\alpha} (C_1', M')}$$

Fig. 1. The operational semantics of Gamma.

3 Transition Assertions

Hoare introduced a logic of **while** programs based on pre- and post-conditions. He showed how partial correctness of programs could be proved by structural induction using rules derived from the relational semantics of the language. His logic was *compositional* in the sense that the meaning of a syntactic construct was defined in terms of its constituents. See the overview by Cousot [Cou90] for more on Hoare logics.

Extending Hoare logic to parallel languages has proved difficult and generally requires abandoning compositionality by introducing auxiliary variables or requiring interference freedom. In contrast, Brookes [Bro92] has defined an axiomatic framework in which compositionality is preserved. Rather than basing the axiomatic definition on the relational semantics, Brookes argues that the transition system defining the operational semantics should be used as basis for reasoning about programs. Instead of asserting pre- and post-conditions of a command, in Brookes' logic one writes pre- and post-conditions for each transition. This reflects the fact that what holds after one command has been executed does not necessarily hold before the next command is executed since another process could have changed the state in-between. In the paragraphs which follow we present the variant of Brookes' logic we will need in the next section to give the semantics of Gamma.

3.1 Syntax and Semantics

Transition assertions have the following syntax:

$$\begin{array}{rlr} \mathbf{TA} \ni \phi ::= & P\sum_{i=1}^{n}\alpha_i P_i \phi_i & \textit{branching} \\ \mid & P\bullet & \textit{terminal} \\ \mid & \theta & \textit{meta-variable} \\ \mid & \mu\theta.\phi & \textit{recursion} \end{array}$$

where P and P_i range over predicates on a multiset expressed in ordinary predicate calculus and α_i are atomic actions. We write $M \models P$ if the multiset M satisfies the condition P. This definition differs from that used by Brookes in two respects. First, Brookes distinguishes termination from deadlock and for this he requires two forms of terminal assertions. In Gamma, deadlock is not a possibility and we need only one. Brookes also defines conjunction for transition assertions which we have chosen to omit.

When a program C *satisfies* a (closed) assertion ϕ we write

$$C \textbf{ sat } \phi$$

We now define validity for such formulae. Validity of a branching assertion is defined by appealing to the operational semantics. C **sat** $P\sum_{i=1}^{n}\alpha_i P_i \phi_i$ is valid if, when a multiset satisfies the condition P, then $\{\alpha_i\}_{i=1}^n$ is the set of possible actions and each transition α_i leads to a multiset satisfying P_i and a (possibly modified) program satisfying ϕ_i.

More formally,

$$\models C \text{ sat } P\sum_{i=1}^{n}\alpha_i P_i\phi_i$$

if and only if the following conditions are satisfied

1. $M \models P \wedge (C, M) \xrightarrow{\alpha} (C', M') \Rightarrow \exists i \leq n \;.\; \alpha = \alpha_i \wedge M' \models P_i \wedge C' \text{ sat } \phi_i$
2. $M \models P \Rightarrow \forall i \leq n \;.\; \exists C_i, M_i \;.\; (C, M) \xrightarrow{\alpha_i} (C_i, M_i)$

A program satisfies a terminal assertion if and only if the program terminates for every multiset satisfying the condition:

$$\models C \text{ sat } P\bullet \iff M \models P \Rightarrow (C, M) \xrightarrow{\delta} (\mathbf{nil}, M)$$

Validity of a formula involving a recursive assertion requires validity with respect to all finite unfoldings of the assertion. The finite unfoldings are defined as follows:

$$\theta_0 = \{\mathbf{false}\}\bullet$$
$$\theta_{n+1} = \phi[\theta_n/\theta] \quad \text{for } n \geq 0$$

where $\phi[\psi/\theta]$ denotes the result of substituting ψ for each free occurrence of θ in ϕ, renaming bound variables where necessary to avoid variable capture. Using this, validity of a recursive assertion is defined such that

$$\models C \text{ sat } \mu\theta.\phi \iff \forall n \geq 0.(\models C \text{ sat } \theta_n).$$

3.2 Composing Assertions

We now introduce two operations for composing transition assertions ϕ and ψ. The first, written $\phi||\psi$, yields an assertion which is satisfied by the parallel composition of two programs satisfying ϕ and ψ respectively. First, we define the auxiliary operator $\Delta : \mathbf{TA} \rightarrow \mathbf{Pred} \times \wp(\mathbf{Lab} \times \mathbf{Pred} \times \mathbf{TA})$ which maps a transition assertion to all the assertions to which it can evolve in a single transition.

$$\begin{aligned}
\Delta\,(P\textstyle\sum_{i=1}^{n}\alpha_i P_i\phi_i) &= (P, \{(\alpha_i, P_i, \phi_i) \mid 1 \leq i \leq n\}) \\
\Delta\,(P\bullet) &= (P, \emptyset) \\
\Delta\,(\mu\theta.\phi) &= \Delta\,(\phi[\mu\theta.\phi/\theta])
\end{aligned}$$

The parallel composition $\phi||\psi$ of two formulae is defined to be a recursive assertion obtained by interleaving transitions from ϕ and ψ. Both ϕ and ψ are unfolded as needed (by Δ). An environment, ρ, which maps formulae to meta-variables, is used to prevent infinite unfoldings.

$$(\phi\|\psi)\ \rho = \begin{cases} \rho[\phi\|\psi] & \text{if } \phi\|\psi \in \mathit{Dom}\ \rho \\ \mu\theta.(P \wedge Q)\left[\begin{array}{l} \sum\{\alpha_i P_i\ ((\phi_i\|\psi)\ \rho[\phi\|\psi \mapsto \theta]) \mid (\alpha_i, P_i, \phi_i) \in T_\phi\} \\ + \sum\{\beta_j Q_j\ ((\phi\|\psi_j)\ \rho[\phi\|\psi \mapsto \theta]) \mid (\beta_j, Q_j, \psi_j) \in T_\psi\} \end{array}\right] \end{cases}$$

where $(P, T_\phi) = \Delta\ \phi$, $(Q, T_\psi) = \Delta\ \psi$ and θ is a new meta-variable not appearing in ϕ or ψ.

We conclude our discussion of the parallel composition operator for transition assertions by relating it to Gamma's parallel composition operator.

Theorem 1. *If* C_1 **sat** ϕ *and* C_2 **sat** ψ *then* $C_1 + C_2$ **sat** $\phi\|\psi$.

Proof. The proof is by induction over the structure of transition assertions. We will consider only the case where ϕ and ψ are branching assertions. Let $\phi = P\sum_{i=1}^{n} \alpha_i P_i \phi_i$ and $\psi = Q\sum_{j=1}^{m} \beta_j Q_j \psi_j$. Now suppose there is a multiset M such that $M \models (P \wedge Q)$. Therefore $M \models P$ and since C_1 **sat** ϕ, by the definition of **sat**, there exists a transition α_i such that $(C, M) \xrightarrow{\alpha_i} (C_i, M_i)$, $M_i \models P_i$ and C_i **sat** ϕ_i. Note that the same transition is possible in $\phi\|\psi$. What remains to be shown is that C_i **sat** $(\phi_i\|\psi)$ which we can get by a second induction over paths in assertion trees. ■

The second operator defined by Brookes is for the sequential composition of transition assertions. Intuitively the sequential composition $\phi;\psi$ replaces the terminal assertions in the assertion tree for ϕ with a copy of ψ. Like the parallel operator, sequential composition is defined recursively over the various combinations of ϕ and ψ which we list below.

$$\begin{array}{lll} P\bullet; (Q\sum_{j=1}^{m} \beta_j Q_i \psi_j) & = (P \wedge Q)(\sum_{j=1}^{m} \beta_j Q_j \psi_j) & \\ (P\sum_{i=1}^{n} \alpha_i P_i \phi_i); \psi & = P\sum_{i=1}^{n} \alpha_i P_i(\phi_i; \psi) & \\ P\bullet; Q\bullet & = (P \wedge Q)\bullet & \\ (\mu\theta.\psi); \phi & = \mu\theta.(\psi; \phi) & \\ P\bullet; (\mu\theta.\psi) & = P\bullet; \psi[\mu\theta.\psi/\theta] & \\ \theta; \phi & = \theta & \theta \text{ a bound meta-variable} \end{array}$$

As with parallel composition, we relate the sequential composition operator for transition assertions with the corresponding Gamma operator.

Theorem 2. *If* C_1 **sat** ϕ *and* C_2 **sat** ψ *then* $C_1 \circ C_2$ **sat** $\psi; \phi$.

3.3 Implication

Finally, still following Brookes, we introduce implication, $\phi \Rightarrow \psi$ for transition assertions. The intuition is that for all programs C, if C **sat** ϕ then C **sat** ψ.

This permits strengthening pre-conditions and/or weakening post-conditions. It is defined in terms of the other operators and in terms of standard implication in the predicate calculus.

$$P\sum_{i=1}^{n}\alpha_i P_i\phi_i \Rightarrow Q\sum_{i=1}^{n}\alpha_i Q_i\psi_i \iff (Q \Rightarrow P) \wedge \bigwedge_{i=1}^{n}(P_i \Rightarrow Q_i) \wedge \bigwedge_{i=1}^{n}(\phi_i \Rightarrow \psi_i)$$

$$P\bullet \Rightarrow Q\bullet \iff Q \Rightarrow P$$

Finally, we introduce the following inference rule:

$$\frac{\psi \Rightarrow \theta \;\vdash\; \psi \Rightarrow \phi}{\psi \Rightarrow \mu\theta.\phi}$$

4 The Proof System

The formulation of the proof system for the satisfaction relation **sat** assumes that we are given a formal system for reasoning about multisets and substitutions on multisets. We shall not address the issue of how to construct such a system but just assume that we can prove assertions of the form $\{P\}\ A(\overline{x})/\overline{x}\ \{Q\}$ meaning that if P holds of a multiset M then Q holds of the multiset obtained by substituting $A(\overline{x})$ for $\overline{x}$ in M. Specifically,

$$\{P\}\ A(\overline{x})/\overline{x}\ \{Q\} \iff \forall M.M \uplus \overline{x} \models P \Rightarrow M \uplus A(\overline{x}) \models Q$$

This will be used in the rule for reasoning about the basic rewrite construct (R, A).

$$\frac{\{P\}\ A(\overline{x})/\overline{x}\ \{P\} \qquad \forall\overline{x}\ .\ R(\overline{x}) \Rightarrow Q(A(\overline{x}))}{(R,A)\ \mathbf{sat}\ \mu\theta.\{P \wedge \exists\overline{x}.R(\overline{x})\}A(\overline{x})/\overline{x}\ \{P \wedge \exists\overline{x}.Q(\overline{x})\}\theta}$$

$$\frac{}{(R,A)\ \mathbf{sat}\ \{\forall\overline{x}.\neg R(\overline{x})\}\bullet} \qquad \frac{C\ \mathbf{sat}\ \phi \qquad \phi \Rightarrow \psi}{C\ \mathbf{sat}\ \psi}$$

$$\frac{C_1\ \mathbf{sat}\ \phi \qquad C_2\ \mathbf{sat}\ \psi}{C_1 + C_2\ \mathbf{sat}\ \phi \| \psi} \qquad \frac{C_1\ \mathbf{sat}\ \phi \qquad C_2\ \mathbf{sat}\ \psi}{C_1 \circ C_2\ \mathbf{sat}\ \psi;\phi}$$

Fig. 2. Proof System for Gamma

The soundness of the two rules for rewrites, (R, A), follows from the operational semantics. Soundness of the rules for parallel and sequential composition follows from theorems 1 and 2 respectively.

5 A Pre-Congruence

In this section we define two orderings on Gamma programs: one derived from the operational semantics and one based on the axiomatic semantics of transition traces. The former will provide a definition of what it means for a program to be a "correct" implementation of another program, *i.e.*, when we can replace one program by another without changing their behaviour observed from an external viewpoint. The latter relation will be contained in the former relation and thus still convey correct information about when a program implements another but it will not record all correct implementations. In return for this loss of precision we get that the relation is a pre-congruence which means that the relation can be used to transform programs in a modular fashion. We discuss the importance of congruence relations first.

The task of optimising a program is eased considerably if the optimisation can be done by optimising a small part of the program which may then be inserted into the original program to obtain an optimised version of the program. In order to formalise this notion we define contexts to be programs with holes in them. The hole is where the component will be inserted. Formally we have

Definition 3. A *context* is a term containing holes [ ]:

$$\mathbf{K} \ni K ::= [\,] \mid (R, A) \mid K + K \mid K \circ K$$

We write $K[P]$ to denote the program obtained by inserting program P in the holes in context K. If $\leq$ is an "optimises"-relation then we can express that $\leq$ allows local optimisation by saying that $\leq$ satisfies

$$P \leq Q \;\Rightarrow\; K[P] \leq K[Q]$$

for all contexts $K[\,]$. If a relation satisfies this property it is called a pre-congruence.

The relational ordering defined by Hankin et.al. [HLS92] provides us with the definition of when one program is a correct implementation of another program. First we introduce the notion of a divergent program:

$$(P, M)\uparrow \stackrel{\text{def}}{=} \exists\{(P_i, M_i) | i \in \omega\}.(P_0, M_0) = (P, M) \text{ and } (P_i, M_i) \rightarrow (P_{i+1}, M_{i+1}).$$

Definition 4. The *relational ordering*, $\sqsubseteq_R$, is given by

$$\begin{aligned} P_1 \sqsubseteq_R P_2 \iff & \forall M.((P_1, M)\uparrow \Rightarrow (P_2, M)\uparrow \\ & \text{and } (\forall N.(P_1, M) \rightarrow^* (\mathbf{nil}, N) \Rightarrow (P_2, M) \rightarrow^* (\mathbf{nil}, N)) \end{aligned}$$

As was already observed in [HLS92] this is not a congruence relation. Using the proof system introduced in the previous section, we will now define a ***satisfaction ordering*** on programs and show that it is a pre-congruence. The idea is that a program P approximates program Q if all properties that P satisfies are satisfied by Q as well.

Definition 5. The *satisfaction ordering*, $\sqsubseteq_S \subseteq \mathbf{C} \times \mathbf{C}$ is given by

$$C_1 \sqsubseteq_S C_2 \iff \forall \phi. \vdash C_1 \textbf{ sat } \phi \Rightarrow \vdash C_2 \textbf{ sat } \phi$$

Theorem 6. *The relation $\sqsubseteq_S$ is a pre-congruence.*

Proof. Structural induction on contexts. Let $K[\ ]$ be a context. We have to check that under the assumption $P_1 \sqsubseteq_S P_2$ and $\vdash K[P_1]$ **sat** φ we can prove $\vdash K[P_2]$ **sat** φ. This is done by simultaneous induction on the structure of $K[]$ and the depth of the proof tree verifying $\vdash K[P_1]$ **sat** φ. ∎

Claim: $\sqsubseteq_S \subset \sqsubseteq_R$

By consideration of the definitions of the relations involved, it is straightforward to justify that $\sqsubseteq_S \subseteq \sqsubseteq_R$. In support of the stronger claim we recall an example from Hankin et.al. [HLS92] which shows that $\sqsubseteq_R$ is not a pre-congruence. Consider:

$$C_1 = \langle x, y \rangle \rightarrow \langle x + y \rangle$$
$$C_2 = \langle x \rangle \rightarrow \langle x - 1, 1 \rangle \Leftarrow x > 1$$
$$C_3 = \langle x \rangle \rightarrow \langle x + 1 \rangle \Leftarrow x < 10$$

We have that $C_1 \circ C_2 \sqsubseteq_R C_1$ (in fact $C_1 \circ C_2 \equiv_R C_1$) but $(C_1 \circ C_2) + C_3 \not\sqsubseteq_R C_1 + C_3$ since in the latter, the left hand side can diverge but the right hand side cannot.

As already stated the relational ordering provides the basis for a fairly standard notion of "correct" implementation. Since we conjecture that our congruence is stronger than the relational ordering, $P \sqsubseteq_S Q$ implies that P is a correct implementation of Q. Our programme is to develop an algebra of programs, based on $\sqsubseteq_S$ and the derived equivalence $\equiv_S$, that can be used as a basis for program transformation. This was also the main goal of [HLS92, San93a]. As an example, we consider one of the laws from [HLS92]: the commutativity of $+$. First we need a simple lemma, the proof of which follows directly from the definition of the operator $\|$.

Lemma 7. *Interleaving of transition assertions (i.e. the operator $\|$) is:*
(a) commutative
(b) associative
(c) idempotent

Proposition 8. $P + Q \equiv_S Q + P$

Proof. The relation $P + Q \sqsubseteq_S Q + P$ is proved by induction over the structure of the proof of $(P + Q)$ **sat** ϕ. The only interesting case is the rule $(+)$ where we use the lemma. The relation $Q + P \sqsubseteq_S P + Q$ is established in a similar way. ∎

Other properties, such as associativity of $+$ and $\circ$, are easily verified in the same way.

We close this section with a slightly more interesting example from [HLS92]. This law states that a program composed in parallel with itself is correctly implemented by a single instance of the program.

Proposition 9. $P \sqsubseteq_S P + P$

Proof. We have $\vdash P$ **sat** $\phi \Rightarrow \vdash P + P$ **sat** $\phi \| \phi$. The idempotency of $\|$, lemma 7(c), implies $\vdash P + P$ **sat** ϕ. ∎

6 Related approaches

Sands [San93a] has suggested another ordering on Gamma programs derived from a denotational semantics of transition traces.

Definition 10. The *transition trace function*, $\mathcal{TT}[\![.]\!] : \mathbf{C} \rightarrow \wp((\mathbf{M} \times \mathbf{M})^{+})$ is given by

$$\begin{aligned} \mathcal{TT}[\![C]\!] = \{ & (M_0, N_0)(M_1, N_1) \ldots (M_k, N_k) \mid \\ & (C, M_0) \rightarrow^* (C_1, N_0) \wedge \\ & (C_1, M_1) \rightarrow^* (C_2, N_1) \wedge \ldots \wedge (C_k, M_k) \rightarrow^* (\mathbf{nil}, N_k)\} \end{aligned}$$

Transition traces deal with the interaction of the environment in the same way as transition assertions do by accepting that the multiset changes between two rewrites. Note that a non-terminating computation is assigned the empty set of transition traces in this model, thus it is not possible to distinguish between different non-terminating programs.

Definition 11. The *transition trace ordering*, $\sqsubseteq_T$, is given by

$$C_1 \sqsubseteq_T C_1 \iff \mathcal{TT}[\![C_1]\!] \subseteq \mathcal{TT}[\![C_2]\!]$$

Theorem 12. $\sqsubseteq_S \subseteq \sqsubseteq_T$.

Proof. Assume $C_1 \sqsubseteq_S C_2$ *i.e.*, $\forall \phi \,.\, \vdash C_1$ **sat** $\phi \Rightarrow \vdash C_2$ **sat** ϕ and let the trace $(M_0, N_0), \ldots, (M_n, N_n)$ be a trace of C_1. To each pair (M_k, N_k) there exists a vector of actions $\overline{\alpha_i}$ and intermediate multisets M^i such that

$$M_k = M^0 \overset{\alpha_1}{\rightarrow} M^1 \overset{\alpha_2}{\rightarrow} \ldots \overset{\alpha_n}{\rightarrow} M^n = N_k.$$

Given this we can construct a transition assertion ψ_k that records these transitions. The ψ_k can be constructed so that $\vdash C_1$ **sat** $\psi_1; \ldots; \psi_n$. From the assumption we then get that $\vdash C_2$ **sat** $\psi_1; \ldots; \psi_n$ from which we can conclude that $(M_0, N_0), \ldots, (M_n, N_n)$ is a trace of C_2, *i.e.*, the set of traces of C_1 are included in the set of traces of C_2. ∎

To see that $\sqsubseteq_T \not\subseteq \sqsubseteq_S$, consider the following two Gamma programs:

$$C_1 = \langle x \rangle \rightarrow \langle x, x \rangle$$
$$C_2 = \langle x \rangle \rightarrow \langle x + 1 \rangle$$

Neither program terminates and thus they cannot be distinguished by their transition traces but they are distinguished by the satisfaction ordering (for example by the transition assertion that states that all elements in the multiset are equal).

There appears to be some empirical evidence that stronger congruences such as $\sqsubseteq_S$ are easier to check automatically. An interesting research problem is to modify the language of transition assertions and to investigate the effect of this on the congruence and its relationship to $\sqsubseteq_T$.

7 Conclusion

In this paper we have demonstrated how an axiomatic semantics for Gamma based on transition assertions induces a relation on programs that allows us to speak about when one program approximates another. This relation can therefore be used to validate laws for program transformation. We showed that the relation forms a pre-congruence for Gamma programs which has the important consequence that program transformation can be done locally. Unlike other congruences proposed in the literature, our relation can distinguish between non-terminating programs. This means that there are laws verifiable by the other relations that we cannot prove but it also means that our relation will be potentially applicable to reactive systems and other systems where non-terminating computations are the norm.

References

[BL90] Jean-Pierre Banâtre and Daniel Le Métayer. The Gamma model and its discipline of programming. *Science of Computer Programming*, 15:55–77, 1990.

[BL93] Jean-Pierre Banâtre and Daniel Le Métayer. Programming by multiset transformation. *Communications of the ACM*, 36(1), January 1993.

[Bro85] S.D. Brookes. A fully abstract semantics and proof system for an ALGOL-like language with sharing. In A. Melton, editor, *Prooceedings of the First International Conference on Mathematical Foundations of Programming Semantics*. Springer-Verlag, LNCS 239, 1985.

[Bro86] S.D. Brookes. A semantically based proof system for partial correctness and deadlock in CSP. In *Proceedings of the IEEE Symposium on Logic in Computer Science*, pages 58–65. IEEE Computer Society Press, 1986.

[Bro92] S.D. Brookes. An axiomatic treatment of partial correctness and deadlock in a shared variable parallel language. Technical Report CMU-CS-92-154, School of Computer Science, Carnegie Mellon University, June 1992.

[Bro93] S.D. Brookes. Full abstraction for a shared variable parallel language. In *Proceedings of the IEEE Symposium on Logic in Computer Science*. IEEE Computer Society Press, July 1993.

[Cou90] Patrick Cousot. Methods and Logics for Proving Programs. In Jan van Leeuwen, editor, *Handbook of Theoretical Computer Science*. Elsevier Science Publishers, 1990.

[EHJ93] Lindsay Errington, Chris Hankin, and Thomas P. Jensen. Reasoning about Gamma programs. In *Proc. of the First Imperial College Department of Computing Workshop on Theory and Formal Methods. To appear in the Springer-Verlag series "Workshops in Computer Science"*, 1993.

[HLS92] Chris Hankin, Daniel Le Métayer, and David Sands. A calculus of Gamma programs. Technical Report 1758, INRIA, October 1992.

[San93a] David Sands. A compositional semantics of combining forms for Gamma programs. In *International Conference on Formal Methods in Programming and Their Applications*. Springer-Verlag, 1993.

[San93b] David Sands. Laws of parallel synchronised termination. In *Proc. of the First Imperial College Department of Computing Workshop on Theory and Formal Methods. To appear in the Springer-Verlag series "Workshops in Computer Science"*, 1993.

Usage Analysis with Natural Reduction Types

David A. Wright
Department of Computer Science
University of Tasmania
Hobart 7001
AUSTRALIA

Clement A. Baker-Finch
Information Sciences and Eng.
University of Canberra
Canberra 2616
AUSTRALIA

Abstract

In a functional program the value of an expression may be required several times. If a *usage analysis* can determine how many times it will be required, certain optimisations are possible, such as converting *lazy* parameter passing to call-by-name or call-by-value, compile-time garbage collection and in-place update. This paper presents a method for deducing usage information in the λ-calculus, based on a type logic employing *reduction types*. A system is presented wherein function type constructors are annotated with expressions over the natural numbers to indicate the usage behaviour of λ-terms. This system is shown to be correct by interpreting the type language over a semi-model of the λ-calculus and demonstrating soundness and completeness. Furthermore, we show how the Curry-Howard interpretation naturally relates such types to relevant logic.

1 Introduction

Modern implementations of functional languages rely heavily on compile-time program transformation techniques to obtain acceptable run-time efficiency. In their turn, program transformation techniques depend on knowing detailed information about the program being transformed. Obtaining this information is the province of much ongoing research worldwide. The main approaches to obtaining information about programs can be categorised by the representation of this information, as follows: abstract lambda terms, see for example Cousot and Cousot [12], Mycroft [26], Burn et al [8] and Hudak and Young [20]; types, as used by Kuo and Mishra [25], Wright [32, 33, 34], Coppo [11] and Wadler [31]; and relations, see Mycroft and Jones [27]. In general, types have the advantage of being first-order notations which describe the higher-order properties of functions in a succinct and clear manner.

Reduction types ([32, 33, 34]) are a novel way of expressing various properties of λ-terms. The main idea is to distinguish between sets of terms based on an extended notion of type. In particular, an instance of reduction types is defined by associating a *separate function type constructor with each class of terms to be distinguished.* For example, functions strict on their argument might have a type constructor $\rightarrow_{\perp}$ associated with them, whereas functions lazy on their argument would then have a different type constructor, say $\rightarrow_?$, so as to distinguish them from those functions definitely known to be strict. The main advantages of using the reduction type framework are that information about higher-order terms is captured very precisely (and very naturally) and that advantage may be taken of the well established implementation technologies existing for types and for unification (see Siekmann [30]).

In this paper we utilise the reduction type framework to develop an analysis of *usage* information in λ-terms. We define usage information for a redex subterm to be the number of times that copies of the redex are reduced during the head reduction of a term. This information is particularly useful to the optimisation phases of a compiler as it allows the compiler to implement "update of structures in place" and "compile-time garbage collection". In addition to the above, a discussion is given of how the logic of our instance of reduction types is related to a non-standard version of *relevant logic*, via the well known Curry-Howard isomorphism.

2 Preliminaries

The reader is assumed to be familiar with the basics of the λ-calculus (Barendregt [4]). Some possibly less familiar notions concerning the λ-calculus are outlined in this section.

β-reduction will be the main form of reduction considered, and so unless otherwise qualified "reduction" will mean β-reduction, "redex" will mean β-redex and "normal form" will mean β-normal form.

The concept of *head normal form* plays a central role in the λ-calculus, in particular, a term has a head normal form iff it is *solvable*, see Barendregt [4] pp41–42 for discussion. Associated with the notion of head normal form is a particular reduction strategy known as *head reduction*. Later, head reduction will be used to define a property called *strong head neededness*.

Definition 2.1 *A subterm N of a term M is at the* head *of M if*

- $M \equiv N$, *or*
- $M \equiv \lambda x.N'$ *and N is at the head of N', or*
- $M \equiv N_1 N_2$ *and N is at the head of N_1.*

Suppose M is not in normal form. The *leftmost* redex of M is the redex whose binder is to the left of the binder of every other redex in M. The leftmost redex, R, of M is a *head* redex of M if R is at the head of M. M is in *head normal form* if it has no head redex. The *head reduction path* of a term M is a sequence of reduction steps in which every redex which is reduced is a head-redex.

Suppose $M \twoheadrightarrow_\beta N$, then the *descendants* of some subterm M' of M can be found in N (if any exist), by marking M' and following it through the reduction from M to N. Each time a marked redex is reduced during this reduction its mark is eliminated. (A more formal definition is available on page 19 of Klop [24]).

Any descendent of a redex, R, is itself a redex, and is called a *residual.* This is so since if R is contracted in $M \rightarrow_\beta N$, then clearly R has no descendants in N.

3 Strong Heed Neededness

Strong head neededness is a variation of the idea of *head neededness* introduced by Barendregt et al [6]. (Barendregt et al [6] show that head neededness and strictness are equivalent concepts).

Definition 3.1 (Barendregt et al [6]) *Suppose R is a redex of M, then R is* head needed *in M if every reduction path of M to head normal form reduces a residual of R.*

Our variation on this concept is that we insist that a (sub)term is contracted in order for it to be considered to be strongly head needed. In contrast, all redex subterms of a term without head normal form are considered to be head needed by Barendregt et al [6]. Thus, strong head neededness gives more detailed information than head neededness about terms which have no head normal form. This has a practical impact on the implementation of functional languages on parallel machines as it reduces the possibility that a non-terminating term will be selected for evaluation—thus moderating the chance that the machine may become overloaded with the computation of non-terminating tasks (this is further discussed in Wright [34]). Strong head neededness can be defined as follows:

Definition 3.2 *Suppose R is a redex subterm of $M \in \Lambda$, then R is* strongly head needed *in M if the head reduction path of M reduces a residual of R.*

In this paper we describe an extension to this idea of strong head neededness. This extension determines more detailed information than the previous definition by recording the *precise number of times* that the residuals of a redex are contracted. This is exactly the information which a usage analysis of terms seeks to deduce.

Definition 3.3 *Let R be a redex subterm of M. R is a* strongly head needed redex of degree n *in M ($n \geq 0$) if exactly n residuals of R are reduced on the head reduction path of M. We say that R is an* irrelevant *redex of M if R is a strongly head needed redex of degree 0 in M.*

4 Reduction Types

Reduction types are a class of notations for specifying the reduction behaviour of λ-terms (Wright [34]). These notations are all a form of type in which a *set* of function type constructors is introduced to depict a particular kind of reduction behaviour.[1] The key idea can thus be summarised by the phrase "functions should be classified by *function type constructors*". For example, in [32, 33] *boolean reduction types* were introduced to describe strong head neededness information. Boolean reduction types are built from a Boolean algebra of function type constructors in which the "true" function type constructor (written as $\Rightarrow$) constructs sets of functions which strongly head need their argument.[2] In contrast, the "false" function type constructor (written as $\not\twoheadrightarrow$) builds sets of functions which ignore their argument. Thus the term $\lambda x.x$ would be assigned a type of the form $\sigma \Rightarrow \sigma$, where σ is any boolean reduction type. Similarly, the term $\lambda xy.x$ would be assigned a type of the form $\sigma \Rightarrow \tau \not\twoheadrightarrow \sigma$, for any types σ and τ.

[1] Typically, the set of function type constructors will form an algebra.

[2] For a complete description of the semantics of boolean reduction types, see Wright's thesis.

Higher-order terms may also be treated in this manner. For these, dummy variables must be introduced, as is illustrated by the following example. Consider the term $\lambda fx.fx$, in which a term variable is treated as a function. Writing dummy variable function type constructors ("arrow variables") as $\rightarrow_i$, $\rightarrow_j$ and $\rightarrow_k$, we can express the type of this term as being:

$$(\sigma \rightarrow_i \tau) \Rightarrow \sigma \rightarrow_i \tau,$$

for any types σ and τ. Such arrow variables are intended to be understood as being implicitly universally quantified over the algebra of ground function type constructors. Of course, under the standard laws for any Boolean algebra there are only two such ground terms, namely the values "true" and "false" (here represented by $\Rightarrow$ and $\not\rightarrow$).

In general, an algebra of function type constructors must be introduced to describe the behaviour of terms. This necessitates the introduction of *function type constructor builders*. For example, an appropriate type for the $\mathbf{S} \equiv \lambda fgx.fx(gx)$ combinator is

$$(\rho \rightarrow_i \sigma \rightarrow_j \tau) \Rightarrow (\rho \rightarrow_k \sigma) \rightarrow_j \rho\ (\rightarrow_i \vee (\rightarrow_j \wedge \rightarrow_k))\ \tau.$$

See [34] for an in depth investigation of several systems based on boolean reduction types.

In this paper we extend boolean reduction types to *natural reduction types* which use an algebra of function type constructors over the natural numbers (rather than the truth values as in boolean reduction types). This allows us to express strong head neededness *of degree n* information. Then by simply following the framework of Wright we produce a system of logic for deducing natural reduction types for λ-terms.

4.1 Natural Reduction Types

In natural reduction types the exact number of uses of a subterm are kept, rather than just "none" ($\not\rightarrow$) or "more than zero" ($\Rightarrow$). This corresponds to the *use-count* generalisation of strictness analysis (see Sestoft [29], Jensen and Mogensen [23] and Goldberg [15]). The set of function type constructors that we use is now defined.

Definition 4.1 *Let* $\Delta_v = \{\rightarrow_i, \rightarrow_k, \rightarrow_j, \ldots\}$ *be a sufficiently large set of* arrow variables, *where* $i, j, k, \ldots$ *are dummy variables over the natural numbers, and let* $\Delta_g = \{\rightarrow_0, \rightarrow_1, \ldots\}$ *be a set of* ground arrows, *(one for each natural number). Now some operators over sets of arrows are defined. Let* $\rightarrow_i + \rightarrow_j = \rightarrow_{i+j}$ *and* $\rightarrow_i \times \rightarrow_j = \rightarrow_{i \times j}$. *In the right-hand sides of these definitions + is ordinary addition and × is ordinary multiplication (both operators are defined only over the natural numbers). The set of* natural arrow expressions *is the algebra of arrows generated by × and + over* $\Delta = \Delta_g \cup \Delta_v$. *Let the meta-variables over arrow expressions be* $\mathrm{b}, \mathrm{b}', \ldots$. *Let the meta-variables for elements of* Δ_g *be* $\rightarrow_m, \rightarrow_n, \ldots$. *Occasionally the multiplication symbol (×) will be replaced by juxtaposition.*

The intention is that irrelevance is now represented by the ground arrow $\rightarrow_0$ and the various other degrees of strong head neededness are represented by the arrows $\rightarrow_1, \rightarrow_2, \ldots$.

Various sets of types may now be constructed from these function type constructors. In this paper we consider the set of *intersection natural reduction types*. (Intersection types are described in several places, for example, Coppo [10] and Barendregt et al [5]).

Definition 4.2 *Let τ_v denote a set of* type variables *with sufficiently many elements. The set of* intersection natural reduction types *is the set T_I defined by:*

1. *$\alpha \in \tau_v$ implies $\alpha \in T_I$, and*

2. *$\sigma, \tau \in T_I$ and $\mathrm{b} \in \Delta$ implies $\sigma \,\mathrm{b}\, \tau \in T_I$ and $\sigma \cap \tau \in T_I$.*

As in Barendregt et al [5], it is natural to introduce an ordering on the types which intuitively corresponds to a notion of subset.

Definition 4.3 *1. The relation $\leq$ on T_I is inductively defined to be the least relation satisfying: $\tau \leq \omega$; $\omega \leq \omega \,\mathrm{b}\, \omega$; $\tau \leq \tau$; $\tau \leq \tau \cap \tau$; $\sigma \cap \tau \leq \sigma$, $\sigma \cap \tau \leq \tau$; $(\sigma \,\mathrm{b}\, \rho) \cap (\sigma \,\mathrm{b}\, \tau) \leq \sigma \,\mathrm{b} (\rho \cap \tau)$; $\sigma \leq \tau \leq \rho$ implies $\sigma \leq \rho$; $\sigma \leq \sigma'$, $\tau \leq \tau'$ implies $\sigma \cap \tau \leq \sigma' \cap \tau'$; and $\sigma \leq \sigma'$, $\tau \leq \tau'$ implies $\sigma' \,\mathrm{b}\, \tau \leq \sigma \,\mathrm{b}\, \tau'$.*

2. $\sigma = \tau$ iff $\sigma \leq \tau \leq \sigma$.

As stated in Barendregt et al [5], the pre-order $\leq$ defined above is a partial order when the set of types, T_I, is factored by $=$. In the following it will be assumed that T_I is indeed factored by $=$.

4.2 A Type Deduction System: The Intersection System

A *type assumption* is a statement of the form $x : \tau$, where $x \in X$ and $\tau \in T_I$. An *assumption set* is simply a set of type assumptions, with the restriction that no term variable occurs more than once in the assumption set. The letter A (possibly with subscripts) will be used to denote an arbitrary assumption set. Write A_x for the assumption set equal to A except that any occurrence of a type assumption containing the variable x in A is removed.

In order to construct a type assignment system the notion of *variable strong head neededness function* is required. A variable strong head neededness function (or, for conciseness, *variable neededness function*) is a function of type $X \rightarrow \Delta$, which denotes to what degree a free term variable is strongly head needed in a term (that is, the degree to which the term resulting by abstracting that free variable strongly head needs its argument). Variable neededness functions are denoted by the letter V (possibly with subscripts). Let V_0 denote the variable neededness function with the property that $\forall x \in X. V_0(x) = \rightarrow_0$. For example, the expression x should have the variable neededness function $V_0[x := \rightarrow_1]$ assigned to it, since $\lambda x.x : \sigma \rightarrow_1 \sigma$ and for all variables $y \not\equiv x$, $\lambda y.x : \tau \rightarrow_0 \sigma$.

A *typing statement* is a quadruple of an assumption set A, a variable neededness function V, a term M, and a type τ. A typing statement will be written as $A \vdash^I_V M : \tau$. (The I reminds us that the reduction types employed are *intersection* natural reduction types). The term logic for our system appears as Figure 1.

4.2.1 An Example

Consider the term $Twice \equiv \lambda fx.f(fx)$. This term has the following deduction using the type assignment system of Figure 1. Let $A = \{f : (\alpha \rightarrow_i \beta) \cap (\beta \rightarrow_j \gamma), x : \alpha\}$, then using VAR and LEQ we obtain deductions of: $A \vdash^I_{V_0[x := \rightarrow_1]} x : \alpha$, $A \vdash^I_{V_0[f := \rightarrow_1]} f : \alpha \rightarrow_i \beta$ and $A \vdash^I_{V_0[f := \rightarrow_1]} f : \beta \rightarrow_j \gamma$.

VAR	$A_x \cup \{x:\sigma\} \vdash^I_{V_0[x:=\rightarrow_1]} x:\sigma$
APP	$\dfrac{A \vdash^I_{V_1} N_1 : \sigma\, \mathrm{b}\, \tau \quad A \vdash^I_{V_2} N_2 : \sigma}{A \vdash^I_V N_1 N_2 : \tau}$ $(V(x) = V_1(x) + (\mathrm{b} \times V_2(x)))$
ABS	$\dfrac{A_x \cup \{x:\sigma\} \vdash^I_{V[x:=\mathrm{b}]} N : \tau}{A \vdash^I_{V[x:=\rightarrow_0]} \lambda x.N : \sigma\, \mathrm{b}\, \tau}$
MEET	$\dfrac{A \vdash^I_V N : \sigma \quad A \vdash^I_V N : \tau}{A \vdash^I_V N : \sigma \cap \tau}$
LEQ	$\dfrac{A \vdash^I_V N : \sigma \quad \sigma \leq \tau}{A \vdash^I_V N : \tau}$

Figure 1: The Rules for deducing Intersection Natural Reduction Types

Now two instances of the APP rule apply. The interesting part of this is the construction of the variable neededness functions in these two instances of APP. In the deduction of a type for fx the calculation is, for f: $\rightarrow_1 + (\rightarrow_i \times \rightarrow_0) = \rightarrow_{1+i\times 0} = \rightarrow_1$, and for x: $\rightarrow_0 + (\rightarrow_i \times \rightarrow_1) = \rightarrow_{0+i\times 1} = \rightarrow_i$. In the deduction of a type for $f(fx)$, the calculations are, for f: $\rightarrow_1 + (\rightarrow_j \times \rightarrow_1) = \rightarrow_{1+j\times 1} = \rightarrow_{j+1}$, and for x: $\rightarrow_0 + (\rightarrow_j \times \rightarrow_i) = \rightarrow_{0+i\times j} = \rightarrow_{i\times j}$. Consider the final type for *Twice*:

$$((\alpha \rightarrow_i \beta) \cap (\beta \rightarrow_j \gamma)) \rightarrow_{j+1} \alpha \rightarrow_{i\times j} \gamma.$$

Firstly, notice that the strong head neededness of f is of non-zero degree. Moreover, if the first occurrence of f in $f(fx)$ strongly head needs fx a total of j times then f is strongly head needed a total of $j+1$ times—once for the first occurrence of f in $f(fx)$ and j times for each use of the second occurrence of f in $f(fx)$.

Similarly, the strong head neededness given for x reflects the intuition that *both* occurrences of f must strongly head need x in order for x to be strongly head needed in the overall expression.

5 An Isomorphism with Relevant Logic

The aim here is to establish a logical foundation for the term logic employing reduction types by applying the Curry-Howard isomorphism [19] to ***relevant logic*** [1, 14]. The implicational fragment of relevant logic is denoted $R_{\rightarrow}$. This system was also studied by Church [9] who called it ***weak implicational logic***. It turns out that the '$\rightarrow$' of relevant logic corresponds to the '$\Rightarrow$' of boolean reduction types. Without trying to be precise about terminology, our claim is that relevance types are a form of reduction type.

The reasons for expecting some connections between relevance and neededness can be outlined as follows. The essence of relevant logic is that, in deducing $A \rightarrow B$,

Axiom

$A \vdash A$

Structural rules

$$\frac{\Gamma, A, B, \Gamma' \vdash C}{\Gamma, B, A, \Gamma' \vdash C} \text{ (Permutation)} \qquad \frac{\Gamma, A, A \vdash B}{\Gamma, A \vdash B} \text{ (Contraction)}$$

Operational rules

$$\frac{\Gamma, A \vdash B}{\Gamma \vdash A \rightarrow B} \; (\rightarrow I) \qquad \frac{\Gamma \vdash A \rightarrow B \quad \Gamma' \vdash A}{\Gamma, \Gamma' \vdash B} \; (\rightarrow E)$$

Figure 2: Natural Deduction System for $R_{\rightarrow}$

the antecedent A *really is used in* (and hence is *relevant* to) the derivation of the consequent B. The idea, generally attributed to Heyting, that a proof of $A \rightarrow B$ is some 'function' f taking each proof p of A to some proof $f(p)$ of B, can also be applied to relevant logic. However, for f to qualify as a relevant proof of $A \rightarrow B$, f must use the proof p of A; that is, f *must depend on its argument.*

Type assignment systems are generally given as formulations corresponding to natural deduction. In relevant logic, as in all other 'resource' logics, the structural rules are of paramount importance and must be explicitly stated. Figure 2 is a natural deduction system for $R_{\rightarrow}$, in sequent form.

It is reasonably well-known that the terms with relevant types are exactly the Curry typable subset of the λI-terms. It is easily demonstrated that the $R_{\rightarrow}$-typable terms are the 'hereditarily strict' ones, recalling the close correspondence with λI-calculus. That is, no sub-term of a hereditarily strict λ-expression is erasable [17, 16].

Relevant types alone contribute little to our enterprise since the aim of the analysis is to *distinguish* functions which strongly head need their arguments from constant functions, whereas the effect above is to merely *exclude* the constant ones.

The Deduction Theorem for relevant logic [9] is as follows: if $A_1, A_2, \ldots, A_n \vdash B$, then either $A_1, A_2, \ldots, A_{n-1} \vdash A_n \supset B$ or $A_1, A_2, \ldots, A_{n-1} \vdash B$. This suggests the concept of a deduction being *relevant with respect to a given hypothesis.* Dunn [14] formalises this concept by 'tagging' a hypothesis, say with a #, and passing the tag along with each application of modus ponens. Then, if the tag turns up on the conclusion, the deduction is relevant with respect to that hypothesis. This idea of tagging carries over to natural deduction and allows us to distinguish relevant and *irrelevant* hypotheses. By then permitting either tagged or untagged items to be discharged, we may distinguish relevant and irrelevant implications, respectively denoted $\Rightarrow$ and $\rightsquigarrow$. Thus there are two conditional proof rules and two versions of modus ponens. The resulting system is denoted $R_{\rightsquigarrow}$ and dubbed *irrelevant logic.* Fundamentally, the difference is that in $R_{\rightsquigarrow}$ weakening is permitted but it introduces only untagged hypotheses. This system closely corresponds to boolean reduction types [3]. In the term logic using reduction types, the tagging is denoted by the variable head-neededness function V, presented separately from the assumption set.

As indicated earlier in section 4, the extension from neededness to a usage analysis is straightforward and the logical framework extends in a corresponding way. The contraction rule is the key here. To use two identical hypotheses and then discharge them together requires that they first be contracted to a single hypothesis. This indicates more than one occurrence of the bound variable in the body of a λ-expression. However, to get information about *usage*, relevance must also be taken into account. For example, $\lambda x.\mathbf{K}xx$ corresponds to a proof where the hypothesis labelled x is contracted before being discharged. Nevertheless only one of those is relevant so only one is *used*.

This leads to the following decisions regarding the monitoring of usage in proofs. The natural deduction system is given in Figure 3. First, each relevant use of a hypothesis attracts a use-count annotation of 1. This is handled in the axiom. Second, each weakening introduces an irrelevant hypothesis, hence it is tagged with a 0. Finally, contraction takes the *sum* of the annotations on the two hypotheses and, on discharging a hypothesis the annotation is transferred to the introduced arrow. The notation $m \times \Gamma$ indicates that all annotations in Γ are to be multiplied by m.

Axiom

$$A^1 \vdash A$$

Structural rules

$$\frac{\Gamma, A^m, B^n, \Gamma' \vdash C}{\Gamma, B^n, A^m, \Gamma' \vdash C} \text{ (Permutation)} \qquad \frac{\Gamma, A^m, A^n \vdash B}{\Gamma, A^{m+n} \vdash B} \text{ (Contraction)}$$

$$\frac{\Gamma \vdash A}{\Gamma, B^0 \vdash A} \text{ (Weakening)}$$

Operational rules

$$\frac{\Gamma, A^m \vdash B}{\Gamma \vdash A \to_m B} \ (\to I) \qquad \frac{\Gamma \vdash A \to_m B \quad \Gamma' \vdash A}{\Gamma, m \times \Gamma' \vdash B} \ (\to E)$$

Figure 3: Natural Deduction System, monitoring uses

By now permitting dummy variables as arrow annotations in the hypotheses we get a logic which, via the Curry-Howard interpretation, corresponds to the term logic of Figure 1 (without the rules MEET and LEQ).

6 A Semantics for Natural Reduction Types

The unique aspect of the semantics for reduction types is the need to look at the behaviour of a function as it is transformed by applying it to a sequence of arguments.

Both the number of arguments and the properties of these arguments are used to collect together functions into the interpretation of types. Thus the semantics for reduction types is *context-sensitive*, a fact which we feel makes them of particular interest.

6.1 Semi-models of the λ-calculus

Plotkin [28] has introduced the notion of *semi-model* in order to conduct a semantic analysis of Curry's original system of F-deducibility [13]. The key step in this work is the emphasis on modelling *reduction* rather than conversion. In order to avoid introducing an EQ rule in the manner of Hindley [18] we will follow Plotkin's approach to interpreting terms.

A $\lambda\beta$-semi-model of the λ-calculus is a triple, $\langle D, \bullet, [\![\cdot]\!].\rangle$, where D is a partial order, $\bullet : D \times D \to D$ is a map called *application* and $[\![\cdot]\!].$ is another map which assigns each term $M \in \Lambda$ to an element $[\![M]\!]_\mu \in D$, for an environment $\mu : X \to D$. The ordering on D will be written as $\leq$ and for two environments μ and μ' write $\mu \leq \mu'$ iff $\forall x \in X.\mu(x) \leq \mu'(x)$. Furthermore, the map $[\![\cdot]\!].$ must satisfy, for each $M \in \Lambda$ and each environment $\mu : X \to D$, the following list of properties (Plotkin [28]):

1. $[\![x]\!]_\mu = \mu(x)$,
2. $[\![MN]\!]_\mu = [\![M]\!]_\mu \bullet [\![N]\!]_\mu$,
3. $[\![\lambda x.M]\!]_\mu \bullet d \leq [\![M]\!]_{\mu[x:=d]}$, for every $d \in D$,
4. if $[\![x]\!]_\mu = [\![x]\!]_{\mu'}$ for all $x \in \mathrm{FV}(M)$, then $[\![M]\!]_\mu = [\![M]\!]_{\mu'}$,
5. if $y \notin \mathrm{FV}(M)$, then $[\![M[x := y]]\!]_\mu = [\![M]\!]_{\mu[x:=\mu(y)]}$, and
6. if $\forall d \in D.[\![M]\!]_{\mu[x:=d]} \leq [\![N]\!]_{\mu[x:=d]}$, then $[\![\lambda x.M]\!]_\mu \leq [\![\lambda x.N]\!]_\mu$.

Theorem 6.1 (Plotkin [28]) *$M \twoheadrightarrow_\beta N$ iff in all semi-models and for every environment μ, $[\![M]\!]_\mu \leq [\![N]\!]_\mu$*

Semi-models do indeed model the syntactic process of reduction (but not conversion). This means that they are an appropriate choice for testing the correctness of the information deduced by our term logic. Furthermore, Plotkin's semi-models allow the type deduction systems to be shown to give *complete* information with respect to reduction.

6.2 A Semantic Notion of Strong Head Neededness

The following definition provides a semantic analogue of the syntactic notion of strong head neededness of degree m.

Definition 6.2 *Let $\langle D, \bullet, [\![\cdot]\!].\rangle$ be a semi-model of the λ-calculus. For any interpretation of term variables μ, write $[\![M]\!]_\mu$ strongly head needed to degree m in $[\![N]\!]_\mu$ if*

$$\left.\begin{array}{l} [\![N]\!]_\mu \\ < [\![\lambda x_1 x_2 \ldots x_{n_1}.MN_1 \ldots N_{k_1}]\!]_\mu \\ < [\![\lambda y_1 y_2 \ldots y_{n_2}.MP_1 \ldots P_{k_2}]\!]_\mu \\ \vdots \\ < [\![\lambda z_1 z_2 \ldots z_{n_m}.MQ_1 \ldots Q_{k_m}]\!]_\mu \end{array}\right\} m \textit{ times.}$$

$$\mathcal{I}[\![\cdot]\!]_{\cdot} : T_I \to \mathbf{TEnv} \to \mathcal{P}(D)$$
$$\mathcal{I}[\![\sigma]\!]_\nu = \bigcap_{\sigma_i \in G_I(\sigma)} \mathcal{G}_I[\![\sigma_i]\!]_\nu$$

$$\mathcal{G}_I[\![\cdot]\!]_{\cdot} : T_I \to \mathbf{TEnv} \to \mathcal{P}(D)$$
$$\mathcal{G}_I[\![\sigma \cap \tau]\!]_\nu = \mathcal{G}_I[\![\sigma]\!]_\nu \cap \mathcal{G}_I[\![\tau]\!]_\nu$$
$$\mathcal{G}_I[\![\alpha]\!]_\nu = \nu(\alpha)$$
$$\mathcal{G}_I[\![\sigma_0 \to_m \sigma_1\, \mathrm{b}_1\, \sigma_2 \ldots \sigma_n\, \mathrm{b}_n\, \alpha]\!]_\nu$$
$$= \{d \in D | \forall d_i \in \mathcal{G}_I[\![\sigma_i]\!]_\nu, 0 \leq i \leq n. \; d_0 \text{ strongly head needed to degree } m \text{ in } d \bullet d_0 \bullet d_1 \bullet \ldots \bullet d_n; \; d \bullet d_0 \in \mathcal{G}_I[\![\sigma_1\, \mathrm{b}_1\, \sigma_2 \ldots \sigma_n\, \mathrm{b}_n\, \alpha]\!]_\nu\}$$

Figure 4: The Semantics of Intersection Natural Reduction Types

Theorem 6.3 *$[\![M]\!]_\mu$ strongly head needed to degree m in $[\![N]\!]_\mu$ iff M strongly head needed to degree m in N.*

6.3 What is a Type Interpretation?

A type interpretation is a pair $\mathit{Ty} = \langle \mathrm{Ty}, [\![\cdot]\!]_{\cdot} \rangle$, where Ty is a set of subsets of the domain of the chosen (semi-) model of terms which satisfies certain closure properties and $[\![\cdot]\!]_{\cdot}$ is an interpretation function from types and type environments to elements of Ty.

The interpretation of types is given modulo the interpretation of type variables. A *type environment* is a function ($\in \tau_v \to \mathcal{P}(D)$) which maps each type variable to an element of the (semi-) model of terms. The letter ν is used to range over type environments.

Definition 6.4 *Let $\mathcal{M}$ denote a model or semi-model of terms. The notion of* semantic satisfaction *can be defined in the following manner:*

1. *$\rho, \nu, \mathcal{M}, \mathit{Ty} \models M : \sigma$ if $[\![M]\!]_\rho \in [\![\sigma]\!]_\nu$,*
2. *$\rho, \nu, \mathcal{M}, \mathit{Ty} \models A$ if for each $x : \sigma \in A$, $\rho, \nu, \mathcal{M}, \mathit{Ty} \models x : \sigma$, and*
3. *$A \models_V M : \sigma$ if $\rho, \nu, \mathcal{M}, \mathit{Ty} \models A$ implies $\rho, \nu, \mathcal{M}, \mathit{Ty} \models M : \sigma$ and $\forall x \in X. \rho, \nu, \mathcal{M}, \mathit{Ty} \models \lambda x.M : A(x)\, V(x)\, \sigma$.*

6.4 The Semantics of Natural Reduction Types

Definition 6.5 *Write $\sigma \trianglelefteq_I \tau$ if there is a substitution, R, of arrow expressions for arrow variables homomorphically extendible such that $\tau = R(\sigma)$. Let $G_I(\sigma) = \{\tau | \sigma \trianglelefteq_I \tau; \tau \in T_I\}$.*

Figure 4 contains the semantics of intersection natural reduction types. Note that this covers all cases as $\rho\, \mathrm{b}(\sigma \cap \tau) = (\rho\, \mathrm{b}\, \sigma) \cap (\rho\, \mathrm{b}\, \tau)$.

Lemma 6.6 *$\sigma \leq \tau$ implies $\forall \nu. \mathcal{I}[\![\sigma]\!]_\nu \subseteq \mathcal{I}[\![\tau]\!]_\nu$.*

Let $\mathrm{Ty} = \mathcal{P}(D)$, where D is the domain of a semi-model of terms, and $\mathcal{I}[\![\cdot]\!]_{\cdot}$ be as defined in Figure 4, then the following Theorem holds.

Theorem 6.7 (Correctness) *$A \vdash_V^I M : \tau$ iff $A \models_V M : \tau$.*

7 Conclusion and Related Work

We have introduced an original method for reasoning about *usage* in the λ-calculus. This method is based on a new instance of Wright's reduction type framework and employs a polynomial algebra over the natural numbers to deduce type expressions which describe the usage behaviour of terms. We have presented a term logic for these types and shown this logic to be semantically correct by first interpreting natural reduction types over a semi-model of the λ-calculus and then providing a correctness proof. Furthermore, we have shown that a natural extension of *relevant logic* can be related to our term logic via the Curry-Howard isomorphism.

During the development of this work, we became aware of Wadler's investigation of the use of linear logic as a basis for sharing analysis (see Wadler [31]). Wadler introduces *linear types* in which the modal '!' operator of linear logic is interpreted as indicating a shared argument. The relation between relevant and linear logic is well-known (for example [2]) so a comparison of natural reduction types with linear types seems appropriate.

At the level of the logics, the only difference is that linear logic disallows contraction except in the scope of a '!'. At the level of the types themselves, it is clear that natural reduction types contain strictly greater information than linear types, since the linear function type constructor (on its own) corresponds to the type constructor $\rightarrow_1$ and the shared argument operator '!' (which is always used in conjunction with the linear function type constructor) is modelled by the use of a variable arrow.

The basic shortcoming with linear types is that '!' indicates a non-linear type, thus confusing *sharing* with *absence*, though there has been recent work on separating '!' into relevant and affine versions [21]. Also, through the promotion and dereliction rules, even linear arguments can be annotated with '!'. In fact, at best '!' indicates several *occurrences* rather than several uses, as in $\lambda x.Kxx : !\sigma \multimap \sigma$. In comparison, the natural reduction type for this term is $\sigma \rightarrow_1 \sigma$, correctly indicating that the argument is *used* exactly once (ideally the linear type should be $\sigma \multimap \sigma$). It also appears that the promotion and dereliction rules complicate the notion of principal type.

Less closely related to our work is the work of Kuo and Mishra [25] and the similar method of Coppo [11]. These works are based on introducing certain non-standard constants to represent the set of strict functions and the set of all functions, and then constructing types over these constants using the standard function type constructor. Of course, no attempt is made in these works to treat the generalisation to usage information, as has been done for reduction types in this paper. However, their approach also seeks to capitalise on type inference technology in its implementation. In addition, Benton [7] and Jensen [22] provide a discussion of the relationship of the approach of Kuo and Mishra with that of the abstract interpretation method of Burn et al [8].

References

[1] A. R. Anderson and N. D. Belnap, Jr. *Entailment: The Logic of Relevance and Necessity*. Princeton University Press, 1975.

[2] A. Avron. The semantics and proof theory of linear logic. *Theoretical Computer Science*, 57:161–184, 1988.

[3] C. A. Baker-Finch. Relevant logic and strictness analysis. In *Workshop on Static Analysis, LaBRI, Bordeaux*, pages 221–228. Bigre 81–82, 1992.

[4] H.P. Barendregt. *The Lambda-Calculus: its Syntax and Semantics*, volume 103 of *Studies in Logic and the Foundations of Mathematics*. North-Holland, second edition, 1984.

[5] H.P. Barendregt, M. Coppo, and M. Dezani-Ciancaglini. A Filter Lambda Model and the Completeness of Type Assignment. *Journal of Symbolic Logic*, 48(4):931–940, December 1983.

[6] H.P. Barendregt, J.R. Kennaway, J.W. Klop, and M.R. Sleep. Needed Reduction and Spine Strategies for the lambda-calculus. Technical report, Centre for Mathematics and Computer Science, May 1986.

[7] P.N. Benton. Strictness Logic and Polymorphic Invariance. In *Logical Foundations of Computer Science*, pages 33–44, 20–24 July 1992.

[8] G.L. Burn, C.L. Hankin, and S. Abramsky. Strictness analysis for higher-order functions. *Science of Computer Programming*, 7:249–278, 1986.

[9] A. Church. The weak theory of implication. In Menne, Wilhelmy, and Angsil, editors, *Kontrolliertes Denken, Untersuchungen zum Logikkalkül und der Logik der Einzelwissenschaften*, pages 22–37. Kommissions-verlag Karl Alber, 1951.

[10] M. Coppo. An Extended Polymorphic Type System for Applicative Languages. In *Mathematical Foundations of Computer Science*, number 88 in Lecture Notes in Computer Science. Springer-Verlag, September 1980.

[11] M. Coppo. Type Inference, Abstract Interpretation and Strictness Analysis. Draft manuscript, 1992.

[12] P. Cousot and R. Cousot. Abstract interpretation : A unified lattice model for static analysis of programs by construction or approximation of fixpoints. In *ACM Symposium on Principles of Programming Languages*, pages 238–252. ACM, 1977.

[13] H.B. Curry and R. Feys. *Combinatory Logic, Volume 1.* Studies in Logic and the Foundations of Mathematics. North-Holland, 1958.

[14] J. M. Dunn. Relevance logic and entailment. In D. Gabbay and F. Guenthner, editors, *Handbook of Philosophical Logic, Vol. III.* D. Reidel, 1986.

[15] B. Goldberg. Detecting Sharing of Partial Applications in Functional Programs. In *Functional Programming Languages and Computer Architecture*, volume 274 of *Lecture Notes in Computer Science.* Springer-Verlag, 1987.

[16] G. Helman. Completeness of the normal typed fragment of the λ-system U. *Journal of Philosophical Logic*, 6:33–46, 1977.

[17] G. Helman. *Restricted Lambda Abstraction and the Interpretation of Some Non-Classical Logics.* PhD thesis, University of Pittsburgh, 1977.

[18] J.R. Hindley. The Completeness Theorem for Typing λ-terms. *Theoretical Computer Science*, 22:1–17, 1983.

[19] W. A. Howard. The formulae-as-types notion of construction. In J. P. Seldin and J. R. Hindley, editors, *To H. B. Curry: Essays on Combinatorial Logic, Lambda Calculus and Formalism*, pages 479–490. Academic Press, 1980.

[20] P. Hudak and R.Young. Higher-order strictness analysis in untyped lambda calculus. In *ACM SIGACT-SIGPLAN Symposium on Principles of Programming Languages*, pages 97–109. ACM, 1986.

[21] Bart Jacobs. Semantics of weakening and contraction. Technical report, Department of Pure Mathematics, University of Cambridge, 1992.

[22] T.P. Jensen. Strictness Analysis in Logical Form, 1991.

[23] T.P. Jensen and T.A. Mogensen. A Backwards Analysis for Compile-time Garbage Collection. In N.D. Jones, editor, *European Symposium on Programming*, volume 432 of *Lecture Notes in Computer Science*. Springer-Verlag, 1990.

[24] J.W. Klop. *Combinatory Reduction Systems*. PhD thesis, State University of Utrecht, 1980.

[25] T-M. Kuo and P. Mishra. Strictness Analysis: A New Perspective based on Type Inference. In *FPCA'89*, pages 260–272, London, United Kingdom, September 1989.

[26] A. Mycroft. The theory and practice of transforming call-by-need into call-by-value. In *International Symposium on Programming*, volume 83 of *Lecture Notes in Computer Science*, pages 269–281. Springer-Verlag, 1980.

[27] A. Mycroft and N. Jones. A relational framework for abstract interpretation. In *Workshop on Programs as Data Objects*, volume 217 of *Lecture Notes in Computer Science*, pages 156–171. Springer-Verlag, 1985.

[28] G.D. Plotkin. A Semantics for Type Checking. In *Theoretical Aspects of Computer Science*, volume 526 of *Lecture Notes in Computer Science*, pages 1–17. Springer-Verlag, 1991.

[29] P. Sestoft. *Analysis and Efficient Implementation of Functional Programs*. PhD thesis, DIKU, University of Copenhagen, 1991.

[30] J.H. Siekmann. Unification Theory. *Journal of Symbolic Computation*, 7:207–274, 1989.

[31] P. Wadler. Is there a use for Linear Logic? In *Partial Evaluation and Program Manipulation*. ACM Press, 1991.

[32] D.A. Wright. Strictness Analysis Via (Type) Inference. Technical Report TR89-3, University of Tasmania, September 1989.

[33] D.A. Wright. A New Technique for Strictness Analysis. In *Theory and Practice of Software Development*, number 494 in Lecture Notes in Computer Science. Springer-Verlag, April 1991.

[34] D.A. Wright. *Reduction Types and Intensionality in the Lambda-Calculus*. PhD thesis, University of Tasmania, 1992.

Polymorphic Types and Widening Operators

B. Monsuez

Laboratoire d'Informatique de l'École Normale Supérieure. (LIENS)
45, rue d'Ulm 75005 Paris, FRANCE
monsuez@dmi.ens.fr
(Extended Abstract)

Introduction

In the general case, the type inference problem is not decidable. In other words, it is not possible to compute the principal type. Undecidability of the type inference problem does not only affect complex type systems like Girards system F, or Coppo-Dezanis intersection types[2]. Really simple type systems like ML+ — the Hindley/Milner type system with recursively-defined polymorphic constants[11]— have the principal type property, but the principal type is not always computable.

Considering Type Inference as an *abstract interpretation* of the dynamic semantics of the language raises new opportunities[6]. The principal type is defined as the greatest fixpoint in the abstract interpretation framework. If the type inference problem was undecidable in the traditional framework, it still remains undecidable, but since undecidability is characterized by infinite decreasing chains, we can define some tactics to avoid those chains:

> The first and simplest solution is to restrict the type algebra to lattices that verify the descending chain condition. Doing so will reject the most commonly used type algebras.
> The second approach consists of using an heuristic to decide when the iteration sequence should stop. Such a strategy is used by Karnomori and al to compute Prolog types [9], or by Aiken and Murphy to compute polymorphic types for FL [1]. This kind of heuristics is not based on any theoretical framework, it requires to proof that the approximate result preserves the soundness property—every well-typed program cannot lead to an erroneous state—and it only works as a two states operator: either we continue the iteration sequence or we stop it.
> The third method consists of using widening operators. In their seminal presentation of the formalism of Abstract Interpretation, the Cousots introduced a speed-up operation for iteration sequences called a widening operator. Widening operators take an infinite iteration sequence and returns a finite iteration sequence. This is achieved by replacing the small steps that can be found in the first iteration sequence with real big steps such that the greatest fixpoint — or a lower approximation of the greatest fixpoint — can be reached within a finite number of those big steps.

In the general case, widening operators do not allow to get the greatest fixpoint, but a lower approximation of the greatest fixpoint. Therefore, there is no best widening operator, but some widening operators are good compromise between the precision of the analysis and the computation time.

In this paper, we present some widening operators that are well suited for polymorphic types. Starting from the type system described in [6] — it is the ML+ type system built using Abstract Interpretation — we define widening operators that mimic the heuristics used with the ML [5] and the Miranda languages [12]. We then show how it is possible to extend those type systems by refining the widening operators.

1 Preliminaries

1.1 Type inference by Abstract Interpretation

With respect to the formalism of *abstract interpretation*, a type is an abstraction of a set of values ensuring an error-free execution.

On the one hand, a type can be interpreted as an upper approximation. Saying that: $\lambda x.1/x$ has the type num $\rightarrow$ num doesn't mean that for all numerical values its evaluation will be error-free. For instance, 0 leads to an error. The function $\lambda x.1/x$ actually maps[1] num* to num*, and so is num $\rightarrow$ num the smallest approximation including num* $\rightarrow$ num*.

On the other hand, a type cannot always be interpreted as an upper approximation. The ML-expression $(\lambda fx.f(fx))(\lambda x.0)$ has the type "num $\rightarrow$ num". Since this function returns the numerical value 0 for any kind of arguments, this type is certainly not the most general. The previous expression has the far more general type: "$\alpha \rightarrow$ num". This time, we observe that the ML principal type is a subset of a more general type.

The framework of *abstract interpretation* requires an abstract value to be either an upper or lower approximation. In [6], we have shown that characterizing a type as a well-behaved abstract value is much more subtle. We split the abstraction into two steps (*i.e.* an upper approximation followed by a lower approximation). First we define a huge type system T_g whose elements are the closest upper approximation of the set of values insuring an error-free execution. These general types are not effective in general, so that we can neither infer types nor perform type-checking. In order to define a useful type system, we have to restrict ourselves to less general types. Thus, we have to abstract the general types to smaller type — like ML-types.

To summarize, a type is an abstract value obtained by combining two pairs of abstraction functions. The first one is an upper approximation, the second one is a dual lower approximation.

$$\text{Set of Values} \underset{\alpha}{\overset{\gamma}{\leftrightarrows}} T_g \underset{\gamma^*}{\overset{\alpha^*}{\rightleftarrows}} T_{ML}$$

[1] num* denotes the numerical values different from 0.

1.2 ML† type system—a polymorphic type system built by Abstract Interpretation

Using this abstraction scheme, we have built in [6] a type system of a small λ-calculus with "`let`" and "`letrec`". Since the purpose of the paper is not to present the construction of this type system, we only summarize the required notions to understand how this small type system works.

- We define the set of monomorphic types **M** as the set of terms:

$$\mathbf{M} : \mathsf{num}|\mathsf{bool}|\mathbf{M} \rightarrow \mathbf{M}.$$

- We define the set of polymorphic types **S** as the set of terms:

$$\mathbf{S} : \mathbf{M}|\alpha, \beta, \gamma \ldots |\mathbf{S} \rightarrow \mathbf{S}.$$

  Our type schemes have implicit "quantification" at the outermost level. Sometime, to avoid any confusion, we denote this implicit quantification by writing the type σ as $\forall(\sigma)$.
- We identify a polymorphic type schemes with the set of his generic monomorphic instances. ("$\alpha \rightarrow \alpha$" $\equiv \{\mathsf{num} \rightarrow \mathsf{num}, \mathsf{bool} \rightarrow \mathsf{bool}, (\mathsf{num} \rightarrow \mathsf{num}) \rightarrow (\mathsf{num} \rightarrow \mathsf{num}), \ldots\}$).

Lemma 1. *The codomain of this injection T_{ML} ordered by inclusion and completed downwards with the empty set is a complete lattice.*

Because of the implicit quantification, we need to collect the equality relations between all the subterms of the types stored in the environment. For example, the assertion:

$$\rho(x \leftarrow (\forall \alpha.\alpha)) \vdash x \Rightarrow \forall \alpha.\alpha$$

is a safe assumption, but does not mean that the function $\lambda x.x$ has type $\forall \alpha.\alpha \rightarrow \alpha$. To conclude that $\lambda x.x$ has type $\forall \alpha.\alpha \rightarrow \alpha$, we need the additional clue that the output of the function $\lambda x.x$ has always the same monotype as the input, *i.e.* the variable x.

For these reasons, the type system we have built using *abstract interpretation* in [6] defines a polymorphic type as the pair of a type scheme σ — *i.e.* a set of monotypes — and a set $\Re$ or relations $\mathcal{R}$ that denote the equality relations between the subterms of σ and the subterms of the types stored in the environment.

$$\mathrm{TYPE} = (\sigma, \Re).$$

The rules that describes the type system are listed on figure 2. With the exception of the abstraction and application rules, we can notice that the rules are similar to the one of the **ML+** type system. Abstraction and application rules are more complex because the abstraction rule includes the type generalization process and the application rule includes the type instanciation process. Consequently, every pair $(\sigma, \Re)$ denotes a polymorphic type, and the "`letrec`" constructor allows recursively-defined polymorphic constants. Henceforth, this type system can be shown to be equivalent to the **ML+** type system.

More precisely, the abstraction rule computes the type of a λ-expression. If the function $\lambda P.E$ maps the pair $(\sigma_1, \Re_1)$ to the pair $(\sigma_2, \Re_2)$ then the type of the function is the pair $(\sigma, \Re)$ where:

fun$((\sigma_1, \Re_1), (\sigma_2, \Re_2)) = (\sigma, \Re)$ **such that:**
$\forall\sigma'$ **subterms of** σ, **if it exists** σ'' **subterms of** σ, **and an equality relation between** σ **and** σ' **then** $\sigma = \sigma'$.
$\Re$ **inherited relations from** $\Re_1, \Re_2$.

apply$(\rho, (\sigma_1, \Re_1)), (\sigma_2, \Re_2)) = (\sigma, \Re)$ **such that:**
instantiate$(\rho, (\sigma_1, \Re_1)) = (\sigma_1', \Re_1')$ **instantiate**$(\rho, (\sigma_2, \Re_2)) = (\sigma_2', \Re_2')$ **and** $(\sigma_2' \to \sigma) = \sigma_1'$
$\Re$ **inherited relations from** $\Re_1', \Re_2'$.

instantiate$(\rho, (\sigma_1, \Re_1)) = (\sigma, \Re)(\sigma', \Re)$ **such that:**
$\forall\sigma_i$ **subterm of** σ **such that** σ_i **is not equal to any variable in the environment** ρ, $\sigma_i' \sqsubseteq \sigma_i$.

$$\sigma' = \sigma[\sigma_1'/\sigma_1, \ldots, \sigma_i'/\sigma_i, \ldots]$$

Fig. 1. Some additional definitions

- $\sigma' \equiv \{(\tau_i \to \tau_i') \mid \tau_i \in \sigma,\ \tau_i' \in \sigma_1$ and the relations in $\Re_1$ and $\Re_2$ are verified $\}$,
- $\Re'$ is the subset of $\Re_1' \cup \Re_2'$ applicable to the term σ.

The application rule ensures that the function can handle correctly the argument and returns the type of the output if the evaluation does not fail. The application process obeys to the following rules:

- The types of a variable are monomorphic types. If we apply a function stored in a variable to an argument stored in a variable as well, and the function is of type $\sigma_1 \to \sigma_2$ and the argument is of type σ_3, then we have to insure that for all possible program executions the monomorphic instances of σ_1 are equal to the monomorphic instances of σ_3. In other words:
  - $\sigma_1 \equiv \sigma_3$
  - we have equality relations between each instance of σ_1 and σ_3.
- A subterm of the type scheme of a constant can be equal to a subterm of the type of a variable. We handle this subterm like the terms of types of variables.
- Subterms of the types of a constant that are not equal to subterms of the type of a variable can be freely instantiated.

The set of rules does not define one type, but a set of types for each expression. In [6], we have found that the principal type is the greatest fixpoint of the equation system inferred from the set of abstract rules.

Theorem 2. *The principal type of an expression is the greatest fixpoint of the equation system inferred from the set of abstract rules.*

Example 1. As an example we show how to compute the type of the expression $\lambda xy.x$ with our type system. The store has at least two locations, one for the variable x and one for the variable y. Since we compute the *greatest fixpoint*, we

$$\rho \vdash_{\mathbf{ML}^\dagger} \texttt{Numerical } N \Rightarrow (\mathsf{num}, \emptyset_{\Re}) \quad (1)$$
$$\rho \vdash_{\mathbf{ML}^\dagger} \texttt{true} \Rightarrow (\mathsf{bool}, \emptyset_{\Re}) \quad (2)$$
$$\rho \vdash_{\mathbf{ML}^\dagger} \texttt{false} \Rightarrow (\mathsf{bool}, \emptyset_{\Re}) \quad (3)$$

$$\frac{\rho(P \leftarrow (\sigma_1, \Re_1)) \vdash_{\mathbf{ML}^\dagger} E \Rightarrow (\sigma_2, \Re_2)}{\rho \vdash_{\mathbf{ML}^\dagger} \lambda P.E \Rightarrow (\sigma, \Re)} \ \mathbf{fun}((\sigma_1, \Re_1), (\sigma_2, \Re_2)) = (\sigma, \Re) \quad (4)$$

$$\frac{\rho \vdash_{\mathrm{val\_of}} \texttt{ident } P \Rightarrow (\sigma, \Re)}{\rho \vdash_{\mathbf{ML}^\dagger} \texttt{ident } P \Rightarrow (\sigma, \Re)} \quad (5)$$

$$\frac{\rho \vdash_{\mathbf{ML}^\dagger} E_1 \Rightarrow (\mathsf{bool}, \Re_1) \quad \rho \vdash_{\mathbf{ML}^\dagger} E_2 \Rightarrow (\sigma_2, \Re_2) \quad \rho \vdash_{\mathbf{ML}^\dagger} E_3 \Rightarrow (\sigma_3, \Re_3)}{\rho \vdash_{\mathbf{ML}^\dagger} \texttt{if } E_1 \texttt{ then } E_2 \texttt{ else } E_3 \Rightarrow (\sigma_2, \Re_2) \sqcap (\sigma_3, \Re_3)} \quad (6)$$

$$\frac{\rho \vdash_{\mathbf{ML}^\dagger} E_1 \Rightarrow (\sigma_1, \Re_1) \quad \rho \vdash_{\mathbf{ML}^\dagger} E_2 \Rightarrow (\sigma_2, \Re_2)}{\rho \vdash_{\mathbf{ML}^\dagger} E_1 E_2 \Rightarrow (\sigma, \Re)} \ \mathbf{apply}(\rho, (\sigma_1, \Re_1), (\sigma_2, \Re_2)) = (\sigma, \Re) \quad (7)$$

$$\frac{\rho \vdash_{\mathbf{ML}^\dagger} E_1 \Rightarrow (\sigma_1, \Re_1) \quad \rho(P \leftarrow (\sigma_1, \Re_1)) \vdash_{\mathbf{ML}^\dagger} E_2 \Rightarrow (\sigma, \Re)}{\rho \vdash_{\mathbf{ML}^\dagger} \texttt{let } P = E_1 \texttt{ in } E_2 \Rightarrow (\sigma, \Re)} \quad (8)$$

$$\frac{\rho(P \leftarrow (\sigma_1, \Re_1)) \vdash_{\mathbf{ML}^\dagger} E_1 \Rightarrow (\sigma_1, \Re_1) \quad \rho(P \leftarrow (\sigma_1, \Re_1)) \vdash_{\mathbf{ML}^\dagger} E_2 \Rightarrow (\sigma, \Re)}{\rho \vdash_{\mathbf{ML}^\dagger} \texttt{letrec } P = E_1 \texttt{ in } E_2 \Rightarrow (\sigma, \Re)} \quad (9)$$

Fig. 2. The $\mathbf{ML}^\dagger$ type system

start from $\top$: (*i.e.*variables and expressions have the most general type denoted by $\forall(\alpha)$ and there are no relations among variables at all):

$$P_0^1 = [x = (\forall(\alpha), \emptyset_{\Re}), y = (\forall(\beta), \emptyset_{\Re})] \vdash_{\mathbf{ML}^\dagger} \lambda xy.x \Rightarrow (\forall(\gamma), \emptyset_{\Re})$$
$$P_0^2 = [x = (\forall(\alpha), \emptyset_{\Re}), y = (\forall(\beta), \emptyset_{\Re})] \vdash_{\mathbf{ML}^\dagger} \lambda y.x \Rightarrow (\forall(\delta), \emptyset_{\Re})$$
$$P_0^3 = [x = (\forall(\alpha), \emptyset_{\Re}), y = (\forall(\beta), \emptyset_{\Re})] \vdash_{\mathbf{ML}^\dagger} x \Rightarrow (\forall(\epsilon), \emptyset_{\Re})$$

Using the rules of Figure 2 we compute a new set of assumptions. For instance, rule 4 transforms the initial assumptions as follows:

$$\frac{P_0^2 \ = \ [x = (\forall(\alpha), \emptyset_{\Re}), y = (\forall(\beta), \emptyset_{\Re})] \vdash_{\mathbf{ML}^\dagger} \lambda y.x \Rightarrow (\forall(\delta), \emptyset_{\Re})}{[x = (\forall(\alpha), \emptyset_{\Re}), y = (\forall(\beta), \emptyset_{\Re})] \vdash_{\mathbf{ML}^\dagger} \lambda xy.x \Rightarrow (\forall(\gamma_1 \rightarrow \gamma_2), \emptyset_{\Re})} \quad (4)$$

$$\frac{P_0^3 \ = \ [x = (\forall(\alpha), \emptyset_{\Re}), y = \forall(\beta), \emptyset_{\Re})] \vdash_{\mathbf{ML}^\dagger} x \Rightarrow (\forall(\epsilon), \emptyset_{\Re})}{[x = (\forall(\alpha), \emptyset_{\Re}), y = (\forall(\beta), \emptyset_{\Re})] \vdash_{\mathbf{ML}^\dagger} \lambda y.x \Rightarrow (\forall(\delta_1 \rightarrow \delta_2), \emptyset_{\Re})} \quad (4)$$

From rule 5, we extract the additional information:

$$\frac{[x = (\forall(\alpha), \emptyset_{\Re}), y = (\forall(\beta), \emptyset_{\Re})](x) = (\forall(\epsilon), \{\alpha = \epsilon\})}{[x = (\forall(\alpha), \emptyset_{\Re}), y = (\forall(\beta), \emptyset_{\Re})] \vdash_{\mathbf{ML}^\dagger} x \Rightarrow (\forall(\epsilon), \{\epsilon = \alpha\})} \quad (5)$$

From the above, we deduce the set of assumptions inferred after the first iteration:

$$\begin{array}{l} P_1^1 = [x = (\forall(\alpha), \emptyset_{\Re}), y = (\forall(\beta), \emptyset_{\Re})] \vdash_{\mathbf{ML}^\dagger} \lambda xy.x \Rightarrow (\forall(\gamma_1 \rightarrow \gamma_2), \emptyset_{\Re}) \\ P_1^2 = [x = (\forall(\alpha), \emptyset_{\Re}), y = (\forall(\beta), \emptyset_{\Re})] \vdash_{\mathbf{ML}^\dagger} \lambda y.x \quad \Rightarrow (\forall(\delta_1 \rightarrow \delta_2), \emptyset_{\Re}) \\ P_1^3 = [x = (\forall(\alpha), \emptyset_{\Re}), y = (\forall(\beta), \emptyset_{\Re})] \vdash_{\mathbf{ML}^\dagger} x \quad\quad \Rightarrow (\forall(\epsilon), \{\epsilon = \alpha\}) \end{array}$$

After the second iteration, we obtain the following set of assumptions:

$$\frac{P_1^2 \ = \ [x = (\forall(\alpha), \emptyset_{\Re}), y = (\forall(\beta), \emptyset_{\Re})] \vdash_{\mathbf{ML}^\dagger} \lambda y.x \Rightarrow (\forall(\delta_1 \rightarrow \delta_2), \emptyset_{\Re})}{P_2^1 \ = \ [x = (\forall(\alpha), \emptyset_{\Re}), y = (\forall(\beta), \emptyset_{\Re})] \vdash_{\mathbf{ML}^\dagger} \lambda xy.x \Rightarrow (\forall(\gamma_1 \rightarrow \gamma_2 \rightarrow \gamma_3), \emptyset_{\Re})} \quad (4)$$

$$\frac{P_1^3 \ = \ [x = (\forall(\alpha), \emptyset_{\Re}), y = \forall(\beta), \emptyset_{\Re})] \vdash_{\mathbf{ML}^\dagger} x \Rightarrow (\forall(\epsilon), \{\epsilon = \alpha\})}{P_2^2 \ = \ [x = (\forall(\alpha), \emptyset_{\Re}), y = (\forall(\beta), \emptyset_{\Re})] \vdash_{\mathbf{ML}^\dagger} \lambda y.x \Rightarrow (\forall(\delta_1 \rightarrow \delta_2), \{\delta_2 = \alpha\})} \quad (4)$$

$$\frac{[x = (\forall(\alpha), \emptyset_{\Re}), y = (\forall(\beta), \emptyset_{\Re})](x) = (\forall(\epsilon), \{\alpha = \epsilon\})}{P_2^3 \ = \ [x = (\forall(\alpha), \emptyset_{\Re}), y = (\forall(\beta), \emptyset_{\Re})] \vdash_{\mathbf{ML}^\dagger} x \Rightarrow (\forall(\epsilon), \{\epsilon = \alpha\})} \quad (5)$$

To reach the greatest fixpoint, only one more iteration is needed. As expected we find the ML-polymorphic type of the expression:

$$\frac{P_2^2 \ = \ [x = (\forall(\alpha), \emptyset_{\Re}), y = (\forall(\beta), \emptyset_{\Re})] \vdash_{\mathbf{ML}^\dagger} \lambda y.x \Rightarrow (\forall(\delta_1 \rightarrow \delta_2), \{\delta_2 = \alpha\})}{P_3^1 \ = \ [x = (\forall(\alpha), \emptyset_{\Re}), y = (\forall(\beta), \emptyset_{\Re})] \vdash_{\mathbf{ML}^\dagger} \lambda xy.x \Rightarrow (\forall(\gamma_1 \rightarrow \gamma_2 \rightarrow \gamma_1), \emptyset_{\Re})} \quad (4)$$

$$\frac{P_2^3 \ = \ [x = (\forall(\alpha), \emptyset_{\Re}), y = \forall(\beta), \emptyset_{\Re})] \vdash_{\mathbf{ML}^\dagger} x \Rightarrow (\forall(\epsilon), \{\epsilon = \alpha\})}{P_3^2 \ = \ [x = (\forall(\alpha), \emptyset_{\Re}), y = (\forall(\beta), \emptyset_{\Re})] \vdash_{\mathbf{ML}^\dagger} \lambda y.x \Rightarrow (\forall(\delta_1 \rightarrow \delta_2), \{\delta_2 = \alpha\})} \quad (4)$$

$$\frac{[x = (\forall(\alpha), \emptyset_{\Re}), y = (\forall(\beta), \emptyset_{\Re})](x) = (\forall(\epsilon), \{\alpha = \epsilon\})}{P_3^3 \ = \ [x = (\forall(\alpha), \emptyset_{\Re}), y = (\forall(\beta), \emptyset_{\Re})] \vdash_{\mathbf{ML}^\dagger} x \Rightarrow (\forall(\epsilon), \{\epsilon = \alpha\})} \quad (5)$$

1.3 Widening approach to Abstract Interpretation

The widening operator as defined by the Cousots [4][3] is an operation $\underline{\nabla} \in L \times L \longmapsto L$ such that:

- $\forall x, y \in L : x \underline{\nabla} y \sqsubseteq x \sqcap y$,
- for all iteration sequences $x^0 \sqsupseteq x^1 \sqsupseteq \ldots$, the decreasing chain defined by $y^0 = x^0, \ldots, y^{i+1} = y^i \underline{\nabla} x^{i+1}, \ldots$ is not strictly decreasing.

It follows that the downward iteration sequence with the widening:

$$\begin{array}{rll} X^0 & = \top & \\ X^{i+1} & = X^i & \text{if } X^i \sqsubseteq F(X^i) \\ & = X^i \underline{\nabla} F(X^i) & \text{otherwise} \end{array}$$

is stationary, and its limit is a sound lower approximation of the greatest fixpoint of F.

To use widening operators, we slightly modify the previous analysis by collecting the instantiations of types. We abstract the type of a constant to the tuple $(\sigma, \Re, \mathcal{I})$ where $\sigma, \Re, \mathcal{I}$ denote respectively the type scheme, the set of relations and the set of the instances of σ used during program execution. The emptyset is the top element. The set of all type instances is the bottom element. We define the "intersection" of two tuples $(\sigma, \Re, \mathcal{I})$ and $(\sigma', \Re', \mathcal{I}')$ as the tuple $((\sigma, \Re) \sqcap (\sigma', \Re'), \mathcal{I} \cup \mathcal{I}')$.

2 ML+ type system + widening operator ⇒ ML type system

Since the type inference problem of polymorphic recursively-defined constants is not decidable, till now the only solution was to restrict the types of recursively-defined constants to monomorphic types. In ML type system, the "`letrec` " is defined as follows:

$$\frac{\rho(P \leftarrow \sigma) \vdash_{\mathbf{ML}^\dagger} E \Rightarrow \sigma \quad \rho(P \leftarrow \sigma_P) \vdash_{\mathbf{ML}^\dagger} E_2 \Rightarrow \sigma}{\rho \vdash_{\mathbf{ML}^\dagger} \texttt{letrec}\ P = E_1 \text{ in } E_2 \Rightarrow \sigma} \quad \sigma_P = \text{gen}(\sigma, \rho)$$

where σ is a monomorphic type and σ, σ_P are polymorphic types. The "gen" function generalizes all the variables of monomorphic type σ that are not bound in the environment ρ. In other words, if it is required to instantiate the type σ of the constant P to the types σ_1 and σ_2, then the Hindley/Milner type of P is the greatest instance of σ, σ_1 and σ_2; that is $\sigma \sqcap \sigma_1 \sqcap \sigma_2$.

Lemma 3. *If $\rho(P \leftarrow (\sigma, \Re, \mathcal{I})) \vdash_{\mathbf{ML}^\dagger} E \Rightarrow (\sigma, \Re)$, and $(\sigma, \Re)$ is the principal type, then it exists $\Re'$ so that $\sigma' = \sigma \sqcap (\sqcap_{\sigma_i \in \mathcal{I}} \sigma_i)$, $\mathcal{I}' = \{\sigma\}$ and*

$$\rho(P \leftarrow (\sigma', \Re', \mathcal{I}')) \vdash_{\mathbf{ML}^\dagger} E \Rightarrow (\sigma', \Re').$$

The previous lemma claims that if a recursively-defined constant P has type $(\sigma, \Re)$, and if $\mathcal{I}$ is the set of all the instances of type σ used during the computation of the principal type of P, then $\sigma \sqcap (\sqcap_{\sigma_i \in \mathcal{I}} \sigma_i)$ denotes a fixpoint too. From this lemma we can deduce a more interesting property:

Lemma 4. *If $\rho(P \leftarrow (\sigma, \Re, \mathcal{I})) \vdash_{\mathbf{ML}^\dagger} E \Rightarrow (\sigma', \Re')$, and $(\sigma', \Re') \sqcap (\sigma, \Re)$, then it exists $\Re''$ so that $\sigma'' = (\sigma \sqcap \sigma') \sqcap (\sqcap_{\sigma_i \in \mathcal{I}} \sigma_i)$, $\mathcal{I}'' = \{\sigma'_i \ : \ \sigma_i \in \mathcal{I} \text{ and } \sigma'_i = \sigma'' \sqcap \sigma_i\}$ and*

$$\rho(P \leftarrow (\sigma'', \Re'', \mathcal{I}'')) \vdash_{\mathbf{ML}^\dagger} E \Rightarrow (\sigma'', \Re'').$$

In other words, if we compute the type of the expression: $\rho(P \leftarrow (\forall(\alpha), \Re, \mathcal{I})) \vdash_{\mathbf{ML}^\dagger} E \Rightarrow (\sigma', \Re')$, then we have found the monomorphic type of the expression since $\rho(P \leftarrow ((\forall(\alpha) \sqcap \sigma') \sqcap (\sqcap_{\sigma_i \in \mathcal{I}} \sigma_i), \Re', \{\sqcap_{\sigma_i \in \mathcal{I}} \sigma_i\}) \vdash_{\mathbf{ML}^\dagger} E \Rightarrow (\sigma', \Re'')$. Finally, to restrict the type of recursively-defined constant in the way Milner does can be achieved by the use of a widening operator:

Definition 5. The operation ∇_{Milner} maps the tuple $(\sigma, \Re, \mathcal{I})$ to the tuple $(\sigma', \Re', \mathcal{I}')$ where:

$$\begin{array}{ll} \text{if } \mathcal{I} = \emptyset & : (\sigma', \Re', \mathcal{I}') = (\sigma, \Re, \mathcal{I}), \\ \text{otherwise} & : (\sigma', \Re') = (\sigma, \Re) \sqcap \bigsqcap_{(\sigma_i, \Re_i) \in \mathcal{I}} (\sigma_i, \Re_i), \\ & \mathcal{I}' = \bigcup_{(\sigma_i, \Re_i) \in \mathcal{I}} (\sigma_i, \Re_i) \sqcap (\sigma', \Re). \end{array}$$

Lemma 6. *The operation $\underline{\nabla}_{\text{Milner}}$ defined as follows:*

$$\begin{array}{l} (\sigma, \Re, \mathcal{I}) \underline{\nabla}_{\text{Milner}} (\sigma', \Re', \mathcal{I}') = \nabla_{\text{Milner}}((\sigma, \Re, \mathcal{I}) \sqcap (\sigma', \Re', \mathcal{I}')) \\ \qquad \textit{if } (\sigma, \Re, \mathcal{I}) \textit{ is the type of a recursive constant,} \\ (\sigma, \Re, \mathcal{I}) \underline{\nabla}_{\text{Milner}} (\sigma', \Re', \mathcal{I}') = (\sigma, \Re, \mathcal{I}) \sqcap (\sigma', \Re', \mathcal{I}')) \\ \qquad \textit{if } (\sigma, \Re, \mathcal{I}) \textit{ it is the type of a non-recursive constant,} \end{array}$$

is a widening operator.

Example 2. We show how to compute the type of the recursively-defined expression: `letrec` $f = \lambda x.f0$. At first glance, this function can take any argument and will loop for ever. Therefore, we would suspect that this function has $\alpha \to \beta$ as the most general type. We start the iteration beginning with the greatest element $\top$:

$$f = (\forall(\alpha), \emptyset_\Re, \emptyset) \ \wedge \ x = (\forall(\beta), \emptyset_\Re).$$

Henceforth, the initial assertions are:

$$\begin{array}{ll} P^0_{\texttt{letrec}\, f=\lambda x.f0} & = () \vdash_{ML^\ddagger} \texttt{letrec}\ f = \lambda x.f0 \Rightarrow (\forall(\gamma), \emptyset_\Re) \\ P^0_{\lambda x.f0} & = (f : (\forall(\alpha), \emptyset_\Re, \emptyset)) \vdash_{ML^\ddagger} \lambda x.f0 \Rightarrow (\forall(\gamma), \emptyset_\Re) \\ P^0_{f0} & = (f : (\forall(\alpha), \emptyset_\Re, \emptyset), x : (\forall(\alpha), \emptyset_\Re)) \vdash_{ML^\ddagger} f0 \Rightarrow (\forall(\delta), \emptyset_\Re) \\ P^0_{f} & = (f : (\forall(\alpha), \emptyset_\Re, \emptyset), x : (\forall(\alpha), \emptyset_\Re)) \vdash_{ML^\ddagger} f \Rightarrow (\forall(\epsilon), \emptyset_\Re) \\ P^0_{0} & = (f : (\forall(\alpha), \emptyset_\Re, \emptyset), x : (\forall(\alpha), \emptyset_\Re)) \vdash_{ML^\ddagger} 0 \Rightarrow (\forall(\varepsilon), \emptyset_\Re) \end{array}$$

Using the abstract rules described on figure 2, we infer a new set of assertions from the set of the initial assertions:

$$\frac{P^0_{\lambda x.f0} = f : (\forall(\alpha), \emptyset_\Re, \emptyset)) \vdash_{ML^\ddagger} \lambda x.f0 \Rightarrow (\forall(\gamma), \emptyset_\Re)}{P^1_{\lambda x.f0} = (f : (\forall(\alpha), \{\alpha = \alpha\}, \emptyset)) \vdash_{ML^\ddagger} \lambda x.f0 \Rightarrow (\forall(\gamma), \emptyset_\Re)} \quad (3)$$

$$\frac{P^1_{0} = (f : (\forall(\alpha), \{\alpha = \alpha\}, \emptyset), x : (\forall(\beta), \emptyset_\Re)) \vdash_{ML^\ddagger} 0 \Rightarrow (\forall(\varepsilon), \emptyset_\Re)}{P^2_{0} = (f : (\forall(\alpha), \{\alpha = \alpha\}, \emptyset), x : (\forall(\beta), \emptyset_\Re)) \vdash_{ML^\ddagger} 0 \Rightarrow (\mathsf{num}, \emptyset_\Re)} \quad (1)$$

$$\frac{P^1_{f} = (f : (\forall(\alpha), \{\alpha = \alpha\}, \emptyset), x : (\forall(\beta), \emptyset_\Re)) \vdash_{ML^\ddagger} f \Rightarrow (\forall(\epsilon), \emptyset_\Re)}{P^2_{f} = (f : (\forall(\alpha), \{\alpha = \alpha\}, \emptyset), x : (\forall(\beta), \emptyset_\Re)) \vdash_{ML^\ddagger} f \Rightarrow (\forall(\varepsilon), \{\alpha = \varepsilon\})} \quad (4)$$

$$\frac{P^2_{f0} = (f : (\forall(\alpha), \{\alpha = \alpha\}, \emptyset), x : (\forall(\beta), \emptyset_\Re)) \vdash_{ML^\ddagger} f0 \Rightarrow (\forall(\delta), \emptyset_\Re)}{\begin{array}{r} P^3_{f0} = (f : (\forall(\alpha), \{\alpha = \alpha\}, \{(\forall(\mathsf{num} \to \alpha_2), \emptyset_\Re)\}), x : (\forall(\beta), \emptyset_\Re)) \\ \vdash_{ML^\ddagger} f0 \Rightarrow (\forall(\delta), \{\delta = \alpha_2\}) \end{array}} \quad (7)$$

After one iteration, we have inferred the type of the function f:

$$f \; : \; (\forall(\alpha \to \beta), \{\alpha \to \beta = \alpha \to \beta\}, \{(\forall(\mathsf{num} \to \alpha_2), \emptyset_{\Re})\}).$$

If we iterate once more, we could notice that we already have reached the fixpoint after only one iteration. But, using the widening operatot $\underline{\nabla}_{\text{Milner}}$, we can now stop the iteration process:

$$\begin{aligned}
(\forall(\alpha), \emptyset_{\Re}, \emptyset)\underline{\nabla}_{\text{Milner}}&(\forall(\alpha \to \beta), \{\alpha = \alpha\}, \{(\mathsf{num} \to \alpha_2\}, \emptyset_{\Re}) \\
= \nabla_{\text{Milner}}((\forall(\alpha), \emptyset_{\Re}, \emptyset) &\sqcap (\forall(\alpha \to \beta), \{\alpha = \alpha\}, \{(\mathsf{num} \to \alpha_2, \emptyset_{\Re})\})) \\
&= \nabla_{\text{Milner}}(\forall(\alpha \to \beta), \{\alpha = \alpha\}, \{(\mathsf{num} \to \alpha_2, \emptyset_{\Re})\}) \\
&= (\forall(\alpha \to \beta \sqcap \mathsf{num} \to \alpha_2), \Re, \{(\mathsf{num} \to \alpha_2, \emptyset_{\Re})\}) \\
&= (\forall(\mathsf{num} \to \alpha), \Re, \{(\mathsf{num} \to \alpha_1, \emptyset_{\Re})\}).
\end{aligned}$$

Using the widening operator $\underline{\nabla}_{\text{Milner}}$ restricts the types of the function f to monomophic types. Since the function f is used with a numerical argument, it have types " $\mathsf{num} \to \tau$" where τ denotes any monomorhic types. Since there is no constraint on this monomorphic type variable τ, the set of monotypes is denoted by the not really "polymorphic" type "$\mathsf{num} \to \alpha$", which corresponds to the solution obtained when using the widening operator $\underline{\nabla}_{\text{Milner}}$.

3 ML+ type system + widening operator ⇒ Miranda type system

Handling recursive definition like Milner does, is certainly not the panacea. For example, we can define the expression:

$$\begin{array}{ll}
\texttt{letrec} & \texttt{map} = \lambda f l.\texttt{if null}(l) \texttt{ then } [] \texttt{ else } f(\texttt{hd}(l)) :: \texttt{map } f \texttt{ tl}(l) \\
\texttt{andrec} & \texttt{minc} = \lambda l.\texttt{map } (\lambda x.x + 1)\ l;;
\end{array}$$

With respect to the ML-type system, the function "map" has type $(\mathsf{num} \to \mathsf{num}) \to \mathsf{num}\ \texttt{list} \to \mathsf{num}\ \texttt{list}$ instead of type $(\alpha \to \beta) \to \alpha\ \texttt{list} \to \beta\ \texttt{list}$. In fact, a simple dependency analysis allows to rewrite the previous expression with no "and" constructor:

$$\begin{array}{ll}
\texttt{letrec} & \texttt{map} = \lambda f l.\texttt{if null}(l) \texttt{ then } [] \texttt{ else } f(\texttt{hd}(l)) :: \texttt{map } f \texttt{ tl}(l) \\
\texttt{in letrec} & \texttt{minc} = \lambda l.\texttt{map } (\lambda x.x + 1)\ l;;
\end{array}$$

With respect to this transformation, the type system will infer the expected types for the "map" and "minc" functions. Miranda is one of the language that includes such a dependency analysis that avoids some arbitrary restriction of the ML-type system.

Again, like the ML-type system, we can deduce the one used in Miranda from the ML+ type system. In the ML-type system if the constant P has type σ and it is required to instantiate this type σ to the types $\sigma_1, \sigma_2, \ldots$, then the type of P is the greatest instance of $\sigma \sqcap \sigma_1 \sqcap \sigma_2 \sqcap \ldots$. In the type system implemented in Miranda, the type of P is the greatest instance of $\sigma \sqcap (\sqcap_{i \in \mathcal{J}} \sigma_i)$, where for all $i \in \mathcal{J}$, the value denoted by the instance σ_i may be used to compute the value of P. In the example above, the type instance $(\mathsf{num} \to \mathsf{num}) \to \mathsf{num}\ \texttt{list} \to \mathsf{num}\ \texttt{list}$

was only used to compute the type of the function "minc". Therefore, we should not intersect the $(\alpha \to \beta) \to \alpha$ **list** $\to \beta$ **list** with the last instance.

Consequently, if $P_1 = E_1, \ldots, P_n = E_n$ is a set of mutually recursive constant definition, then we need to find what are the instances of P_i that could be used to compute the type of the expression E_j. It is true that the type of an expression E_i depends on the type of a constant P_j if and only if it exists a relation between the type of E_i and one of the instance of P_j. But, as long as we have not reached the greatest fixpoint, the absence of such a relation between P_j and E_i does not mean that the type of an expression E_i does not depend on the type of the constant P_j. For example, the type of the expression E_i directly depends on the type of the constant P_k and the type of the expression E_k directly depends on the type of the constant P_j. Finally, the type of the expression E_i indirectly depends on the type of the constant P_j.

Theorem 7. *Let $P_1 = E_1, \ldots, P_n = E_n$ be a set of mutually recursive constant definition, let $(T_i^k, \Re_i^k)$ be the type of the constant P_i after k iterations, if σ_i^k is an instance of the type T_i^k of the constant P_i that is directly or indirectly used to compute the type T_i^{k+1} of the expression E_j, and if $k > n$ then it exists at least one equality relation between some subterms of the instance σ_i^k and some subterms of the expression type T_i^{k+1} in the set $\Re_i^k$.*

As a corollary, we now introduce the widening operator that mimics the behavior of Miranda's type system:

Definition 8. The operation ∇_{Mir} maps the tuple $(\sigma, \Re, \mathcal{I})$ to the tuple $(\sigma', \Re', \mathcal{I}')$ where:

$$\begin{aligned} &\text{if } \mathcal{I} = \emptyset &&: (\sigma', \Re', \mathcal{I}') = (\sigma, \Re, \mathcal{I}) \\ &\text{otherwise} &&: (\sigma', \Re') = (\sigma, \Re) \sqcap \bigsqcap_{(\sigma_i, \Re_i) \in \mathcal{J}} (\sigma_i, \Re_i) \\ & && \quad \mathcal{I}' = \mathcal{K} \cup \{(\sigma', \Re')\}, \end{aligned}$$

and:

$\mathcal{J} = \{(\sigma_i, \Re_i) \ : \ (\sigma_i, \Re_i) \in \mathcal{I}$ and there exists an equality relation between σ_i and σ stored in $\Re\}$,

$\mathcal{K} = \{(\sigma_i, \Re_i) \ : \ (\sigma_i, \Re_i) \in \mathcal{I}$ and there is no equality relation between σ_i and σ stored in $\Re\}$.

Lemma 9. *If the value n denotes the cardinality of the biggest set of mutually recursive constant definition: $P_1 = E_1, \ldots, P_n = E_n$ then the operation $\underline{\nabla}_{\text{Miranda}}$ defined as follows:*

$$(\sigma_i, \Re_i, \mathcal{I}_i)\underline{\nabla}_{\text{Miranda}}(\sigma_{i+1}, \Re_{i+1}, \mathcal{I}_{i+1}) = \nabla_{\text{Mir}}((\sigma_i, \Re_i, \mathcal{I}_i) \sqcap (\sigma_{i+1}, \Re_{i+1}, \mathcal{I}_{i+1}))$$
if $(\sigma_i, \Re_i, \mathcal{I}_i)$ is the type of a recursive constant and $i \geq n$,

$$(\sigma_i, \Re_i, \mathcal{I}_i)\underline{\nabla}_{\text{Miranda}}(\sigma_{i+1}, \Re_{i+1}, \mathcal{I}_{i-1}) = (\sigma_i, \Re_i, \mathcal{I}_i) \sqcap (\sigma_{i+1}, \Re_{i+1}, \mathcal{I}_{i+1})$$
if $(\sigma_i, \Re_i, \mathcal{I}_i)$ is the type of a recursive constant and $i < n$,

$$(\sigma, \Re, \mathcal{I})\underline{\nabla}_{\text{Miranda}}(\sigma', \Re', \mathcal{I}') = (\sigma, \Re, \mathcal{I}) \sqcap (\sigma', \Re', \mathcal{I}')$$
if $(\sigma, \Re, \mathcal{I})$ it is the type of a non-recursive constant,

is a widening operator.

Remark. In fact, the previous defined operator does not exactly mimic Miranda's type system. The dependency analysis of Miranda's type system is a syntactical one. The dependency analysis obtained by iterating the equation is a semantic one. In the common case, it leads to the same result, but in some cases, this can lead to a better result:

$$\begin{array}{ll}\texttt{letrec} & P = \lambda x.\texttt{if } Q(x) = Q(1) \texttt{ then } P(x) \texttt{ else } P(x)\\ \texttt{andrec} & Q = \lambda x.P(1).\end{array}$$

There is a syntactical dependency between P and Q. But this does not imply that the type of P depends on the type of Q — the opposite is true. Because of this syntactical dependency, the expression P and Q has type $\mathsf{num} \rightarrow \alpha$ with respect to Miranda's type system. Using our widening operator, we will find out that the expression P and Q have the more general type: $\alpha \rightarrow \beta$.

4 Partial polymorphic "letrec"

It will be nice to get rid of the restriction of recursively-defined constants to monomorphic types. A solution consists of defining the type of a recursively-defined constant as the most general semi-unifier of all its instances. Like before, we first define the operation $\nabla_{\mathrm{Semi}}(\sigma, \Re, \{(\sigma_1, \Re_1), \ldots, (\sigma_n, \Re_n)\})$ which returns the most general semi-unifier of the type: $(\sigma, \Re)$ with respect to the instances: $(\sigma_1, \Re_1), \ldots, (\sigma_i, \Re_i)$.

Definition 10. The operation ∇_{Semi} maps the tuple $(\sigma, \Re, \mathcal{I})$ to the tuple $(\sigma', \Re', \mathcal{I}')$ where:

$$\begin{array}{ll}\text{if } \mathcal{I} = \emptyset & : (\sigma', \Re', \mathcal{I}') = (\sigma, \Re, \mathcal{I})\\ \text{otherwise} & : (\sigma', \Re') = \mathrm{Semiunifier}((\sigma, \Re), \{(\sigma_1, \Re_1), \ldots, (\sigma_n, \Re_n)\})\\ & \quad \text{where } (\sigma_i, \Re_i) \in \mathcal{I}\\ & \quad \mathcal{I}' = \bigcup_{(\sigma_i, \Re_i) \in \mathcal{I}} (\sigma_i, \Re_i) \sqcap (\sigma', Re)\end{array}$$

Lemma 11. *The operation $\underline{\nabla}_{\mathrm{Semi}}$ defined as follows:*

$$\begin{array}{l}(\sigma, \Re, \mathcal{I}) \underline{\nabla}_{\mathrm{Semi}} (\sigma', \Re', \mathcal{I}') = \nabla_{\mathrm{Semi}}((\sigma, \Re, \mathcal{I}) \sqcap (\sigma', \Re', \mathcal{I}'))\\ \qquad\qquad \textit{if } (\sigma, \Re, \mathcal{I}) \textit{ is the type of a recursive constant.}\\ (\sigma, \Re, \mathcal{I}) \underline{\nabla}_{\mathrm{Semi}} (\sigma', \Re', \mathcal{I}') = (\sigma, \Re, \mathcal{I}) \sqcap (\sigma', \Re', \mathcal{I}')\\ \qquad\qquad \textit{if } (\sigma, \Re, \mathcal{I}) \textit{ is the type of a non-recursive constant.}\end{array}$$

is a widening operator.

The iteration process is no longer infinite, but semi-unification is known to be semi-decidable[10]. Therefore, the previous widening operator is of no practical use.

The two widening operators $\underline{\nabla}_{\mathrm{Milner}}$, $\underline{\nabla}_{\mathrm{Semi}}$ have one thing in common, they compute a fixpoint after *only one iteration* [2]. We now show that iterating more than one time before using a widening operator is much more interesting. In a lot

[2] if we follow the iteration strategy used by Milner

of cases, we reach the fixpoint without having to use the widening operator. If we try to type the expression: $f = \lambda x.(\lambda xy.x)0(f0)$, we find after only two iterations that :

$$f \;:\; (\forall(\alpha \rightarrow \beta), \{\alpha \rightarrow \beta = \alpha \rightarrow \beta\}, \{(\forall(\mathsf{num} \rightarrow \alpha_2), \emptyset_{\Re})\}).$$

is the greatest fixpoint. If we would have used the widening operator $\underline{\nabla}_{\text{Milner}}$ we would have found that f should have the type: $\mathsf{num} \rightarrow \mathsf{num}$. As a consequence of this remark, we propose to apply the previous defined ∇_{Milner} operator after an arbitrary number N of iterations.

Lemma 12. *The operator* $\underline{\nabla}^N_{\text{Milner}}$ *defined as follows:*

$$(\sigma_i, \Re_i)\underline{\nabla}^N_{\text{Milner}}(\sigma_{i+1}, \Re_{i+1}) = (\sigma_i, \Re_i) \sqcap (\sigma_{i+1}, \Re_{i+1})$$
$$(\sigma_i, \Re_i, \mathcal{I}_i)\underline{\nabla}^N_{\text{Milner}}(\sigma_{i+1}, \Re_{i+1}, \mathcal{I}_{i+1}) = (\sigma_i, \Re_i, \mathcal{I}_i) \sqcap (\sigma_{i+1}, \Re_{i+1}, \mathcal{I}_{i+1})$$
if it is the type of a non-recursive constant.
$$(\sigma_i, \Re_i, \mathcal{I}_i)\underline{\nabla}^N_{\text{Milner}}(\sigma_{i+1}, \Re_{i+1}, \mathcal{I}_{i+1}) = (\sigma_i, \Re_i, \mathcal{I}_i) \sqcap (\sigma_{i+1}, \Re_{i+1}, \mathcal{I}_{i+1})$$
if it it is the type of a recursive constant and $i < N$
$$(\sigma_i, \Re_i, \mathcal{I}_i)\underline{\nabla}^N_{\text{Milner}}(\sigma_{i+1}, \Re_{i+1}, \mathcal{I}_{i+1}) = \nabla_{\text{Milner}}((\sigma_i, \Re_i, \mathcal{I}_i) \sqcap (\sigma_{i+1}, \Re_{i+1}, \mathcal{I}_{i+1})$$
if it is the type of a recursive constant and $i \geq N$

is a widening operator.

On the one hand, for all N it exists a recursively-defined expression whose type is more general if computed using the widening operator $\underline{\nabla}^{N+1}_{\text{Milner}}$ instead of the widening operator $\underline{\nabla}^N_{\text{Milner}}$. On the other hand, the smaller the iteration number N, the faster the computation. The choice of the value N of the widening operator is a compromise between computation time that should be short, and the type precision. We have experimented values like $N = 20$ and have obtained accurate responses with really small expenses. More accurate solutions are obtained with a value N proportional to the size of the expression to be typed. For bigger values, the gained accuracy seems to be negligible with respect to the involved computation time.

5 The Two-levels Widening Operator

All the previous widening operators $\underline{\nabla}_{\text{Milner}}$, $\underline{\nabla}_{\text{Miranda}}$, $\underline{\nabla}^N_{\text{Milner}}$ operate like a two-states operator; either we continue the iteration sequence or we stop it. In this section we propose a smarter widening operator that does speed-up the iteration sequence from time to time but don't stop it in such a brutal way.

After a certain number of iterations, we remark that some subterms of the type of the expression are preserved by the iterative process. In fact, it is more or less like we would have reached the fixpoint with respect to those subterms. The idea is to preserve those subterms, and to transform the subterms that are still growing.

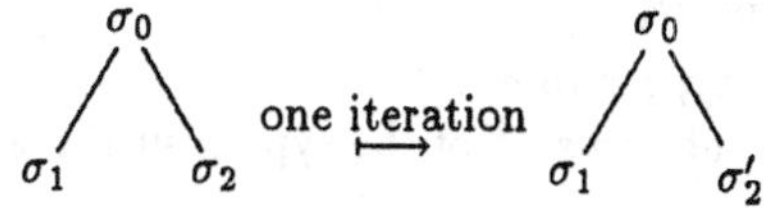

with $\sigma'_2 \sqsubseteq_S \sigma_2$

We can now define an operation $\bowtie$ such that for all $\sigma, \sigma' \in S$, $\sigma \bowtie \sigma' \sqsubseteq \sigma \sqcap \sigma'$. We replace the growing terms σ_2, σ_2' with the term $\sigma_2 \bowtie \sigma_2'$ in the above tree.

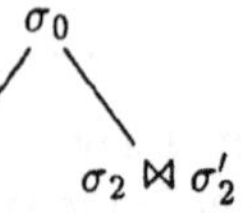

There are many possible choices for the $\bowtie$ operator. Since the motivation is to speed-up the iteration sequence, we propose to restrict the growing subterms to monomorphic subterms. Let $(\sigma, \Re, \mathcal{I})$ be the type of a constant, and σ^0 is the increasing subterm of σ that we want to restrict to a monorphic type. For all $\sigma_i \in \mathcal{I}$ it exists a substitution Π_i such that $\Pi_i(\sigma) = \sigma_i$. To restrict the term σ_2 to a monomorphic one, we need only to compute the greatest instance of the type σ^0 and the types $\Pi_i(\sigma^0)$, that is: $\sigma^0 \sqcap (\sqcap_{\sigma_i \in \mathcal{I}} \Pi_i(\sigma^0))$.

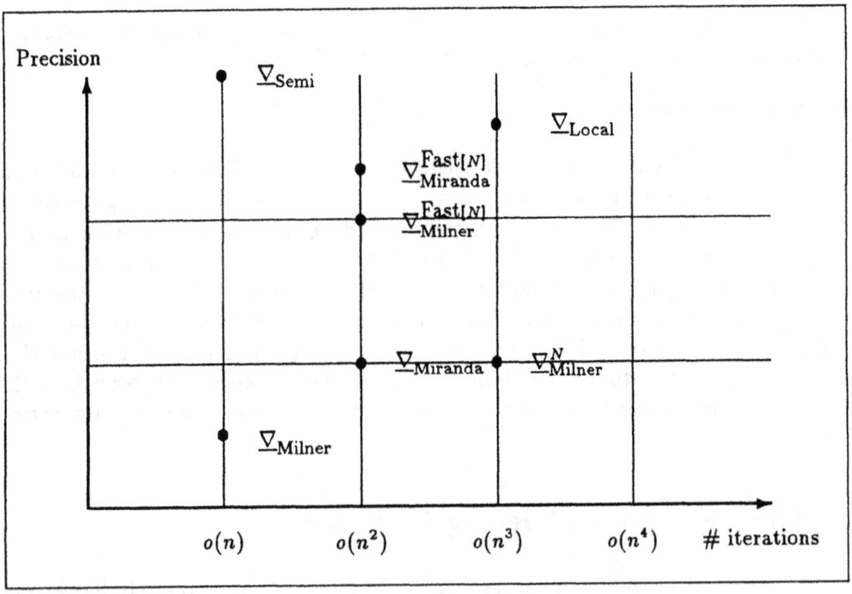

Fig. 3. A classification of widening operators

Definition 13. The operation ∇_{Local} maps the pair of tuples $(\sigma, \Re, \mathcal{I})$, $(\sigma', \Re', \mathcal{I}')$ to the tuple $(\sigma_0, \Re_0, \mathcal{I}_0)$ where:

- $(\sigma'', \Re'', \mathcal{I}'') = (\sigma, \Re, \mathcal{I}) \sqcap (\sigma', \Re', \mathcal{I}')$.
- The substitution Π_0 maps the type σ to σ''.
- The set $\mathcal{J}$ is the set of all the subterms σ^k of the type σ such that:
  - $\Pi_0(\sigma^k) \sqsubset \sigma^k$,

  - $\forall \sigma^*$ subterm of σ^k, $\Pi_0(\sigma^*) \sqsubset \sigma^*$.
- For all $\sigma_i'' \in \mathcal{I}''$ it exists a substitution Π_i such that $\Pi_i(\sigma'') = \sigma_i''$, for all elements $\sigma^k \in \mathcal{J}$, we define the element $\sigma_0^k = \sigma^k \sqcap \Pi_0(\sigma_k) \sqcap (\sqcap_{\sigma_i \in \mathcal{I}} \Pi_i(\sigma''))$.
- $\sigma_0 = \Pi(\sigma'')$ where Π replace all the subterms $\sigma_k \in \mathcal{J}$ with the subterm σ_0^k.
- $\mathcal{I}_0 = \cup_{\sigma_i \in \mathcal{I}''} \{\sigma_i \sqcap \sigma_0\}$.
- $\Re_0 = \Re''$

Using the ∇_{Local} operator, we can define a widening operator. For example we can apply after Nth iterations the operation ∇_{Local} to the pair $(\sigma_{N-1}, \Re_{N-1}, \mathcal{I}_{N-1})$ and $(\sigma'_N, \Re'_N, \mathcal{I}'_N)$. After that, we continue to iterate till we reach a lower approximation of the greatest fixpoint, or the $2 * N$th iterations. Again, we use the operation ∇_{Local} to locally speed up the iteration sequence, and so on. Since the operation ∇_{Local} speeds up the iteration sequence, but does not ensure algorithm termination, we still need to stop the iteration sequence after $N \times M$ iterations, if we have not reached the greatest fixpoint before. This can be done using the standard ∇_{Milner} operation.

$$\underbrace{\underbrace{1 \rightarrow 2 \rightarrow \ldots N}_{\text{first sequence}} \overset{\nabla_{\text{Local}}}{\rightarrow} \underbrace{N+1 \rightarrow 2 \rightarrow \ldots 2 \times N}_{\text{second sequence}} \overset{\nabla_{\text{Local}}}{\rightarrow} \ldots \overset{\nabla_{\text{Local}}}{\rightarrow} \underbrace{(M-1)N+1 \rightarrow 2 \rightarrow \ldots 2 \times M \times N}_{\text{last sequence}}}_{\text{iteration sequences without using } \nabla_{\text{Milner}}} \overset{\nabla_{\text{Milner}}}{\rightarrow} \infty$$

Lemma 14. *The operator $\underline{\nabla}_{Local}$ defined as follows:*

$(\sigma_i, \Re_i) \underline{\nabla}_{\text{Local}} (\sigma_{i+1}, \Re_{i+1}) = (\sigma_i, \Re_i) \sqcap (\sigma_{i+1}, \Re_{i+1})$
$(\sigma_i, \Re_i, \mathcal{I}_i) \underline{\nabla}_{\text{Local}} (\sigma_{i+1}, \Re_{i+1}, \mathcal{I}_{i+1}) = (\sigma_i, \Re_i, \mathcal{I}_i) \sqcap (\sigma_{i+1}, \Re_{i+1}, \mathcal{I}_{i+1})$
if it is the type of a non recursive constant.
$(\sigma_i, \Re_i, \mathcal{I}_i) \underline{\nabla}_{\text{Local}} (\sigma_{i+1}, \Re_{i+1}, \mathcal{I}_{i+1}) = (\sigma_i, \Re_i, \mathcal{I}_i) \sqcap (\sigma_{i+1}, \Re_{i+1}, \mathcal{I}_{i+1})$
if it is the type of a recursive constant and $i \not\equiv 0(N)$
$(\sigma_i, \Re_i, \mathcal{I}_i) \underline{\nabla}_{\text{Local}} (\sigma_{i+1}, \Re_{i+1}, \mathcal{I}_{i+1}) = \nabla_{\text{Local}}((\sigma_i, \Re_i, \mathcal{I}_i), (\sigma_{i+1}, \Re_{i+1}, \mathcal{I}_{i+1}))$
if it is the type of a recursive constant and $i \equiv 0(N)$
$\nabla_{\text{Local}}((\sigma_i, \Re_i, \mathcal{I}_i), (\sigma_{i+1}, \Re_{i+1}, \mathcal{I}_{i+1})) = \nabla_{\text{Milner}}((\sigma_i, \Re_i, \mathcal{I}_i) \sqcap (\sigma_{i+1}, \Re_{i+1}, \mathcal{I}_{i+1}))$
if it is the type of a recursive constant and $i \geq M \times N$

is a widening operator.

6 Conclusion

Because of the ease of use and the versatility of widening operators, there seem to be good candidates for defining new type inference strategy wherever the type inference problem is not decidable.

More precisely, in this paper, we exhibit some widening operators that either mimic some type inference strategy that are already implemented in some languages, or extend the ML-type system. In fact, those widening operators are only selected operators from a much larger family of widening operators listed on figure 3 that works very well on the ML-type algebra.

But widening operators can be used to solve other problems than the termination of the ML+type inference problem. For example, in [7] we have introduced a new type algebra called Fractional Types. Since the intersection of two fractional types is not computable in some cases, we have to use a widening operator to compute a lower approximation of the intersection of two fractional types, and to ensure algorithm termination.

We intend to develop the widening techniques presented in this paper:

- to search for sharper widening than those realized de facto by specific known algorithms, not only in ML, but wherever type inference is possible;
- to bridge the gap between type inference and abstract interpretation techniques.

References

1. A. Aiken, B. Murphy, *Static Type Inference in a Dynamically Typed Language*, Conf. rec of the 18th ACM Symposium on POPL, Orlando Florida 279-290, Jan 1991.
2. M.Coppo, M.Dezani-Ciancaglini, *An extension of the Basic Functionality Theory for the l-Calculus*, Notre Dame, Journal of Formal Logic 21 (4), 1980.
3. P.Cousot, *Méthodes itératives de construction et d'approximation de points fixes d'opérateurs monotones sur un treillis, analyse sémantique des programmes.* Thèse d'Etat, Grenoble 1978.
4. P. & R. Cousot , *Abstract Interpretation: a unified lattice model for static analysis of program by construction of approximate fixpoints*, Conf. rec of the 4th ACM Symposium on POPL, Jan 1977.
5. R. Harper, D. MacQueen, R. Milner *Standard ML* Report ECS-LFCS-86-2, Edinburgh University.
6. B. Monsuez *Polymorphic Typing by Abstract Interpretation* Conf. rec. of the 12th Conference on FST&TCS, December 1992, New Dehli, India, LNCS 652 Springer Verlag.
7. B. Monsuez *Fractional Types* Prooceding of the Workshop on Static Analysis, Septembre 1992, Bordeaux, France, BIGRE 82.
8. N.D. Jones, A. Mycroft, *A relational framework for abstract interpretation* in "Program as Data Objects" Proc. of a workshop in Copenhagen Oct. 1985. Ed. Ganziger and Jones. LNCS 215 Springer Verlag.
9. T. Karnomori, K. Horiuchi *Polymorphic Type Inference in Prolog by Abstract Interpretation*, in Logic Programming '87, Tokyo, LNCS 315, 1988, 195-214.
10. A.J. Kfoury, J. Tiuryn, P. Urzyczyn, *The undecidability of the semi-unification problem* Proc. ACM Symp. Theory of Computing, 1990.
11. A. Mycroft *Polymorphic Types Schemes and Recursive Definitions* in LNCS 167 International Symposium on Programming. 6th Colloquium April 1984, Toulouse.
12. D. Turner, *Miranda, a non-strict functional language with polymorphic types* in Functional programming Languages and Computer Architecture, Nancy, LNCS 201.

Demonstration: Static Analysis of AKL

Dan Sahlin and Thomas Sjöland
dan@sics.se and alf@sics.se

SICS, Box 1263, S-164 28 Kista, Sweden

Abstract. We have implemented a method for analysing programs in AKL which strictly separates the setting up of abstract semantic equations and finding a least fixpoint to these equations. We show a prototype analyser which is entirely coded in AKL.

1 Introduction

The concurrent constraint programming language AKL is defined in [4] by a system of rewrite rules. AKL has deep guards and allows concurrent execution of determinate goals. The interpreter approach for analysis frameworks for Prolog [7] does not seem feasible for AKL, since all possible choices of rewrite rules have to be considered. Previous work on analysis of CCLs [2] assumes flat guard (constraint) expressions and uses a confluent operational semantics which is not applicable to AKL.

We base our approach on abstract interpretation where the semantics of the programming language is abstracted by an equation system containing semantic functions [1]. We set up the equations for the analyser directly, arguing informally for its correctness.

2 Setting up the Semantic Equations

An AKL program is a set of definitions, each a sequence of clauses, each divided into a guard and a body which each contain a set of atoms (constraint atoms or goal atoms).

A set of equations is produced which represents an abstract semantics of the program. In addition to the Pre/Post pairs used in analysis frameworks for Prolog we add a third point, the Susp point (used as an alternative to extending the domain [3]), to model intermediate states. In order to model the concurrent execution we let the value of each Pre-point of an atom depend on the Susp-points of all other atoms in a guard (body) as well as on the input to the clause from the outside. The result of concurrent execution of the atoms in the body is modeled by the function **conj** and the value is stored in the Post-point of the clause. The intermediate results are modeled by the function **disj** and the value is stored in the Susp-point.

The functions **call**, **rename**, **lub**, **conj**, **disj**, **suspunif** and **unif** are parameters to the framework. A domain covering aliasing and type information has been implemented.

3 Solving the Semantic Equations

In abstract interpretation the domain is often quite complex and the functions are expensive to compute [7]. On the other hand most functions just depend on a small subset of the variables, and we utilise this fact. A graph of the functional dependencies can be used to find an efficient order for computing the functions. We identify strongly connected components of the graph as subsystems using Tarjan's algorithm [6], and then sort these topologically to form a partial order (considering each subsystem as a node). The analyser then handles the different subsystems respecting the partial order.

We experiment with heuristics for fixpoint computation based on the dependency graph, and with particular properties of the functions and the domain. Some are shown in the demonstration and are described in [5].

4 Conclusions

Our experience is that the topological sorting described above used together with observations and heuristics described in the report can substantially reduce the number of function applications needed to compute the fixpoint. The implemented tool shows that AKL is a suitable language for the purpose of prototyping analysis algorithms.

References

1. R. Barbuti, R. Giacobazzi and G. Levi, A General Framework for Semantics-Based Bottom-Up Abstract Interpretation of Logic Programs, Univ. of Pisa, *ACM Trans. on Prog. Lang. and Sys.* 15(1):133-181, 1993
2. M. Codish, M. Falaschi, K. Marriott and W. Winsborough, Efficient Analysis of Concurrent Constraint Logic Programs, In *Proc. of ICALP'93*, LNCS 700, 1993
3. M. Hanus, An Abstract Interpretation Algorithm for Residuating Logic Programs, In *Proc. of WSA'92*, Bordeaux, 1992
4. S. Janson and S. Haridi, Programming Paradigms of the Andorra Kernel Language, In *Logic Programming: Proc. of the 1991 Int. Symp.*, MIT Press, 1991
5. D. Sahlin and T. Sjöland, Towards an Analysis Tool for AKL, deliverable no. D.WP.1.6.1.M1.1 in ESPRIT project ParForce (6707), July 1993
6. R. Tarjan, Depth-First Search and Linear Graph Algorithms, *SIAM J. Comput.*, Vol 1., No. 2, June 1972
7. V. Englebert, B. Le Charlier, D. Roland and P. Van Hentenryck, Generic Abstract Interpretation Algorithms for Prolog: Two Optimization Techniques and Their Experimental Evaluation, In *Software Practice and Experience*, Vol. 23(4), 419-459, April 1993

Lecture Notes in Computer Science

For information about Vols. 1–650
please contact your bookseller or Springer-Verlag

Vol. 651: R. Koymans, Specifying Message Passing and Time-Critical Systems with Temporal Logic. IX, 164 pages. 1992.

Vol. 652: R. Shyamasundar (Ed.), Foundations of Software Technology and Theoretical Computer Science. Proceedings, 1992. XIII, 405 pages. 1992.

Vol. 653: A. Bensoussan, J.-P. Verjus (Eds.), Future Tendencies in Computer Science, Control and Applied Mathematics. Proceedings, 1992. XV, 371 pages. 1992.

Vol. 654: A. Nakamura, M. Nivat, A. Saoudi, P. S. P. Wang, K. Inoue (Eds.), Parallel Image Analysis. Proceedings, 1992. VIII, 312 pages. 1992.

Vol. 655: M. Bidoit, C. Choppy (Eds.), Recent Trends in Data Type Specification. X, 344 pages. 1993.

Vol. 656: M. Rusinowitch, J. L. Rémy (Eds.), Conditional Term Rewriting Systems. Proceedings, 1992. XI, 501 pages. 1993.

Vol. 657: E. W. Mayr (Ed.), Graph-Theoretic Concepts in Computer Science. Proceedings, 1992. VIII, 350 pages. 1993.

Vol. 658: R. A. Rueppel (Ed.), Advances in Cryptology – EUROCRYPT '92. Proceedings, 1992. X, 493 pages. 1993.

Vol. 659: G. Brewka, K. P. Jantke, P. H. Schmitt (Eds.), Nonmonotonic and Inductive Logic. Proceedings, 1991. VIII, 332 pages. 1993. (Subseries LNAI).

Vol. 660: E. Lamma, P. Mello (Eds.), Extensions of Logic Programming. Proceedings, 1992. VIII, 417 pages. 1993. (Subseries LNAI).

Vol. 661: S. J. Hanson, W. Remmele, R. L. Rivest (Eds.), Machine Learning: From Theory to Applications. VIII, 271 pages. 1993.

Vol. 662: M. Nitzberg, D. Mumford, T. Shiota, Filtering, Segmentation and Depth. VIII, 143 pages. 1993.

Vol. 663: G. v. Bochmann, D. K. Probst (Eds.), Computer Aided Verification. Proceedings, 1992. IX, 422 pages. 1993.

Vol. 664: M. Bezem, J. F. Groote (Eds.), Typed Lambda Calculi and Applications. Proceedings, 1993. VIII, 433 pages. 1993.

Vol. 665: P. Enjalbert, A. Finkel, K. W. Wagner (Eds.), STACS 93. Proceedings, 1993. XIV, 724 pages. 1993.

Vol. 666: J. W. de Bakker, W.-P. de Roever, G. Rozenberg (Eds.), Semantics: Foundations and Applications. Proceedings, 1992. VIII, 659 pages. 1993.

Vol. 667: P. B. Brazdil (Ed.), Machine Learning: ECML – 93. Proceedings, 1993. XII, 471 pages. 1993. (Subseries LNAI).

Vol. 668: M.-C. Gaudel, J.-P. Jouannaud (Eds.), TAPSOFT '93: Theory and Practice of Software Development. Proceedings, 1993. XII, 762 pages. 1993.

Vol. 669: R. S. Bird, C. C. Morgan, J. C. P. Woodcock (Eds.), Mathematics of Program Construction. Proceedings, 1992. VIII, 378 pages. 1993.

Vol. 670: J. C. P. Woodcock, P. G. Larsen (Eds.), FME '93: Industrial-Strength Formal Methods. Proceedings, 1993. XI, 689 pages. 1993.

Vol. 671: H. J. Ohlbach (Ed.), GWAI-92: Advances in Artificial Intelligence. Proceedings, 1992. XI, 397 pages. 1993. (Subseries LNAI).

Vol. 672: A. Barak, S. Guday, R. G. Wheeler, The MOSIX Distributed Operating System. X, 221 pages. 1993.

Vol. 673: G. Cohen, T. Mora, O. Moreno (Eds.), Applied Algebra, Algebraic Algorithms and Error-Correcting Codes. Proceedings, 1993. X, 355 pages 1993.

Vol. 674: G. Rozenberg (Ed.), Advances in Petri Nets 1993. VII, 457 pages. 1993.

Vol. 675: A. Mulkers, Live Data Structures in Logic Programs. VIII, 220 pages. 1993.

Vol. 676: Th. H. Reiss, Recognizing Planar Objects Using Invariant Image Features. X, 180 pages. 1993.

Vol. 677: H. Abdulrab, J.-P. Pécuchet (Eds.), Word Equations and Related Topics. Proceedings, 1991. VII, 214 pages. 1993.

Vol. 678: F. Meyer auf der Heide, B. Monien, A. L. Rosenberg (Eds.), Parallel Architectures and Their Efficient Use. Proceedings, 1992. XII, 227 pages. 1993.

Vol. 679: C. Fermüller, A. Leitsch, T. Tammet, N. Zamov, Resolution Methods for the Decision Problem. VIII, 205 pages. 1993. (Subseries LNAI).

Vol. 680: B. Hoffmann, B. Krieg-Brückner (Eds.), Program Development by Specification and Transformation. XV, 623 pages. 1993.

Vol. 681: H. Wansing, The Logic of Information Structures. IX, 163 pages. 1993. (Subseries LNAI).

Vol. 682: B. Bouchon-Meunier, L. Valverde, R. R. Yager (Eds.), IPMU '92 – Advanced Methods in Artificial Intelligence. Proceedings, 1992. IX, 367 pages. 1993.

Vol. 683: G.J. Milne, L. Pierre (Eds.), Correct Hardware Design and Verification Methods. Proceedings, 1993. VIII, 270 Pages. 1993.

Vol. 684: A. Apostolico, M. Crochemore, Z. Galil, U. Manber (Eds.), Combinatorial Pattern Matching. Proceedings, 1993. VIII, 265 pages. 1993.

Lecture Notes in Computer Science

For information about Vols. 1–650
please contact your bookseller or Springer-Verlag

Vol. 651: R. Koymans, Specifying Message Passing and Time-Critical Systems with Temporal Logic. IX, 164 pages. 1992.

Vol. 652: R. Shyamasundar (Ed.), Foundations of Software Technology and Theoretical Computer Science. Proceedings, 1992. XIII, 405 pages. 1992.

Vol. 653: A. Bensoussan, J.-P. Verjus (Eds.), Future Tendencies in Computer Science, Control and Applied Mathematics. Proceedings, 1992. XV, 371 pages. 1992.

Vol. 654: A. Nakamura, M. Nivat, A. Saoudi, P. S. P. Wang, K. Inoue (Eds.), Parallel Image Analysis. Proceedings, 1992. VIII, 312 pages. 1992.

Vol. 655: M. Bidoit, C. Choppy (Eds.), Recent Trends in Data Type Specification. X, 344 pages. 1993.

Vol. 656: M. Rusinowitch, J. L. Rémy (Eds.), Conditional Term Rewriting Systems. Proceedings, 1992. XI, 501 pages. 1993.

Vol. 657: E. W. Mayr (Ed.), Graph-Theoretic Concepts in Computer Science. Proceedings, 1992. VIII, 350 pages. 1993.

Vol. 658: R. A. Rueppel (Ed.), Advances in Cryptology – EUROCRYPT '92. Proceedings, 1992. X, 493 pages. 1993.

Vol. 659: G. Brewka, K. P. Jantke, P. H. Schmitt (Eds.), Nonmonotonic and Inductive Logic. Proceedings, 1991. VIII, 332 pages. 1993. (Subseries LNAI).

Vol. 660: E. Lamma, P. Mello (Eds.), Extensions of Logic Programming. Proceedings, 1992. VIII, 417 pages. 1993. (Subseries LNAI).

Vol. 661: S. J. Hanson, W. Remmele, R. L. Rivest (Eds.), Machine Learning: From Theory to Applications. VIII, 271 pages. 1993.

Vol. 662: M. Nitzberg, D. Mumford, T. Shiota, Filtering, Segmentation and Depth. VIII, 143 pages. 1993.

Vol. 663: G. v. Bochmann, D. K. Probst (Eds.), Computer Aided Verification. Proceedings, 1992. IX, 422 pages. 1993.

Vol. 664: M. Bezem, J. F. Groote (Eds.), Typed Lambda Calculi and Applications. Proceedings, 1993. VIII, 433 pages. 1993.

Vol. 665: P. Enjalbert, A. Finkel, K. W. Wagner (Eds.), STACS 93. Proceedings, 1993. XIV, 724 pages. 1993.

Vol. 666: J. W. de Bakker, W.-P. de Roever, G. Rozenberg (Eds.), Semantics: Foundations and Applications. Proceedings, 1992. VIII, 659 pages. 1993.

Vol. 667: P. B. Brazdil (Ed.), Machine Learning: ECML – 93. Proceedings, 1993. XII, 471 pages. 1993. (Subseries LNAI).

Vol. 668: M.-C. Gaudel, J.-P. Jouannaud (Eds.), TAPSOFT '93: Theory and Practice of Software Development. Proceedings, 1993. XII, 762 pages. 1993.

Vol. 669: R. S. Bird, C. C. Morgan, J. C. P. Woodcock (Eds.), Mathematics of Program Construction. Proceedings, 1992. VIII, 378 pages. 1993.

Vol. 670: J. C. P. Woodcock, P. G. Larsen (Eds.), FME '93: Industrial-Strength Formal Methods. Proceedings, 1993. XI, 689 pages. 1993.

Vol. 671: H. J. Ohlbach (Ed.), GWAI-92: Advances in Artificial Intelligence. Proceedings, 1992. XI, 397 pages. 1993. (Subseries LNAI).

Vol. 672: A. Barak, S. Guday, R. G. Wheeler, The MOSIX Distributed Operating System. X, 221 pages. 1993.

Vol. 673: G. Cohen, T. Mora, O. Moreno (Eds.), Applied Algebra, Algebraic Algorithms and Error-Correcting Codes. Proceedings, 1993. X, 355 pages 1993.

Vol. 674: G. Rozenberg (Ed.), Advances in Petri Nets 1993. VII, 457 pages. 1993.

Vol. 675: A. Mulkers, Live Data Structures in Logic Programs. VIII, 220 pages. 1993.

Vol. 676: Th. H. Reiss, Recognizing Planar Objects Using Invariant Image Features. X, 180 pages. 1993.

Vol. 677: H. Abdulrab, J.-P. Pécuchet (Eds.), Word Equations and Related Topics. Proceedings, 1991. VII, 214 pages. 1993.

Vol. 678: F. Meyer auf der Heide, B. Monien, A. L. Rosenberg (Eds.), Parallel Architectures and Their Efficient Use. Proceedings, 1992. XII, 227 pages. 1993.

Vol. 679: C. Fermüller, A. Leitsch, T. Tammet, N. Zamov, Resolution Methods for the Decision Problem. VIII, 205 pages. 1993. (Subseries LNAI).

Vol. 680: B. Hoffmann, B. Krieg-Brückner (Eds.), Program Development by Specification and Transformation. XV, 623 pages. 1993.

Vol. 681: H. Wansing, The Logic of Information Structures. IX, 163 pages. 1993. (Subseries LNAI).

Vol. 682: B. Bouchon-Meunier, L. Valverde, R. R. Yager (Eds.), IPMU '92 – Advanced Methods in Artificial Intelligence. Proceedings, 1992. IX, 367 pages. 1993.

Vol. 683: G.J. Milne, L. Pierre (Eds.), Correct Hardware Design and Verification Methods. Proceedings, 1993. VIII, 270 Pages. 1993.

Vol. 684: A. Apostolico, M. Crochemore, Z. Galil, U. Manber (Eds.), Combinatorial Pattern Matching. Proceedings, 1993. VIII, 265 pages. 1993.